CICERO'S *DE OFFICIIS*

Cicero's *De Officiis*, perhaps his most influential philosophical work, ranges over a wide variety of themes, from the role of the family in society to the question of whether our duties can conflict with one another, and from the moral significance of offence to the question of whether it is right to kill a dictator. This Critical Guide, the first collection of essays devoted to the work, is helpfully organized in thematic sections and aims to illuminate both the main individual topics of *De Officiis* and their interconnections, with essays by an international team of contributors that will allow readers to appreciate the work's distinctive blend of philosophical theory and social and political reality. It will be valuable for a range of readers in fields including philosophy, classics and political theory.

RAPHAEL WOOLF is Professor of Philosophy at King's College London. He is the author of *Cicero: The Philosophy of a Roman Sceptic* (Routledge, 2015), translator of Cicero's *De Finibus* (On Moral Ends, ed. Julia Annas, Cambridge, 2001) and (with Brad Inwood) translator and editor of Aristotle's *Eudemian Ethics* (Cambridge, 2012). He has published articles on Plato, Aristotle, Cicero and Hellenistic philosophy.

CAMBRIDGE CRITICAL GUIDES

Titles published in this series:

Cicero's *De Officiis*
EDITED BY RAPHAEL WOOLF
Kierkegaard's *The Sickness unto Death*
EDITED BY JEFFREY HANSON AND SHARON KRISHEK
Nietzsche's *Thus Spoke Zarathustra*
EDITED BY KEITH ANSELL-PEARSON AND PAUL S. LOEB
Kant's *Metaphysical Foundations of Natural Science*
EDITED BY MICHAEL BENNETT MCNULTY
Aristotle's *On the Soul*
EDITED BY CALEB M. COHOE
Schopenhauer's *The World as Will and Representation*
EDITED BY JUDITH NORMAN AND ALISTAIR WELCHMAN
Kant's *Prolegomena*
EDITED BY PETER THIELKE
Hegel's *Encyclopedia of the Philosophical Sciences*
EDITED BY SEBASTIAN STEIN AND JOSHUA WRETZEL
Maimonides' *Guide of the Perplexed*
EDITED BY DANIEL FRANK AND AARON SEGAL
Fichte's *System of Ethics*
EDITED BY STEFANO BACIN AND OWEN WARE
Hume's *An Enquiry Concerning the Principles of Morals*
EDITED BY ESTHER ENGELS KROEKER AND WILLEM LEMMENS
Hobbes's *On the Citizen*
EDITED BY ROBIN DOUGLASS AND JOHAN OLSTHOORN
Hegel's *Philosophy of Spirit*
EDITED BY MARINA F. BYKOVA
Kant's *Lectures on Metaphysics*
EDITED BY COURTNEY D. FUGATE
Spinoza's *Political Treatise*
EDITED BY YITZHAK Y. MELAMED AND HASANA SHARP
Aquinas's *Summa Theologiae*
EDITED BY JEFFREY HAUSE
Aristotle's *Generation of Animals*
EDITED BY ANDREA FALCON AND DAVID LEFEBVRE
Hegel's *Elements of the Philosophy of Right*
EDITED BY DAVID JAMES
Kant's *Critique of Pure Reason*
EDITED BY JAMES R. O'SHEA
Spinoza's *Ethics*
EDITED BY YITZHAK Y. MELAMED
Plato's *Symposium*
EDITED BY PIERRE DESTRÉE AND ZINA GIANNOPOULOU
Fichte's *Foundations of Natural Right*
EDITED BY GABRIEL GOTTLIEB

(Continued after the Index)

CICERO'S *DE OFFICIIS*

A Critical Guide

EDITED BY

RAPHAEL WOOLF

King's College London

Shaftesbury Road, Cambridge CB2 8EA, United Kingdom

One Liberty Plaza, 20th Floor, New York, NY 10006, USA

477 Williamstown Road, Port Melbourne, VIC 3207, Australia

314–321, 3rd Floor, Plot 3, Splendor Forum, Jasola District Centre, New Delhi – 110025, India

103 Penang Road, #05–06/07, Visioncrest Commercial, Singapore 238467

Cambridge University Press is part of Cambridge University Press & Assessment, a department of the University of Cambridge.

We share the University's mission to contribute to society through the pursuit of education, learning and research at the highest international levels of excellence.

www.cambridge.org
Information on this title: www.cambridge.org/9781009048774

DOI: 10.1017/9781009049375

© Cambridge University Press & Assessment 2023

This publication is in copyright. Subject to statutory exception and to the provisions of relevant collective licensing agreements, no reproduction of any part may take place without the written permission of Cambridge University Press & Assessment.

First published 2023
First paperback edition 2025

A catalogue record for this publication is available from the British Library

ISBN 978-1-316-51801-4   Hardback
ISBN 978-1-009-04877-4   Paperback

Cambridge University Press & Assessment has no responsibility for the persistence or accuracy of URLs for external or third-party internet websites referred to in this publication and does not guarantee that any content on such websites is, or will remain, accurate or appropriate.

Contents

List of Contributors	*page* vii
Acknowledgements	viii
List of Abbreviations	ix

Introduction   1
Raphael Woolf

PART I   THE FRAMEWORK OF *DE OFFICIIS*   13

1. The Family in *De Officiis*   15
   J. P. F. Wynne

2. Conflict of Duties in Cicero's *De Officiis*   42
   Georgia Tsouni

PART II   THE ROLE OF VIRTUE   61

3. *Oikeiōsis* and the Origin of Virtue   63
   Brad Inwood

4. Cicero's Project in Book 2 of *De Officiis*   78
   Malcolm Schofield

5. Cicero's *De Officiis* on Practical Deliberation   97
   Christopher Gill

PART III   EXEMPLARY ETHICS   117

6. *De Officiis* and Exemplary Ethics   119
   Rebecca Langlands

7. Emulation and Moral Development in *De Officiis*   139
   Georgina White

PART IV	SELF AND SOCIETY	161

8 Care of the (Written) Self: Literary and Ethical
  Decorum in *De Officiis*   163
  Caroline Bishop

9 Cicero and the Cynics   182
  Sean McConnell

PART V	POLITICS	201

10 Patriotism and Cosmopolitanism in Cicero's *De Officiis*   203
   Jed W. Atkins

11 Cicero's Extremist Ethics   224
   Ingo Gildenhard

References   243
Index   254

Contributors

JED W. ATKINS is E. Blake Byrne Associate Professor of Classical Studies and Associate Professor of Political Science and Philosophy, Duke University.

CAROLINE BISHOP is Associate Professor of Classics, Texas Tech University.

INGO GILDENHARD is Professor of Classics and the Classical Tradition, University of Cambridge.

CHRISTOPHER GILL is Emeritus Professor of Ancient Thought, University of Exeter.

BRAD INWOOD is William Lampson Professor of Philosophy and Classics, Yale University.

REBECCA LANGLANDS is Professor of Classics, University of Exeter.

SEAN MCCONNELL is Associate Professor of Classics, University of Otago.

MALCOLM SCHOFIELD is Emeritus Professor of Ancient Philosophy, University of Cambridge.

GEORGIA TSOUNI is Assistant Professor of Classics, University of Crete.

GEORGINA WHITE is Assistant Professor of Classics, University of Kansas.

RAPHAEL WOOLF is Professor of Philosophy, King's College London.

J. P. F. WYNNE is Associate Professor of Classics, University of Utah.

Acknowledgements

My sincere thanks to all the contributors for their patience, skill and enthusiasm; to an anonymous reader for helpful suggestions and advice; and to Hilary Gaskin of Cambridge University Press for suggesting the volume and for sympathetic oversight.

Abbreviations

Works by Cicero

Ad Brut.	Epistulae ad Brutum	Letters to Brutus
Am.	De Amicitia	On Friendship
Att.	Epistulae ad Atticum	Letters to Atticus
Balb.	Pro Balbo	On behalf of Balbus
Brut.	Brutus	
Cat.	In Catilinam	Against Catiline
De Or.	De Oratore	On the Orator
Div.	De Divinatione	On Divination
Dom.	De Domo Sua	On his House
Fam.	Epistulae ad Familiares	Letters to his Friends
Fin.	De Finibus	On Ends
Flac.	Pro Flacco	On behalf of Flaccus
Inv.	De Inventione	On Invention
Leg.	De Legibus	On the Laws
Luc.	Lucullus	
Mil.	Pro Milone	On behalf of Milo
Mur.	Pro Murena	On behalf of Murena
ND	De Natura Deorum	On the Nature of the Gods
Off.	De Officiis	On Duties
Or.	Orator	The Orator
Phil.	Philippicae	Philippics
Planc.	Pro Plancio	On behalf of Plancius
Q. Fr.	Epistulae ad Quintum Fratrem	Letters to his Brother Quintus
Rab. Perd.	Pro Rabirio Perduellionis Reo	On behalf of Rabirius Charged with Treason
Red. Pop.	Post Reditum ad Populum	To the People after his Return
Rep.	De Re Publica	On the Republic
Sest.	Pro Sestio	On behalf of Sestius

Sul.	Pro Sulla	On behalf of Sulla
Tusc.	Disputationes Tusculanae	Tusculan Disputations
Verr.	In Verrem	Against Verres

Works by Other Ancient Authors

Anon. Iamb.	Anonymus Iamblichi (*The Anonymous Author in Iamblichus*)
Apul. *Flor.*	Apuleius, *Florida*
Aristotle, *NE*	Aristotle, *Nicomachean Ethics*
Aristotle, *Top.*	Aristotle, *Topics*
August. *Civ. D.*	Augustine, *Civitas Dei* (*City of God*)
August. *Conf.*	Augustine, *Confessions*
Clem. *Strom.*	Clement of Alexandria, *Stromateis*
Dio Chrys. *Orat.*	Dio Chrysostom, *Orations*
DL	Diogenes Laërtius, *Lives and Opinions of Eminent Philosophers*
Epictetus, *Diss.*	Epictetus, *Discourses*
Galen, *PHP*	Galen, *On the Doctrines of Hippocrates and Plato*
Gell. *NA*	Aulus Gellius, *Noctes Atticae* (*Attic Nights*)
Horace, *AP*	Horace, *Ars Poetica*
Il.	Homer, *Iliad*
Lactantius, *Inst. Div.*	Lactantius, *Institutiones Divinae* (*The Divine Institutes*)
Philodemus, *Stoic. Hist.*	Philodemus, *Stoicorum Historia* (*History of Stoicism*)
Plato, *Hip. Maj.*	Plato, *Hippias Major*
Plato, *Phdr.*	Plato, *Phaedrus*
Plato, *R.*	Plato, *Republic*
Plutarch, *Dem.*	Plutarch, *Life of Demosthenes*
Plutarch, *Mor.*	Plutarch, *Moralia*
Seneca, Const.	Seneca, *De Constantia Sapientis* (*On the Constancy of the Sage*)
Seneca, Ep.	Seneca, *Epistulae Morales* (*Letters on Ethics*)
Tac. Ann.	Tacitus, *Annales* (*Annals*)

Modern Works

CIL	*Corpus Inscriptionum Latinarum*
LS	A. A. Long and D. N. Sedley, *The Hellenistic Philosophers*

OLD	*Oxford Latin Dictionary*
SB	D. R. Shackleton Bailey (editions and translations of Cicero's letters)
Sch. Vet. Il.	*Scholia Vetera in Homeri Iliadem*, ed. H. Erbse
SVF	*Stoicorum Veterum Fragmenta*, ed. H. von Arnim
TLL	*Thesaurus Linguae Latinae*

Introduction
Raphael Woolf

1 Preliminaries

This *Critical Guide* both reflects and, I hope, contributes to the ongoing scholarly renaissance of Cicero as a philosophical author. The *De Officiis* is by any reckoning one of Cicero's major philosophical works, and in terms of overall historical impact, probably his most influential. While it would be far-fetched to suppose it likely to regain the kind of prominence it had in, say, the early modern period,[1] it continues to offer fascinating discussion of a wide range of ethical and political topics. Given that, to this point, a collection of essays devoted to the work has been lacking, the time seemed right for a critical and philosophically oriented assessment of some of its main themes; this is what the current volume seeks to provide.

In this Introduction, I shall focus, in Section 2, on Cicero's prefaces to the three books that comprise *De Officiis*,[2] in order both to complement the essays that follow and because the prefaces give important information about the form of the work and about Cicero's methods and motives in composing it. I shall then, in Section 3, say a little for purposes of orientation about the structure of the volume and offer a brief outline of the individual chapters.

2 *De Officiis*: Title, Form and Method

To begin, though, with the title of Cicero's work. Although individual contributors have been free to translate as they see fit, the title of the volume retains the work's original Latin title rather than attempting a translation such as 'On Duties' or 'On Appropriate Actions'. The former,

---

[1] Though see Wynne ch. 1, this volume, p. 16, for its appearance in a recent US Supreme Court decision. Its continuing social and political relevance is highlighted also in the chapters by McConnell (p. 196–200) and Atkins (p. 214–17).
[2] On the prefaces cf. Baraz 2012: 212–23.

I

though useful shorthand, is liable to mislead: the English word 'duties' comes freighted with baggage from the deontological tradition that does not necessarily represent the sense of the Latin term, in particular insofar as Cicero uses *officia* in the work to translate the Greek Stoic technical term *kathēkonta*, now itself standardly translated in English as 'appropriate actions'. While that phrase retains both an accuracy and a neutrality that 'duties' lacks, 'On Appropriate Actions' seems as a rendition of *De Officiis* somewhat cumbersome and (the downside of its neutrality) without a clear meaning in English absent further explication.

Cicero's usage of *officia* belongs, as he tells us near the start of Book 1, in the realm of reasons for action. What he calls a 'middle' *officium* – that is, one whose discharge includes within its scope ordinary agents who have not attained the perfect virtue of the Stoic sage – is an action for which a 'plausible reason' (*ratio probabilis*) can be given (1.8).[3] I take it that this already gives *officium* a wider application than that of 'duty'. Moreover, while 'duty' within the deontological tradition tends to refer to something that by its nature one has an overriding reason to do, a key feature in Cicero's discussion – indeed it structures the whole work – is the question of the relation between what one might call moral and prudential reasons: in his terminology, between what is 'honourable' (*honestum*), on the one hand, and 'expedience' (*utilitas*) on the other.

The main source that Cicero draws on for at least the first two books of *De Officiis* is the Stoic Panaetius' now lost work *peri tou kathēkontos*. Cicero complains (not too despairingly, one feels) that whereas Panaetius promised to consider the question of what to do when the honourable and the expedient course of action are in apparent conflict, he never actually got around to doing so (3.7). Thus, while Cicero broadly follows Panaetius in Book 1, which focusses on what is honourable, and Book 2, which treats of the expedient, the field is clear for him to press ahead in Book 3 and argue that, despite appearances, there is no genuine conflict between what is honourable and what is expedient.[4] Cicero's often intricate discussion is thus underpinned by an ostensibly simple structure.

The literary form that *De Officiis* takes is that of a letter (1.4) from Cicero to his only son Marcus, who is studying at Athens, the cradle of Greek philosophy, with the Peripatetic philosopher Cratippus (1.1). While in substance the work is evidently a treatise, as a letter it differs from a

---

[3] See further Tsouni ch. 2, this volume.
[4] The extent of Cicero's indebtedness to Panaetius is discussed in several chapters of this volume; see esp. those by Tsouni, Inwood, Schofield, Langlands, and Bishop.

straightforward treatise in being personal.[5] Formally, Marcus is its specific recipient. One thing this formal feature may do is remind us that action, one of the basic themes of the work, is personal too, undertaken by specific agents who thereby take responsibility for what they do.

Now *De Officiis* is part of an astonishing burst of compositional creativity that marked roughly the last two years of Cicero's life. And he is clear that this turning to philosophical composition is in part attributable to his inability to partake any longer in public life, thanks to, as he not unreasonably saw it, the effective end of Roman republican government (2.2–4, 3.2–4), despite the work being composed in the wake of Julius Caesar's assassination. Cicero perhaps has a tendency to exaggerate the role of individual agency in the explanation of social and political change. It is characteristic, if understandable, that he places emphasis on the despotism 'of a single individual' (*unius*, 2.2) – that is, Caesar – when he bemoans the fate of the republic. So too he speaks of the individuals (*homines*) bent on upending the republic at 2.3.

By the same token, however, Cicero stresses, in a way that manages to be both moving and self-serving, how such developments have failed to quash his own agency. He tells us at 2.2 that he succumbed neither to grief (in addition to the death of companions in opposition to Caesar that he refers to here, we are no doubt supposed to have in mind the loss of his daughter Tullia after childbirth) nor to pleasure. Refusing to let idleness get the better of him (3.3) he has sought to make the best of things by providing a useful service to 'our people' (*nostris*) the Romans in writing philosophy (2.5).

The latter referent shows that Cicero, in fact and unsurprisingly, intends the work to have much wider reach and readership than Marcus alone. While some parts of it rather touchingly address Marcus' own exploits (e.g. 2.45), they also take pains to remind us of its wider scope (*non de te est, sed de genere toto*, ibid.). Cicero succeeds on the whole in conveying a well-crafted balance between the strictly personal dimension of his son as formal recipient and his wider ambitions for the work. Indeed there is often a distinct note of unease in his addressing of Marcus that highlights both the special importance to him of trying to inculcate in his son something of Cicero's own industriousness and achievements (3.6) and the possibility of failure in that regard. I have, says Cicero, written 'again and again' (*multa ... saepe*, 3.6) to encourage you; and here it is hard not to

---

[5] The letter from father to son as a literary genre continues to have vitality; a recent example, in a very different context, is Coates 2015.

detect a sense that Cicero's efforts to that end may be doomed to failure – as seems to have been the case.[6] Fortunately, Cicero has already made it clear that the work is also intended to foster wider Roman enlightenment. One may speculate that he would have found additional compensatory gratification in its (and in that sense his) endurance far beyond the Roman republican era.

The epistolary form brings out the notion of individual agency in another way too, which connects with issues of philosophical substance that Cicero explores within the main body of the work. While Cicero's exhortations to Marcus no doubt represent a sincere wish on the part of the father for the son to follow in his footsteps, the father-son relationship also features in the discussion in Book 1 of the Stoic *personae* theory, which holds that what it is right for an agent to do depends not just on general features of rationality shared with other humans as such, but also on features specific to individuals (*singulis*, 1.107).

In the context of this theory Cicero notes that while there are many cases of sons who strive for excellence in the same field as their father, some sons decline to do so and follow their own path (1.116). Cicero gives no indication that this latter option is in principle inferior to the former; that would be inconsistent with the theory that Cicero is expounding. So while the drama of the work hints at paternal disappointment, its theoretical discussion suggests that sons are entitled to go their own way. Cicero does not tell us what to make of this juxtaposition; but it provides an indication of how dramatic frame and philosophical content interact to stimulate the reader's own reflections.

The examples that Cicero lists of sons who did seek to emulate their fathers is itself an example of the work's thoroughgoing use of illustrative examples (*exempla*) to support more abstract ethical theory. Cicero's use of *exempla* will be covered in some depth later in the volume;[7] let me just note here that it offers an example of how Cicero artfully constructs his prefaces to anticipate features that turn out to be central to the construction of the main body of the work. In the opening lines of *De Officiis* Cicero reminds Marcus that he has been studying with Cratippus in Athens for a whole year now; and adds that while the former will enrich him in terms of knowledge (*scientia*), the latter will do so in terms of *exempla* (1.1). In the dramatic context this is a perfectly natural thing to say: Athens abounds in examples of great philosophers. But it also reflects a commitment on

---

[6] See Dyck 1996: 12, 15–16.
[7] See esp. the chapters by Langlands and White.

Cicero's part both to the ethical significance of individuals and to the educational role of examples in communicating ethical ideas.

The idea that I mentioned above, of letting the reader reflect and come to their own conclusions, now connects with a fundamental point about Cicero's method. He presents himself in *De Officiis*, as elsewhere in his writings, as an adherent of the sceptical Academy, a stance hinted at at 1.2 and confirmed at 2.7. But this raises a problem: how is this professed stance related to what seems to be a work full of positive philosophical content, chiefly Stoic-inspired? How, moreover, does Marcus' studying with a Peripatetic philosopher bear upon that?

Cicero's first move is to tell Marcus that his own writings do not differ greatly from those of the Peripatetics, seeing that both the latter school and the sceptical Academy claim allegiance with Socrates and Plato (1.2). And while there is no doubt an element of mischief in this – Cicero was well aware of the contested nature of such allegiances – it contains a serious point of method. While perfectly capable of incisively distinguishing and critiquing different schools (as, for example, in *De Finibus*), Cicero is also inclined, when he wishes, to expound philosophical ideas in less critical mode and to play down differences between schools in favour of similarities (the *Tusculan Disputations* may serve as an example here; in contrast to *De Officiis*, it even brings the Epicureans into the fold, e.g. *Tusc.* 3.76, 5.87–9).

At the same time, Cicero tells Marcus (1.2) that as far as philosophical substance (*rebus ipsis*) is concerned, he must use his own judgement (*tuo iudicio*) when reading Cicero's work. Now note, firstly, how this subtly undercuts the idea of similarity: the sceptics and the Peripatetics are at any rate not so similar that one who is undertaking study with an adherent of the latter does not have to use critical judgement in responding to work by an adherent of the former. But what to make of the fact that that work in turn draws heavily on Stoic material? Here too we see a dual response by Cicero. He tells us, on the one hand, that he does not uncritically follow his Stoic sources; in fact, he uses 'my own judgement and discretion (*iudicio arbitrioque nostro*, 1.6)' in this regard. On the other hand, the Stoics and Peripatetics have some relevant similarities: both allot the leading role in their ethics to virtue, albeit to a different extent (3.11, cf. 3.20, 33). Moreover, by speaking at 1.8 of the notion of *officium* as related to what can be given a plausible (*probabilis*) reason, Cicero slyly suggests affinity between Stoicism and, with its criterion of plausibility, Academic scepticism.

Whatever Marcus may have made of all this (if he made anything of it at all), the Ciceronian strategy seems designed, in line with good sceptical

Academic practice, to engage the reader critically. The *De Officiis* is a sceptical work, it seems to me, even as it forges a mainly Stoic path, just to the extent that it draws our attention to questions about the relation between philosophical schools and invites us to use our judgement in assessing similarities and differences. At the same time, in response to objections he says have been raised against him (2.7), Cicero insists that the sceptic is perfectly entitled to follow positions that seem plausible (*probabilia*), while treating, by contrast with the dogmatic schools, nothing as certain (2.7–8). Interestingly, Cicero proceeds to mount a defence of the practice of the sceptical Academy of arguing against every position, claiming that only by this procedure can one determine what is plausible (2.8). One might have thought this part of his defence somewhat gratuitous, given that *De Officiis* is not apparently a work that goes in for such argument. But Cicero thereby signals that what we find in the work is indeed a product of that kind of engagement, and by implication we as readers should, if we are appropriately constituted, seek to emulate Cicero's industriousness and not respond in uncritical fashion to what he has laid out before us.

3 This Volume: Structure and Chapter Outlines

The *Critical Guide* is organised around a series of themes, within which individual chapters are located. The themes are intended to reflect the way *De Officiis* itself is written, in being interconnected and overlapping rather than marking rigid demarcations. They are there to help orient readers and provide some structural backbone, as well as to indicate, non-dogmatically, some of the work's main currents of thought. Part I, 'The Framework of *De Officiis*', comprises a pair of chapters that deal respectively with two of the basic elements in the work's construction, namely family relationships and the nature and status of *officia*.

In Chapter 1, 'The Family in *De Officiis*', John Wynne explores the central role that Cicero allots to the family unit. Beginning at the end, with Cicero's final exhortation to Marcus, Wynne seeks to clarify how Cicero considers the family, and in particular the love of parents for their children, to serve as the origin for other social relationships and ultimately as the foundation of civil society. Wynne argues that while our rational natures are responsible for our concern for others insofar as they too are rational, it is parental love which, in practice, makes us care for at least some other humans as humans rather than just as bare reasoners, and to that extent explains how we are able to come to care for others for their own sake. Wynne goes on to consider how the family fits with Cicero's conception of the social virtues of justice and beneficence, arguing that, in the case of justice, Cicero views parental love as enabling a bridging of that cognitive gulf between awareness of how oneself and others are affected that tends to make us more attentive to our own interests than those of others. In the case of beneficence, moreover, the example of parental love teaches other family members attitudes and behaviour through which bonds that unite human societies more broadly can be forged. Wynne uses these reflections to illuminate how the virtues function for Cicero within the family itself, including, as members of every wealthy Roman's household, in the treatment of slaves.

In Chapter 2, 'Conflict of Duties in Cicero's *De Officiis*', Georgia Tsouni investigates the way in which the work is structured around the themes of what is honourable and what is expedient in action. Tsouni brings out the relevance to Cicero's philosophical project of his characterisation of *officium* as what has a *ratio probabilis* (see above) and goes on to outline the work's relationship with Panaetius' treatise and the significance of the latter work's failure, deliberate or otherwise, to address in detail the question of conflict between *officia*. Tsouni draws attention to the sheer variety of kinds of conflict that Cicero then covers in the work: in addition to the (as Cicero sees it) merely apparent conflict between what is honourable and expedient, this includes the possibility of the 'tragic dilemma', that is, conflict arising from within duties mandated by the virtues, where an agent is unable to perform one duty without violating another. In laying out in some detail the various stratagems that Cicero deploys in an attempt to show that in these cases too conflict is merely apparent, Tsouni demonstrates how extensively the theme of conflict permeates the work. Tsouni argues that this emphasis is in turn a reflection of the dialectical strategy that Cicero is apt to utilise in his more overtly dialogical works. In *De Officiis*, however, it serves above all the aim of preserving republican values and the political community.

While the essays in Part I each offer treatments of virtue in relation to their respective themes, Part II, 'The Role of Virtue', focusses more directly on how *De Officiis* conceives of virtue's nature and role. In Chapter 3, '*Oikeiōsis* and the Origin of Virtue', Brad Inwood argues that at *Off.* 1.11–12 there is an innovative version of the Stoic theory of *oikeiōsis* ('appropriation'), likely deriving from Panaetius himself, that possesses greater explanatory power in tracing how other-regarding attitudes develop from the phenomenon of self-love than other versions of the theory known to us. Inwood then investigates how this theory relates to the establishment of the virtues proper, and argues that while three of the four cardinal virtues are plausibly based in *oikeiōsis*, the fourth, wisdom, is at least initially not presented that way, lacking in particular a connection back to the drive for self-preservation. Only when theoretical and practical wisdom are later distinguished do we find, in the latter case, such a connection. Inwood shows that we can explain both Panaetius' innovations and Cicero's acceptance of them in terms of distinct motivations arising from the respective philosophical contexts in which each author wrote.

Chapter 4, 'Cicero's Project in Book 2 of *De Officiis*' takes us, as the title indicates, from Book 1 to Book 2. Malcolm Schofield begins by outlining the basic agenda of Book 2 as concerned with a question more complex than is sometimes supposed, namely how to acquire the resources that represent the means to the attainment of an agreeable life, with the most important of these resources being human. It is then virtue that enables us to secure from our fellow humans the cooperation needed for our ability to lead a good life. Schofield analyses the central role that Cicero allots to beneficence or liberality in winning the favour of our fellow humans, bringing out in particular how Book 2, in contrast with Book 1, lays emphasis on the *res publica* both as object of beneficence and constraint on the exercise of largesse. Against some interpretations, Schofield argues that, if anything, it is gratitude more than glory that Cicero highlights as the main benefit accruing to the bestower of beneficence, this in turn according with the idea that preservation of the *res publica*, as the entity on which our wellbeing as individuals ultimately depends, serves as the principal reference-point for the exercise of individual virtue.

In Chapter 5, 'Cicero's *De Officiis* on Practical Deliberation', Christopher Gill takes up the question of how virtue figures in practical deliberation in the context of the Stoic ethical theory that Cicero draws on. For the Stoics, virtue is the only good, and as such the sole constituent of happiness; on the other hand, it is the so-called indifferents, items that are neither good nor bad, that provide the Stoics with the material for practical deliberation. Theorists in this tradition are thus faced with the problem of how, if at all, given the categorical difference between them, virtue and the indifferents are supposed to work together in the operation of practical reason. Gill discusses and rejects some scholarly readings that take consideration of virtue to play little or no part in the Stoic agent's practical deliberations. Such readings, Gill suggests, underplay the role of specifically virtuous motivation in Stoicism. Gill proposes that this aspect can be brought out, so as to illuminate the treatment of virtue in *De Officiis*, by appeal to certain features of Rosalind Hursthouse's contemporary virtue theoretical ethics. These features Gill utilises to outline a model of practical deliberation in

Stoicism that coheres with, and is evidenced by, Cicero's discussion of the grounds for appropriate action as it unfolds across the three books.

Part III of the *Guide*, 'Exemplary Ethics', presents a pair of complementary essays devoted to an aspect of *De Officiis* that suffuses the work, namely Cicero's use of illustrative examples (*exempla*) to support and elaborate its positions. In Chapter 6, '*De Officiis* and Exemplary Ethics', Rebecca Langlands brings out the variety of functions that *exempla* serve in *De Officiis*, and the interrelations between them. Taking Cicero's treatment of Regulus in Book 3 as a case study, and drawing in part on Gill's discussion in the preceding chapter, Langlands shows how Cicero's presentation matches dialectical features that are characteristic both of his philosophical procedure elsewhere and of the Stoic debate between Diogenes and Antipater described earlier in the book. This dialectical mode means that the case of Regulus is not offered straightforwardly as a paradigm of admirable behaviour. Rather, the different readings of Regulus' behaviour that Cicero voices have the effect of expressing an anxiety about the difficulty in identifying the truly right thing to do. Exemplarity is thus for Cicero itself a topic for critical reflection, as, Langlands suggests, can also be seen from Cicero's handling of cases in which a moral quality and its opposite each appear as candidates for exemplary status. At the same time Langlands demonstrates how Cicero not only draws on Stoic resources in constructing his *exempla* but introduces dimensions that enable them to do better at capturing virtuous Stoic attributes than the Stoics themselves had hitherto managed. This in turn influences later Stoic-inspired treatments, such as those of Seneca, and aligns with the critical and creative way that Cicero engages with the *exempla* that he draws from Panaetius.

In Chapter 7, 'Emulation and Moral Development in *De Officiis*', Georgina White addresses the question of how precisely Cicero's use of *exempla*, particularly historical *exempla*, are intended to aid moral development. To the extent that they are models to imitate, they would presuppose proper understanding of the ethical theory that they serve to exemplify, given that it is the virtuous nature of the deeds in question rather than the specific actions performed that must carry over. Instead, White shows how Cicero takes pains to warn his readers away from an imitative model by focussing on its liability to lead us into error. Cicero underpins this theoretically by reference both to the idea that no ordinary human *exemplum* embodies the perfected virtue of the Stoic sage, and by appeal to features of the *personae* theory. How, then, do *exempla* serve an agent's moral development? For Cicero, White argues, in three main ways: they improve our capacity for self-analysis by prompting us to analyse the behaviour of others; they bear witness that the kind of ethical deliberation theorised in *De Officiis* has real-world application; and they provide motivating illustration of the idea that moral behaviour brings glory to the agent (and immoral behaviour the opposite) – and do so, moreover, White suggests, in a way designed to mitigate the threat of explanatory circularity arising from Cicero's reconceptualising of traditional Roman ideas of glory to fit the normative theory he expounds.

Part IV, 'Self and Society', also contains two complementary essays, each with a differing focus on the way that *De Officiis* conceives of the nature of the ethical self and its exercise in a social context, in particular with regard to the virtue of *decorum*. In Chapter 8, 'Care of the (Written) Self: Literary and Ethical Decorum in *De Officiis*', Caroline Bishop lays out how Cicero's treatment of *decorum* serves the task of constructing a moral identity suited to an environment in which the crisis of the republic had, for a member of the Roman elite, increasingly shrunk the possibilities for self-expression in the traditional public sphere. Bishop emphasises how the term *decorum*, which Cicero translates from the Greek *to prepon* that featured in Panaetius' treatise, represents a quality to which a notably comprehensive scope is given, as the virtue that encompasses and moderates our speech and actions in such a way that they conform with the other virtues. Moreover, in both the Greek and Latin cases, its usage signals the importation into philosophical ethics of a concept with pervasively aesthetic connotations. Bishop shows how in *De Officiis* it is these aesthetic dimensions, in particular as they relate to the orator's construction of speeches, that Cicero invokes in explaining the concept's applicability to ethics. In keeping with the times, he thus initiates the formation of a more private, inward-looking self, but one which purports to salvage the norms that had applied to the more traditional public roles. As Bishop argues, Cicero thus positions himself to reclaim old elite values for the new reality, and for the generations (Marcus included) to come.

In Chapter 9, 'Cicero and the Cynics', Sean McConnell examines *decorum* as a locus for the relation between self and society in its guise as the virtue by which, bound by a sense of shame (*verecundia*), we avoid giving offence to others. But this raises a problem: why should the attitudes of others have a bearing on the moral status of one's actions? McConnell shows how Cicero responds by grounding the moral significance of offence in nature rather than convention. Cicero mounts his defence principally in opposition to the Cynic view (shared by some Stoics) that nothing is by nature offensive. McConnell analyses Cicero's setting out (in *Fam.* 9.22) of the Cynic challenge that implicates the moral irrelevance of offence in the seeming arbitrariness of which words count as offensive. Since the parties on both sides agree that only things that are by nature offensive have moral significance, Cicero needs to show that there are such things. McConnell emphasises how Cicero's response in *De Officiis* is tailored to Stoic principles of rational design in nature and thus offers a dialectically appropriate defence in terms of the naturalness of *verecundia*. However, Cicero's argument, which centres on the parts and functions of the human body, risks failing to capture swathes of apparently culture-specific conventions about what is offensive. McConnell shows how the *personae* theory offers a framework for him to address this issue and considers how Cicero's discussion in *De Officiis* may provide resources for those of us in modern liberal multicultural societies to navigate the moral complexities of offence.

The previous two chapters veer towards the realm of politics, a realm which forms a continuous backdrop to *De Officiis*. Part V of the *Guide*, 'Politics', foregrounds the political dimension. In Chapter 10, 'Patriotism and Cosmopolitanism in Cicero's *De Officiis*', Jed Atkins explores the relation between two strands of the work's thinking about the civic sphere: on the one hand, a republicanism that sees our greatest allegiance as being to the citizens of our own country (*res publica*); on the other hand, the Stoic cosmopolitan notion that we belong to a society of all humans, to whom we have obligations in virtue of our shared humanity regardless of particular citizenship. Given the latter, how does Cicero argue for the special priority of the former? Atkins notes that Cicero grounds both these strands on the same philosophical basis, namely the naturalness of human sociability, which allows Cicero to develop an account of 'patriotic cosmopolitanism', whereby the *res publica* is the optimal place for developing other-regarding attitudes and meeting human needs, the latter in turn enhancing human sociability. This establishes that the kind of 'thick' allegiance made possible by a *res publica* is the best exemplification of the attachment of human to human that cosmopolitanism rightly upholds. Atkins moves on to discuss some objections to this picture and, in considering possible Ciceronian responses, shows how its problems and prospects continue to offer material for modern cosmopolitans to reflect on.

Chapter 11, 'Cicero's Extremist Ethics', takes as its starting point Cicero's lauding in *De Officiis* of Julius Caesar's assassination. Ingo Gildenhard argues that this endorsement of tyrannicide is not an isolated feature of the work but reflects a broader stance in which the use of force for the common good, up to and including homicide, is seen by Cicero as a legitimate political tool, one that he defends in a multitude of ways. There is thus a tension in the work between the idea that humans are made to be sociable and the reality of the conflict and chaos besetting the republic. Cicero adduces a number of psychological explanations to account for the human propensity to wickedness but, as Gildenhard shows, also wrestles with the paradox that the subversion of the republic had at its root the pursuit of objectives that its own political culture most admired. Cicero's remedy, Gildenhard argues, is the advocacy of both education and, where all else fails, political violence. The latter is given theoretical underpinning in the work's doctrine of passive injustice, that is, failure to prevent others' unjust action. Moreover the demands of justice override other obligations, even, in appropriate circumstances, legal ones. This makes the Cicero of *De Officiis* 'extremist', Gildenhard suggests, not simply in that his position seemed not to find favour with those whom Cicero might have taken to be allies, but because from a theoretical point of view it allows for political killing to be a repeatable action. As Gildenhard observes, it is a grim irony that this portends Cicero's own fate.

Here the *Guide*'s exploration of the long arc of *De Officiis* comes to a close, on a somewhat sombre note, but one perhaps not unsuited either to the times that Cicero was living through, or to our own. Like every great composition, *De Officiis* has a tendency to outrun any particular reading of it. Taken as a whole, the contributors to this volume aim to showcase a work that, in its richness and range, and its synthesis of philosophical theory with social and political reality, retains its vibrancy today.

PART I

The Framework of De Officiis

CHAPTER I

The Family in De Officiis

J. P. F. Wynne

They tuck you up, your mum and dad,
They read you Peter Rabbit, too.
They give you all the treats they had
And add some extra, just for you.
          –From Adrian Mitchell, "This Be the Worst"

1 Introduction

"Marcus my son, you have a gift from your father. In *my* opinion, it is a great one, but it will be just as you take it."[1] "Goodbye, then, [young Marcus], and be assured that you are superlatively dear to me, but that you will be much dearer, if you take delight in such precepts and advice as these" (*Off.* 3.121). *De Officiis*, both a declaration of love and a moral exhortation from father to son, gains significance from what the father, Cicero, advises. For he says that parents' love of their children is one of only a few origins of virtue, that the household of parents and their children is both the origin of settlements and the seedbed of the republic, and that of all humanity our immediate family is "most connected" (*coniunctissimus*) to us and is extraordinarily owed, after only the gods and the republic, our duties of beneficence. To borrow a modern term, in *De Officiis* Cicero promotes "family values."

Today we hear the little society of parents and their children called the "traditional" family. Cicero was and is traditional. We might therefore be unsurprised at Cicero's position. What else could an ancient Roman

---

I am most grateful to Raphael Woolf, whose editorial comments improved this chapter very much. I presented some of this material at a panel organized by Thornton Lockwood at the 2019 Society for Ancient Greek Philosophy meeting at Christopher Newport University, and benefited in particular from discussion with Thornton, Eric Brown, Michael Vazquez, Andree Hahmann, and Clerk Shaw. All remaining errors and weaknesses are my own. To my family, my thanks.

[1] Except when otherwise noted, all translations are my own. My translations here aim first for philosophical clarity.

moralist have said? But while influential Greek or Roman thinkers might have said that "traditional" family life was good, it was unusual that they made it an ideal or a source of virtue.[2] With some allies in the mature Stoa, Cicero represents a high-water mark in the "traditional" family's philosophical reputation for centuries before and after.[3] This has not gone unnoticed today. In the court's opinion in *Obergefell v. Hodges*, where the U.S. Supreme Court found that the U.S. Constitution requires the states to license same-sex marriages, Justice Kennedy wrote, "Since the dawn of history, marriage has ... [bound] families and societies together." For this he cites two ancient authorities: Confucius and *De Officiis*.[4]

Why did Cicero harbor these bourgeois notions? Why not think instead that the family is the mechanism by which man hands on misery to man? In *De Officiis*, Cicero scarcely argues for his position. As suits a work in which he gives advice, rather than the details of how he would justify his advice, arguments full enough to do justice to the complexities of family life are lacking. But it seems to me that in Cicero's other writings we find philosophical doctrines and debates, often on Cicero's mind, that clarify this part of *De Officiis*.

My aim in this chapter is to present briefly some of that background in Cicero's other writings (in Section 2 below), and then, partly in light of this background, to give an interpretation of the role of the family in *De Officiis* (in Sections 3 and 4). My conclusion will be that in *De Officiis* nature gives parental love to humanity to teach us what it is like when people love other people for the others' own sake, and that the family is the school where this lesson is taught.

I close my introduction with two further notes.

First, I give some interpretive principles. Cicero tells us in *De Officiis* to read his speeches and his other philosophical writings *studiose*, "attentively" (1.3). To some degree, that licenses my method in this

---

[2] Here are some examples. In the *Republic*, Plato makes non-"traditional" sex and child-rearing part of the ideal lives of the guardians (457d–461e). Aristotle, it is true, made a social building block of the household of a man, a woman, children – but also slaves (*Politics* 1261a1–9). In their turn, the earlier Stoics are said to have advocated "wives and children in common" (DL 7.131). Epicurus said the virtuous might or might not marry and have children, and discouraged child-rearing (DL 10.119, Epictetus *Diss.* 1.23.3). Plotinus was a guardian to the children of others, but did not himself marry, although some of his close students did (Porphyry, *Life* 9). Church Fathers tended to regard marriage as better than fornication, but less good than chastity attent on God.
[3] I have in mind Stobaeus' selections from Hierocles collected in Ramelli 2009: 73–95 and Musonius Rufus fragments XIIIA–XVI in Lutz and Reydams-Schils 2020.
[4] *Obergefell v. Hodges* 576 U.S. 644 (2015), on p. 657. Kennedy cites Miller's Loeb, but gives his own paraphrase ("The first bond of society is marriage; next, children; and then the family") of part of a sentence that appears below in **T8**. Cf. Chief Justice Roberts' dissent, p. 689.

chapter. But some texts that I cite from Cicero's dialogues are spoken by characters other than Cicero. They may represent schools of thought incompatible with one another or with Cicero's position in *De Officiis*. Further, Cicero was an Academic, as he reminds us in *De Officiis* (3.20). Hence even his own pronouncements at different times are not necessarily parts of the same view of things. Therefore, the material I bring from Cicero's other writings is not necessarily evidence of the *same* philosophy of the family as we find in *De Officiis*. Next, although in my view Cicero was an Academic of a sort who did not assent to what he writes in *De Officiis*, I shall write, as he did, as though what he says there were simply his view. Finally, I take no position on what in *De Officiis* Cicero owed to Panaetius or to other sources. I aim only to interpret Cicero's text as I find it.

Second, imagine a Martian who picked up *De Officiis* as a guide to humanity. It would conclude that people are raised naturally and beneficially in a home with their own, obviously loving, biological parents. In fact, it might well conclude that that is almost always how people grow up. Yet many people do not grow up that way. As is also natural, not least because parents are naturally mortal, many children are raised by foster, adoptive, or stepparents, or in settings that are not families.[5] Some of these experience love and benefits of the sort that Cicero associates with biological parents. Others are raised by biological parents who do not, or do not seem to, love them. We could go on for some time: family life can cause feuds and misery as well as the harmony and happiness for which it is not, in fact, a necessary condition. But that is not the impression Cicero will give to our Martian. Why? My answer will be that *De Officiis* focuses on what Cicero thinks is an *explanatory kind* of family, and what he claims is its naturalness, because he thinks it can help to explain the other loving and beneficial relationships that we meet in real life, which, although Cicero does not mention them much, must include childhoods and private lives of other kinds.

2 Some Background in Cicero's Life and Writings

Cicero's experiences with and reflections on the idea that parental affection is natural will help us to understand the family in *De Officiis*. Therefore, I

---

[5] In Cicero's society legal adoption was generally of older children or adults. But less formal fostering or guardianship of even young children, in ways good or bad, was common. See Rawson 1991: 250–63.

give here some highlights both of what we know of Cicero's experience of parenthood, and of how he tended to reflect on this experience.[6]

2.a Some Background in Cicero's Life

Sometimes, when Cicero as a barrister wished to provoke strong feelings, he would pick up a baby and carry it around the court as he spoke (*Or.* 131, cf. *Flac.* 106). He expected a Roman juryman to be moved by the bonds of love in other people's families, of which the baby was both object and token. No doubt this was a shrewd observation. But from Cicero it was not a cynical one. For he himself looked positively on children and families, as we shall now see.[7]

Hem, mea lux, meum desiderium, "Oh, my light, my desire!" (*Fam.* 14.2.2). Thus wrote Cicero from exile to his first wife Terentia.[8] With Terentia he had two children. Once, when missing his best friend Atticus, Cicero wrote, "I am so deserted by everyone that the only relaxation I have is what I spend with my wife and little daughter and sweet Cicero" (*Att.* 1.18). Despite his dry tone, Cicero communicates that he did, in fact, enjoy at least his children's company, and in his letters at large it is unmistakeable that he was a loving father. Cicero felt pressure to provide for the family. From exile he wrote, "I should have provided for you [to be most happy], and I would have provided it, if I had not been such a coward" (*Fam.* 14.2.1).

His "little daughter" Tullia, apple of her father's eye, was in fact about eighteen at the time when he so described her. Later, married thrice, she died after childbirth. The baby – so far as we know, Cicero's only grandchild – probably died soon too. Cicero's desperate grief is perhaps the episode in his family life best known to his philosophical readers today. It helped to occasion the outburst of philosophical writing in his last years.[9]

"Sweet Cicero" was Cicero's son of the same name, whom I call "young Marcus." He is the addressee of *De Officiis*. At the time when his father

---

[6] Cicero's childhood and relationship with his own parents would be equally relevant. But he wrote so little about his parents that almost any conclusions about that relationship are speculative.
[7] I owe the example of babies in court to Treggiari 2005: 14. Treggiari's chapter shows in detail that Cicero turned to his advantage in his speeches the ideas about the family that I explore here in his philosophy. Cf. also Hall 2014: 85–86.
[8] For Cicero and Terentia, see Treggiari 2007, in which similar expressions of love are collected on p. 160. When Cicero praises wholesome family life in *De Officiis*, we should also remember Publilia, the young woman he married scandalously after his divorce from Terentia, and soon divorced in turn. See Treggiari 2007: 133–41.
[9] For Tullia, see Treggiari 2007: chs. 5–10.

called him "sweet" he was about four (cf. *Att.* 1.2). When Marcus was two or three Cicero privately described the impact on the little boy of his own political misfortunes: "No sooner did he begin to understand, than he saw the most bitter griefs and miseries" (*Fam.* 14.1.1). Cicero's relationship with him grew to be more complex than that with Tullia. Cicero worried that his son lacked his own talent. *De Officiis* was written and is set during young Marcus' time in Athens studying with Cratippus, an anxious effort to develop that potential (3.5–6).[10]

In the last seven years of his life, her first seven, Cicero was friends with Atticus' little daughter, Pomponia (*Att.* 12.3). Cicero nicknamed her Attica. In letters to her father, Cicero fusses about her health (12.1, 12.6a). He accepts wrongdoing for not saying goodbye to her properly. He asks Atticus to beg her forgiveness: *commotiunculis sumpaskhō*, "I sympathize with little tantrums" (12.11).

Of particular interest is a letter that Cicero wrote to Atticus when Attica was a few months old, and therefore about five years before Cicero wrote works such as *De Finibus* and *De Amicitia*, and about six years before *De Officiis*. This is **T1**:

> I'm so pleased that you are delighted (*delectari*) by your little daughter and that it proves to you that 'affection for one's children is natural' (*phusikēn esse tēn <storgēn tēn> pros ta tekna*). For indeed if it's not so, there can be no linkage (*adiunctio*) by nature of human being with human being. Take that away, and the society of life (*vitae societas*) is refuted.
>
> "We should be so lucky!" says Carneades. Filthy! But still, wiser than our friend Lucius [Saufeius], or Patro, who, since they refer everything to themselves and think nothing done for the sake of another and say furthermore that a man should be good so as not to have evil, and not because it's right by nature, don't understand that they're talking about a cunning person, not a good man. (*Att.* 7.2.4)

Evidently, Atticus had written to Cicero about the affection that Attica elicited from Atticus. As a result, at least in Cicero's opinion, Atticus conceded a philosophical thesis to Cicero. One gets the impression this thesis

---

[10] Plutarch (*Cicero* 24.5–6) says Cicero had arranged for Cratippus to become a Roman citizen. A now lost inscription at Cratippus' home city of Pergamon recorded a family of Tullii Cratippi (*CIL* III.399). Perhaps Cratippus took Cicero's *nomen* when Cicero arranged his citizenship. If so, he may have been closer to the Cicero family than might appear in *De Officiis*. Young Marcus wrote to Cicero's secretary that he was like Cratippus' *filium* ... *coniunctissimum*, "closest son" (*Fam.* 16.21.3). *Coniunctus* would become the term of art in *De Officiis* that I translate as "connected" in this chapter. One wonders if Cicero took Marcus' remark to heart and felt some paternal rivalry with Cratippus. For a collection of Cicero's correspondence about Marcus' education in Athens, see Shackleton Bailey 1971: 237–42.

was a standing point of disagreement between the two men. That Cicero gives it in Greek suggests that the phrase was debated in philosophical culture at large.[11]

Let us see what Cicero thought he won in his victory over Atticus.

Atticus was sympathetic to Epicureanism. Saufeius and Patro were Epicureans.[12] The Epicurean position was that human parents come to affection for their children easily and voluntarily but not naturally. Many others disagreed and argued that human parental affection is natural. The debate is documented over several centuries.[13] It was vigorous in Italy during Cicero's life. For the Epicureans, one argument at that time was that if parental affection is natural, then it is not voluntary, but parental affection is voluntary.[14]

In the century after Cicero, a Stoic opponent hinted, I think, at a deeper Epicurean motivation: "Even Epicurus understands that we are by nature social, but once he put our good in the husk [i.e. in the body], he could no longer say anything other than *that*. ... Yet he knows that once a child is born, it is not in our power not to have affection (*stergein*) for them or not to give thought to them" (Epictetus, *Diss.* 1.23.1–6). Epictetus' point, I think, is this: Epicurus held that each of us should pursue the good of *our own* pleasure. Thus, he put the good for each person in that person's own body. But if, on becoming a parent, affection moves me to care for my child ultimately for its own sake rather than ultimately for my own pleasure (for as we shall see, Epicurus' opponents thought that was part of the claim that parental love is "natural"), then suddenly I have *two* places to look for my ultimate Epicurean goods: my body and my child's. The Epicurean parent has become a sort of limited utilitarian. She seeks the greatest pleasure for the greatest number in the little circle of parent and children. The hostile Epictetus says that Epicurus was not ready to concede this consequence, and that therefore Epicurus stuck stubbornly to a view that Epicurus knew was false, that sociability and parental affection are not natural.

An Epicurean, of course, would deny that her view is implausible or stubbornly held, and that parental affection is as involuntary and selfless as Epictetus suggested. Is it not gladly given and a source of a parent's rejoicing, she might say, rather than nature's way of enslaving us to a shrieking

---

[11] Modern editors provide the supplement that Cicero indeed had in mind, *storgēn tēn*. But I suspect Cicero himself left these words out because the thesis he intended would be so obvious to Atticus.
[12] See *Att.* 4.6.1, 5.19.3; *Fam.* 13.1.2–5; *Q. Fr.* 1.2.14.
[13] On Lucretius' contribution to this debate, see McConnell 2018. See also Plutarch's work often called *On Parental Affection* (*Peri philostorgias pros ta eggona*); *Against Colotes* 1123a; cf. *On Stoic Self-Contradictions* 1038b; Lactantius, *Inst. Div.* 3.17.5.
[14] Demetrius Lacon, P. Herc. 1012 ed. Puglia coll. 66 and 68; see McConnell 2017.

baby? Nevertheless, I think Epictetus put his finger on the deepest question in this debate: does one human ever love another ultimately for the other's own sake? If a parent loves a child ultimately for the child's own sake, then by example the answer is "yes."

The second paragraph of **T1** suggests Cicero, too, thought this was the point of the question of the naturalness of parental affection. Carneades, a gleeful critic of any proposition whatever, would delight in the "refutation" of the "society of life." But the Epicureans Saufeius and Patro had their own views at stake. First, they believed that, psychologically speaking, we *do* not do anything ultimately for the sake of another person. Second, they believed that we *should* not do anything ultimately for the sake of another person, and instead themselves referred everything to their own benefit. The letter implies that Cicero thought Atticus' experience deprived Patro and Saufeius of evidence for their views. If parental affection were *not* natural, then they would infer correctly that we *cannot* love another ultimately for the other's own sake. For Cicero's movement from the first paragraph of **T1** to the second suggests to me that love of another for the other's sake is what he means by the "linkage" (*adiunctio*) of one person to another, which is, in turn, a condition for "the society of life." But Atticus' experience suggested that parental affection *is* natural. Therefore, it was still defensible to hold that we are by nature social, rather than merely weak beings who must strike cunning deals to survive.[15]

To sum up: Cicero was soft-hearted about children. Parenthood was a powerful force in his emotional life. He expected it to be so for others. As a result, even in his private life, he advocated the philosophical thesis that parental affection is natural and among the roots, or even a necessary condition, of human society.

But this philosophical reaction on Cicero's part is in many ways mysterious. How could it be plausible that parental love is the, or even a, basis for society at large? Certainly, to say that "everyone is some mother's son" is a way to recognize the weight of another's humanity by adopting the perspective of a parent. Reverence for parental love, as with the Madonna and Child, is traditional. (If these examples seem questionably gendered – Where are the daughters? What price a father's love? – I find that many such examples in modern culture are like that. It is Cicero who is resolutely gender neutral in his description of parental love.) Yet the relation between a biological parent and child seems unique. It seems implausible that it could or should obtain between others. Reader, I do not want you

---

[15] Cicero also contrasts natural love with love from need at *Am.* 27.

to love me as your child. Further, parental love has its faults. We fear that it smothers – a psychoanalyst stereotypically starts with your parents. We exclude the defendant's mother from the jury – the parental perspective can be wrong as well as right. In Sections 3 and 4 I unravel this mystery for the case of *De Officiis*. But first, I leave Cicero's biography, to present some background in Cicero's philosophical and rhetorical writing.

2.b Some Background in Cicero's Theoretical Works: The Origins of Society

In Cicero's *Republic*, Scipio says he will not begin his political theory as far back as learned Greek philosophers do, "from the first mating of male and female, then from offspring and biological relationships" (*Rep.* 1.38). But in the treatises that Cicero wrote late in life he had exactly this habit, expressed either in his own words or through what he wrote for characters of various philosophical persuasions.[16] Scipio's remark shows that the habit was not original to Cicero. Indeed, in *De Finibus*, Cicero says that it was Plato's students who first taught that parental love is natural.[17] Nevertheless, that the later Cicero routinely began even divergent treatments from this point shows that he himself found it a helpful place to start thinking about society. I will begin this subsection with an example of that habit, relevant to *De Officiis* in that it advocates a Stoic position.

My example is from Cato's speech in *De Finibus*. Cato defends the Stoics against the charge that they posited two sorts of highest good, virtue and what is according to nature. His defense is that from birth we adopt certain *indifferents* as according to our nature, but that the only *good* is to be virtuous. Here Cato begins to tell Cicero how creatures like us can come to treat others well:

> **T2** We must understand this first from the shape and members of our bodies, which themselves announce that the plan for procreation comes from nature. Nor indeed would the following claims be coherent: that nature both wills procreation and does not take care that those procreated are objects of affection (*diligi*). And in fact the force of nature can be perceived even in beasts. When we see them toil in birth and in bringing up the young we seem to hear the voice of nature itself. Therefore, just as it is obvious that we recoil from pain naturally, just so it is clear that by nature itself we are pushed to love (*amemus*) those whom we have begotten.

---

[16] In addition to **T2** and **T4**, Cicero in his late *philosophica* began a discussion of social ethics with parental love on three other occasions, at *Am.* 27 and twice in *Fin.*, 4.17 and 5.65.

[17] Specifically, he attributes this to Speusippus, Aristotle, Xenocrates, Polemo, and Theophrastus (*Fin.* 4.3, 4.17).

From this is born the fact that even the shared appeal (*commendatio*) of humans among other humans is natural. As a result, due to this very fact, that he is a human being, it should not seem that a human being is foreign to a human being (*oporteat hominem ab homine ... non alienum videri*). (*Fin.* 3.62–63)

Thus Cato for the Stoics, like Cicero in **T1**, traces certain aspects of human society back specifically to the *naturalness* of parental affection and love.[18] Cato adds two arguments for this naturalness that do *not* depend on Atticus', or anybody's, experience of being a parent.

First, Cato says that nonrational animals visibly have affection for their children. In them, this can only be nature's doing. From this we generalize, to conclude that all animals naturally have affection for their children. But since we too are animals, parental affection must be natural in us too.

Second, we must consider our own bodies. Here we should recall that, for the Stoics, through life from the earliest stage we are "appropriated" – we go through *oikeiōsis*, to our own bodies and their parts. We recognize what they are and their purpose. To conserve our own nature we must conserve them and meet their purposes. Cato means, I think, that when we recognize that our reproductive organs have a purpose, to have children, we come to see children we might have as our own concern, part of what we, and our reproductive organs, can naturally achieve. Thus, parents' affection for their children arises naturally, just as our concern for ourselves, or for our kidneys, arises naturally. On this point, we know that Cato agrees with the seminal Stoic Chrysippus. For in Plutarch's *On Stoic Self-Contradictions* we read, "So why does [Chrysippus] wear himself out, writing again in every book about physics and, by Zeus, about ethics too, that we are appropriated to ourselves as soon as we are born, and our parts, and our own offspring?" (1038b). Therefore, we shall, and should, regard indifferents that accord with our children's nature as according to our own nature.[19]

In the second paragraph of **T2**, Cato alludes to very well-known words spoken by the comic playwright Terence's character Chremes: "I think nothing human foreign to me (*humani nil a me alienum puto*)" (*Heauton Timorumenos* 77). For Cato says that the naturalness of parental love has a

---

[18] For analysis of this passage, see Inwood 2016.
[19] **T2** is a key text for our understanding of Stoic *oikeiōsis*, a notion subject to a good deal of debate in recent scholarship. For a summary of the debate, see Klein 2016, whose conclusions I am in substantial agreement with. See also Inwood ch. 3, this volume. A discussion of the role of parental love in particular is Blundell 1990.

result. The result is that we *should* (*oporteat*) see other people as Chremes says he does, such that no human seems foreign. Now Cato's goal is to describe the Stoics' highest good, virtue. If no human should seem foreign, we may assume that no human will seem foreign to the virtuous person. Therefore, what Cato implies is that a result of natural parental love is that a human sage will not find *any* human foreign to herself. In practice, of course, we fools (non-sages) do overlook other human beings' natural needs. But whereas Epictetus pointed out that parenthood threatened to turn an Epicurean into a limited utilitarian, Cato welcomes the thought that a parent has become at least a sort of limited Chremes. For nothing to do either with the parent or with the parent's children seems foreign to the parent. Nature gives humanity at least that much head start towards the achievement and spread of justice, and Cato implies (mysteriously) that justice, or an impulse towards it, does indeed spread from parents to other people (cf. p. 32–34 and n. 32 below).

3   The Family in *De Officiis*

De Officiis gives advice, but not on how to act with the perfect virtue of a Stoic sage. Instead, when he speaks there of "the virtues" and so on, Cicero does not mean Stoic virtue proper, the *perfection* of reason. Rather he means what Stoics elsewhere would call progress towards wisdom, an ability to return rational justifications for one's actions (cf. 1.8, 1.46, 3.15–16). From now on I shall use "virtue," terms for virtues, and their cognates in this looser sense, except where I specify "perfect" virtue and so on.

3.a   The Family and the Origins of the Virtues

In exploring the origins of the virtues, Cicero assumes that what is natural tends to what is good. He does not justify this assumption at any length. It seems to me that the shrewdest hint comes at *Off.* 3.23, where he remarks that "nature's reason itself ... is divine and human law." Thus (a) nature has reason, and (b) nature's reason is right reason, such that it could serve as law even for the gods. Therefore, if we look for guidance from perfectly virtuous reason but will not find that among humans, we can look to nature.

I will discuss two origins of society and social virtue that Cicero says nature has put in us. These are, in no particular order, (1) the desire to have and raise children and (2) reason.

As to (1), Cicero says that nature brings about parental love in us as follows. First:

> **T3** But the appetite for union for the sake of procreation is common to all animals, and care (*cura*) of some kind[20] for those things that are procreated. (*Off.* 1.11)

Second:

> **T4** And this same nature by the force of reason brings human together with human (*hominem conciliat homini*) for society of speech and of life, and engenders above all a particular extraordinary love (*praecipuum quendam amorem*) towards those who have been procreated, and drives a person to desire that there should be meetings and crowds of human beings and that he should go to them. By these same causes, it drives a person to be eager to provide whatever supplies plenty in nourishment and in lifestyle, not only for himself, but also for his spouse, and children, and for others whom he holds dear or ought to keep safe … . (*Off.* 1.12)

To someone who read *De Officiis* on its own, Cicero's bald assertions about parenthood might seem undertheorized. In Section 2 I have shown that they are not. Cicero takes a position in the well-known debate: parental love is natural. His first readers knew that arguments like Cato's, and experiences like Cicero's and Atticus', stand behind it.

How, then, should we understand what Cicero says here about parental love? It is tempting to put together **T3** and **T4** in the following, mistaken way: Cicero (we would say) thinks that, like other animals, adult humans are moved by a nonrational desire to have and to care for children. This is what I called parental "affection" in Section 2, translating the Greek *storgē* and its cognates. A parent's reason then serves this nonrational desire but has no share in setting the objects to which it moves us. After all, Cato in **T2** compared parental love to the way that we recoil from pain, a reflex reaction.[21]

We should avoid that tempting interpretation. For Cicero in **T4** says that it is "by the force of reason" that we are brought to love our children.

---

[20] "care *of some kind*" (*cura quaedam*) addresses in **T3** an objection raised to **T2** by Gábor Betegh and Brad Inwood at Inwood 2016: 161, that Cato cannot explain why some animals of some species are *not* social by nature. By adding *of some kind*, Cicero allows that for some animals parental care could be minimal, temporary, or indirect, such that not every animal will become social.

[21] Inwood 2016 raises the problem that a Stoic would not think human parental love is a mere nonrational reflex. I agree that the Stoics would not think that. I suggest Cato means that what love of children shares with how we recoil from pain is that both are *natural*, not that both are nonrational reflexes. This is clear if we distinguish a natural nonrational affection which we share with all other animals, from a rational love at which human parents arrive partly in response to feeling the nonrational affection.

Indeed, since *De Officiis* is written from a broadly Stoic point of view (1.6), that must be so. For the Stoics held that rational animals act only rationally, and Cicero thinks of loving parental behavior as a sequence of responsible actions. Thus, I think Cicero in **T4** means that human parents come to be disposed to love their children when they come to have a rational attitude in favor of caring for them. The role in human life that Cicero intends for parental affection, the nonrational drive to procreate and care for offspring he described in **T3**, is probably that (consciously or otherwise) we tend to notice this drive in ourselves, along with the associated parts and purposes of our anatomy, as we develop our concepts and beliefs. From this appreciation of our own nature we will tend to derive a belief (whether we are conscious of it or not) that it is appropriate for us to have children and to raise them to thrive, even at great cost and effort, a belief described as "extraordinary love" in **T4**. Note that, given the Stoic explanation of the emotions, if Cicero means here that parental love, and a disposition to it, are rational attitudes, he need not deny that these attitudes are part of, or that they cause, warm emotions.[22]

Cicero can now answer two puzzles I mentioned above.

First, Cicero can explain the variety we observe in children's lives, of which he left the Martian ignorant (see p. 17 above). According to the Stoics, humans naturally develop reason. Given the rest of our nature, this natural development *tends* to result in a true belief that it is natural to have and raise children. But this natural development is such that we do not all share in this belief, or the same form of this belief, for at least two reasons. First, when we first become rational, we become foolish. Foolishness is various. Thus, the Stoics predict that a natural development will result in a great variety of attitudes to parenthood, or towards caring for children not one's own. Second, as Cicero is especially keen to emphasize in *De Officiis*, in Stoicism we may take into account our own circumstances, personalities, attachments, and so on, when we make decisions (1.107–125). Even what perfectly virtuous people will know about their own nature, history, and vocations will differ from sage to sage. Therefore, people might virtuously decide they should not have children.

Second, Cicero has an answer to the charge of the Epicureans, that if parental love is natural, then it is involuntary in some way that we should find implausible (p. 20–21 above). Cicero can agree with the Epicureans and Epictetus that nonrational parental affection is involuntary, but add that the "extraordinary" parental love that motivates family life is not this

---

[22] Here I use "emotion" loosely, to include human affects in general, foolish or wise.

affection, but rather a rational attitude. For the Stoics, rational attitudes are all voluntary (LS 62).

In order to discern the role of parental affection and love in **T4**, notice that it is certainly not the only origin of society and social virtue described there. For Cicero says (2) *reason* alone leads us to wish to meet, to speak to each other, and so on. Indeed, it would seem that even if humans had no children, reason would still do this. For in *De Officiis* Cicero makes use of the wide range of meaning of the Latin *ratio*, "reason." It has meanings such as the capacity to think or the desire for the truth (1.11, 1.13). But it also means the ability to use language, to signify, and to communicate (1.12). The latter, linguistic aspects of rational life are dominant in *De Officiis*. It is by a shared language that "human beings are most of all united" (1.53). Sages given solitude in which to do nothing but contemplate the truth would flee back to society (1.158). Thus, says Cicero, reason pursues truth, but does so for the sake of its social needs (1.157). None of these social relations would seem to need parental affection to prompt them.

Just as with parental love, in his earlier writing Cicero often raised this idea that reason, or reason developed into eloquence, philosophy, or wisdom, first brought human society together.[23] In *De Officiis*, then, Cicero described together the two origins of human society that in previous writings he had returned to separately: reason and parental love. From a Stoic point of view, one way to state the complementary nature of these two origins is the following.

Reason *per se* is the origin of the society of all rational beings, such as rational humans. We wish to share reason's projects – communication, learning, lawgiving, and so on – with other reasoners. But reason does not make us social with other *humans* as such. For example, it will not draw us into society with little children who, in Stoic thinking, are not rational. No doubt as our offspring, developing towards reason and starting to mimic it in their utterances, small children have a special relationship with the society of the rational. But they are not part of it. Cicero was not bound by it to "sweet" little Marcus (p. 18–19 above). Meanwhile, reason *will* draw us into society with rational beings who are not human, such as nature or the gods (*Off.* 1.160). But we cannot attend to nature's or the gods' human needs. They have none. The bond of reason, then, gives common goals to all the rational, but does not necessarily lead each rational

---

[23] The first words we have from Cicero's pen, the opening of *De Inventione*, dwell on this theme (*Inv.* 1.1–4). In his speech *Pro Sestio*, Cicero said publicly that this was a common opinion in Rome (*Sest.* 91). Cf. *De Or.* 1.33, *Tusc.* 5.5.

being to attend to the needs of another rational being in the way it attends to its own. It might, therefore, bring a human to regard another human as a fellow reasoner, a floating mind, but not to care about all the other person's human needs.

By contrast, parental love necessarily makes some humans care for at least some others *as humans*, rather than as reasoners. It leads parents to plan for such natural needs as their families' nourishment and living conditions, just as they do for their own needs, and perhaps also for their small children's development towards reason with a view to their eventual development towards wisdom. In this particular sense, parental love introduces care for other people not only for reason's goals, but for those others' own sake.[24]

This concludes my discussion of Cicero's introduction of parental love into *De Officiis*. An objection that Cicero invites here and in his subsequent discussion of human procreation (see **T8** below) is that his can seem a bizarrely limited account of the human desire for sex, or romance, or marriage. People often desire these things without desiring to have and raise children as a result. Cicero wrote to Terentia, "Oh my light, my desire!" not "I wish we could have more kids!" Meanwhile, some people do not desire these things at all. But Cicero's aim is not to give a complete account of attitudes towards sex and romance. Rather, his aim is to describe the kind of case that interests him as an origin of society, namely, the case where a man and a woman have children and then raise them. By describing this case, he does not deny all the other aspects of human romantic and sexual desire, nor that children are often raised in other ways.

In **T1** Cicero said that if parents do not naturally have affection for their children, there *can* be no linkage of human to human. In *De Officiis* he gives a different view. For suppose that we changed the world of *De Officiis* only so that nonrational parental affection were not natural. Reason is flexible enough, I assume, that people could still arrive in other ways at a sincere, moving belief that they should attend to the human needs of their children – or, indeed, of anyone else. But, without the prompt of natural parental affection, these attitudes would be less common. Thus, in *De Officiis* natural parental affection is not a necessary condition for genuine human social links. Rather, parental affection and the family are a way that, in practice, nature *does* commonly bring these links about. This is its explanatory power and moral importance.

---

[24] For a different analysis of the origins of justice in *Off.* 1.11–12, see Schofield 1995: 199–204.

3.b The Family and the Virtues and Vices

Cicero would not count the origins of the virtues as such if they tended equally towards virtue or vice. They point us more towards virtue. But the origins of the virtues are not virtues. They can lead us to do ill. For example, the love of one's children could lead one to steal for them. Thus, the path to virtue is not simply to allow ourselves to be driven by the origins of virtue that nature has put in our souls. Rather, we must regulate rationally our response to these desires and promptings, in order to achieve, or at least make progress towards, perfect virtue. Cicero's subsequent discussion in Book 1 is intended to help us with this task. Here I examine what he says about social virtue, the part of virtue in which the family is involved.

3.b.i The Family, Justice, and Injustice

Cicero names two species of social virtue. First, there is justice (*iustitia*). To be just is not to harm anyone unless provoked by injustice, and to treat what is common as common and what is private as private. (Since the question of what is common and what private arises also under beneficence, I will focus in this subsection on the "harm" criterion for justice.) Second, there is "beneficence" (*beneficentia*) (*Off.* 1.20). Rather than regulating harm and theft, beneficence regulates the benefits we give to others (1.42). Let us see first how justice relates to the family.

The family has no special place in the general demand of justice to refrain from harm unless provoked by injustice. We are not to harm anyone unprovoked. Thus, we should not harm our family unprovoked, but neither should we harm anyone else. "He who does not defend against or hinder injustice when he can is at fault as though he abandoned his parents or friends or country" (*Off.* 1.23). That might sound like hyperbole, but Cicero puts the point even more starkly later, when he implies that we should endure "death, poverty, pain, even loss of children, of close relatives (*propinquorum*), or of friends" rather than commit "an act of injustice against anyone" (3.26). Tullia, the child he lost, and her baby, the grandchild he probably lost, must have been on Cicero's mind as he wrote these words.

Although the family has no special place in the general demand to refrain from harm, I presume Cicero would concede it a special place among our thoughts about the justice of some particular actions. For we can harm our relatives in special ways. If some relatives, like children or elderly parents, have needs that only we can meet, and we do not, then we harm them. Often one can harm a close relative simply by saying things that would harm nobody else. If I tell you, dear reader, that I do not love you as a father should, I do not harm you. But if I said that to my children, I might well harm them.

Now I move to Cicero's explanation of *in*justice. For it sheds considerable light on his view of the family in *De Officiis*. We can see this by the comparison of **T5** and **T6**, as follows.

First, justice in *De Officiis* as it relates to harm seems simple to grasp: never harm anyone unprovoked. Yet unjust harm is common enough, even from those who accept such a principle. Why is that, Cicero?

> **T5** [Now we that we have outlined justice, injustice, and its causes] we shall be able easily to adjudicate the thing we ought to do (*quod ... officium sit*) at each moment – *if* we do not love ourselves too much, for to care about the affairs of others (*rerum alienarum*) is difficult. Albeit that Terence's character Chremes "thinks nothing human is foreign (*alienum*) to him", nevertheless, because we perceive and we feel things that result in our favour, or against us, more than we do things that come out that way for others, which we see as though across a wide gulf, we form judgments about others differently than we do about ourselves. (*Off.* 1.30)

Cicero agrees with Cato in **T2**: we *should* be the way Chremes claims to be in his famous line. Moreover, if we saw the consequences of our actions for other people as we see the consequences of events for ourselves, it would be *easy* to be like Chremes. The obstacle, Cicero says, is cognitive. Either we are unaware of how events impinge on others, or when we are aware of what someone else suffers, we do not feel its impact as we feel what happens to ourselves. It is hard to be like Chremes and therefore to be just.

Second, Cicero describes people who try to make family limit their duties of justice.

> **T6** For the thing some people say is stupid: that they will not take anything from a parent or a brother for their own advantage, but that they have another attitude to the rest of their fellow citizens. They decide that there is for them no justice with their fellow citizens, no society for sharing what is useful. This opinion pulls apart the whole society of the city. (*Off.* 3.28)

In Cicero's view, these people are not just. For they think it is acceptable to harm some others unprovoked. But even they will not harm those closer to themselves. Why? I suggest that Cicero can interpret the data in **T6** in light of **T5**. In the case of our families, Cicero thinks that it is easier to leap the cognitive gulf that separates us from others. For, first, the needs of those we are close to come easily to our attention. Second, when we love them, we perceive accurately the value of the help and harm we can give them. Notice that (according to Cicero) parental love is responsible for both of these cognitive advantages. For parental love is not only the origin of the love within the family, it is also what led the parents to make any family home at all (see **T8** below).[25]

3.b.ii The Family and Beneficence

Than beneficence, says Cicero, "nothing is more appropriate (*accommodatius*) to human nature" (*Off.* 1.42). Our instinct, he implies, is or should be to be open-handed. But the *virtue* of beneficence imposes "wariness" (*cautiones*) of three sorts. First, our giving should not harm those to whom we give. Second, our giving should not exceed our ability to give. Third, we should give to each according to "desert" or "standing" (*dignitate*) (ibid.). Cicero's discussion of wariness about "standing" contains much about the family. I concentrate on that kind of wariness here.

Cicero gives four criteria by which to determine "standing." I give these criteria in **T12** below (p. 37). Cicero says that these four criteria might yield different decisions. Therefore, with beneficence we must become "good calculators of our *officia* by adding and subtracting." We must call on experience and adapt our decisions to circumstance (*Off.* 1.59–60). In consequence, we should read much of what Cicero has to say about the *officia* of beneficence with an "all else equal" clause attached.

Cicero gives most space to his treatment of criterion **3**. He introduces this treatment as follows:

> **T7** But human society and connection (*coniunctio*) will best be preserved if, the more connected (*coniunctissimus*) each person is, the more kindness (*benignitatis*) is conferred upon him. But it seems we should look again more deeply at what the natural starting points of human society and community (*communitas*) might be. (*Off.* 1.50)

Cicero therefore returns to the topic of my Subsection 3.i above, the *natural origins* of society, this time in order to establish the natural facts about to whom each of us is more "connected." A consideration on which Cicero focuses in these sections is how much we hold in common with others. He says that originally and by nature, everything was held in common. But people have by use of their shared reason deemed some property private, or the possession of some city or group, and that we should respect these decisions (1.50–53).

---

[25] Cicero had not always thought that parents would naturally make a home, or at least not that fathers would do so. As a young man, in *De Inventione*, his guess was that before eloquence brought society together, "no one had seen children certainly his own" (*Inv.* 1.2).

Cicero's renewed discussion of the natural origin of society is a key passage on the family in *De Officiis*. Therefore, I shall quote from it at length, and comment on each part as we go.

> **T8** Indeed the binding of the society of relatives (*propinquorum*) is tighter, for out of that boundless society of the human race is enclosed something little and narrow. For since by nature it is common to animals, that they have the desire to procreate, the first society is in the coupling (*coniugio*) itself, the next in children, then one home, everything in common. (*Off.* 1.54)

Cicero begins to trace what I have suggested is a source of human society distinct from the desire to pursue the goals of reason together, namely, the nonrational desire for procreation and to care for children.

The process by which some aspects of society emerge from the desire to procreate starts from the "coupling" of a man and a woman. The word Cicero uses, *coniugium*, can bear many meanings.[26] It could apply to the coupling of animals or to "wedlock (considered in a physical point of view …)," to quote Lewis and Short's Victorian dictionary *sv*. But equally it could refer to a marriage, including legal Roman matrimony: *coniuges*, meaning those joined by a *coniugium*, was an ordinary word for legally married spouses.

Hence we must ask what Cicero means by *coniugium* in **T8**. The couple he describes has more than one child and builds a home in which to raise the children. Thus, in this case, *coniugium* must refer to more than sex, but rather to a relationship which, whether it began as a one-night stand or with a long-term commitment, is or becomes lasting and deliberate, with child-rearing among the couple's goals, at least eventually. On the other hand, this home is supposed to be (at least explanatorily or potentially) prior to the development of *conubium*, the right to marry legally, which is no surprise when (as we shall see) it is also prior to the formation of the sort of cities that can make laws.[27] Therefore, *coniugium* here is not necessarily legal matrimony. Thus, my translation "coupling" should be read in this light: a man and a woman deliberately forming a long-lasting sexual couple, not necessarily married in civil law, with care for their children on their mind.

Cicero says that in the family home, everything is in common. Inside its walls, so to speak, the original, natural condition of communism is

---

[26] See *TLL* and *OLD sv.*, Treggiari 1991: 6.
[27] On *conubium* see Treggiari 1991: 43–49. There is a well-known tale about the development of *conubium* at Rome. It was when nearby cities refused Romulus' request for *conubia*, rights of legal intermarriage, to the men of the newly founded Rome, that the Romans kidnapped the Sabine women, establishing Rome's own, internal marriage rights (Livy 1.9).

preserved, or perhaps reinstituted, by contrast to society outside the home where people have deemed some property private. Why this contrast? As we saw, the "extraordinary love" of parents for children leads "a person to be eager to provide whatever supplies plenty in nourishment and in lifestyle, not only for himself, but also for his spouse, and children ..." (See **T4** above.) Naturally, then, the mother and father regard their possessions as open to the children's and each other's use.[28]

In **T8**, Cicero does not say only that parents regard the home as a little society where they share everything with their children. He writes as though everyone in the home is a member of the society, using everything in common. Thus, we confront here a new mystery. For I have argued that Cicero roots parental love, and in a different way the love of parents for one another, in our reproductive anatomy and biology. But that explanation does not apply to a child's love of a parent, a sibling's love of a sibling, and so on. Nor, so far as I can see, does Cicero anywhere suggest an equivalent biological origin for these other kinds of love. Yet Cicero evidently thinks that children, siblings, and so on will love their families if not in the extraordinary manner of parents, nevertheless in some way that is similar enough for most of his purposes in *De Officiis*. How does he think this comes about?

I conjecture that Cicero means that it is from the parents that the children, and others in the home, *learn* to regard and behave towards the parents, each other, and the rest of family in something like the way that the parents regard the children. In loving families of the sort on which Cicero has focused, the children all their lives will have seen and benefited from parents who behave towards them with "extraordinary love." As they develop towards reason, the children acquire memories, concepts, and eventually beliefs and emotions in part as a result of these experiences. Their attitudes and behavior towards their siblings, and back towards their parents, are shaped to become like their parents' attitudes and behaviour towards themselves, to one degree or another. Others within the home, to one degree or another, are influenced to have similar rational or prerational attitudes. Of course, parents and the family home are not the only

---

[28] In Roman marriage, some couples shared their property legally, or more precisely, used property held by one *paterfamilias*, typically the husband or his father. But often the wife kept her own (or her father's) property distinct from her husband's. Furthermore, in law spouses were *unable* to give each other gifts (see Treggiari 1991: 365–96). Thus, even happily married Roman couples often did not share everything legally speaking. It is clear in this context that Cicero's aim is not to give the natural starting points of Roman law specifically. Further, when he says that everything in the home is in common, he does not necessarily mean common property legally speaking.

influence on the children or others in the home. Cicero's point is not that a loving family life mechanically, inevitably, or invariably induces children or others in the home to love the rest of the family.[29] Nevertheless, we commonly accept that parents and the family home are very often an important influence at least on the children of the family. Hence, nature's gift of parental affection is an elegant piece of design: it ensures that others who care for them for their own sake, and a little society within which people find it easy to act as though they were just and beneficent, even holding all in common, loom large in many people's most formative cognitions. In this way, nature gives many of us a helping hand in the hard but obligatory task of bridging the cognitive gulf between ourselves and at least some other people.

If I am right with this conjecture, I can solve the mystery I mentioned at the ends of Subsections 2.a and 2.b above, at least for the case of *De Officiis*. Cicero thinks parental affection is an origin of society. But he thinks that parental affection, grounded in the parents' own anatomy, is indeed unique to parents and does not itself spread to draw people into other kinds of love. Rather, what spreads are the attitudes and behavior for which parents are the model. They spread by the ability of human beings to learn. Nor need Cicero think parental love is without its problems. The role he gives it is consistent with the way that loving but flawed parents may put it into practice ineptly. Furthermore, we now see more of Cicero's answer to the questions with which I ended my introduction. Cicero can say that the loving "traditional family" of *De Officiis* could influence the social attitudes and behavior even of those who do not grow up in one, in that such family life, because natural, is a part of common human experience, seen at least in the homes of others, or in literature and art. It is the main way nature puts in most people at least a sleeping sense not only of life lived according to love, but also of the difference they could make by loving others.

Cicero goes on:

> **T9** But this is a starting point of a settlement (*principium urbis*) and as it were a seedbed of a republic (*seminarium rei publicae*). There follow the connections between brothers, afterwards between cousins on both sides, who, when one home can no longer hold them, go out into other homes as though to colonies. There follow rights of marriage (*conubia*), and relationships by marriage (*affinitates*), and from these still more relatives. This planting-out and propagation is the origin of republics (*origo ... rerum publicarum*). But connection by blood binds humans with good will

---

[29] See Cicero's account of the role of parental influence in a young adult's choice of lives, *Off.* 1.118.

(*benevolentia*) and dearness (*caritate*). For it is a great thing to have the same monuments of one's ancestors, to practice the same rites, to have tombs in common.[30] (*Off.* 1.54–55)

Cicero says the home is the "starting point" of an *urbs* and the "seedbed," *seminarium*, of the republic. I think these are two different relations, as follows.

First, *urbs* is only one of Cicero's words for a city. By contrast with *civitas* (the city of its own citizens), *patria* (one's country), or *res publica* (the republic, the people's commonwealth), Cicero tends to use *urbs* for the built settlement of houses, streets, people, temples, and so on.[31] The home is the *starting point* of such a settlement, presumably because it comes about when parents decide to build their homes near one another and to share streets, a water supply, temples, and so on. Such a settlement is not necessarily a republic, a true political community. It might be mediated purely by agreements, stemming from reason and the ability to communicate.

Second, a *seminarium* or "seedbed" was a plant nursery, where plants were grown in order to be planted out elsewhere or to provide seed for propagation (see *TLL sv*). It is the *propagation* from the *seminarium*, out of the home, that is the origin of the republic, of a *political* community. That is to say, the propagation stands to the republic as the home stands to the settlement. This propagation takes place when the home overflows, beloved people move into other homes like colonists on the family's behalf, and family relations of various sorts thus arise between people in one home and people in other homes. In consequence, the little circle of relations, who have familial love towards one another and recognize one another's human needs, spreads. These households, many of which one presumes will also be part of the same material settlement, thus start to form a political community, a republic.

Family relationships bring with them good will (*benevolentia*) and dearness (*caritas*). *Caritas* later came to be used for selfless, Christian love, Greek *agapē*, and is the source of the English "charity." But in Cicero it is the property of one who is *carus*, "dear," that is, is the property of the one loved, not of the lover. It is translated most accurately with the awkward word "dearness." Good will and dearness are paired properties:

---

[30] For what Cicero means by connection by ancestors, rites, and tombs, see his description of his own *two* countries (*patriae*) at *Leg.* 2.3–5. He was connected by such things to his Volscian home city, Arpinum, his "country by birth" (*germana patria*), but to Rome by citizenship. He says that for him the Roman republic as a whole, which contained Arpinum, must rank first in dearness (*caritate ... praestare*), though not by much.

[31] See *Rep.* 1.41, cf. *Sest.* 91.

the one who loves has good will towards the one who is dear. We see this, for example, in the definition of friendship Cicero gives to the speaker Laelius in his *De Amicitia*: "agreement on all matters human and divine with good will and dearness" (*Am.* 20).

Cicero continues:

> **T10** But when you have examined everything with reason and the soul, no society is more weighty, none is dearer, than that which there is for each one of us with the republic (*re publica*). Parents are dear, children, relatives, and friends are dear, but everyone's every dearness is embraced by one country (*patria*). Should it profit his country, what good man would hesitate to face death? (*Off.* 1.57)

Cicero does not say here that we find our fellow citizens dear, unless they happen to be our relatives or our friends. Rather he says that each of us individually enjoys a social bond, of the sort we have with an individual relative or friend, but with the republic corporately.[32] Here, at least, he attributes none of this bond to a rational agreement with the laws or the culture handed down by our fellow citizens. Rather, it stems from the dearness to us of our relatives and our friends, all of whom are included in our country.[33] We therefore find the republic as a whole at least as dear to us as our parents, children, or friends severally, for it is, to quote E. M. Atkins, "the stage and setting for all of [our] deepest loves."[34]

We have now reached the end of Cicero's description of the natural roots of human society, by which he determines with whom we are naturally more connected, one criterion for the third "wariness" by which we should confine virtuous beneficence, the criterion of standing. Now I turn to the *officia* of beneficence within or from the family that Cicero generates from this and his other criteria.

---

[32] This passage appears to contrast strikingly with some of what we saw in Section 2 above. In **T2** Cato said for the Stoics that the "shared appeal" of humanity in general was born from parental love. Meanwhile, elsewhere in *De Finibus*, Piso says for Antiochus of Ascalon that dearness creeps out from the household "to embrace the whole human race (*totius complexu gentis humanae*)" (*Fin.* 5.65, cf. Schofield 2012a: 176–79). By contrast, in **T10**, "everyone's every dearness is embraced by one country (*patria una complexa est*)". Thus for Cato and Piso, parental love ultimately draws all humanity together, but it appears that in *De Officiis* its effect goes no further than one's country. What to make of this apparent difference is a vexed question, but beyond the scope of the family and therefore of this chapter.

[33] This part of Cicero's description seems odd. Perhaps we always share a country with our families. But we can be friends with foreigners. Cicero had a friend in Tiro, his secretary and confidant, who was a slave until Cicero freed him, and who was therefore not a citizen of the republic until then. Why would Cicero think that *any* friendship is embraced by one country? Perhaps he means *res publica* or *patria* here in a more flexible way than we are used to, such that any foreign friends we have are in some loose sense part of our country, connected to it through us.

[34] Atkins 1990: 275.

This last section of Cicero's treatment of beneficence begins as follows:

> **T11** But should there be a competition and a comparison over to whom we should give more of our duty (*officium*), first on the list would be country and parents, to whom we are obligated by the very great benefits (*beneficiis*) they have given, children would be next and the whole household that looks to us alone and cannot have any other refuge, and thereafter relatives with whom we are on good terms, with whom even our fortunes are for the most part in common. For that reason, the necessities that support life are owed most of all to those I have just mentioned. But a common life and lifestyle, planning, conversations, consolations, sometimes even reproaches flourish most in friendships, and the most pleasant is the friendship that is joined by similarity of character. (*Off.* 1.58)

This is not one ranked list. The first ranking given is only of people to whom we owe "necessities to support life" (*necessaria praesidia vitae*). Other things, like our conversation, are most fruitfully given to people not placed in the first ranking, to friends. In principle, then, we might decide correctly and consistently, for example, to make our parents and children the priority for the money we spend, but our close friends our priority in how we spend our leisure time. As we saw, Cicero himself preferred Atticus' company even to that of his wife and children (p. 18 above).

I shall interpret the ranking of those to whom we most owe necessities to support life using the criteria that Cicero himself gave us. We can begin with the three kinds of "wariness" (see p. 31 above). Whether the benefit given will in fact help will depend on the particular circumstances of a particular gift, so I presume it does not help with this ranking. Whether the gift is beyond the ability of the giver will often be beside the point within family, since there property is regarded as common, so the giver will often not simply lose what is given. In any case, this second kind of wariness again seems unhelpful for establishing the ranking. Thus, the third kind of wariness, whereby we apportion our generosity according to the "standing" of the receiver, seems likely to be what governs the ranking in **T11**.

As to standing, here are Cicero's four criteria (cf. p. 31 above):

> **T12** We must look to
> 1. the character of him to whom we might give the benefit,
> 2. and his attitude towards us,
> 3. and his community and society of life [*sc.* with us],
> 4. and the services (*officia*) that he has previously conferred for our use.
>
> We may hope that these all coincide. If they don't, the greater and more numerous grounds will have more weight. (*Off.* 1.45)

Let us now apply the four criteria to the various parts of the family in T11, to see why Cicero might have ranked our *officia* towards them as he did. I will take these in reverse order.

First, consider the part of the family ranked last in T11, "relatives" other than our children or parents "with whom we are on good terms." From context we may infer that these are relatives in other households, including perhaps such close relatives as siblings, or any in our own households who have means independent of our own. We have seen how nature has connected us to these people and inclined us to share our property with them. Thus, we share "even our fortunes" with them. Therefore, it is no doubt by criterion 3 above all that their claim on our generosity ranks so high. Still, Cicero's addition, "with whom we are on good terms," points to more. It suggests that there could be relatives in other households to whom we are by nature strongly connected, but who should fall below the ranking in T11 because we are *not* on good terms with them. This is explicable by the other criteria. We can see how such people might fall afoul of criterion 1 (perhaps we fell out because we perceived flaws in their characters), 2 (since we are on bad terms, they may well be hostile to us), or 4 (perhaps they have given us less than they should).

In second place come "children ... and the whole household that looks to us alone and cannot have any other refuge." Note that this sentence is written narrowly from Cicero's point of view, a Roman *paterfamilias* upon whom his household depended legally and economically, and who expects young Marcus, to whom the sentence is addressed, to become a *paterfamilias* in turn. To address explicitly the *officia* of readers not in that position, Cicero would need to have said more. Here criterion 3 is plainly dominant given the strength of the natural connection from parent to child in particular, and from householder to household in general, that we have explored. As to those in the household who love "us," criterion 2 is also at work.

"The whole household" for a wealthy Roman like Cicero included his slaves. Indeed, there were probably whole unfree families living beside the free family of the *paterfamilias*.[35] Slaves often go unmentioned in *De Officiis* – shamefully so. But of course they were human beings too, and Cicero therefore insists that they are owed justice like anybody else (1.41). Now we learn, perhaps surprisingly, that a *paterfamilias* also owes to them the same level of beneficence as he does to his own children.[36]

---

[35] The Latin *familia* referred to all the dependents of the *paterfamilias*. It is a much broader term than the English "family": a *familia* could include many families.

[36] If the *paterfamilias* had married his wife under the arrangement known as *cum manu*, then she too was his dependent. If not, then she was not.

Some clarification follows in 1.59: "But in paying all our duties (*officiis*) we shall have to see what each person most needs and what each can or cannot attain without us." In the latter respect, the children and the slaves of a *paterfamilias* resemble one another, for they "look to [him] alone." We might also reflect that by criterion 4, many slaves, at least those who (heroically, in their circumstances) strove to act thoughtfully, would have given many *officia* to the *paterfamilias*.

Now Cicero surely did not expect free and unfree people in the same household dependably to find one another dear as he expected each family to do. Nor, surely, can he have hoped that heads of households would share their property as though in common with their slaves. Thus these brief, glib allusions to all the people who lived in Cicero's legal power demand clarification. It is a tragic sign of the thoughtlessness and injustice of Roman slavery that this was all he had to say. But it could be that (however hypocritically, patronizingly, and mistakenly) Cicero thought it was relatively easy for somebody like him to grasp rationally the needs even of the legally unfree people with whom he shared a household – whose children played with his children, perhaps – and therefore that it was relatively easy for him to be just and beneficent towards those people. In these remarks, we also see that like justice at large, beneficence in the household has nothing to do with nationality, so that each household is (so to speak) a miniature cosmopolis. For slaves were, by definition, not citizens of the same republic as the householder, but rather aliens under the same roof. Yet it is the roof, not the republic, that defines this second rank among those humans to whom we, or at least heads of households, owe beneficence.

I end with the first rank: parents. That parents rank first is most revealing. For if we attended only to the origins of virtue, and the extraordinary love to which parental affection leads, it might seem that the voice of nature tells parents to put their children first. Yet Cicero implies that someone who has both parents and children should give to parents before children. It would seem that the most choiceworthy actions to which nature leads us by the gift of parental love are not a parent's care for children, but rather the children's *response* to that care. Why?

In T11, Cicero points us to criterion 4: we should respond to all the benefits parents have given us. As the donors of life, of all a child's necessities, and of upbringing at large, among individual humans parents win on this score. On criterion 3, a child's natural connection and community of life with a parent ranks high. As to criterion 2, Cicero says the kind of attitude that we should look for is not to be judged by warm feelings: "We should give more to him who has more affection for us (*diligamur*), but let us not judge benevolence in the manner of adolescents, by some ardor of love" (*Off.* 1.47). Parents of the sort Cicero is focused on demonstrate by their actions stable, planned, generous care for their children. For many people, then, their parents will win by criterion 2.

What about criterion 1, "character"? At first sight, it might seem that even the loving parents of *De Officiis* on the whole will do no better or worse than any other group of people. For in truth, such parents are no better or worse than any other group of people. But, as we have seen, loving parents, even when they are thoroughly vicious people, tend to act justly and beneficently towards their children, or more precisely in the case of vicious parents, to act as though they were just and beneficent. Cicero says in **T11** that children should respond to parents' *beneficiis*, their beneficent, which is to say their virtuously given, gifts, and not merely to their *officia* or to the useful things they have given. So, from the point of view of their children, loving parents on the whole *do* score well on criterion 1.

But on reflection, we can go further. Cicero points out that, aside from nature itself, in the world of *De Officiis* we will not encounter perfect virtue, and therefore we are doing well if we find *simulacra*, "images" of virtue (1.46). The word *simulacra* suggests in particular the stone or paint images of the gods which, however flawed as images, allowed Romans to imagine divinities they never saw. Consider that, strictly within the family, loving parents of the sort Cicero describes seem to be as Chremes claims to be, and as Cato implies the sage will be in general, with nothing human foreign to them. By the standards of fools, they seem to be constant: they make and keep long-term plans for the basic needs, education, or lifestyle of the family, upending their previous lives as though they care about their children in the same way they care about themselves. They seem to hold property in common as nature originally gave it. Like statues of the gods, at least from the point of view of their children, and strictly within a loving family of the sort Cicero describes in *De Officiis*, parents are images (however flawed) of the *perfectly* virtuous, and their family home is an image of a more virtuous society than is the foolish world. Nature is the artist who makes the image for us.

4 Friends and Family in *De Officiis*

Cicero discusses friendship in *De Officiis* immediately after his discussion of the strong natural connections in the family. He describes it as another occasion of very strong love, between two virtuous people who recognize a similar character in each other (1.55–56).[37] A full discussion of Cicero on friendship, a topic to which he previously devoted his *De Amicitia*, would be out of place here. But it is worthwhile to close this chapter with what friendship shows us about familial love in *De Officiis*. I have argued that the family teaches us about loving others. A word whose presence in that thesis might seem no more than trivial is "others." But in Cicero's writings it carries unexpected weight.

Dearness, *caritas*, in friendship (cf. **T10** above) cannot arise only out of familial love, and often will not do so at all, since many friends are unrelated. Rather, it arises out of a rational recognition of one's friend's character. Cicero says that friendship is special in that it can bring together "one person" (*unus*) out of more than one (*pluribus*). As Cicero puts it in *De Amicitia*, my friend is *alter idem*, "another self" (*Am.* 80). I care about my friend as I care about myself. Now, in one sense, since my friend is *another* myself, this is altruism on my part, care for the *alter*, the other. But in another sense, it is not altruism, because my friend is another *myself*. In that sense, when I care for my friend, I do not care for someone altogether other than me.

By contrast, family love is not unitive. It does not make (for example) parent and child into one person. Parents might love children who they find are very dissimilar from themselves, emphatically other. Yet, according to Cicero, parents still care for such children as they care for themselves. This is, emphatically and literally, altruism, in a way that friendship is not.

This observation helps us to understand the quotations with which I began this chapter. Those quotations seem double-edged, perhaps shockingly so. Cicero assures his son that he loves him very much. This seems heart-warming. But he says he would love his son much more if he should delight in his father's precepts. This conditional part of Cicero's love seems cold, even cruel. I suggest that Cicero wishes by means of *De Officiis* to make a friend of his son. Marcus, the damaged but sweet toddler whom he has now raised into an undergraduate of doubtful promise, is extremely dear to Cicero in the manner of a son, an other. But what his parental love leads Cicero to offer now to young Marcus, the budding philosopher in search of self-improvement, is the hope and the material to achieve what Cicero would recognize as "the fine in another" (*honestum ... in alio*), and thus to unite himself in friendship with his father (1.55).

---

[37] Konstan 2017: 304 argues that there is a tension between Cicero's respect for friendship as a recognition of virtue, and his sense that human love is "as unconstrained and instinctive as that of tigress for its cub." He suggests (plausibly) that such a tension may have been heightened in Cicero by Tullia's death (cf. Konstan 2015). But it seems to me that Cicero can account for both, at least in *De Officiis*, as stemming from rational interaction and natural parental affection, respectively, but as arriving in common at a response to the *caritas* that the lover perceives in the loved.

CHAPTER 2

Conflict of Duties in Cicero's De Officiis

Georgia Tsouni

1 Cicero's *De Officiis* and the Greek Concept of Duty

Cicero's *De Officiis* offers the most extensive discussion of the Stoic concept of duty (Greek *kathēkon*). This chapter addresses the way Cicero discusses in that work the topic of conflict between different duties. It proceeds in three steps: The first part of the chapter discusses Cicero's relation to his Greek sources and the extent to which Cicero diverged from Panaetius' treatise 'On Duty' in his treatment of conflict of duties. The second part analyses how, in case of conflict, duties are prioritized in *De Officiis* according to the specific circumstances of action. It is thereby shown that conflict of duties in *De Officiis* excludes 'tragic dilemmas'. Finally, the third part presents the conflict between the 'expedient' and 'honourable' courses of action in the third book of *De Officiis* and Cicero's attempt to present such a conflict as merely apparent.

Treatises on duty had an already long philosophical tradition by the time of Cicero's writing of *De Officiis*, spanning from the early Stoa down to the Roman era. Thus, treatises 'On Duty' (*Peri tou kathēkontos*)[1] are attested for both Zeno and his successor Cleanthes, as also for Sphaerus and Chrysippus.[2] Numerous titles of works on duty also survive from the post-Chrysippean era of the Stoic school down to Panaetius and his pupils, Posidonius (DL 7.124; 7.129) and Hecato of Rhodes (*Off.* 3.63).[3]

---

[1] Although 'On Duties' is the standard way of rendering the title of Cicero's work, there is a debate as to whether 'duty' is an appropriate translation for the Greek term *kathēkon*. Many scholars, including Long and Sedley, have opted for a more general rendering such as that of 'appropriate action' on the assumption that the (modern) sense of duty is too narrow to convey the Stoic term. Cf. Dyck 1996: 8. A lot depends on how narrowly we understand the notion of duty, cf. Woolf (2015: 171): "'duties' has a rather narrower range in English, with its specific connotations of moral obligation'. The case for a translation of *kathēkon* as 'duty' has been defended again by Visnjic 2021: 139–52, who draws attention to the normative connotations of the term already in its pre-Stoic use.

[2] DL 7.4 (for Zeno), 7.174 (for Cleanthes), 7.177 (for Sphaerus) and Plutarch, *De Stoicorum Repugnantiis* 1045e, 1047f (for Chrysippus).

[3] *Hecatonem quidem Rhodium, discipulum Panaetii, video in iis libris, quos de officio scripsit Q. Tuberoni.* Cf. *Off.* 3.89.

Suggestive of the considerable popularity that such treatises enjoyed in Rome is that M. Brutus, as referred to in Seneca *Ep.* 95.45, had written a treatise *Peri kathēkontos* (in Greek), where he gave practical advice (*praecepta*) to 'parents, children and brothers'.[4] In line with this, Cicero, at the beginning of *De Officiis*, presents the handing down of advice concerning which action is dutiful as common among all philosophers and as a most popular philosophical topic.[5] While admittedly using Greek treatises on duties as a model, Cicero's discussion of duties extends far beyond a mere imitation of his Greek sources. Cicero's contribution is evident not only in the framing of the treatise as a letter to his son Marcus, thereby giving to the discussion a pedagogical and protreptic function as well, but also in the way he relates the topic of duty to his peculiar epistemological assumptions, adjusting it to the dialectical structure of his dialogues.

This becomes clear if we consider Cicero's rendering of the definition of the Stoic concept of duty. The 'standard' definition of the early Stoic *kathēkon*, as 'what is consistent [sc. with nature] in life, which, after having been done, admits of a well-reasoned defence'[6] (a definition which, as Cicero notes at *Off.* 1.7, Panaetius strikingly did not mention in his treatise) is explicitly alluded to at *Off.* 1.8 and is given more attention at *Fin.* 3.58, where Cicero provides a Latin translation of the second part of the definition.[7] Cicero translates the 'well-reasoned' (*eulogon*) in the Greek definition of duty with the – more permissive – adjective *probabilis* which is also used by Cicero to translate Carneades' epistemological criterion of the *pithanon*, meaning 'worthy of approval', 'likely' or 'persuasive', an adjective frequently used in Cicero in relation to his allegiance to the 'New Academy'.[8] Thus, his translation of the term blurs the distinction between the epistemological commitments of the Stoa and Academic scepticism but, additionally, it places the focus on the psychological and rhetorical effect of a judgement linked to the justification of a duty.[9]

---

[4] *M. Brutus in eo libro quem* περὶ καθήκοντος *inscripsit dat multa praecepta et parentibus et liberis et fratribus.*

[5] *Off.* 1.5: *Quis est enim, qui nullis officii praeceptis tradendis philosophum se audeat dicere?* Seneca *Ep.* 94.1–17 gives us a glimpse of the way early Stoics treated the part of philosophy which handed down advice for conduct.

[6] *to akolouthon en zōē, ho prachthen eulogon apologian echei*, Stobaeus 2.85.14–15 = *SVF* 1.55.13–14. See also DL 7.107 = *SVF* 1.55.6–8.

[7] *Est autem officium, quod ita factum est, ut eius facti probabilis ratio reddi possit.*

[8] Cf. *Luc.* 32.

[9] On the rhetorical origin of the word *probabilis* and its positive connotations in Latin, see Görler 2004: 69–71. For the meaning of *eulogon* in the 'New Academic' Arcesilaus, see Brennan 1996: 334. For a defence of the rendering of *eulogon* as 'well-reasoned', ibid. 328.

Further, Cicero makes clear at *Fin.* 3.58–59 that in rendering the Stoic definition of duty he refers to the so-called middle duty (*medium officium*). Accordingly, in *Off.* 1.8 Cicero mentions the following division (which he ascribes to the Stoic philosophers): duties can be either 'perfect', in which case they are the actions of the sage (in Greek *katorthōmata*), or 'middle' (*media*) and 'common' (*communia*) both to the sage and to the non-sage. It is to this latter category of 'middle' duties that a 'reasonable (or persuasive) account' (*ratio probabilis*) is linked and, as Cicero makes clear, they are the object of discussion in *De Officiis*.[10] Elsewhere in the work (2.7), Cicero claims that his project of supplying advice regarding duty is compatible with that of a follower of Academic scepticism, as long as one understands the difference between 'certain' (*certa*) and 'persuasive' (*probabilia*).[11] The search for a *probabilis* account of duty in *De Officiis* thus incorporates not only Stoic doctrine but also numerous historical *exempla*, legal rules and the presentation of opposed views, something particularly linked to the topic of conflict of duties.

Cicero's work explicitly relies on a treatise 'On Appropriate Action' (*Peri tou kathēkontos*) of the (Middle-) Stoic Panaetius. Thus, Cicero writes to Atticus in 44 BCE that he finished a work on appropriate action, so far as Panaetius goes, in two books, whereas Panaetius treated the same topics in three books.[12] From the independent evidence of Aulus Gellius, we know that Panaetius wrote his work with the purpose of leading people towards virtuous actions, thereby also using rhetorical means, as the powerful analogy of the prudent agent with a 'pancratist' suggests.[13] His treatise seems to have been geared towards the 'paraenetic' aspects of duty, those related to advice (*praecepta*) and instruction on how to lead one's life. In line

---

[10] *Off.* 1.8: *medium autem officium id esse dicunt, quod cur factum sit, ratio probabilis reddi possit.* The topic is treated more elaborately at *Fin.* 3.58–59. Cicero attests clearly at *Off.* 3.14 that the topic of *De Officiis* are the 'middle' duties: *Haec enim officia, de quibus his libris disputamus, media Stoici appellant.*

[11] *Nos autem, ut ceteri alia certa, alia incerta esse dicunt, sic ab his dissentientes alia probabilia, contra alia dicimus.* Cf. also *Off.* 1.18, where Cicero criticises 'rash assent' (*temere assentiamur*). For the sceptical orientation of the *De Officiis*, cf. also Woolf 2015: 187.

[12] τὰ περὶ τοῦ καθήκοντος, *quatenus Panaetius, absolvi duobus; illius tres sunt, Att.* 16.11.4. Later on in the same letter, Cicero praises Panaetius' exposition (*de duobus primis praeclare disserit*). However, he is also keen to note that despite his dependence on Panaetius, he is not performing the task of a mere translator, see *Off.* 2.60: *ut et hic ipse Panaetius, quem multum in his libris secutus sum, non interpretatus.* Cf. also 3.7, where Cicero says that he followed Panaetius but also applied some 'amendment' (*correctio*) to his work. Panaetius' treatise as a source for *De Officiis* is discussed by Dyck 1996: 17–29.

[13] *NA* 13.28. For a hypothesis about the original context of the passage in Panaetius' treatise, see Dyck 1979b.

with this is Cicero's evidence in *Off.* 1.9 that Panaetius offered a division of ways of deliberation concerning which course of action to follow (*consilii capiendi deliberatio*) which involved doubt (*dubitant … tertium genus dubitandi*) about which course of action is the one to be deemed dutiful. The emphasis on doubt in deliberation suggests that Panaetius conceived his treatise as a guiding aid for those who, evidently, do not possess the wisdom which guarantees unerring action.

Panaetius divided enquiry or deliberation into the appropriate action into three categories (*tria genera exquirendi*): the first category concerns the question whether a duty is virtuous or not (*honestum an turpe*), the second concerns whether it is expedient or inexpedient (*utile an inutile*), whereas the third concerns which way to judge in case there is an (apparent) conflict between the virtuous and the expedient courses of action.[14] The structure of Cicero's *De Officiis* reflects the division of Panaetius; thus, in the first book, it is shown how *kathēkonta* derive from each of the four fundamental virtues towards which we are drawn by nature, namely wisdom, justice, courage and temperance. Particular emphasis is put here on the virtues which preserve the 'fellowship of human beings' (*hominum inter homines societas*), and especially on those which derive from justice (*iustitia*) and the related virtue of beneficence (*beneficentia*) (*Off.* 1.20). The second book of Cicero's treatise discusses the way duties aimed at acquiring 'the expedient' (*utile*) *also* rely on the principles of virtue. The identification of special duties aimed at expediency seems again to draw on Panaetius' discussion, which most probably diverged from the earlier Stoics on this point.[15] Panaetius seems also to have grounded the virtues in nature as the extensive references to the mechanism of natural appropriation in Cicero's work suggest.[16]

Regarding the kind of deliberation about duties which involves the conflict between the expedient and the honourable, Cicero underlines that Panaetius did not develop in his (lost) treatise this third kind of enquiry into duties, although he promised to do so in the future.[17] We cannot be entirely sure whether Panaetius, by addressing such a conflict, merely alluded to ordinary ways of thinking about duty (without a wish to expand on it further) or, as Cicero implies, his treatise was left incomplete on this point (see *Off.* 3.33), either due to the difficulty of the subject or out of

---

[14] *cum haec inter se pugnare videantur, quo modo iudicandum sit*, *Att.* 16.11.4; cf. *Off.* 1.9, 3.7.
[15] Cf. Dyck 1996: 17. On the coherence of Panaetius' discussion of duties, see Veillard 2014: 101–7.
[16] *Off.* 1.11–14.
[17] *Att.* 16.11.4: *de duobus primis praeclare disserit, de tertio pollicetur se deinceps scripturum sed nihil scripsit.* Cf. *Off.* 3.7: *de tertio autem genere deinceps se scripsit dicturum nec exsolvit id, quod promiserat.*

negligence.[18] The information that Panaetius lived on for thirty years after the completion of the three books that Cicero used (mentioned at *Off.* 3.8) suggests a deliberate rather than an unintentional omission. The remarks at *Off.* 3.9–10 reveal that there was a relevant discussion already in the time of Posidonius regarding the incompleteness of the work, with some defending an intentional omission of the third part of the division of the enquiry into duty and others an unintentional one.[19] Cicero himself notes the incompatibility of a conflict between the *honestum* and the *utile* with the Stoic view which postulated that these two notions are coextensive.[20] He therefore concludes at *Off.* 3.12 that Panaetius should not have introduced the sort of deliberation where that which may appear useful is compared to what is honourable.[21] He goes on to specify, however, that Panaetius referred only to an *apparent* conflict between what *seems* expedient and the *honestum* and did not thereby mean to say that we should place expediency above the principle of virtue (thus breaching Stoic commitments); according to Cicero, Panaetius suggested only that one should know how to adjudicate correctly between these two things, whenever they happen to occur in one's mind.[22] Cicero feels free to develop the topic far further than Panaetius did by presenting the possibility that *honestum* and the *utile* may function as two conflicting principles of action (a possibility that he at the same time condemns).[23] The expansion of such a discussion is seen as an original contribution on Cicero's part which is meant to complete Panaetius' discussion on duty.[24]

Further, Cicero announces the discussion of what is among two honourable courses of actions the 'most honourable' (1.152–61) as an original *supplement* to Panaetius' division on duty which constitutes his model in

---

[18] For the incompleteness of Panaetius' work, see also Dyck 1996: 24.

[19] *Off.* 3.9: *Minime vero assentior iis, qui negant eum locum a Panaetio praetermissum, sed consulto relictum.*

[20] *Off.* 3.11: *Cui quidem ita sunt Stoici assensi, ut et, quicquid honestum esset, id utile esse censerent, nec utile quicquam, quod non honestum.* On the Stoic views cf. LS 60 G, I.

[21] *non videtur debuisse* (sc. Panaetius) *eiusmodi deliberationem introducere, in qua quod utile videretur cum eo, quod honestum est, compararetur.*

[22] *Off.* 3.34.

[23] It is suggestive that Cicero projects at *Off.* 3.13 the possibility of conflict also onto the Stoic ethical theory by presenting the ideal of a life according to nature as 'choosing the things which are according to nature unless they conflict with virtue' (*cetera autem, quae secundum naturam essent, ita legere, si ea virtuti non repugnarent*). This may be reflecting a Peripatetic division between the 'virtuous' and 'expedient' things (cf. *Off.* 3.20) but does not do justice to the way Stoics regard the unique value of the *honestum*. For a critique of this way of presenting Stoic theory (the so-called *salva virtute* model), see the discussion in Brennan 2005: 220–26.

[24] Suggestive in this regard is Cicero's use at *Off.* 3.34 of a proverbial expression when saying that he is going to 'fight his own battle' (*Marte nostro*), without the use of other writers, regarding the issue apparently first raised by Panaetius.

the first two books of De Officiis.²⁵ Thus, there is an explicit reference to a 'comparison' (*comparatio*) or, even, 'competition' (*contentio*) among duties that derive from the four cardinal virtues at *Off.* 1.58.²⁶ This is a topic that Cicero exploits for his own purposes: such a 'comparison' of duties gives, for example, the opportunity for Cicero to show his preference for the active/political action against the pursuit of theoretical studies in case of conflict.²⁷ Thus, Cicero states at *Off.* 1.154 that there is no one who wouldn't cast aside even the most dignified objects of learning if 'one's country were suddenly and critically endangered and one could come to its aid'.²⁸ This seems to reflect Cicero's own stance in the period of writing of *De Officiis* and his renewed political involvement after Caesar's assassination.²⁹

Another aspect with which Cicero supplements the Panaetian discussion on duty is that of the discussion of duties under particular circumstances which was, according to the testimony of Cicero, absent from Panaetius' work on duty.³⁰ This topic had been discussed, however, in other Greek sources: Cicero tells us that Posidonius' treatise on the *kathēkon* contained a section 'on the appropriate action according to circumstances' (*peri tou kata peristasin kathēkontos*) (*Att.* 16.11.4),³¹ a category that he conveys in Latin with the expression *ex tempore officium* (*Off.* 3.32). Also, a 'casuistic' approach seems to have been central to Hecato's (lost) treatise *On Duty* as well, which Cicero mentions at *Off.* 3.63 but for which no fragments

---

²⁵ *Off.* 1.152: *Eorum autem ipsorum, quae honesta sunt, potest incidere saepe contentio et comparatio, de duobus honestis utrum honestius, qui locus a Panaetio est praetermissus.* Cf 1.58. See also 1.7: *num quod officium, aliud alio maius sit.* There is a similar *comparatio* raised in the domain of the *utile* at 2.86–90.
²⁶ The rhetorical origin of an argument based on *comparatio* may be traced at *De Partitione Oratoria* 66.
²⁷ The defence of the priority of duties which are aimed at preserving human fellowship is contained at *Off.* 1.152–60. To that effect, Cicero uses both rhetorical means (like a 'thought experiment') (1.153) but also the Aristotelian idea, shared by the Stoics as well, that humans are 'political' animals (1.157–8). Cicero also (following Posidonius) mentions a possible conflict between duties deriving from seemliness and those which aim at preserving human fellowship but he dismisses the (real) possibility of such a conflict without further explanation at 1.159.
²⁸ *Quis enim est tam cupidus in perspicienda cognoscendaque rerum natura, ut, si ei tractanti contemplantique res cognitione dignissimas subito sit allatum periculum discrimenque patriae, cui subvenire opitularique possit, non illa omnia relinquat atque abiciat?*
²⁹ The superiority of political and practical action against the pursuit of theoretical studies comes to the fore at *Off.* 1.19, where Cicero claims that theoretical studies should only be pursued when political engagement has been interrupted: *omnes artes in veri investigatione versantur, cuius studio a rebus gerendis abduci contra officium est. Virtutis enim laus omnis in actione consistit, a qua tamen fit intermissio saepe multique dantur ad studia reditus.* See also 1.28 (with the example of Plato's philosopher-kings and their devotion to theoretical studies); 1.70. Cf. Dyck 1996: 38.
³⁰ *Off.* 3.33.
³¹ Posidonius' treatise is referred to explicitly also at *Off.* 1.159 and 3.8.

survive. The discussion of particular cases, by highlighting the various contingent parameters that impinge on our actions, brings to light the idea that in many cases we will have to choose among the various duties that impinge on us and that in many cases as well, it will be impossible to *simultaneously* fulfill all the duties that derive from the virtues. The use of numerous particular case studies and *exempla* drawn from Roman history bring to the fore, perhaps even more than the Greek treatises did, the possible conflict between duties. Whether this amounts to a real conflict, involving 'tragic dilemmas', for a moral agent remains to be seen.

2   Conflict between Duties of Honourableness and (Seeming) Tragic Dilemmas in *De Officiis*

The focus in the first two books of Cicero's treatise on duties lies in the specification of the actions that are dutiful in different domains of life, and, thus, may be recommended, even to those who do not yet possess a virtuous disposition. The specification of what an appropriate action is in each individual case depends on a number of factors; Cicero's emphasis on the particular circumstances or 'occasions' (*tempora*) of actions[32] maps onto a Stoic distinction which is known from Diogenes Laërtius (DL 7.109) between *kathēkonta* 'independent of circumstances' (*aneu peristaseōs*) and those 'dependent on circumstances' (*peristatika* or *kata peristasin*).[33]

This already suggests a certain idea of 'conflict' which was accommodated in Stoic thought by means of the proposed distinction. For if it is a duty to preserve one's health, according to the 'good reasoning' exemplified by a teleological and providential nature, does it not constitute a contradiction that in some cases it is a duty to harm our health, or even to kill ourselves? Specifying duty within the particular circumstances of action suggests that it is not.[34] For there is no conflict at the level of 'token' duties but only at the level of 'types' of duties, which are, however, seen independently of dutiful *action*. An example of a seeming dispute concerning which action is appropriate is provided in a Stoic source, where it is mentioned that to tell the truth may seem in some cases to be in conflict with helping someone, as in the case of a doctor who uses lies in order to

---

[32] See *Off.* 1.31; 1.115. Cf. 1.59, where it is stated that the degrees of relationships and those of circumstances are not the same: *ita non idem erunt necessitudinum gradus qui temporum*.

[33] Visnjic 2021: 42–44 understands *peristasis* more narrowly as 'emergency/crisis/dire circumstance'.

[34] The difficulty to formulate a single rule or principle of Stoic deliberation is thematised in Barney 2003. See also Woolf 2007, who refers to the 'particularist' outlook of the Stoic theory of *kathēkonta* on the basis of Cicero's *De Officiis*, and Klein 2015: 274–75.

convince a patient for a treatment which is necessary for his or her health.[35] The Stoics resolve such a potential conflict by identifying the *kathēkon* not on the basis of the falsehood of the statement it is accompanied by but on the basis of the *intention* that the utterance of the statement serves. In the case of the doctor mentioned, his act of lying does not constitute a violation of duty (despite the fact that in general truth-telling is a duty), since it is in this case a (necessary) means to discharging the actual duty of helping the patient.

Accordingly, Cicero alludes to such cases when duties undergo a change and 'the opposite becomes the case' (*commutantur fiuntque contraria*),[36] giving the example of not returning a deposit as an example of a dutiful action, in case the returning of the deposit produces more harm than benefit (3.95). The benefit implied in this case does not refer to the individual benefit of the agent but to the benefit of all those affected by the action. This complies with what Cicero repeatedly calls, using a judicial metaphor, a 'rule of procedure' (*formula*) according to which we should resolve conflicts regarding duties.[37] According to this, a dutiful action should be based on a judgement as to whether the common good or the 'fellowship of the human race' (*societas generis humani*) is best preserved in this way. This principle is further justified in *De Officiis* on the basis of a Stoic line of reasoning.[38] If it turns out that a generic duty needs to be violated under the particular circumstances in order to preserve justice towards others, then that action should be chosen. Accordingly, Cicero states that a wise man is not allowed to steal other people's resources in order to survive, unless by remaining alive he or she *intends* to confer a great benefit to his state or to the human community.[39] Only in this latter case is stealing not reprehensible.

A case study from *Off.* 1.32 serves to illustrate the point that there is no real conflict between (Stoic) duties. The example is particularly pertinent because it thematises the act of promising, a paradigmatic case of duty in the modern sense of the word. Given its judicial context, it may as well be an original Ciceronian contribution to the debate in addition to Panaetius'

---

[35] For the example, see Philo *On the Cherubim* 15 = LS 59H.
[36] *Off.* 1.31: *Sed incidunt saepe tempora, cum ea quae maxime videntur digna esse iusto homine, eoque quem virum bonum dicimus, commutantur fiuntque contraria.* Cf. *Off.* 3.19, 3.96.
[37] See *Off.* 3.19.
[38] See *Off.* 3.21–25.
[39] *Off.* 3.30. This is also shown with an example taken from Hecato at 3.90. In the hypothetical case sketched there, when two sages can have access to a single plank after a shipwreck and can contribute equally to the republic's and their own interests, Hecato suggests that 'they will give in to the other as if losing by lot or by playing odds and evens'.

Greek examples. In the relevant scenario that Cicero discusses, the benefit ensuing to a friend, whom we have promised to advocate for in court, is weighed against the loss incurred by neglecting another course of action, that of attending to one's son who has, in the meantime, fallen seriously ill. The example clearly suggests that, taking into account the harm produced to both parties, it is not against duty to break one's promise to a friend on this occasion[40] and, furthermore, suggests that there is only *one* appropriate action to be performed in this case, namely that of attending to one's sick child. Cicero's additional remarks at 1.32 that the person to whom one had made the promise 'would be failing in his *officium* if he complained that he had been abandoned'[41] are further suggestive of a lack of regret on the part of the agent, something which corroborates the assumption that no duty has been omitted in this case and that no *absolute* value is assigned to the act of promise keeping.[42] The same applies to cases when one has promised something which proves harmful either to oneself or to another, in which case it is again dutiful to act against what one has promised with the proviso that one does not thereby harm the other party.[43] Thus, the fact that some courses of action, which are generally considered duties, are not appropriate under particular circumstances does not signify any real conflict among *kathēkonta*, or any conflict in the soul of the sage. It rather suggests that there is only *one* appropriate action under the particular circumstances, the one that the sage would perform,[44] and that performing one appropriate action does not leave another appropriate action undone.

The specific parameters which impinge on our actions take into account internal factors as well, such as our own character traits. Cicero, borrowing again from Panaetius, discusses the way one's *individual* nature, or 'role' (*persona*, Greek *prosōpon*), impinges on the actions that are 'proper' at a particular moment.[45] Thus, given his austere character, it was proper

---

[40] On the appropriateness of violating a promise under particular circumstances, see also *Off.* 3.92–95. For a discussion of promise keeping in *De Officiis*, see also Woolf 2007: 321–30.

[41] *magisque ille, cui promissum sit, ab officio discedat si se destitutum queratur.*

[42] See, however, the example of Regulus (*Off.* 1.39; 3.100) which speaks for the absolute value of keeping oaths, independently of circumstances. Swearing an oath represents a particular case of promise giving. Cicero remarks at 3.104 that a sworn oath is 'religious affirmation' (*affirmatio religiosa*) with the gods as witnesses, which explains the force of keeping oaths even towards enemies in war. Exceptions are mentioned in this case as well, as in the case of oaths towards pirates (3.107) which may be violated without this resulting in a dishonourable action.

[43] See *Off.* 3.92–95.

[44] Cf. Brennan 1996: 332.

[45] The idea that in our pursuit of a life which is 'according to nature', our 'common' human nature (the first *persona*) should be supplemented by our 'individual' nature (the second *persona*) is introduced at *Off.* 1.107. On the 'role' (*personae*) theory developed there, see Gill 1988.

for Marcus Cato to commit suicide after his defeat by Caesar, but the same did not apply to his companions. This suggests that Cato's suicide should not be understood as a general rule suggesting the way in which everyone should have reacted under those circumstances, nor does it mean that Cato's companions were wrong in handing themselves to Caesar. Their behaviour does not exhibit conflicting approaches to duty, rather they were making the right decisions given their individual natures and their more 'easy-going' attitudes towards life.[46] The same applies to big 'lifetime' decisions, such as the decision whether to devote oneself to politics, to a military career or to philosophy, a particularly pertinent question given the educational character of Cicero's work. Cicero, projecting his own convictions, shows a clear preference for the practical/political life over the theoretical/leisurely one. He suggests at *Off.* 1.71 that political engagement is justifiably avoided only in case someone gives clear signs of excellence in a 'theoretical' subject or when one is prevented by reasons of health or some other 'weightier' cause from practicing politics.[47] Despite Cicero's expectation that his son follow and imitate his example and glory at 1.78,[48] Cicero (following Panaetius) also states at 1.110 that the decision about which path of life to follow should be in line with one's natural inclinations, even if this means abandoning things which are 'weightier and better' (*graviora atque meliora*) and restricting oneself to a private life. To this effect, Cicero urges that we abstain from passively imitating others (even one's own father) and engage in gaining true knowledge of oneself.[49] Again, the message here is that there is no tragic dilemma involved in choosing between, say, a life devoted to politics and one devoted to science, but that one course of life is more suitable than other alternatives given one's particular natural inclinations.

An area where Cicero particularly explores the tensions, and possible conflicts, between duties is that of human relationships. Stoics made explicit that our duties are embedded in a nexus of different relationships, which comply with our nature and are ultimately grounded in a natural

---

[46] *Off.* 1.112: *atqui ceteris forsitan vitio datum esset, si se interemissent, propterea quod lenior eorum vita et mores fuerant faciliores.*

[47] *Quapropter et iis forsitan concedendum sit rem publicam non capessentibus, qui excellenti ingenio doctrinae sese dediderunt, et iis, qui aut valitudinis imbecillitate aut aliqua graviore causa impediti a re publica recesserunt, cum eius administrandae potestatem aliis laudemque concederent.* With regard to the superiority of the active/political life, cf. also *Off.* 1.92.

[48] *Licet enim mihi, M. fili, apud te gloriari, ad quem et hereditas huius gloriae et factorum imitatio pertinet.* Cf. 1.121: *Optima autem hereditas a patribus traditur liberis omnique patrimonio praestantior gloria virtutis rerumque gestarum, cui dedecori esse nefas et vitium iudicandum est.* See also the comments at 2.44 and 3.6.

[49] *Off.* 1.118; 119: *in qua deliberatione ad suam cuiusque naturam consilium est omne revocandum.*

mechanism of social appropriation (*oikeiōsis*).⁵⁰ The most extensive treatment of the social dimension of *kathēkonta* survives in the fragments of the late Stoic Hierocles (second century CE), which possibly derive from a treatise *Peri kathēkontos*. One of the fragments features an image of concentric circles; the different circles extend from the centre, which stands for one's mind (*dianoia*), outwards, including first one's own body, then one's parents, siblings, spouse and offspring, further out one's closer and more distant relatives, one's fellow-citizens and people of the same ethnicity and, ultimately, humanity as whole.⁵¹ Although the model illustrates the progressive degrees of intensity of our goodwill,⁵² starting with ourselves and ending with humanity at large, Hierocles suggests that one should strive to contract the diverse circles of association in which one is embedded inwards, and thus attempt to effect an 'assimilation' (*exomoiōsis*) of those who stand at a larger distance from oneself. Thus, Hierocles' scheme integrates both an empirical model based on progressive proximity to our own selves and a normative model which inverts this 'natural' extension of proximity.

Cicero refers extensively to the way *officia* apply to different degrees of human society (*gradus ... societatis hominum*). In line with the scheme of successive circles surviving in Hierocles, Cicero mentions at *Off.* 1.54 the 'first fellowship' (*prima societas*) to one's spouse which arises through marriage and the successive fellowships towards one's children and extended family; he thereby mentions the love and goodwill which arises through the blood ties.⁵³ This scheme is supplemented by references to the fellowship towards friends and one's city and nation. Although Cicero praises, at 1.55, as the 'most preeminent and firm' the friendship that arises between 'good men' tied together by similarity of conduct,⁵⁴ the fellowship of every citizen with the Roman republic (*res publica*) is deemed to be the *most* eminent and dear one (*nulla est gravior, nulla carior*).⁵⁵ Finally, Cicero discusses the appropriate duties of liberality towards humanity as a whole (the widest possible degree of *societas*), that is, towards people to whom one stands in no special relation, at. 1.51–52.⁵⁶ Such duties seem to be restricted

---

⁵⁰ Cf. *Off.* 1.12: *Eademque natura vi rationis hominem conciliat homini et ad orationis et ad vitae societatem.*
⁵¹ Stobaeus 4.671.7–672.6 = LS 57G.
⁵² See ibid. 4.672.16–17: *aphairēsetai men gar ti tēs eunoias to kath' haima diastēma pleon on.*
⁵³ *Off.* 1.54: *Sanguinis autem coniunctio et benivolentia devincit homines et caritate.*
⁵⁴ *Sed omnium societatum nulla praestantior est, nulla firmior, quam cum viri boni moribus similes sunt familiaritate coniuncti.*
⁵⁵ *Off.* 1.57 seems to argue that the *res publica* includes in itself the affections towards all other particular fellowships: *cari sunt parentes, cari liberi, propinqui, familiares, sed omnes omnium caritates patria una complexa est.*
⁵⁶ Cf. *Off.* 3.28.

to 'humanitarian' actions, like providing basic means of subsistence and advice to those in need.[57]

Whereas these different spheres of action, related to different senses of 'community', are discussed separately, Cicero also mentions a 'comparison' (*comparatio*) among them, namely which one seems to have priority over the other spheres in cases of conflict. Thus, at 1.58 he mentions that the greatest assistance towards living should be provided to one's fatherland and parents, due to what we owe them for the kindness we have received from them, whereas next we should prioritise aid to one's children and household, due to their dependence upon us, and finally to one's close relatives, because we share a common fortune with them.[58] On the other hand, social intercourse and conversation is mostly owed to friendships and, in particular, to those which are based on similarity of conduct. Cicero also mentions that consideration of what is dutiful in human relationships depends on the specific circumstances of an action, which may lead to an inversion of the priorities that he has laid out in his general presentation of the degrees of fellowship. For example, one should give precedence to a neighbour rather than to one's relatives, when asked to assist in gathering the harvest, but one should prioritise one's relatives when it comes to defending them in lawcourt.[59] In the case of acting for the sake of humanity as such, envisaging a possible conflict, Cicero advises that any bestowing of such duties should take into account whether harm is inflicted on oneself through the provision of help, as also the extent to which bestowing such duties impinges on our ability to help those 'closer' to us.[60]

In case of a conflict between acting for the sake of one's country or for the sake of one's family, Cicero suggests that the *res publica* should have priority in one's deliberations, proposing at 1.160 a ranking which (in accordance with a scheme we later find in Hierocles)[61] places the immortal gods first, followed by one's country, whereas one's parents are ranked at the third place.[62] The potential of a conflict comes most prominently to the fore when Cicero is talking about the duty of tyrannicide, alluding thereby to the assassination of Julius Caesar, which he

---

[57] See *Off.* 1.52.
[58] On family relationships see further Wynne ch. 1, this volume.
[59] *Off.* 1.59.
[60] *Off.* 1.52: *Sed quoniam copiae parvae singulorum sunt, eorum autem, qui his egeant, infinita est multitudo, vulgaris liberalitas referenda est ad illum Ennii finem 'nihilominus ipsi lucet', ut facultas sit, qua in nostros simus liberales.*
[61] Stobaeus 4.671.4–6. Cf. DL 7.120.
[62] *In ipsa autem communitate sunt gradus officiorum, ex quibus quid cuique praestet intellegi possit, ut prima diis immortalibus, secunda patriae, tertia parentibus, deinceps gradatim reliquis debeantur.*

openly approved:[63] in case a close friend, or even one's parents, threaten to overthrow the *res publica* it is a duty to undertake action against them, and, if necessary, to kill them.[64] The priority given to duties towards one's country is also exemplified by Cicero's own actions just before undertaking the writing of *De Officiis*; while his initial intention in July 44 BCE was to sail to Athens and visit his son Marcus, in the midst of his journey he decided to go back to Rome in order to take part in a meeting of the senate, which ultimately led to his fiery attack against Antony.[65] The epilogue to the work suggests that the writing of *De Officiis*, from September 44 onwards, functions as a substitute for Cicero's absence from Athens and for his choice to place political action over parental duties.[66]

3 Conflict between Duties of Expediency and Duties of Honourableness in *De Officiis*: A False Dilemma

Contrary to the conflict described in the previous section, the conflict of duties in the third book of *De Officiis* suggests a more fundamental idea of conflict, that is, one that may amount to conflicting principles of action. Cicero introduces the relevant part of Panaetius' division in 1.9, describing it it in terms of a conflict which impinges on the soul and is felt like a division in it:

> *Tertium dubitandi genus est, cum pugnare videtur cum honesto id, quod videtur esse utile. Cum enim utilitas ad se rapere, honestas contra revocare ad se videtur, fit ut distrahatur in deliberando animus afferatque ancipitem curam cogitandi.*

> The third type of uncertainty arises when something apparently beneficial appears to conflict with what is honourable. For when benefit seems to snatch you to its side, and honourableness in its turn to call you back, it comes about that the mind is pulled this way and that in its deliberation and it arouses in its reflection a care that is double-edged. (Trans. E. M. Atkins)

Cicero is addressing here the vast majority of non-wise agents, who do not possess the unerring judgement of the wise person (for whom the

---

[63] See further Gildenhard ch. 11, this volume.
[64] *Off.* 3.19: *Num igitur se adstrinxit scelere, si qui tyrannum occidit quamvis familiarem? Populo quidem Romano non videtur, qui ex omnibus praeclaris factis illud pulcherrimum existimat.* Cf. 3.90: *ad extremum, si ad perniciem patriae res spectabit, patriae salutem anteponet saluti patris.* The justification of tyrannicide is sharpened at 3.32, where the tyrant is likened to a beast in human form threatening the common 'body' of humanity. Similarly, at 3.83 Cicero likens Caesar's actions to the 'most disgusting parricide', that of one's fatherland (*taeterrimum parricidium patriae*).
[65] See *Att.* 16.7.
[66] See *Off.* 3.121. Cf. Dyck 1996: 8 n. 20; 12.

expedient and the virtuous action always and unhesitatingly coincide).[67] Cicero describes how this is manifested as a confusion in one's deliberation.[68] While 'confusion' may suggest puzzlement about whether a (perceived) expedient course of action can be discharged in a way that does not conflict with the *honestum* (without questioning the priority of the latter principle), Cicero also mentions the cases of 'wicked' persons for whom there is a conscious choice and prioritisation of the expedient over the *honestum*.[69] Accordingly, he refers at *Off.* 3.37 to those who 'knowingly contaminate themselves with wickedness' (*se scientes scelere contaminent*) as to people who may be deemed fully responsible for their bad actions. In this case expediency takes the form of one's *personal* or *individual* good, as opposed to the common good, and *utilitas* is not any more measured in terms of the common good as in the Stoic theory. While this is not manifested as a psychological conflict, since Cicero, following the Stoics, does not explain such cases in terms of weakness of will, a 'wicked' behaviour based on ill will (*malitia*) does manifest a fundamental conflict between two different principles of action: one that aims at the maximization of one's individual profit and one that aims at the common benefit (in accordance with a principle of virtue).

The references to a potential conflict between the *utile* and the *honestum* in *De Officiis* reveal a dialectical context which serves the aims of the philosophical dialogues of Cicero; the readers of these dialogues are asked to make a judgement on what appears most persuasive (*probabilis*) and similar to the truth (*veri simile*) after opposed views on a question have been exposed.[70] Accordingly, the conflict between expediency and honourableness is discussed not only from a Stoic perspective (where it is reduced to a merely apparent conflict) but also from the perspective of other philosophical positions (for which the conflict is real). Thus, such a conflict is thematised in *De Officiis* also with regard to the Epicurean ethical theory which measures the value of virtue by the benefit or pleasure it brings about.[71] According to Cicero's critique, the Epicurean view that pleasure (or the absence of pain)

---

[67] See *Off.* 3.15.
[68] Thus, at *Off.* 3.35 Cicero refers to the way one is affected (*commoveri*) by the appearance of expediency and mentions how the mind may detect something dishonourable attached to what appears expedient. See also the use of *conturbent* at 3.40 and 3.81.
[69] *Off.* 3.40.
[70] *Off.* 2.8: *Contra autem omnia disputantur a nostris, quod hoc ipsum probabile elucere non possit, nisi ex utraque parte causarum esset facta contentio.*
[71] *Off.* 3.117: *Nam si non modo utilitas, sed vita omnis beata corporis firma constitutione eiusque constitutionis spe explorata, ut a Metrodoro scriptum est, continetur, certe haec utilitas et quidem summa, – sic enim censent – cum honestate pugnabit.* The Epicureans are alluded to also at *Off.* 3.12, 1.5.

is the highest good is in fundamental conflict with honourable action.[72] For, despite the fact that the Epicureans make the virtues necessary for a happy life, acting dutifully, that is, acting honourably, presupposes that virtue be chosen for its own sake and not instrumentally.[73] A still more fundamental conflict between honourableness and expediency was sketched in the third book of Cicero's *De Re Publica*. In Philus' speech in the third book of this work, which conveys one part of Carneades' famous disputation for and against justice, expediency was explicitly juxtaposed to justice.[74] Thus, Carneades is reported to have shown there that someone is either 'wise' or 'just' but cannot be both at the same time. Wisdom or prudence is in this case associated with the multiplication of wealth and empire and the enjoyment of pleasures, contrary to the functions ascribed to justice, including the consideration of the interests of the entire human race and the respect for what belongs to others.[75] This leads to a distorted notion of 'wisdom' (*sapientia*) and its dissociation from justice,[76] with (provocatively) the very example of Rome's policy being given in Philus' speech in order to exemplify this dissociation.[77] Philus' speech is reminiscent of the greed for wealth and power that Cicero criticizes at *Off.* 3.36, a critique associated with Caesar's seizure of power.[78] Further, some of the Carneadean examples used to show the conflict between wisdom and justice, like that of a prospective seller who has an interest in selling a house with serious faults to an ignorant purchaser, are reminiscent of Cicero's examples in the third book of *De Officiis*.[79] It seems, therefore, that the Carneadean challenge lurks in the background of Cicero's staging of a potential conflict between honourableness and expediency.

---

[72] See *Off.* 3.120.
[73] *Off.* 3.118: *Neque enim bonitas nec liberalitas nec comitas esse potest, non plus quam amicitia, si haec non per se expetantur, sed ad voluptatem utilitatemve referantur.*
[74] *Rep.* 3.8.
[75] Ibid. 3.24.
[76] See e.g. *Rep.* 3.16, where the Roman practice of forbidding the peoples beyond the Alps to grow vines and olives is deemed 'prudent' but not 'just', so that one may think that 'wisdom and equity disagree' (*ut intellegatis discrepare ab aequitate sapientiam*). It is Carneades that may be alluded to (and criticised) at *Off.* 2.10: *Quod qui parum perspiciunt, ii saepe versutos homines et callidos admirantes, malitiam sapientiam iudicant.* Cf. 2.34. For a similar critique of the way *malitia* is associated with either practical wisdom (*prudentia*) or 'intelligence' (*intellegentia*), see *Off.* 3.71–72.
[77] *Rep.* 3.24.
[78] *hinc opum nimiarum, potentiae non ferendae, postremo etiam in liberis civitatibus regnandi existunt cupiditates, quibus nihil nec taetrius nec foedius excogitari potest.* This chimes with the limitless desire for power and glory that Cicero (implicitly) ascribes to Caesar at *Off.* 1.26.
[79] A significant part of Philus' report of Carneades' defence of injustice is lost but we have the evidence of Lactantius *Inst. Div.* V, 16, 5–13 on it. According to this evidence, Carneades used the example of a man who knows of serious faults in something he has for sale and reveals them to a prospective purchaser in order to show the incompatibility of justice and wisdom. Cf. Annas 1989: 156–57.

While the kind of malicious intention which prioritises one's self-interest above all else, and which is sophistically associated with prudence by Carneades, is presented as reprehensible and as a violation of the rules of human community established by nature, Cicero presents also a more subtle kind of conflict between expediency and honourableness. The 'good man' (*vir bonus*),[80] to whom Cicero refers in this case, is one who may not possess the unerring judgement of a sage[81] but he also differs from the person who measures everything by his or her own (individual) profit, juxtaposing the latter to honourableness.[82] Thus, the hesitation and conflict seems in the case of the *vir bonus* to entail no *intention* to harm another person for the sake of pursuing one's personal interest. On this latter point, Cicero invokes an alleged dispute, cast as a discussion *in utramque partem*, between two heads of the post-Chrysippean Stoa, Diogenes of Babylon and Antipater of Tarsus (*Off.* 3.49–55).[83]

The Stoic Diogenes may have attempted to show on the basis of relevant examples, perhaps in direct response to Carneades' challenges,[84] that the sage is justified in engaging in ordinary transactions and in pursuing advantages, like money or other necessary resources. In line with this, Diogenes would have granted that in doing so the sage will rely on a certain institutional and legal framework, as, for example, that of private property and the rules regulating commercial transactions.[85] Diogenes seems to suggest that there is no contradiction there with (standard) Stoic views: even though one could help people in need by giving away one's resources, a sage is justified in possessing private property, and acquiring other means of subsistence with the proviso that he or she does not thereby harm others.[86] A similar view is ascribed to Panaetius' pupil

---

[80] For the use of the expression *vir bonus* in Roman law, see e.g. *Digest* 19.2.24.
[81] See *Off.* 3.16–17.
[82] *Off.* 3.18.
[83] On Cicero's role in constructing the debate between Diogenes of Babylon and Antipater of Tarsus, see Annas 1989: 154–55. Annas goes so far as to say (165) that Cicero wholly fabricated the Diogenes-Antipater debate creating a 'non-existent conflict' out of the opinions of the two philosophers. For Cicero's reliance on Hecato for the construction of the debate between the two philosophers, see Dyck 1996: 557–8. For a defence of the historicity of the 'controversy' between Diogenes and Antipater, see Schofield 1999: 144.
[84] See Schofield 1999: 146–47.
[85] At *Off.* 1.21 Cicero claims that private property arises from what has been by nature 'common property' but also states that not violating property rights is essential for the preservation of human fellowship. Cf. *Fin.* 3.67.
[86] On the justification of securing for oneself, rather than for another, the 'necessities of life' see *Off.* 3.22: *Nam sibi ut quisque malit, quod ad usum vitae pertineat, quam alteri adquirere, concessum est non repugnante natura*. This is also exemplified at 3.42 with Chrysippus' famous simile of the stadium.

Hecato.[87] This again could invite 'particularistic' objections of the sort that Antipater seems to have raised against his teacher. In some cases, as the one presented at *Off*. 3.50, discharging duties through commercial transactions, such as the sale of necessary commodities (like corn), might, under particular circumstances, result in harm, as when the buyers are starving and could acquire more of the necessary resources with less money, if the seller would reveal that he or she is not the only one supplying corn (since the scenario presupposes that more merchants are on the way with the same commodity). Antipater implies (3.52) that in this case it is an honourable, and thus dutiful, thing to reveal this information to the buyers, despite the fact that this will have as a consequence sale at a smaller price. The idea is that by caring for other peoples' interests one preserves the human fellowship that has been established by nature. Diogenes could have in his own right answered that if the sage had no *intention* to profit from the other's disadvantage this should not count as against duty;[88] disadvantage to others seems to occur in this case from other contingent reasons independent of the sages' intention. Accordingly, the sage's action should in this case not count as concealing (which implies intention) but as 'keeping silent' (3.52).[89] Diogenes' defence concludes by saying that if the sage is in all respects not to care for his advantage, then the very institution of selling and buying should be abolished for the sake of giving away all resources.[90] It is important to note that the dispute that Cicero sketches turns on whether not revealing information in this case is or is not a dishonourable thing and not on whether one should *do* a dishonourable thing or not (since it is clear that this latter is reprehensible).[91]

Cicero moves next to discussing cases where the conflict between personal expediency and an honourable course of action comes more clearly to the fore. The case discussed is whether someone who sells his house (a topic particularly relevant to the Roman elite and to Cicero himself) should conceal from the prospective buyer some serious faults of the house in order to

---

[87] *Off*. 3.63: *Hecatonem quidem Rhodium, discipulum Panaetii, video in iis libris, quos de officio scripsit Q. Tuberoni, dicere, sapientis esse nihil contra mores, leges, instituta facientem habere rationem rei familiaris.* See also the casuistic examples at 3.89.
[88] This is corroborated by the statement at 3.51 that the person is not selling the produce 'for more than others do' (*vendo meum non pluris, quam ceteri*).
[89] Annas 1989: 161, on the other hand, understands 'concealing' here as not telling someone something which the person has the *right* to know. She thereby concludes (164) that the debate that Cicero has constructed is 'a spurious one, since the alleged opponents are not talking about the same thing'. Against Annas' interpretation, see Schofield 1999: 145–46.
[90] *Off*. 3.53: *Quod si ita est, ne vendendum quidem quicquam est, sed donandum.*
[91] *Off*. 3.50: *de eius deliberatione et consultatione quaerimus, qui celaturus Rhodios non sit, si id turpe iudicet, sed dubitet, an turpe non sit.* Cf. 3.53.

achieve a better price for it than he would if he had revealed its faults.⁹² In this case, both the intention of achieving greater profit and the harm incurred to the other party of the transaction are more explicit. Arguing pro and contra the honourableness of the action is again assigned to Diogenes and Antipater. The latter underlines that the action is dishonourable because it involves consciously misleading someone.⁹³ Cicero gives to the dispute a legalistic twist, when ascribing to Diogenes for his alleged defence of the honourableness of the action, the invocation of the principle *caveat emptor*, which transfers responsibility for the recognition of the faults of the house to the judgement of the buyer.⁹⁴ Cicero adjudicates at 3.57 that, when something is kept silent from other parties for the sake of increasing one's own individual profit, this constitutes a case of wickedness resulting from a bad intention and cannot, thus, be deemed a dutiful action. Such examples culminate with the narration of the story of Canius and Pythius (3.58–59), a clear case of malicious fraud (*dolus malus*), which manifests how one can harm another person 'actively' by deceiving through lying, as Pythius did when selling a house to Canius.

Cicero goes on at 3.72 to defend the view that one should not act in a way that involves exploitation of another person's ignorance, showing on the basis of historical examples how Roman civil law supports such a conclusion as well, by placing, for example, particular importance on the injunction of 'good faith' in contracts regulating dealings and transactions.⁹⁵ Similarly, numerous examples from Roman history, such as that of Regulus, assert that the forefathers prioritized the honourable course of action over the (apparently) beneficial.⁹⁶ The dialectical context in which the conflict between expediency and honourableness is presented leads in this way to the reaffirmation rather than to the subversion of the values of Roman civil society.⁹⁷ Cicero concludes, in Stoic fashion, that a conflict between 'the virtuous' and 'the expedient' is only apparent and that the rule (*regula*) of the virtuous and the expedient courses of action should always be the same,⁹⁸ leading to one single appropriate action in each case. Such a rule foresees that the personal *utilitas* is limited by the preservation of *societas*, in particular the preservation of the *res publica*, and ultimately that personal

---

⁹² *Off.* 3.54: *quaero, si haec emptoribus venditor non dixerit aedesque vendiderit pluris multo quam se venditurum putarit, num id iniuste aut improbe fecerit?*
⁹³ *Off.* 3.54: *Plus etiam est quam viam non monstrare; nam est scientem in errorem alterum inducere.*
⁹⁴ *Off.* 3.55: *Ubi enim iudicium emptoris est, ibi fraus venditoris quae potest esse?* The principle is invoked in Roman law, see *Digest* 18.1.43.
⁹⁵ *Off.* 3.65–68 and 3.70 for the example of Scaevola. Cf. 3.61 on other formulations from Roman legal history and practice which suggest the disapproval of fraud and untruthfulness in dealings.
⁹⁶ See e.g. *Off.* 3.86 for the story of Fabricius in the war against Pyrrhus.
⁹⁷ Cf. Dyck 1996: 31.
⁹⁸ *Off.* 3.74: *eadem utilitatis quae honestatis est regula.* Cf. 3.81.

and common expediency should coincide.[99] Cicero's pedagogical, but also political motives, for writing the *De Officiis* become in this way apparent. Contrary to theoretical questions about what constitutes a happy life, or what are the specific attributes of the divine, the discussion of how one should appropriately behave in all aspects of social life conveys throughout the attempt of Cicero at the resolution of the possible conflicts surrounding the notion of duty for the sake of the preservation of civil society.

4 Conclusion

Cicero's extensive discussion of the topic of conflict of duties in *De Officiis* seems to supplement Panaetius' discussion of duty, which formed one of the most important sources for Cicero's work. Cicero discusses in Book 1 how in particular circumstances it is impossible to discharge all duties that are generally in accord with honourableness; this does not result, however, in 'tragic dilemmas' but suggests that duty should in every case be identified, through the exercise of good judgement, according to the specific circumstances at hand. In Book 3 of *De Officiis* Cicero moves to the discussion of a more fundamental conflict between principles of duty, which challenges the Stoic identification of 'honourable' and 'expedient' courses of action. While revealing the tensions between personal expediency and an honourable course of action, Cicero condemns the prioritization of individual profit over 'common utility' or 'human society' and attempts to offer a 'rule' for the resolution of such conflicts surrounding duties. Despite its reliance on Stoic philosophical sources, the persuasive force of Cicero's attempt at resolution of conflicts surrounding duties rests to a considerable extent on the Roman traditional examples that it supplies. This seems ultimately to be linked to Cicero's attempt to promote, through the writing of *De Officiis*, the traditional 'republican' values in an era characterized, in his view, by excessive individual ambition and moral decline.

Even if Cicero's appeal to the 'common good' may not conclusively resolve interpersonal conflicts (not even those pertaining to the intricate political reality of the last years of the Roman republic), his treatise lays out some of the main areas in human life where conflicts about values and principles of action are prone to arise and offers testimony to the way the particular circumstances of an action affect our decisions. The aforementioned aspects make the work especially attractive for a modern reader as well.

---

[99] *Off.* 3.26: *Ergo unum debet esse omnibus propositum, ut eadem sit utilitas uniuscuiusque et universorum.* See also the references to the common benefit at 3.21–28 and 3.101 with particular reference to the *res publica*.

PART II

The Role of Virtue

CHAPTER 3

Oikeiōsis *and the Origin of Virtue*

Brad Inwood

1 Introduction

Views differ about how closely Cicero's *De Officiis* tracks Panaetius' work *On Appropriate Actions*, and the degree of closeness certainly varies from one part of the work to another. In one sense this is an unimportant issue. The question about Cicero's sources may ultimately be insoluble, especially if it is handled at too general a level, and perhaps it is not even that important if one's interest is in the content and historical impact of the work. To someone with those interests what matters most is that Cicero as author adopted certain views and puts his own name behind the claims made in the book. Views on how he uses his sources differ considerably: one could be, like Peter Brunt,[1] convinced that Cicero follows Panaetius closely; or one could, rather, be a sceptic on such matters, as I normally tend to be. Nevertheless, when it comes to the foundational structure of the discussion in book 1 it seems likely that Panaetius' plan did in fact shape Cicero's strategy. In what follows I will argue that the basic strategic moves made at the outset of Cicero's *De Officiis* are in fact Panaetius', at least in outline, although Cicero's reasons for embracing the theory were different from Panaetius' for developing it.

2 Theories of *Oikeiōsis*

In *De Officiis* Cicero is (for once in the *philosophica*) speaking in his own voice and not as a character in a dialogue.[2] And no matter what his

---

I would like to thank Raphael Woolf for a number of constructive challenges and suggestions. His input has helped to improve this chapter; I am responsible for the remaining defects and limitations.

[1] See Brunt 2013.
[2] To be sure, in the prefaces Cicero also speaks in his own voice rather than as a character; but the substantive philosophical claims he makes in the dialogues are mostly made by the characters, including the character named Cicero.

inspiration or sources are he is not speaking as a Stoic. How could he? He is directly addressing his son and was himself a lifelong Academic. But Cicero did believe that on many fundamental issues in ethics there was a high degree of convergence between Academics, Peripatetics and Stoics.[3] This no doubt made it more congenial for him to embrace Panaetius' strategy as a framework for his own discussion. Recognition that this is the case will, I suggest, add some significant philosophical depth to our appreciation for the theory in book 1.

The stretch of text I want to focus on is from 1.11 to 1.20. Here Cicero sets out certain fundamental features of human nature which he says are the basis of the virtues. His investigation into what is honourable (*honestum*) rests on the claim that it is composed of and produced by the particular virtues.[4] The bulk of book 1 consists of accounts of those four cardinal virtues: *sapientia* or *prudentia*; *iustitia* and its related virtues such as generosity; *magnitudo animi*; and *moderatio* (1.15–17). The four cardinal virtues are, of course, ultimately Platonic in origin (with the common Hellenistic substitution of greatness of soul for courage).[5] They are mutually entailing (*inter se colligata atque implicata* 1.15) but distinct. Their origins are in different aspects of human nature and each virtue generates distinct kinds of *officia* (*tamen ex singulis certa officiorum genera nascuntur* 1.15). Though the cardinal virtues are Platonic in origin, the sharp distinction between the theoretical virtue of *prudentia* or *sapientia* and the other three practically oriented virtues (Cicero refers to the non-theoretical virtues as "the remaining three" at 1.17 and 1.20) seems more likely to be Peripatetic in its ultimate inspiration.

The adoption of the four Platonic cardinal virtues was a long-standing feature of Stoicism,[6] but the privileged treatment of theoretical virtue is

---

[3] At 3.20 Cicero identifies himself with the sceptical Academy, as usual in his philosophical works. (For the lifelong commitment of Cicero to Academic scepticism see Görler 1995.) In the same chapter Cicero refers to the Peripatetics as the school of his son, who is the addressee of the work, and explains that he is following Stoic principles in dealing with the issues of book 3 because their ethical position is compatible with both Old Academic and Peripatetic doctrines. Antiochus of Ascalon, whose philosophy had a great influence on Cicero, held that Academics, Peripatetics and Stoics all held very similar views in many areas of philosophy. For Cicero's relationship to Antiochus, see Barnes 1989: 51, 61.

[4] *Quibus ex rebus conflatur et efficitur id quod quaerimus honestum* (1.14) and *sed omne quod est honestum id quattuor partium oritur ex aliqua* (1.15).

[5] Woolf 2015: 173 notes that each of these virtues is described in broader terms than is often the case, to emphasize both their complexity and the essentially social context of all four.

[6] See Plutarch *On Moral Virtue* 440f–441a: Aristo recognized *phronēsis*, justice, temperance and courage; Zeno demarcated *phronēsis* itself into justice, temperance, and courage by reference to the domain where it operated. Zeno's defenders claim that he used *phronēsis* as an equivalent for *epistēmē*.

not a consistent feature of Stoic doctrine. Cicero puts a version of it into Cato's mouth at *Fin.* 3.17 when he acknowledges a drive for learning in young children that is parallel to the drive for self-preservation,[7] and Seneca is often drawn towards this stance, at least when it comes to physics and especially cosmology.[8] But many Stoics, from Aristo to Marcus Aurelius, went so far as to reject theoretical wisdom altogether, far from just denying it a special status among the virtues. Despite this possibly non-standard feature, Cicero's account in *De Officiis* 1 is of direct Stoic inspiration. The key Stoic feature, of course, is seen in the foundational role played by the universal drive to self-preservation, something seen in the so-called *oikeiōsis* theory found in many sources for Stoic ethics, including DL 7.85, *Fin.* 3.16 ff., and Seneca, *Ep.* 121.

Reliance on a version of *oikeiōsis* theory is a clear mark of Stoicism, even though it came ultimately to have influence on other schools as well, as, for example, in the Peripatetic account of *De Finibus* 5.[9] But no other version of the Stoic theory purports to derive the basic virtues directly from the primitive drive for self-preservation which lies at the heart of the theory of *oikeiōsis*. The version we see at *De Officiis* 1.11 ff. is an ambitious and original basis for the presentation of a distinctively Stoic ethical theory, so much so that it is hard to doubt that at least this feature should be attributed to Panaetius rather than to Cicero himself. In other areas Panaetius was an innovative Stoic theorist (doubting conflagration and divination,[10] for example, not to mention his distinctive focus on the *prepon* (or *decorum*) and on *prosōpa* (or *personae*) which we see in *De Officiis* itself) and it seems perfectly plausible that he should have proposed a creatively expanded role for *oikeiōsis*.

Similarly, one might also suspect that another feature of Cicero's account here is in some measure the work of Panaetius. In 1.11 Cicero immediately juxtaposes the universal animal drive for procreation and care of offspring with the motivation for self-preservation. The connection is not made explicitly in Seneca or Diogenes Laërtius, and in *De Finibus* 3 these two aspects of *oikeiōsis* are widely separated and weakly coordinated (the significance of love for one's offspring only comes in at 3.62 and there is no attempt to connect it closely with the motivations posited at 3.16 ff.).

---

[7] Epictetus, *Diss.* 1.18.1–2, also sets the drive for truth in parallel with the drive for what is personally beneficial.
[8] See Inwood 2009: 212–222.
[9] This has been a highly contentious issue with no final consensus as yet. See most recently Tsouni 2019. Also Inwood 2014: ch. 3.
[10] See Stobaeus 1.171.5–7; Philo *On the eternity of the cosmos* 76–78; Cicero, *Luc.* 107.

By contrast, in *De Officiis* 1.11–12 there is a direct and serious attempt to integrate these two potentially conflicting motivations (self-preservation and care for offspring and hence other human beings). It seems to be an attempt to resolve a potential tension in Stoic ethics between a fundamentally self-oriented approach and their deep commitment to the interests of others.[11] There is good reason to suppose that this reconfiguration is the work of Panaetius rather than Cicero (who, after all, had passed up an opportunity to resolve the tension when writing *De Finibus* 3). This second innovation on earlier Stoicism by Panaetius is characterized by an impressive theoretical richness. In *Off.* 1.11–12 it is the centrality to human nature of rationality and communication that resolves the potential tension between the drive for self-preservation and intrinsic social concerns.

A commented translation of Sections 11 and 12 will illustrate the point:

> First of all, nature has bestowed on animals of every species the inclination to protect themselves, their life and their body and to steer clear of things which seem likely to harm them; and to pursue and procure all the necessities of life, such as food, shelter and things of that sort. (*Off.* 1.11)

This is the standard drive for self-preservation that turns up in all *oikeiōsis* accounts. The triplet "themselves, their life and their body" could well be a Ciceronian elaboration rather than indicating three distinguishable objects for the protective instinct. The motivation to protect oneself extends automatically to instruments necessary for that protection.

> Moreover, all animals share a desire for mating in order to produce offspring and a particular concern for those offspring. (*Off.* 1.11)

The reproductive drive is not subordinated here in any way to the self-preservation drive, as food, shelter etc. are, and it covers all animals rather than just human beings. This drive is appropriately indicated by the term *appetitus*. By contrast, at *Fin.* 3.62, where Cato is introducing the foundations of human social bonding, he skips over other animals and deals immediately with the relationship of human parents to their children. Cato claims explicitly that parental love for offspring is the basis for social bonding among humans and, as I have said, there is no attempt to connect the claims made here with the account of *oikeiōsis* at *Fin.* 3.16 ff. Things are quite different in *De Officiis*:

> But the most significant difference between humans and beasts is this: since beasts are only affected by the senses they only respond to what is at hand in the present and are aware of the past and future to a very limited degree.

---

[11] See Inwood 1983.

> But human beings have a share in reason and as a result they perceive consequences, discern causes and are not unaware of the preconditions and results of things. They make comparisons between things that are similar and draw connections between future situations and the present; they can readily see the whole course of life and make the necessary preparations for living that life. (*Off.* 1.11)

Up to this point the attributes of self-preservation and drive for and protection of offspring have been asserted of all animal species. But now the special status of human beings is explained by their possession of reason; this is what enables them to be more efficient in the pursuit of those objectives shared with the other species. Awareness of time and the relations of cause and effect enable planning and deliberation on a long timescale. So far, though, there is still no distinctively human mode of interaction in play. But that changes in Section 12:[12]

> The same nature connects human beings one to another through the power of reason so they can share both speech and life. First of all, it creates in human beings an extraordinary love for their offspring and drives them to desire that there should be social interaction and gatherings, and to participate in them; this is why people are eager to provide for the care and feeding not just of themselves but also of their wives, their children and everyone else whom they love and are obliged to defend. This commitment stirs their spirit and renders them better at getting things done. (*Off.* 1.12)

In addition to making humans into more efficient pursuers of self-preservation, the same rational capacity enables speech and social life. Though the connections are not fully explicit, the causal dependencies seem clear enough. When Cicero says that "the same nature" connects human beings to each other, he refers to rational nature. It is reason that makes possible speech (a shared activity), which further makes it possible to share life (*vitae societas*). The concern (*cura*) for offspring which obtains for all animals (1.11) now manifests itself in human beings as a powerful love (*amor*) for those offspring. Reason is apparently what it takes for mere concern, which animals also manifest, to become love in human beings.[13] Cicero does not elaborate on the difference between *cura* and *amor* that reason makes possible, but one might speculate that the former is merely an observed behavioural tendency while the latter is infused with cognitive

---

[12] On this passage compare Wynne ch. 1, this volume: 25–28.
[13] There is, as Raphael Woolf points out *per litteras*, a clear echo of the phrasing in 1.11 (*cura quaedam*) in that of 1.12 (*quendam amorem*). We are meant to notice both the parallel and difference between animals and humans in this regard.

content (just as all emotions are in Stoicism). The same rationality which distinguishes human concern for offspring from that of mere animals also generates a wider drive for social group interaction. Just when we might begin to wonder how all of this fits together as a coherent account of varied human motivations, Cicero connects the dots. It is reason with its associated power of speech (an intrinsically interpersonal activity) that enables us to extend our care of self to the concern for others, beginning with our mates, the resultant children, and everyone else we love – which must include some if not all of those involved in the social group interaction we are drawn to. And once members of our social group beyond the nuclear family are drawn into the ambit of our concern, we need to look out for them in various ways.

In contrast to the relationship between the drive for self-preservation and for social bonding of *De Finibus* 3, where the connection is scarcely noticed let alone explained, Cicero here provides an integrated account of the natural drive for self-preservation and reproduction shared by all animals and the distinctively rational motivations of human beings. Reason doesn't just make us more efficient at pursuing animal goals. It also transforms our attachment to our offspring into a love which mere animals are not capable of. And because it gives us the power of speech it creates society and the extended motivations which constitute our being as social animals. It doesn't strictly follow that animals are not social, but it does follow that they are not social in the way that we are, since our sociability depends on the possession of speech and rationality. Stoics (and Peripatetics) are steadfast in their belief that animals lack reason, which is why any natural sociability they possess would have to be different in principle from ours.

This version of *oikeiōsis* is distinctive among the various Stoic or Stoically inspired theories we know of. The way in which other Stoics integrated social bonding with the self-oriented drives that are basic in all animals is sometimes a matter for reconstruction and speculation. One suggestion for Chrysippus' version is that we generalize from attachment to our offspring to an attachment to other people and that we are attached to our offspring because they are in a sense parts of our own selves, to which our attachment is primary. As we have seen, Cicero's account in *De Finibus* 3 leaves the connection unclear; the issue is not even addressed in Diogenes Laërtius, Seneca or Hierocles.[14] It is certainly true that all Stoics hold that

---

[14] Hierocles' account of the varied degrees of human attachments (Stobaeus 4.84.23) does not offer a theory of how the motivations for self-preservation and for social bonding are related to each other.

our drive for social bonds is natural and that in mature humans it can be as strong as the drive for self-preservation. But few provide us with a *theory* of how that turns out to be the case and no one provides an account that is as plausibly integrated as Cicero's account in *De Officiis* 1.[15]

3 The Origin of the Virtues

That is the first distinctive feature of the account of foundations in *De Officiis*. As far as I can see, this is the best framed account of the two applications of the *oikeiōsis* theory that we know of. This level of sophistication and originality makes it more likely to have originated with Panaetius than to be Cicero's invention.[16] I would say the same for the other feature of these sections, the derivation of four cardinal virtues from our basic drive to self-preservation. If this theory is regarded as successful, it would be one of the most plausible accounts of the naturalness of the specific virtues known to us from the ancient world. Let's look more closely at the way this account is developed.

We begin with the final sentences of 1.12. There is perhaps a foreshadowing of justice in the claim that there is an obligation to defend those whom we have come to love through shared social interaction – it is not just our wives and children but also "everyone else whom one loves and is *obliged* to defend [*tueri debeat*]." It is far from explicit, but there is a hint of the basis for justice here. In the next sentence there is a similarly inchoate suggestion of courage and practical wisdom. Our commitment to defending others "stirs their spirit and renders them better at getting things done." This is not yet a story about the origins of all four cardinal virtues, but it clearly points to starting points for justice and courage (or spiritedness or greatness of soul) in the social commitments that emerge integrally from our fundamentally rational nature.

---

[15] McCabe 2005 explores just how complicated and, in her view, internally inconsistent the different strands of *oikeiōsis* theory are in the Stoic tradition. When dealing with the evidence of Cicero she discusses only *De Finibus* 3 and nowhere considers the significantly different version in *De Officiis*, which is the focus of the present discussion. Her discussion is, however, very enlightening with regard to the complexities of Stoic theory as found in the wide range of sources available to us and helpfully emphasizes the variety of theories within the school. In her view the account in *De Finibus* is heir to two different versions and so does not cohere; I agree with her on that point. (See Inwood 1983.) In the present discussion I argue that one of the virtues of the account in *De Officiis* is precisely its internal cohesion.

[16] In 1.9 and 1.10 Cicero attributes specific doctrines directly to the book of Panaetius. At various points in the work Cicero remarks on what Panaetius included or omitted from his book: 1.7, 1.90, 1.152, 1.161, 2.16, 2.35, 2.51, 2.76, 2.99, 3.8–11, 3.18, 3.33–34. At 2.60 Cicero generalizes: "Panaetius, whom I have followed a great deal in these books, though not merely translated."

The account of how these foundational natural commitments relate to the virtues begins properly in Section 13. The most important feature of this account, though, is that one of the cardinal virtues, wisdom, is not presented as being derived from the basic drive introduced in Sections 11–12. When the natural human drive for enquiry and pursuit of truth not for practical purposes is introduced in 1.13, there is no attempt to link it to *oikeiōsis* or to the social commitments that have been presented as developing in virtue of our rationality. Indeed, theoretical enquiry is described as something we are eager for precisely when practical obligations are in abeyance. In place of an integrated account, we are given a flat assertion that this is a proper and natural feature of human beings:

> It is above all characteristic of human beings to enquire into and probe for the truth. Consequently, when we are free of our essential obligations and concerns we are eager to see, hear, and learn, and we believe that learning matters that are arcane or amazing is essential for the happy life. From this we see that what is true, simple and pure is best suited to our human nature. (*Off.* 1.13)

Nothing in the *oikeiōsis* account of 1.11–12 provides a context for this; there is no allusion here to the role of reason in grounding speech and social interaction. In contrast, when Cicero moves on to the next virtue (greatness of soul) we can recognize that the life of social interaction and obligations already sketched provides the context for this virtue:

> This desire for seeing the truth is accompanied by a definite lust for leadership: no mind that has been properly educated is prepared to yield to anyone except an adviser, a teacher or a commander duly appointed under law for the sake of general utility. This is the basis for greatness of soul, that is, the capacity to treat merely human matters with disdain. (*Off.* 1.13)

The value of being able to treat what is merely human with disdain might seem to be in tension with our basically social nature. But this need not be so. The capacity to rise above the trials and tribulations that come with our being human does not require us to disvalue other people and their interests. What *magnitudo animi* usually looks down on are difficulties and challenges in carrying out our responsibilities and activities.[17] Similarly for *moderatio* in 1.14. The aesthetic appreciation which is such an important feature of this virtue might in principle be socially detached, as theoretical reason is, but in fact it is accompanied by a clear emphasis

---

[17] See, for example, *Fin.* 2.95, 4.17, *Tusc.* 1.64, 2.53. In *Fin.* 4.11 the character Cicero refers to how the *explicatio naturae* conduces to various virtues, including *moderatio* and justice, alongside *magnitudo animi*.

Oikeiōsis *and the Origin of Virtue* 71

on the role of *moderatio* in guiding our actions and social interactions. I highlight here the references to behaviour that are absent from the account of theoretical reason:

> And it is an important result of our rational nature that human beings are the only species that can see what orderliness is, what it is that is fitting, and what limits there should be in our *words and actions*. And so no other species sees what it is in visible things that is beautiful, charming and harmonious. Our rational nature transfers an image of this from the visual realm to the mental and holds that the preservation of beauty, stability and orderliness is even more important in the domain of our thoughts and *actions*; and it is careful to avoid *doing* anything that is undignified or effeminate and likewise to avoid *doing* or even thinking about anything that is motivated by lust. (*Off.* 1.14)

The fact that three of the four cardinal virtues are plausibly related to the *oikeiōsis* account which sets up this discussion is striking – but equally important is the fact that theoretical wisdom and philosophical enquiry are not connected to it in a comparably obvious way. The drive for *veri inquisitio* is simply asserted as a basic motivation without context or any effort to connect it to *oikeiōsis*. And yet this could have been done. If self-preservation were linked to self-enhancement, as it is in other Stoic accounts such as Seneca's in letter 121 and in Piso's account in *De Finibus* 5, it could be argued that the drive for knowledge emerges from our commitment to our self, this self now being a rational animal which naturally desires to know; this would echo the Aristotelian commitment from the opening of the *Metaphysics*. But Cicero shows no inclination here to follow this line of thought.

De Officiis 1.15 pauses to make explicit that the four virtues are the parts of what is *honestum*: *omne quod est honestum, id quattuor partium oritur ex aliqua*. These virtues are parts of a single whole and, as he goes on to say, interlocked with each other: *inter se conligata atque implicata*. This seems closely compatible with what we learn elsewhere about Panaetius' views:

> For all the virtues consider what belongs to all of them and the issues governed by the various virtues. For Panaetius said that the situation with the virtues was as though there were a single target set up for several archers and this target had on it lines of different colours. Each archer would then aim at hitting the target, but one would do so directly by way of hitting, for example, the white line, another by way of hitting the black line, and another by way of hitting a line of some other colour. For just as they make hitting the target the highest goal while each archer aims directly to do so in a different way, so too all the virtues make the goal happiness, which consists in living in harmony with nature, but each virtue achieves it in a different way. (Stobaeus 2.63–64)

The single target is the whole of what is *kalon* or (in Cicero) *honestum*. The various lines on the target are the four parts mentioned in Cicero. Each virtue governs a domain of its own, hitting the mark in which it makes its contribution to achieving the goal of happiness. We have functional differentiation and complementarity for the four cardinal virtues, much as we find in Cicero's account.

The ensuing discussion in Cicero of the particular virtues underscores the special position of theoretical virtue. In 1.15 the interconnection of the virtues and their functional differentiation is highlighted:

> Although these four [virtues] are connected and intertwined with each other, nevertheless from each of them distinct kinds of responsibilities [*officia*] emerge. For example, the first part of virtue that I outlined, where we located wisdom and prudence,[18] involves the investigation and discovery of truth and this is the proper function [*munus*] of this virtue. (*Off.* 1.15)

By contrast, the account of the other three virtues in 1.17 is emphatic about their connection to the principle of self-preservation and the derived social interactions:

> The other three virtues have as their objects the things we need for attaining and retaining what is essential for the activities of life: the preservation of a unified human society and the manifestation of an outstanding greatness of soul both in enhancing wealth and other advantages for oneself and one's family and even more importantly in the ability to despise these same benefits. Moreover, a certain orderliness, stability, moderation and other similar characteristics are involved in areas where one needs to take action as well as to have a kind of mental activity. For it is by deploying a measure of balance and orderliness in the practicalities of life that we will be able to maintain our honour and dignity. (*Off.* 1.17)

We may note the emphasis on acquiring and maintaining activities needed for life and the preservation of society.

---

[18] *Sapientia* and *prudentia*, terms which would ordinarily indicate distinct theoretical and practical knowledge. But in this context the terms taken together seem to refer to theoretical virtue. The two descriptions of this virtue in 1.15 are *perspicientia veri sollertiaque* and *sapientiam et prudentiam*, but the second description is augmented by the statement that this virtue contains *indagatio atque inventio veri*. If this is right, we should interpret the pair as a mere Ciceronian doublet. When Cicero turns to practical knowledge in 1.19 the term *prudentia* is not used. Elsewhere, as at 1.81, *prudentia* has its more usual reference specifically to practical intelligence. Woolf 2015: 173 holds that the virtue cited here is "surely meant to include both the contemplative … and practical … forms of wisdom." I am not persuaded by his interpretation, though it is certainly true that in his initial reference to intellectual virtue Cicero already has in mind the more complex issues that are soon brought to the surface. See Woolf 2015: 173–176.

Oikeiōsis *and the Origin of Virtue*

In 1.18–19 Cicero focusses on the first virtue, theoretical wisdom and enquiry. He again underlines its privileged and superior position in human nature:

> The first topic, which consists in the knowledge of the truth, engages most directly with human nature. For we are all attracted, indeed drawn to a desire for knowing and understanding; we think it is wonderful to excel in this and take it to be bad, disgraceful in fact, to be in error, to be ignorant and to be led astray. This branch of virtue is both natural to us and honourable. (*Off.* 1.18)

This is the point where Cicero begins to provide a more detailed account of each of the virtues, beginning with wisdom. He proceeds by outlining the two mistakes people make in this domain, the first of which reflects Cicero's Academic commitments:

> First, we should not mistake what we don't know for what we do know and so rashly give our assent to it; those who want to avoid this mistake (and that should be everyone) will take their time and exercise caution when assessing things. (*Off.* 1.18)

Precipitancy, rushing to faulty conclusions and failing to distinguish what we know and what we don't – these are cardinal failings in the Academic tradition, inspired originally no doubt by Socrates' insistence on knowing only that he doesn't know. The second failing is perhaps more reflective of Cicero's commitments as a practical agent and also reflects a tendency in later Stoicism that we see with particular clarity in Seneca, squandering precious time and energy on unimportant enquiries:

> The second mistake is that some people are overly enthusiastic about devoting their energies to the investigation of arcane and difficult problems which aren't essential. (*Off.* 1.19)

This consideration triggers, for the first time in this discussion, serious reflection on the place of practical knowledge and its relationship to theoretical enquiry:

> If those mistakes are avoided then all the care and attention devoted to honourable matters that are worth knowing will be praised, and rightly so. For example, I've heard about Gaius Sulpicius, an astronomer, and I know first-hand Sextus Pompeius, the geometer, as well as many dialecticians, several eminent legal theorists – all of which are subjects that involve ascertaining the truth. To be diverted from taking action by one's enthusiasm for theory is a violation of our *officia* – for action is the essence of what is praiseworthy in a virtue. Still, one can often take a break from action and there are many opportunities to retreat to one's studies – and our ceaseless

mental energy can keep us going in our enthusiasm for learning even when we don't devote our efforts to it. All mental activity and thinking, though, will either deal with deliberation about issues which are honourable and conduce to a good and happy life or will focus on the enthusiastic pursuit of understanding and knowledge. (*Off.* 1.19)

The combination of astronomy, geometry, and dialectic with legal theory opens the door to considering the balance of theoretical and practical knowledge. Even with the *ius civile* the focus is not on the practical utility of legal knowledge – it is on the list of "subjects that involve ascertaining truth." In the sentences which follow Cicero is clearly preoccupied with the balance between the urgency of practical obligations, diversion from which is *contra officium*, and the permissible attractions of theoretical enquiry. This is, of course, an issue which dogged Cicero through his whole career. If any aspect of this section is a direct reflection of Cicero's own personal perspective, rather than Panaetius' organization of the virtues, this would be it. The topic concludes with a clear distinction between theoretical and practical mental activities along lines that might well seem to be Peripatetic in inspiration – a distinction that might better have been introduced at the outset, instead of the rather stark contrast between intellectual virtue on the one hand and the other three more practical virtues on the other.

At 1.20 Cicero reverts to the initial framework (one theoretical virtue in opposition to the other three that are socially oriented and practical). He begins with justice ("of the other three, the most comprehensive is the line of reasoning which grounds social bonds among people and a kind of shared life") and its associated virtue, beneficence. This discussion runs from here to Section 60, and it is followed by a comparably extended account (61–92) of courage, greatness of soul, and associated virtues; the essentially social and political context of these virtues is clear. Much of the rest of the book is taken up by discussion of the fourth virtue (or family of virtues) – *verecundia, temperantia, modestia* are listed here, whereas *ordo, constantia* and *moderatio* were the terms used in 1.17, with the discussion of *personae* beginning at 105 and running to 121. From 122 to the end of the book a series of issues relevant to determination of *officia* in general are dealt with, but at this point Cicero has left behind the organization of topics that began with the account of *oikeiōsis* at 1.11.

4 Cicero and Panaetius Revisited

Let me here take stock and draw tentative conclusions. At the beginning of his theorization of the virtues in *De Officiis* 1, Cicero makes two striking moves that stand in an interesting contrast to other Stoic accounts. (1) He develops a more explicit account of the relationship between the natural drive for self-preservation and the natural social drive in humans; this involves an emphatically explicit contrast between humans and non-rational animals. (2) He begins by treating wisdom separately from the other three cardinal virtues, as though it developed from a different psychological tendency in us; only later does he disentangle theoretical from practical wisdom, making it clear that the latter is more closely linked to the other virtues than the former is. This feature seems more like what we see in Aristotle than what is found elsewhere in Stoicism.

The significance of these two moves deserves a bit of reflection. The first seems to me to be an innovative move within the Stoic theory of *oikeiōsis*. Cicero (no doubt thanks to Panaetius) offers an explicit and theoretically satisfying account of the relationship between so-called personal and social *oikeiōsis*, filling a gap in Stoic theory that an alertly critical Stoic might easily have noticed and wished to address. Such a move would fit well with Panaetius' other well-documented critical departures from the doctrines of the Chrysippean school. Cicero's embrace of this Panaetian move, assuming that that is what it is, need not have been motivated by the same considerations. The central role played by *ratio* and *oratio* would no doubt be an attractive feature of the move, as would its general acceptability to other Socratic schools of thought.

The second innovation, however, does not seem to emerge so obviously from a need to resolve difficulties within the Stoic system. Setting the disinterested drive for truth for its own sake over against the three more practical virtues and then subsequently distinguishing practical reason from its purely theoretical counterpart seem to be moves which reflect the influence of Aristotelian thought. Assuming that these moves were made by Panaetius, it is tempting to account for the openness to such non-Stoic influence by reference to the active engagement with a revived Aristotelian philosophy in Panaetius' day, stimulated by the emergence of Critolaus as a key figure in the debates of the second century BCE.[19] I see no reason to doubt that a philosopher of Panaetius' independent-minded tendencies would be deterred by dogmatic resistance from accepting what seemed to be a good argument of Peripatetic origin. At the same time, though, it does not follow that Cicero's readiness to adopt such a move in his own work was motivated by the same considerations. As an Academic and a sceptic, Cicero comfortably allowed himself to accept what seemed like

---

[19] See Inwood 2014 and Hahm 2007.

the best arguments at a given moment, independently of school connections. He had a strong and persistent interest in the commonalities of the main Socratic schools, influenced to a considerable extent by the example of Antiochus of Ascalon.[20] It is not hard to imagine that a philosophical accommodation attractive to Panaetius because of dialectical debate in the second century BCE might have appealed to Cicero for quite different reasons, considerations more pertinent to the philosophical situation of his own day.

Among other things, I have suggested that Panaetius proposes and Cicero accepts a significant and interesting change in the Stoic theory of *oikeiōsis*. Let me close by asking from another point of view whether this is a plausible supposition. After all, if the change in the Stoic theory is not originally the work of Panaetius, then we would have to attribute the move in its entirety to Cicero. In fact, though, I think there is a further reason for supposing that the innovation came originally from Panaetius. The further consideration I want to adduce comes from the work of one of Panaetius' most important students, Posidonius, who seems to have made a similarly dramatic change in the standard Stoic theory.

As a part of his attack on Chrysippus for departing from the wisdom of the ancients, Galen (*PHP* 5.5.8–9 = p. 318.12–24 de Lacy, F 160 E-K) invokes Posidonius, paraphrasing his doctrine of *oikeiōsis* in a move that brings his theory very close to the Platonic tripartition favoured by Galen himself:

> We have, then, by nature three affinities (*oikeiōseis*) corresponding to the three parts of the soul: to pleasure because of the appetitive part, to victory because of the spirited part, and to the fine because of the rational part. Thus Epicurus recognized only the affinity of the worst part of the soul, Chrysippus only that of the best part (as he claimed that we only have an affinity to the fine, which, obviously, is the good). Only the ancient philosophers were able to see that we have all three affinities. Since Chrysippus dismissed two of these affinities it makes sense that he was at a loss about the source of badness, not being able to specify its cause or the ways it exists in us, and being unable to discover how it is that children go wrong. It is reasonable, I think, that Posidonius criticized and blamed him for all of this.

If Posidonius did in fact criticize Chrysippus for recognizing only one *oikeiōsis* and held that a proper account of human nature has to recognize that our basic drives are more varied than that, then he can be seen as

---

[20] See his remarks at *Off.* 3.20: Academics and Peripatetics would accept the *formula* he offers, which is nevertheless closest to that of the Stoics. Cicero invokes his Academic *licentia* to justify pursuing this convergence.

doing something similar to but distinct from what I am supposing that Panaetius did. Responding critically to what he regarded as an excessively unitary theory of *oikeiōsis*, Posidonius (like Panaetius) retains the basic Stoic move of grounding ethical theory in an account of innate natural drives in human beings but insists that those drives are more complexly articulated than Chrysippus thought. According to Galen, this enabled Posidonius to provide a markedly better account of the nature of the passions. It seems that Panaetius' own innovation enabled him to provide what he (and Cicero) took to be a better integrated account of the four cardinal virtues.

If this is right, then we have tentative confirmation of the traditional view that Cicero adopted at least the main philosophical structure of book 1 of *De Officiis* from Panaetius' work, but this comes with both a better appreciation of how that structure relates to other versions of Stoic ethics and a recognition that Cicero had good philosophical reasons of his own for adopting a theory developed in a very different context under different dialectical pressures over a hundred years before.

CHAPTER 4

Cicero's Project in Book 2 of De Officiis

Malcolm Schofield

1 Human Resource, and How to Harness It

Early in Book 1 of *De Officiis*, Cicero explains the way the material he plans to investigate in the treatise was described and organized in his model, a work by the second-century BCE Stoic Panaetius (*Off.* 1.9):

> Triplex igitur est, ut Panaetio videtur, consilii capiendi deliberatio. Nam aut honestumne factu sit an turpe dubitant id, quod in deliberationem cadit; in quo considerando saepe animi in contrarias sententias distrahuntur. Tum autem aut anquirunt aut consultant, ad vitae commoditatem iucunditatemque, ad facultates rerum atque copias, ad opes, ad potentiam, quibus et se possint iuvare et suos, conducat id necne, de quo deliberant; quae deliberatio omnis in rationem utilitatis cadit. Tertium dubitandi genus est, cum pugnare videtur cum honesto id, quod videtur esse utile; cum enim utilitas ad se rapere, honestas contra revocare ad se videtur, fit ut distrahatur in deliberando animus afferatque ancipitem curam cogitandi.

> There are in consequence, as it seems to Panaetius, three questions to deliberate when deciding upon a plan of action. In the first place, men may be uncertain whether the thing that falls under consideration is an honourable (*honestum*) or a dishonourable thing to do; often, when they ponder this, their spirits are pulled between opposing opinions. Secondly, they investigate or debate whether or not the course they are considering is conducive to the advantageousness and pleasantness of life, to opportunities and resources for doing things, to wealth and to power, all of which enable them to benefit themselves and those dear to them. All such deliberation falls under reasoning about what is beneficial (*utilitas*). The third type of uncertainty arises when something apparently beneficial appears to conflict with what is honourable: benefit seems to snatch you to its

---

Earlier versions of some of the material in this chapter were presented to colloquia at Cornell and Oxford. My gratitude particularly to Charles Brittain, Brad Inwood, and Lesley Brown for the invitations to do so. My thanks also to Raphael Woolf, whose editorial attentions have led to some clarifications and other adjustments in this present version, for his invitation to contribute to the volume.

side and honourableness in its turn to call you back; consequently the mind is pulled this way and that in its deliberation, resulting in troubled irresolution. (Trans. E. M. Atkins (adapted))

My focus here will be on the second of the topics specified: deliberation about *utilitas* – 'expediency', as the Loeb translator renders it, or better 'the useful' (Walsh), or as in Griffin and Atkins's edition, reproduced above, 'what is beneficial'. Cicero turns to explore this subject in Book 2, corresponding – it is generally supposed – to the third book in Panaetius's three book treatise περὶ τοῦ καθήκοντος, 'On appropriate behaviour', his main model and source for his own first two books (*Off.* 3.7).

The list of questions that Cicero mentions under the second topic to help the reader grasp the scope of such deliberation contains a structural complexity it is easy to miss on a first quick look. He starts by indicating the ultimate general concern of questions of this type: *vitae commoditatem iucunditatemque*, 'the advantageousness and pleasantness of life' (in contrast with *honestum*, 'the fine or honourable thing to do', the subject of Panaetius's first topic of deliberation, examined in Book 1 of *De Officiis*).[1] The remaining questions on Cicero's list – relating to the acquisition of 'opportunities for things and resources, wealth and power' – pertain to some key capabilities conceived as necessary or helpful if people want for 'themselves and those dear to them' a life that will be advantageous and agreeable to live. In other words, these are questions framed not with reference directly to ultimate goals of deliberation – advantage and pleasantness – but with regard to means of securing them: how to tackle the problem of securing what will benefit us and ours in our search for the resources requisite for the final objective, which in the introduction to Book 2 Cicero will speak of as *vitae cultus*, 'civilised living' (*Off.* 2.1). The major part of Book 2 will accordingly be devoted to specifying the principal means for acquiring such resources, chief among them the human resource – the support of other people – needed if one is to achieve high public recognition and political impact. The project undertaken in Book 2 – as adumbrated in the prospectus at the beginning of Book 1 – would therefore not be adequately described as enquiry into the means required if those aspirations are to be realised. What is envisaged is something less straightforward. It is to be

---

[1] Andrew Dyck points out (Dyck 1996: 81) that in Stobaeus's treatment of the τέλος (goal of living), Aristotle is said to have posited three targets on which human desires are focused: τὸ καλόν (the noble), τὸ συμφέρον (i.e. *utilitas*, what is advantageous), τὸ ἡδύ (the pleasurable, Stobaeus 2.51.18–52.1). We might also be reminded of τὸ ὠφέλιμον (the beneficial) καὶ τὸ ἡδύ (in contrast with τὸ καλόν), a trio which figures memorably in one of Socrates' trickier arguments with Polus in Plato's *Gorgias* (474c–475e).

an investigation into the means for getting the means (the capacity and resource) necessary for realising the ultimate aim: to live advantageously and agreeably, particularly (it will transpire) enjoying political power and public standing.

None of this sounds very like the Stoicism of Zeno or Chrysippus. The Stoics had a notion of 'preferred indifferents': things of value such as life, health, strength, wealth, public esteem, whose possession however makes no ultimate difference to happiness. The stress Panaetius seems to have put on capabilities and resources, and on means of acquiring those, is not something we find in orthodox accounts of Stoic ethics. In fact, Cicero's presentation in *Off.* 1.9 of the three basic types of deliberative question that he identified points us away from any idea that early Stoic doctrine was the basis on which he made the classification. The impression conveyed is rather that the questions human beings in general typically ask themselves in considering how to act are what Panaetius meant to be putting into his three categories, presumably reflecting the Peripatetic influence often detected in the ethical thought of this φιλοαριστοτέλης or 'philaristotelian' Stoic (fr.57 van Straaten).[2] The classification seems designed to capture and crystallise ordinary discourse about practical questions, as asked by people at large: an approach which fits with the general enterprise of discussing 'shared, and widely accessible' obligations that he was undertaking in the treatise to which Cicero was making recourse (see *Off.* 3.14–16). If Stoicism is to come into play in the treatment of the topic, it will therefore have to figure in the answers to such questions that it goes on to give, and in the way those answers are tackled and formulated.

When Cicero in Book 2 – after preliminaries – gets down to discussion of *utilitas*, resources that make for the maintenance of human life are what he proceeds to discuss. His first move is to sketch a hierarchy of such resources, beginning with minerals and crops,[3] rising through animals such as horses, cattle and the like, to rational beings (gods and humans): in short, a *scala naturae*. There then follows an extended passage, for whose length he apologises, arguing and illustrating the thesis that human activity and cooperation are the essential prerequisite without which nothing else could function *as* a resource. Human civilisation in all its many dimensions depends on human exploitation of minerals, plants, and other animals, and on the development of arts and crafts and cooperative endeavour for its

---

[2] Cf. Dyck 1996: 357–8. See also Inwood ch. 3, this volume: 75–6.
[3] Dyck 1996: 378 thinks that Cicero inadvertently omits plants. But he includes 'produce from the earth' (2.11), presumably counting it within the class of inanimate things, opposed to which are animals with 'drives and impulses'. See also (with Walsh 2000: 160) *ND* 2.150–2.

creation and preservation. In short, human beings themselves are the No.1 human resource (*Off.* 2.11–15).

It seems likely that Cicero is here reproducing Panaetius's own line of argument, as the commentators agree (the coupling of gods and humans certainly strikes a thoroughly Stoic note) – although Panaetius was probably drawing on some earlier treatment of the invention of the technical and civilised arts: the sort of 'Kulturgeschichte' most familiar from Protagoras's myth in Plato's *Protagoras*, the preface to Diodorus's universal history, or Book 5 of Lucretius's *De Rerum Natura*.[4] What makes Panaetian provenance particularly likely is first, Cicero's apology for going on longer than necessary, not something that usually ever troubles him; and second, an immediate subsequent reference explicitly to Panaetius, criticising him for labouring – with far too many examples – the obvious fact that no general or statesman could have performed great exploits without committed endeavours from other humans (2.16), but thereby himself simultaneously giving the point extra emphasis.[5] In truth it seems probable, as Miriam Griffin argues,[6] that a main reason why Cicero was attracted into using Panaetius's treatise as his model was precisely his shared interest in politics and public life, as evidenced also by the reference subsequently made to Panaetius's discussions of the conduct of advocates (2.51) and of public building programmes (2.60). In sum, it sounds very much as though at 2.16 Cicero is mentioning, only to abbreviate, a further instalment of the same general Panaetian treatment of the indispensability of human activity for preserving each and every aspect of civilised human life. He then deals very briskly with the complementary point, credited to the early Peripatetic Dicaearchus, that humans have also wrought more destruction of other humans than has resulted from any natural disasters (2.16).

A conclusion is now drawn: it is humans who are both humans' greatest asset and their greatest problem. That being so, Cicero declares, he counts it 'the special property of virtue to win over the hearts and minds of men and to enlist them in one's own[7] service'. This, he says, explains why, while securing the necessities of life is the business of expert crafts such as mining and agriculture, 'it is the wisdom and virtue of outstanding men that inspire

---

[4] Cole 1967 remains a valuable study of this topic.
[5] Cicero also seems mildly critical of the admiration Panaetius expressed for Scipio's incorruptibility (*abstinentia*), which he represents as something characteristic of Romans of that era in general, when Scipio had other and greater virtues (2.76).
[6] Griffin and Atkins 1991: xx; cf. also Dyck 1996: 354–5, Brunt 2013: 217–18.
[7] I follow here the Loeb rendering of *ad suos usus*. Atkins (Griffin and Atkins 1991) has 'its own', i.e. 'virtue's'; so also Walsh 2000.

people to be prompt, ready, and devoted in the further advancement of our affairs' (2.17). Cicero expands later on the power of virtue to inspire, in terms familiar from the theory of virtue he has expounded in Book 1 (2.32; cf. e.g. 1.55–6, 98): 'Because that very thing which we call the honourable and fitting (*decorum*) is inherently pleasing to us, and moves the hearts of all by its nature and appearance, shining out brightly, so to speak, from the virtues that I have mentioned – because of that, when we think people possess these virtues, we are compelled by nature itself to love them'.[8]

The notion of virtue (*virtus*) is now, therefore, introduced into the argument for the first time, and with it a first indication of how a distinctively Stoic perspective will shape the treatment of the topic. Commentators express surprise that the service in which virtue enlists the hearts of those attracted by it is specified as something so apparently remote from virtue as 'advancement of our affairs' – which recalls the focus on benefiting 'themselves and those dear to them' that Panaetius was said to have identified as characteristic of deliberation about *utilitas* (1.9). But Cicero's train of thought reflects a stance actually quite close to the outlook of Stoicism as it was developing in the second century BCE, in the context of debate between the Stoics Diogenes of Babylon and Antipater of Tarsus (with both of whom Panaetius is said to have studied) and the great Academic scholarch Carneades. Thus Stobaeus tells us that Antipater often used to define the goal as 'doing everything so far as one can oneself continually and unswervingly to achieve the things that are naturally the most salient' (πᾶν τὸ καθ' αὑτὸν ποιεῖν διηνεκῶς καὶ ἀπαραβάτως πρὸς τὸ τυγχάνειν τῶν προηγουμένων κατὰ φύσιν: Stobaeus 2.76.13–15) – so that a distinction has to be made between the goal (acting virtuously) and its focus or target (achieving what is naturally salient).[9] Cicero's claim is effectively a corollary of this conception of virtue and the goal. Since our own interests and affairs are the things that human nature finds most salient, and since as he has just argued at length, human support is what is needed if the enterprise of advancing our affairs is to succeed, virtue will accordingly be focused on securing such support, as something appropriate to its special function. And just because virtue shines out with an attractive force, it is in fact able to inspire other humans too to assist in the endeavour.

After further comment on virtue, Cicero turns to his main project in Book 2 of the treatise: determining 'the methods by which we can acquire the capacity to embrace and retain the support of other humans' (2.19) – or

---

[8] On the *decorum*, see Schofield 2012b, and the chapters by Bishop and McConnell, this volume.
[9] For discussion of this subtle distinction, see Long 1967 and Striker 1996: 298–315.

at any rate, he will do so once he has reminded the reader of 'the great power of fortune' (that is to say, sheer luck) in human affairs (2.19–20). By now we are primed to expect that virtue will be key to the answers he gives: but in what specific ways, and why alternatives to virtuous conduct will not be as effective, remains to be explored. His account of the methods he will consider has a fairly straightforward structure. It begins with a sketch of the main motivations that prompt human beings to give someone else the kind of support that will advance that person's political standing and the esteem in which he is held (*ad eum augendum atque honestandum*).[10] Cicero lists six: (i) goodwill (e.g. out of gratitude for kindnesses shown); (ii) a desire to honour virtue; (iii) trust, and the belief that this person will take good care of the supporter's interests; (iv) fear of his power; (v) expectations, as when kings or populist politicians make lavish promises; (vi) finally and disreputably, but sometimes unavoidably, bribery (2.21–2).[11]

The detailed exposition of the way these motivations operate in attracting support occupies the bulk of the rest of Book 2. Thus (iv) fear is first discussed, only for its sustained effectiveness to be decisively rejected (2.23–9). It gives Cicero his first opportunity in this book to resume his attack on tyranny and corruption in the Roman politics of his own time, above all by Julius Caesar and now, after his assassination, his political heirs. Perhaps the most important passage in the discussion of fear is the argument that ruthless oppression and exploitation of Rome's allies under the dictatorships of Sulla and most recently Caesar have fostered the inordinate ambitions of warlords. Rewarding such megalomania has backfired by generating the calamity of civil wars. Fostering rapacity abroad has in the end imperilled the *res publica* at home. *iure igitur plectimur*, is the verdict: 'So it's justice, that we are feeling the lash' (2.28).[12] Rejection of terror as an appropriate method for winning allegiance leaves ways of inspiring affection as the preferred approach (2.29–31), and after brief comment on friendship (where Cicero notes that he has provided a discussion in his dialogue *Laelius (De Amicitia)*, which had been composed earlier in the same

---

[10] It goes without saying that Cicero writes in a social, political, and cultural milieu in which only males of citizen status are conceived as his target readership.

[11] An abbreviated version of this same list, now presented as giving reasons why people submit to *imperium* and *potestas*, follows immediately (2.22). Winterbottom 1994: 77 deletes it in his Oxford Classical Text edition, as an insertion of authentic Ciceronian material not belonging to *De Officiis*; Walsh 2000: 61 with 162 follows suit. Dyck 1996: 387–90, however, points out reasons for thinking that, although clumsily presented and not best thought through in content or expression, it is needed in the context to prepare the transition to the treatment of fear that now follows and to the position which that occupies in the argument of Book 2 (cf. also Griffin and Atkins 1991: 70 nn. 2–3).

[12] See Griffin 2008.

year 44 BCE), he duly makes observations in sequence on (i) goodwill (2.32), (iii) trust (2.33–5), and (ii) esteem (2.36–8), all advertised at the beginning of the section 2.31–51 as jointly required if 'the peak and perfection of glory (*gloria*)' is to be achieved. It will naturally only be conduct or achievement of quite exceptional calibre that will attract such responses to a degree that constitutes glorification. He follows these with remarks on the importance of justice, whose importance has been indicated throughout discussion of (i) to (iii) (2.39–43), and advice to the young on behaviour that 'may be effective in securing glory' (2.42–51). The account is rounded off by what is billed at the outset as a treatment of liberality, which deals in effect also with (v) expectations of lavish expenditure. (vi) Bribery, and the need for it *faute de mieux*, seems not to be dealt with at all in the event (2.52–85; but after all *De Officiis* is a work on how one *ought* to behave).

Such an overall structuring of the main body of Book 2 would presumably have derived from the treatise of Panaetius that Cicero was using. Whether he also got from Panaetius the list of motivations at 2.21, and his delivery of the detailed programme for exploiting them that he works out at 2.23–85, is a question to which no very securely based answer is likely to be found. It is presumably significant that at the end of Book 2, Cicero records the objection – by Antipater of Tyre, a recently deceased Stoic – that Panaetius had omitted in his coverage two key topics: care of health and financial management (2.86). That seems to suggest that up to that point the programme under discussion was at least broadly Panaetian, although many of the illustrative examples of conduct he cites are taken from Roman political life, clearly his own contribution, as may also be (for example) the somewhat awkwardly introduced and positioned discussion (2.42–3) of the difference between true and counterfeit *gloria*, one of Cicero's own longstanding favourite themes.[13] Indeed, such was the dominance of *gloria* in Roman political ideology, with its demand for 'both achievement in public life' – especially military achievement – 'and public recognition of that achievement',[14] that its emphatic prominence in this part of Book 2 may likewise be due to Cicero himself, as will no doubt have been true of most of his specific advice on how a young man should develop his career (2.44–51).[15] For a good deal of the detailed development

---

[13] See Dyck 1996: 411–12, 422–5.
[14] Long 1995: 216.
[15] Cicero does explicitly appeal to Panaetius's authority here on one point in particular: to try to forestall any philosophical disquiet over his remark that it is sometimes an advocate's job to argue in defence of a client something plausible, even if it falls short of the truth (2.51). From this mention of Panaetius it is impossible to infer anything more general about how much else in the passage depends on him – perhaps only that he too had discussed legal advocacy at this juncture in his treatise.

of the material he presents, however, Miriam Griffin's conclusion to her treatment of the nature and extent of his dependence in *De Officiis* on Panaetius's περὶ τοῦ καθήκοντος, 'On appropriate conduct', seems eminently sane: 'When we consider how marked the work is by contemporary events and how closely it mirrors Cicero's views elsewhere, we must conclude that Panaetius's work was too thoroughly digested and reworked by Cicero for us to separate the contributions of the two authors now'.[16]

2 Liberality and Largesse

Cicero marks the break between the two major sections of Book 2 with the words (2.52, in Walsh's translation with an adaptation): 'Now that I have explained these obligations of young men which are effective in gaining glory, I must next discuss beneficence and liberality'. It was only the final part (2.44–51) of the section concerned with acquisition of glory (2.31–51) that was devoted to the career development of a young man, and only its final piece of advice that explicitly spoke of 'a piece of advice on one's obligation' (*praeceptum officii*, 2.51). But throughout, the accent has been on the virtues that one needs to exhibit in conduct, and particularly on justice at 2.31–43, where in summing up Cicero says, referring back to Book 1 (2.43; cf. 1.20–41): 'Anyone who wants to gain true glory must discharge the obligations of justice'. More specifically, he has said of justice (2.38), it secures '(i) goodwill, because it desires to benefit many; and for the same reason (iii) trust; and (ii) admiration, because it scorns and ignores the very things towards which most men, inflamed by greed, are dragged'.[17] An obligation of justice is clearly what he means at 2.51, too, since the piece of advice he goes on to dispense forbids one to indict an innocent person on a capital charge.

So although at 2.31–51 he is in the first instance sketching the way someone bidding for glory should attempt to foster (i) goodwill, (ii) a desire to honour virtue, and (iii) trust, the major underlying theme has been the need to act in all things with justice. And that is the final note struck, with the reference at 2.52 to 'obligations', i.e. the obligations of justice. Justice is in truth the principal ethical concern of this first main section of Book 2.

---

[16] Griffin in Griffin and Atkins 1991: xxi.
[17] As Dyck 1996: 418 notes, Cicero in the discussion at 2.32–7 to which this summary relates has mostly spoken only of a reputation for justice (*fama, opinio iustitiae*, 2.32; cf. 2.39, 42), not justice itself, as exerting this sort of impact. But he appeals to Socrates' dictum that the short cut to glory is to so behave that you are the sort of person you wish to be thought, and argues that if you take any other route you will go badly wrong (2.42).

A similar approach is indicated in Cicero's programmatic formulation there of 'beneficence and liberality' as the focal concern of 2.52–85. That section is where he will deal with item (v) of the agenda at 2.21, largesse and the hope or expectation of it. The implication already is that the prime concern must be to exercise the other main social virtue besides justice – beneficence or liberality – as first expounded also in Book 1 (1.42–60). Largesse must be under the control of that virtue so far as possible, even if political necessity may sometimes require one to exceed the appropriate limits that largesse's proper exercise should observe.[18]

The organisation and conceptual distinctions of 2.52–85 are rather more complex than those of 2.31–51 (already indicated in Section 1 above), so the rest of Section 2 will be mostly devoted to exploring them. But there is another more substantive difference. Justice is a guiding theme in the discussion of ways of achieving glory at 2.31–8. At 2.52–85 beneficence is the quite explicit focus. Here Cicero is exploring the virtue at length for itself as well as for its pay-offs for the donor (which do not always receive much emphasis); and while preoccupation with distinguishing it from largesse dominates in the opening pages (2.52–60), largesse drops out of sight for much of the rest of this second main section – as to an extent do the specifics of the programme for career advancement set out at 2.21–2.

Liberality and largesse are often treated by Cicero as mutually exclusive modes of conduct, while at the same time he shows himself well aware that there can be a fine line between them. For example, he writes (*De Or.* 2.105): 'When someone is charged with corrupt electoral practice, there is seldom the possibility of separating liberality (*liberalitate*) and generosity (*benignitate*) from corruption (*ambitu*) and largesse (*largitione*)'. Here the largesse of *largitio* is virtually equivalent to bribery, one of the distinct senses of the term identified in the lexica.[19] A similarly fine line is also suggested by the way Cicero treats the root adjective *largus*. In the section of *De Officiis* with which we are primarily concerned, he begins one subsection with a division of the *largi*, those who give amply, into two species: *prodigi*, 'lavish' or 'extravagant', and *liberales*, 'generous' (2.55). Examples are now given:

---

[18] Cf. Atkins 1990: 260: 'If the discussion of *gloria* was intended to argue pragmatically for the importance of justice ..., the discussion of liberality provides the pragmatic argument for observing the guidance about *beneficentia* given in 1.42–60'.

[19] But it can be used simply in a descriptive way to mean 'gift' or 'bestowal', as when, in celebrating the Romans' tradition of extending citizenship to communities they conquered, Cicero speaks of *largitio et communicatio civitatis*, 'the bestowal and sharing of citizenship' (*Balb.* 31).

The extravagant squander their money on civic feasts, distributions of meat [after public sacrifices], gladiatorial shows, promotion of games and wild-beast chases, all outlays for which they will be remembered briefly or not at all. Generous people, on the other hand, apply their resources to redeeming captives from pirates, relieving friends from the burden of debt, or helping them to provide dowries for their daughters, or aiding them in the acquisition or extension of property. (*Off.* 2.55) (Trans. P. G. Walsh (adapted))

Cicero likewise thinks of matching species of *largitio*, as is indicated by disapproving talk of that *genus largitionis*, 'species of largesse', which 'robs Peter to pay Paul' (2.85, as Walsh translates the Latin). But there is another such *genus largiendi* which is prompted by true liberality (2.61), 'more important and more beneficial', which *boni viri* ('good men') should supply provided it is within their means, such as the unspecified form of entertainment for popular consumption that he himself laid on as expected of an aedile in his year of office (2.58), but notably also in assisting individuals (2.61-4).[20] In general, the rationale for *largitio* should be that it is 'either necessary (*necesse*) or beneficial (*utile*)' (2.59). Cicero's main examples here of the beneficial are city walls, docks, harbours, aqueducts. But expenditure on theatres, colonnades, and new temples, though not to be considered virtuous, and disapproved of by Panaetius, is the sort of financial outlay that may be justified as necessitated by political circumstances, provided that it is within one's means and neither cheese-paring nor extravagant (2.60).

Here, as often in the section, Cicero means 'beneficial to the *res publica*' (2.85; cf. e.g. 2.58, 60, 63, 64, 72), much although by no means all of his concern being with the conduct of politicians operating on the public stage, as in earlier sections of Book 2. As the translators and commentators explain, this section divides into two parts, each further divided, but in a way that yields a chiastic overall structure. Cicero begins with gifts of money or expenditure (*largitio*, as a neutral general category) from one's own finances, first in the public arena, then in assistance to individuals (2.52-64). After that he turns to provision of personal efforts (*opera*, neuter plural noun), first for individual citizens, whether by legal advice,

---

[20] If Cicero carried through the programme he set out when in 70 BCE he was aedile elect, these were various traditional games dedicated to different deities in the Roman pantheon, customarily provided by an aedile (see *Verr.* 2.5.36, where he lays heavy and insistent emphasis on the solemn obligations of piety to be observed). The proviso about sufficiency of means (*facultates*) is an application of the second rule for caution in exercise of beneficence stipulated in the Book 1 discussion (1.44).

advocacy in the courts, or other favours, then comparable actions ideally for the entire *res publica* on the part of those in public office (2.65–85), although the different categories of benefit and constituencies of recipients are in practice not always kept distinct or clearly identified and demarcated. At the outset of the whole section (2.52–85), he makes clear his emphatic general view of the comparative merits of generosity through financial means as against personal service. Money is easier to provide, but service is 'nobler, more impressive, and worthier of a courageous and eminent man'. The one draws on family coffers, the other on virtue (2.52).

The final part of the section dealing with generosity by efforts made (*opera*), is perhaps the best known passage of Book 2, on account of its vigorous defence of the inviolability of ownership of private property, rejection of any property tax except in dire national emergency, and hostility to introduction of measures for debt relief (2.72–85).[21] Cicero focuses here on those *beneficia* or acts of beneficence that have in view citizens generally (*universos*), rather than particular individuals (*singulos*), and the *res publica* (2.72), performed by those persons in public life who have responsibility for 'managing the *res publica*' (2.73). He observes that nonetheless (*autem*) among these very *beneficia* (*eorum ipsorum*) for the general citizenry, there are those that partly (*partim*) affect people generally in that mode (*eius modi*), partly particular individuals.[22] He rules that in having regard to the interests of individuals (just as important as those of the *res publica*), 'the provision should be to the advantage, or definitely not the disadvantage, of the *res publica*' (2.72).

It becomes clear that the term 'individuals' (*singulos*) in the particular examples he now proceeds to give is to be construed as identifying

---

[21] Neal Wood saw the philosophy of *De Officiis* as motivated by a proto-Lockean 'enlightened economic individualism', and as affirming 'unequivocally that the basic purpose of the state is the protection of private property' (see especially Wood 1988: 111–15, and – for the remark about private property – 132). His interpretation is briefly discussed in Schofield 2021: 163–4; Barlow 2012 offers an extended critique. Cicero clearly believed that citizens of a *res publica* could have no confidence that it enshrined a just social order unless the common interest in the protection of everyone's private property were maintained (but Garnsey 2009 argues that he abandoned his commitment to Stoic ideals of community and sociability when his own class interests pointed in another direction; see also Long 1995: 233–40). Dyck 1996: 470–9 provides a helpful discussion of the treatment of debt-relief at 2.78–85 and elsewhere in Cicero.

[22] The main modern English translations (the Loeb, Atkins, Walsh; Dyck 1996: 462 likewise) all misleadingly treat Cicero as dividing these general acts of beneficence exhaustively, between some that affect people in general as against others that affect individuals (which seems to imply muddle on Cicero's part: how could general acts of beneficence not affect people in general?). The Latin is not as clear or determinate as it might be, but as much of the rest of the subsection (2.72–85) shows, what clearly concerns him is legislation that has general effect beneficial or damaging to the *res publica*, but impacts unfairly on different individuals, depending on their economic position within the society.

members of one particular sector of society, the *plebs*, as principal beneficiaries of legislation (*de facto* at least), in contrast with the *res publica* itself. Cicero refers to laws introducing free distribution of grain promoted by C. Gracchus and M. Octavius. He predictably disapproves of Gracchus's law, which he describes as an act of *largitio* (pejorative connotation), damaging to the public treasury, and so in breach of the prescription he has just enunciated. The expenditure authorised by Octavius's measure, on the other hand, was something the *res publica* was capable of bearing, while at the same time being necessary for the *plebs*. It therefore sustained the well-being of citizens – members of the *plebs* – and *res publica* alike (2.72). Here the efforts (*opera*) these magistrates performed seem to be treated as *de facto* acts of financial assistance, in Gracchus's case extravagant largesse (*largitio*). It might appear that the only distinction now seems to be in the source of funding: public treasury vs. family coffers. The only way, however, in which such moneys from the treasury could have been authorized was by the service to the *res publica* rendered, wisely or otherwise, by a magistrate initiating legislation – i.e. by his efforts (*opera*, neuter plural). It is perhaps indicative that fairly early in this subsection, Cicero begins some remarks on property taxes by saying that 'effort (*opera*, feminine singular noun) should be invested' in avoiding the levying of property taxes, and in making provision long in advance to forestall that eventuality (2.74).

In Book 1 the discussion of beneficence and liberality (1.41–60) was entirely and exclusively devoted to the exercise of these virtues in assisting individuals. There was no mention of a species of benefit and *beneficentia* directed towards the *res publica*, nor of any distinction between individuals and the commonwealth as objects of support. Legal provisions initiated by politicians were not their personal benefactions, though might be remembered as their work and invoked by their names, as when Cicero in the last of his Verrines apostrophises liberty, the rights of citizenship, and 'law of the Porcian clan, laws of the Sempronian family' (*lex Porcia legesque Semproniae, Verr.* 2.5.163).[23] Nonetheless it seems highly likely that it was not just Cicero, but Panaetius, too, who had focused discussion in this final part of the treatment of the *utile* on action for the community on the part of those holding political responsibility. As Dyck and Brunt suggest, the probability is that Cicero reproduced from Panaetius his reference to Spartan avarice as well as the explicitly attributed commendation of Scipio's integrity (2.76–7), but also his discussion of the Spartans

---

[23] Even in our own day, those with long memories may treat legislative provisions they applaud or deplore as the responsibility of particular politicians.

Lysander and Agis and of Aratus of Sicyon as exemplars respectively of vice and virtue in their policies on land distribution and ownership (2.80–2).[24]

Whatever we might conjecture about the provenance of that material, it is striking that Cicero highlights conduct of the responsibilities of those entrusted with the management and administration of the *res publica* as a central theme of this subsection. After his introductory remarks (2.72) on the *beneficia* for which citizens at large become eligible through efforts made by politicians (rather than by largesse), he makes a sequence of points all focused on those who bear those responsibilities. First and most important is to see that everyone keeps what is his, with no encroachment by public act on goods owned by private persons (2.73). Next to avoid imposition of property taxes (2.74). Then to ensure that there is a sufficient supply of life's necessities (2.74). Finally, and paramount (*caput*), to banish even the slightest suspicion of personal avarice (2.75–7).

Cicero's strategy here is not hard to fathom. The generally available benefits for citizens in general he has solely or primarily in mind are economic. What he therefore makes the focus of his discussion are precepts specifying the constraints that must be observed by those who, by virtue of public office, are in a position to make the efforts needed to make such benefits available.[25] The subsection ends with eloquent and increasingly rousing elaboration of the first of these precepts, where the material on the Greek statesmen Lysander, Agis, and Aratus is included, and where Cicero takes one more opportunity to laud his own performance as consul, on this occasion particularly of the problem of debt that acted as a trigger for the Catilinarian conspiracy (2.78–85).[26]

3 Gratitude and Glory

The account I have been giving of the scope and shape of the argument of Book 2 of *De Officiis* should not, I would have hoped, be thought particularly controversial. It is broadly in line with (for example) that given

---

[24] Dyck 1996: 461–2, Brunt 2013: 197–8.

[25] Whether or not by design, the two chief parts of the main body of Book 2 both therefore conclude with specific advice or prescriptions, addressed first to those young men wanting to achieve glory (2.45–51), then to those charged with the administration of the *res publica* (2.73–85).

[26] These are not the only prescriptions Cicero enunciates on the obligations of those in government: see especially 1.85, deriving from Plato, and 1.124, which became particularly salient in the Western tradition of political theorizing. But it is no accident that it is in the course of brief introductory comments on Book 2 in general and 2.72–85 in particular that Miriam Griffin (in Griffin and Atkins 1991: xxv) writes: 'It would not seriously misrepresent *De Officiis* to describe it as a handbook for members of the governing class on their duties to their peers in their private life and to their fellow-citizens in public life'.

by Griffin in the English edition of Cicero's work, which since she and Margaret Atkins published it in 1991 has done so much to make *De Officiis* more read and appreciated by a range of scholarly and student constituencies. But readers of the subsequent commentary by Andrew Dyck and the monograph of Eckhard Lefèvre would get a very different impression of its trajectory. Griffin and Atkins take the general subject of paragraphs 23–85 of Book 2 to be 'Acquiring the support and esteem of others', to be followed by brief non-Panaetian sections on 'Acquiring health and money' (2.86–7) and on comparison of benefits (2.88–90). They divide the long treatment of the main topic into four sections: the ineffectiveness of fear (2.23–9), the acquisition of glory (2.30–51), financial liberality (2.52–64), and liberality by service (2.65–85). Peter Walsh, in his English edition of 2000, names the main sequence (2.23–85) 'Gaining popular support', and identifies under slightly different descriptions the same four sections.[27] In this identification of the main topic of Book 2, he and likewise Griffin and Atkins were doubtless guided by various formulations, particularly in paragraphs 19–23, which speak consistently of enlisting resources (*opes*) and support (*studia*) for our interests (*utilitates*) and influence (*opes*). Political standing and esteem (*augendum atque honestandum*) are the particular focus in the list of motivations that need to be harnessed for the purpose (2.21).

Dyck, by contrast, makes the pursuit of glory 'the real subject' of Book 2 as a whole, and sees Cicero's treatment of it as occupying all of paragraphs 2.31–85. 'First the discussion focuses', he suggests, 'on the man engaged in a political career; second it is argued that such a man obtains the *utile* by means of glory but glory by means of virtuous action'.[28] Lefèvre takes the same view. He actually extends the relevant passage, to constitute the whole of paragraphs 2.23–85.[29] But there is no sign of preoccupation with glory in the discussion of fear (2.23–9), which ends with Cicero concluding that they should instead turn to 'the means by which we can most easily attain with honour and good faith the affection (*caritas*) which we desire' (2.29, Walsh's translation). Glory (*gloria*) is first mentioned only at 2.31, and then in a list sandwiched between honour (*honor*) and the goodwill of the citizens. It becomes a dominant focus only from that point on, until Cicero signals an end to its treatment in the section 2.31–51, at the beginning of 2.52. By then it has become clear that glory is not just esteem, but what is attained when people 'look up to and lavish abundant praise on

---

[27] Griffin and Atkins 1991: l; Walsh 2000: l–li.
[28] Dyck 1996: 355.
[29] Lefèvre 2001: 96–7.

those in whom they think they see particular outstanding and unique (*singulares*) virtues' (2.36). In short, it is something more special than esteem, or even than fame – which was the Loeb editor's shot at capturing *gloria* on that first mention (2.31). An apt modern comparison might be the lustre generated by and around an exceptional Olympic record-breaker.

The treatment of 'liberality and the conferring of benefits', which Dyck and Lefèvre agree in making the topic of the subsequent paragraphs 2.52–85, Dyck counts as the last, longest, and most elaborately structured section of Cicero's advice on the way to achieve glory.[30] He does not offer much in the way of a defence of this articulation of the material as all of it focused on *gloria*; Lefèvre simply takes over the interpretation without further argument. I have not found it much anticipated in any previous scholarship on *De Officiis*,[31] although A. A. Long, in an article that repays particular attention, claims likewise – without going into any detail – that focus on glory 'controls the discussion throughout' the main body of Book 2, while yet pointing out that 'Cicero presents it as a subordinate value', and in particular 'enormously helpful in conducting affairs of state (2.31)'.[32]

First recourse in evaluating this assessment must be a further look at the detail of the section 2.52–85. It begins (as noted above, p. 85) with the transitional sentence (2.52): 'Now that I have explained these obligations of young men which are effective in gaining glory, I must next discuss beneficence and liberality'. The formula introducing the section which now concerns us neither asserts that it too (as well as 2.31–51) will present its material as enabling the pursuit of glory, nor does it preclude the possibility that that will prove likewise to be the main objective (although at 2.31 Cicero spoke only of 'touching upon' glory there). As we read on, a distinctly variegated picture emerges. When Cicero makes his initial comparison and contrast between monetary gifts and personal efforts on behalf of others, he argues that the greater the number of people you give money to, the less able to give to many you will be, through having exhausted your coffers; whereas the more people you help by your efforts and your

---

[30] Dyck 1996: 356.
[31] Thus (for example) Max Pohlenz in *Antikes Führertum* (1934) proposes an arrangement for Cicero's overall argument in Book 2 differing in some respects from that adopted by Griffin and Atkins and by Walsh, but – as his title already indicates – takes political leadership, and legitimate ways of influencing people in order to be able to acquire and exercise it, as the main theme.
[32] Long's whole discussion of the material in Book 2 on glory is of the first importance (Long 1995: 224–33; quotations are from 228–9, where it is also noted that Cicero presents attainment of glory as a means of gaining friends and supporters (2.31)). Since galvanising such support is also treated there as the way to achieve glory in the first place, a feedback mechanism seems to be the logical implication.

virtuous nature, you will end up having more assisting you in acting generously, and through growing the habit of beneficence you will become readier and, so to speak, more practised in earning the gratitude of many (2.52–3). Here he talks more like a modern charity fundraiser[33] than an exponent of an honour culture, although as he continues with this train of thought he stresses that beneficence by one's own efforts of this kind is also more honourable than providing largesse (2.54).

Much of Cicero's emphasis in the section on financial liberality (2.52–64) is simply on doing the right thing rather than gratifying the populace by extravagant spending. But towards the end of his treatment of expenditure in the public sphere, he does talk of the 'greater and more advantageous (*utilior*)' outcomes for a donor who gives within his means. He instances Orestes, who won great honour for laying on public dinners on the streets; Marcus Seius, who dispelled his own great and deep-seated unpopularity by supplying cheap grain at a time of high market prices; and (rather less credibly) Milo, who won great honour by employing gladiators as vigilanti against Clodius's 'insane schemes' (2.58).[34] Largesse right now is (like cash in hand) more agreeable, but money spent on public works earns greater gratitude with posterity (2.60).

When Cicero turns to giving to individuals, the accent is similarly on making sure that the beneficiary and the rationale are appropriate. The pay-off (*fructus*) for the donor that is stressed is gratitude, and praise for someone seen as a 'common refuge of all' (2.63). If hospitality is provided to distinguished visitors from abroad, then for those who 'wish to exercise honourably a lot of power (*posse multum*)' it is 'emphatically advantageous' (*vehementer utile*) to 'wield influence and command gratitude' (*valere opibus et gratia*) among foreign peoples through those whom they hosted (2.64).[35]

The same sort of outcome is stressed in Cicero's opening remarks in the second major subsection, on benefits provided by personal effort, initially to individuals (2.65–85). Here he makes the point that safeguarding someone's legal interests, assisting them with advice, and giving 'emphatically as many people as possible' the benefit of legal knowledge, contributes to expanding influence and fostering gratitude (2.65). Closely aligned with that is ability

---

[33] Even if he is playing variations on now traditional material (cf. e.g. *Anon. Iamb.* 97.27–9 for the first limb of the argument).

[34] The praetor Milo was charged with compassing Clodius's murder (52 BCE), but despite Cicero's efforts as his advocate failed to secure an acquittal.

[35] 'Influence' is the rendering of *opes* here and in 2.65 favoured by Atkins and the Loeb. Walsh opts for 'resources'. Given that power is the goal envisaged, influence seems the likelier meaning, particularly since one's power base abroad is the focus at 2.64.

in public speaking, which 'attracts more gratitude and makes more of a show' (*et gratior et ornatior*).³⁶ It has an exceptional capacity to win admiration from those who hear it, hope from those in need, and gratitude from those defended (2.66). Gratitude is the outcome mentioned again in this connection (2.67), and with assistance more generally to appropriately chosen individuals – poor but honest, for preference (2.69). Protecting people from injustice is the ultimate rule: justice is the foundation of an enduring good name and celebrity (*commendationis et famae*, 2.71).

In the long concluding passage on service by the personal efforts of those holding public office to citizens at large (2.72–85), the emphasis is placed insistently (as we noticed in Section 2 above) on securing the good of the *res publica*, protecting the rights of individuals, particularly security of their property, and avoiding any suspicion of avarice. Cicero is fierce in his attacks on populist politicians who undermine the foundations of the *res publica*: concord, which cannot survive when some have others' money donated to them; and fairness, if any individual cannot keep what belongs to him (2.78).³⁷ By contrast, 'there is no easier way for those who have management of the *res publica* to gain the goodwill (*benevolentia*) of the masses than by incorruptible abstemiousness' (2.77). Very little else is said about the advantages someone gets from their public efforts, perhaps not surprisingly given that those of them which impact on individuals are said to attract more gratitude (2.72). But Cicero rounds off his discussion with a resounding climax, which concludes his entire treatment of beneficence and liberality. The 'great gratitude and great glory' a truly distinguished public figure will earn can be achieved only in conjunction 'with supreme *utilitas* for the *res publica*' (2.85).

Glory for the greatest achievers in public life is the final note Cicero wants to strike, just as it was a good name and celebrity at the end of his treatment of efforts of personal support made for individuals (2.71). In the light of his arguments in the previous section (2.31–8), honour, admiration, hope, popularity, praise, and goodwill, all mentioned in the passages we have just reviewed (but perhaps not necessarily influence, also important), should doubtless also be seen as belonging to the same cluster of responses to beneficence, although presumably in most cases falling well short of conferring celebrity (*fama*), mentioned only at 2.71, let alone

---

³⁶ With the Loeb editor, I follow Lambinus's deletion (perhaps right, in the opinion of the OCT editor) of *gravior*.

³⁷ Here we seem to be in the same theoretical territory as in *De Re Publica*'s definition of a people (*populus*: the collective body to which the *res publica* belongs): 'an assemblage of a *multitudo* which forms an association through the consensus of justice (*ius*) and through sharing in advantage (*utilitas*)' (*Rep.* 1.39).

glory, attributed only at 2.85 to really significant achievers on the public stage. Gratitude, however, is coupled there with glory as something to be expected for such service, and they are both made conditional on the conferring of exceptional benefit upon the *res publica*. Gratitude, indeed, is what has emerged as a constant and perhaps the main pay-off from beneficence, particularly when extended by personal efforts made for individual citizens (2.72), even to the point of suggesting that it will have the effect of making the grateful generous themselves (2.53). It could hardly have been otherwise. The social system of ancient Rome, like the ancient Greece πόλις, was glued together by the reciprocity of gift exchange: *gratia*, like Greek χάρις, is at once the favour granted and the thanks, in whatever form, thereby evoked.[38] The philosophers accordingly wrote reams about the ethics of beneficence, although only fragments survive apart from Aristotle's discussions of advantage friendship, the treatment of the topic in *De Officiis*, and Seneca's major seven book treatise *De Beneficiis*. Seneca, too, who restricts himself to beneficence to individuals, has much to say on gratitude.[39] His strict Stoic emphasis on mental attitude, not deeds, is even at one point anticipated by Cicero when he refers to a saying he likes to use and reuse:[40]

> Someone put it well when he says that the person who keeps his money has not repaid it, and he who has repaid it does not keep it; but the man who repays gratitude keeps it, and in keeping it has repaid it. (*Off.* 2.69) (Trans. P. G. Walsh)

Most of Cicero's attention is given, nonetheless, to the right and wrong ways to behave if engaging in acts of liberality and beneficence, not to their pay-offs for the donor. For his treatment of beneficence by purely financial means, we noted this focus already. The same is no less true of his approach to beneficence by personal effort, particularly where beneficence directed to citizens in general is concerned. *De Officiis* is a work on obligations or duties – or often more generally on the appropriate behaviour expected of a citizen of substantial means, especially in public life (as Panaetius's Stoic term *kathēkon*, appropriate conduct, better indicates than the Latin *officium*).

---

[38] See (most pertinently to its philosophical treatment at Rome) Griffin 2003.
[39] See especially Inwood 1995.
[40] Dyck 1996: 457–8 notes that Cicero also quotes this saying in slightly different forms elsewhere: *Red. Pop.* 23 and *Planc.* 68. Indeed he toys with the idea that it may be interpolated from *Pro Plancio* here and in *Post Reditum ad Populum*, on the perhaps slender basis of its citation only from *Pro Plancio* by Gellius (*NA* 1.4.2).

4 Conclusion

'*Utilitas* for the *res publica*' is what has to control the performance of obligations or appropriate behaviour that affects citizens in general – and their performance will bring great glory and gratitude only if the benefit to the *res publica* is commensurately great (2.85). And as we have seen, 'an enduring good name and celebrity' have to be built on a foundation of justice: in other words, on the *honestum* (2.71; cf. 2.31–8). The honourable (*honestum*) and the beneficial (*utile*) are those two contrasted categories structuring Cicero's division of material between the three books of *De Officiis*. But as we have been seeing, pursuit of the beneficial has at every point to be guided by what will make conduct honourable, except when necessity dictates some dilution of its demands. And Book 3 will argue at length that what is truly beneficial will always be honourable too. Although 'these two seem discordant verbally, they seem in substance to sound a single note' (3.83). 'We all seek what is beneficial, we are pulled towards it, we can do nothing else. … But we can never find beneficial things except in what is praiseworthy, seemly, and honourable' (3.101). More particularly, 'what was beneficial for the country (*patriae*) was for that reason honourable' (3.40; cf. 3.19: in a similar context, 'honourableness (*honestas*) has followed upon advantage').[41]

What goes for the honourable in general goes for social virtue – justice and beneficence – in particular. Social virtue's prime focus is presented as safeguarding human community (1.15, 20), and 'of all communities none has more weight, none induces more affection than that which each one of us has with the *res publica*' (1.57). It is accordingly to our country and our parents that we most owe obligation (1.58). In other words, locus of the greatest social benefit to which we are attracted, and focus of the prime obligations of justice and beneficence, are one and the same. Book 1 of *De Officiis* explains why that should be so. Book 2 then explains how a citizen of the *res publica* might harness the human resources needed to make an optimal contribution to maximising the benefit, abiding by the aims and obligations of justice and beneficence which must guide the whole enterprise, if it is not to founder.

---

[41] Dyck 1996: 519, like many scholars in the past (but not Winterbottom in the OCT, nor the translations of Atkins and Walsh), would wish to emend the text at 3.19, without noting the parallel at 3.40. Examples of the honourable following advantage or benefit could be multiplied: for example, in a discussion of the obligation to keep a promise: 'Many things that seem honourable by nature become through circumstances honourable no longer. To keep promises, to stand by agreements, to return deposits become no longer honourable, if benefit changes' (3.95).

CHAPTER 5

Cicero's De Officiis *on Practical Deliberation*

Christopher Gill

1 Introduction

One way of reading *De Officiis* is as a work of guidance in practical deliberation, based on Stoic principles of what counts as ethically well-judged decision-making. In this chapter, I begin by discussing Stoic thinking on this subject, as far as we can reconstruct this. I review some recent scholarly treatments of the topic, and then offer my own account. Subsequently, I correlate Cicero's *De Officiis* with this interpretation, referring both to the overall structure of the work and salient passages which illustrate Cicero's approach.[1]

2 Stoic Thinking on Practical Deliberation

Determining Stoic ideas on this subject is not entirely straightforward. The topic does not figure as one of the standard themes of Stoic ethics, nor is it analysed in the context of Stoic ethical psychology (by contrast with Aristotle's presentation, for instance).[2] However, there is no doubt that the question of what constitutes properly conducted deliberation was important in Stoic thought. The topic is central for *De Officiis*, based on a Stoic treatise; it underlies Seneca's *De Beneficiis*, shaped by Stoic thinking;[3] and it informs other, practically oriented, Stoic writings, such as Epictetus' *Discourses* and Marcus Aurelius' *Meditations*. The two ethical categories most relevant for deliberation are those of 'appropriate actions' (*kathēkonta*) and 'indifferents' (*adiaphora*), both innovative concepts within ancient philosophy, which reflect distinctive features of Stoic thought.[4] They express, on the one hand, the broadly naturalistic approach

---

[1] This chapter draws on material developed more fully in Gill 2022, chs. 2 and 8.
[2] For the standard Stoic ethical topics, see LS 56 A. For Aristotle on deliberation, see *NE* 3.3, 6.9.
[3] On Seneca's work and its Stoic character, see Griffin 2013: 19–20, 25–9.
[4] On these concepts, see LS 58–9; also, on *kathēkonta*, Gourinat 2014; on indifferents, Klein 2015.

of Stoic ethics. Appropriate actions are ones which human beings naturally perform, in relation to themselves and others. Human beings are also naturally motivated towards 'preferable' indifferents, such as life, health, property and the wellbeing of their families, and away from 'dispreferable' ones, such as death, illness, and so on. In this respect, both appropriate actions and preferable indifferents are viewed as positive features of human life.[5] On the other hand, Stoic thinking on these concepts also expresses their radical theory of value, according to which only virtue and happiness count as 'good', in a strong sense, and happiness depends solely on virtue. Hence, in comparison with virtue and virtue-based happiness, both appropriate actions and indifferents count as 'neither good nor bad'. Whether or not appropriate actions and indifferents contribute to a happy life depends on the exercise of virtue, seen as a form of expertise in living. A related idea is that only an appropriate action shaped by virtue counts as a 'perfectly correct' action (*katorthōma*), whereas other appropriate actions count only as prima facie reasonable ones.[6] These points underpin the crucial role of virtue in Stoic practical deliberation (and also Cicero's guidance in *De Officiis*), which I stress in this essay. But how, more precisely, is well-conducted deliberation conceived, in Stoic terms? I consider three recent scholarly treatments, which address two different areas of debate, both bearing on *De Officiis*. I also discuss an analysis of deliberation in contemporary virtue ethics, which, I suggest, is illuminating both for Stoic thinking and *De Officiis*.

Brad Inwood (1999) addresses the question whether Stoic practical reasoning, including deliberation, should be conceived in terms of the application of universal rules or not. Stoic deliberation has sometimes been interpreted in this way; this view is sometimes combined with the idea that proper deliberation expresses the application of natural law (a well-marked Stoic concept).[7] A rule-based analysis of moral deliberation is quite common in modern ethical theory, typically coupled with a focus on the specification of what counts as right action. The roots of this approach are sometimes traced to the natural law tradition, which, in modern Western thought, has a Judaeo-Christian background.

---

[5] See LS 58 C–E, 59 B–E.
[6] See LS 58 A–B, 59 B, F-H. On virtue as expertise or knowledge in living, see LS 61 A, C–D, G–H; on 'good' in Stoic ethics, see LS 60.
[7] On natural law, see LS 67 R–S. For 'rule-based' approaches to Stoic ethics, see Mitsis 1986, 1999, and Striker 1996: 215–20; on scholarly debate on this topic, and positions on either side, see Inwood 1999: 96–8, esp. n. 5.

However, Inwood argues strongly against this interpretation of Stoic practical reasoning. A substantial problem for this view is that its supporters struggle to identify any universal rules in Stoic ethical writing, beyond the rather obvious idea that we should always act in line with virtue.[8] It is yet harder to discern signs of a systematic application of such rules. Rather than looking for universal rules of this kind, Inwood proposes that Stoics operate with forms of guidance or 'rules of thumb', which are applicable for the most part; that is, they are 'defeasible' rules, subject to modification in different contexts.[9] He highlights features of the Stoic presentation of deliberation which indicate an awareness of the ethical significance of situational variation and context; these features include their extensive use of case-studies and illustrative examples or narratives. In defining a Stoic framework for deliberation, he points to Seneca's recommendation of a combination of *decreta* and *praecepta*. Although one or other of these terms (or both) has sometimes been interpreted as 'rules', Inwood maintains that *decreta* signify 'doctrines' and *praecepta* (relatively specific) 'guidance'. Taken together, these ideas provide a basis for the kind of context-sensitive guidelines that he thinks Stoic ethics aim to offer. Inwood holds that *De Officiis* illustrates these features and that the work can be taken as a representative example of Stoic guidance in practical reasoning.[10]

I think that, on the question he addresses, Inwood's view is highly convincing. However, his account leaves open another important question. What are the respective roles of the factors of indifferents and virtue in practical deliberation (that is, in determining what counts as a correct 'appropriate action')? Two, related, treatments by Rachel Barney (2003) and Tad Brennan (2005) have raised this question. While differently framed, and reaching different conclusions, these two accounts have certain common features. Although I have significant reservations about these two treatments, I think they are very useful in articulating an important set of questions raised by Stoic deliberation.

Both discussions accentuate the role of indifferents in soundly conducted Stoic deliberation and are sceptical that the idea of virtue forms part of Stoic practical reasoning. Barney offers a general model of deliberation based on two key points. One is the claim that (properly conducted) Stoic practical deliberation consists entirely of consideration

---

[8] See DL 7.109; also Inwood 1999: 102–4, esp. n. 28.
[9] See Inwood 1999: 107–9, referring to Schauer 1991 on 'rules of thumb'.
[10] See Seneca, *Ep.* 94–5; taken with Inwood 1999: 106–8, 113–20; and 112–13, 120–7, on *De Officiis*.

of indifferents, viewed as indifferents, that is, as bearers of positive or negative value. They are not being considered, for instance, as vehicles for performing virtuous acts. The other is that the person concerned is (properly) concerned only with maximising preferred indifferents, such as health or property, and minimising dispreferred ones, and doing so for herself.[11] Brennan also regards this account of Stoic deliberation (which he terms 'indifferents only') as one that merits serious consideration, though he does not, in the end, adopt it. On the face of it, their view is a surprising one. As both scholars acknowledge, it runs counter to certain prominent strands in Stoic ethical discussion, including the commendation of an exemplary figure, Regulus, in Book Three of *De Officiis*, for a decision which involves giving up all preferable indifferents, including life itself.[12] However, there are certain features of Stoic ethical theory which seem to lend support to this view. One is the presentation of instinctive attraction to preferable indifferents as a natural human motive and one that plays a key role in the development towards virtue and happiness. More precisely, the 'selection' of indifferents plays this role, in the course of the rational development of a human being.[13] A second factor is the prominence, in our evidence for second-century BCE Stoic theory, of the idea that happiness consists in the 'selection' (and adoption) of indifferents, meaning, apparently, preferable indifferents for the agent.[14] A third point is that, in summaries of Stoic ethical theory, the concepts of appropriate actions and indifferents are closely linked. Cicero, for instance, in Book Three of *De Finibus*, twice stresses the importance of the virtuous person taking account of the factor of the preferability of indifferents in performing correct actions. In one passage, he appears to present the maximisation of preferred indifferents as the main factor that a wise person should consider in making decisions.[15] Hence, the emphasis by Barney and Brennan on this idea, while in some ways unexpected, is not without basis.

Their stress on this point goes along with their belief that consideration of the idea of virtue plays no part in (soundly conducted) practical

---

[11] For this model, which she terms that of 'deliberative sufficiency' (of indifferents) and 'maximisation', see Barney 2003: 324, more broadly 304–25.
[12] *Off.* 3.99–108 (see also text to nn. 80–1 here). See Barney 2003: 319–20, 324–5; Brennan 2005: 203–4.
[13] See *Fin.* 3.16–22, esp. 3.20: also LS 59 D, and LS, vol. I, 357–9, 368. 'Selection' (*eklogē*) is a Stoic term of art for adoption of indifferents, by contrast with 'choice' (*hairesis*) of the good; see Inwood 1985: 201–15.
[14] See LS 58 K; and LS 64 on the ancient debate provoked especially by this formulation of the goal of life; also Barney 2003: 305–19.
[15] *Fin.* 3.22, 3.59–60: also Barney 2003: 312–14; Brennan 2005: 195–6, 218–19.

deliberation. Barney, for instance, cites, approvingly, John Cooper's view that 'virtue' constitutes a 'third-personal' description of deliberation which is conducted entirely, by the deliberating person, in terms of selecting preferable indifferents.[16] Brennan gives special emphasis to this point. He argues against the idea that acting according to virtue can usefully function as a criterion for deliberation either for the wise or the non-wise progressor (the two main positive types of person recognised in Stoic ethics). The non-wise are unable to discern what should count as virtue, whereas the wise person's actions are virtuous by definition.[17] Both Brennan and Barney, in particular, argue against a particular interpretation of Stoic deliberation in which virtue plays a significant part in the agent's considerations. Brennan takes a passage in Cicero's *De Officiis* (3.13) as expressing this view: 'The Stoics define the highest good as "being in conformity with nature"', and what I think this means is that we must always align ourselves with virtue, and choose all else which accords with nature [that is, preferable indifferents] so long as it does not militate against virtue'.[18] Brennan takes this passage as expressing Cicero's interpretation of what constitutes proper deliberation in Stoic thought. According to this view, proper deliberation consists, first, in determining actions in line with virtue and then selecting preferable indifferents if they do not conflict with virtue. However, neither Brennan nor Barney accept this as a valid, or at least widely accepted, model of Stoic deliberation, at least in mainstream Hellenistic thought, even if Cicero presents Stoic thinking in this way. Their reasons for this view centre on their denial that the idea of virtue can play a meaningful role in the Stoic concept of deliberation for the wise or the non-wise person.[19]

Despite rejecting this account as representative of Stoic thought, Brennan adopts a model of deliberation which, as he recognises, has points in common with it. The model is one that Brennan calls 'no shoving'; and it is based on a passage in *Off.* 3.42 ascribed by Cicero to the major Stoic theorist Chrysippus: 'Runners in a race ought to compete and strive to win as hard as they can, but by no means should they trip up their competitors or give them a shove (*manu depellere*). So too in life; it is not wrong for each person to seek after the things useful for life, but to do so by depriving

---

[16] Cooper 1999: 533–4, cited by Barney 2003: 314.
[17] Brennan 2005: 184–94; also 216–18, 220–6.
[18] Trans. Walsh 2000.
[19] Brennan 2005: 182–94: he describes this as the *salva virtute* ('virtue excepted') model of deliberation. See also Barney 2003: 330–2, criticising what she calls the 'dualist model' on similar grounds, though she takes *Off.* 3.13 as indicative of a third model, 'degree of nature' (Barney 2003: 334–6).

others is not just'.²⁰ Brennan's model is based on the assumption, shared with Barney, that the virtuous person is (properly) motivated primarily to maximise her own preferable indifferents. However, there are situations in which this motive needs to be checked or modified by consideration of what is required by just treatment of other people. Hence, he identifies a three-stage process for proper deliberation, which consists in (1) maximising preferred indifferents but (2) avoiding injustice to other people, and (3) taking account of the interests of the community or state. This is the model that Brennan sees as implied in the passage of Chrysippus cited, and in other passages in Book Three of *De Officiis*, which are taken by him as representing mainstream Stoic thought.²¹ Thus, by contrast with Barney, who is, in the end, uncertain whether we can identify a single overall Stoic position on sound deliberation, Brennan thinks that his model provides a pattern that is consistent with other Stoic evidence on this question.²²

Brennan's 'no shoving' model is, in some ways, suggestive as an interpretation of Stoic deliberation, and one which might illuminate the kinds of cases explored in Book Three of *De Officiis*. However, I think there are also significant problems with his view, including the presentation of motivation and the scope of the grounds for 'not shoving'. The only positive motivation Brennan seems to recognise is that for maximising preferable indifferents; he does not consider the question of the motivation that leads someone to restrain this maximising motive.²³ However, Stoic thinking on ethical development (conceived as 'appropriation', *oikeiōsis*) identifies two relevant forms of positive motive. For instance, in Cicero's account of appropriation in *Fin*. 3.16–22, the primary human motive to go towards, and 'select', preferable indifferents is transformed through rational development into a motive directed towards the good, that is, towards acting in line with virtue.²⁴ In the treatment of appropriation in *Off*. 1.11–15, each of the four virtues is represented as the developed form of one of four primary human motives.²⁵ So there is no lack in Stoic theory

---

²⁰ Trans. Griffin and Atkins 1991.
²¹ Brennan 2005: 204–15; other passages cited in support of this view include *Off*. 1.20–1, 1.31, 3.13, 3.21, 3.29–30. Brennan's aim is to reconstruct early (Chrysippean) Stoic thought on this subject, not to analyse Cicero's approach, though he draws freely on Cicero's evidence.
²² Brennan 2005: 216–20; contrast Barney 2003: 337–9. However, in (2014), Brennan adopts a different model again, based on the agent following indications of the will of Zeus or Fate.
²³ Brennan 2005: 204–5, also 206–14.
²⁴ *Fin*. 3.20–2, esp. 3.22: '[the good'] stimulates us to desire it far more strongly than we are stimulated by all the earlier objects' (LS 59 D(6), their trans.).
²⁵ See Striker 1996: 252–3. See also Stobaeus' summary of Stoic ethics, based on Arius Didymus, section 5b3 (trans. Inwood and Gerson 2008: 126).

of ideas that could explain the motivation involved in acting in line with the principles Brennan associates with 'no shoving'. Secondly, Brennan's account of those restraining principles seems to be very incomplete. He recognises indications of justice, or at least, avoiding injustice, but takes no account of indications of any of the other three cardinal virtues identified by Stoic theory.[26] This selectiveness is the more problematic because Stoics conceive all four virtues as either making up a unified set or as interdependent.[27] Hence, Brennan's analysis of Stoic well-conducted motivation is unconvincing, taken as a whole, though there are some suggestive features. As noted earlier, Barney herself highlights difficulties in her (maximising) account, while also finding any alternative model incapable of explaining all the relevant features of Stoic ethical theory.[28] Overall, their discussions break new ground in examining the possible forms of Stoic deliberation and the difficulties of our evidence for this. However, we are still some way from defining a wholly credible pattern.

Given this, I think we have good reason to widen the range of conceptual options brought to bear on this question. I think that certain ideas in Rosalind Hursthouse's (1999) contemporary version of virtue ethics offer the basis of an explanatory framework. In modern moral theory, a standard form of enquiry is the question what should count as a right action; more precisely, what are its criteria and what kind of guidance (or 'rule') is needed to enable people to perform this kind of action. Typically, the criteria and guidance are framed in terms of fulfilling duties or obligations, or of bringing about consequences that are beneficial for those involved or affected. It has often been argued, or assumed, that a virtue ethical framework cannot provide the requisite kind of criteria or guidance; but Hursthouse maintains that this is not the case. The formulation she proposes is that: 'an action is right iff [if and only if] it is one a virtuous agent would characteristically do in the circumstances', coupled with a specification, in general terms, of what it is to be a virtuous agent.[29] She maintains that this formulation is similar in type to that which can be offered for deontological (duty-centred) or consequentialist theory, and that guidance offered in terms of the virtues is no less helpful than that offered in alternative terms. Indeed, she characterises this guidance as 'v-rules' (that is, virtue rules), arguing that this

---

[26] Brennan 2005: 207–14.
[27] LS 61 B–F. The interconnection is recognised in *Off.* 1.15, and in the fact that all four virtues are used to structure the whole work, even if Cicero, typically, considers one virtue at a time.
[28] Barney 2003: 337–9.
[29] Hursthouse 1999: 28–9.

kind of advice is as widely applicable and as capable of codification as other types of moral rule.³⁰

A second feature of Hursthouse's account is her discussion of the virtuous agent's reasons for action. She begins with the Aristotelian idea that a virtuous person chooses a virtuous action 'for its own sake' and explains this idea as acting 'for at least one of a certain type of range of reasons'. She considers for this purpose two types of reason. One type is that of reasons which are specific to particular situations, and which explain or justify the virtuous person's acting in a specific way. The other type is that of the general principle on which the virtuous person acts. There is a range of possible principles, including ones such as duty or benefit which are typically taken as characteristic of frameworks other than that of virtue ethics. However, she argues that there is no reason why virtue ethics cannot also refer to such principles to explain the virtuous person's reason for acting. Hence, in saying that a virtuous person performs an action for its own sake, we mean that her actions respond to relevant specific features of the situation, which may be combined with the idea that her actions are based on a general principle relevant to the situation and her action. As Hursthouse formulates this point, the v-person is one who does a v-action for x-reasons, that is reasons of one or both of these two types.³¹

Hursthouse's discussion is, obviously, intended as a contribution to modern moral theory and offers ideas, from a virtue ethical standpoint, germane to that context of debate.³² My interest here, however, lies in drawing on her ideas to inform scholarly discussion of the general form of Stoic thinking on virtuous practical deliberation. I think that, in this context too, it is reasonable to suggest that a right or correct action is one that a virtuous person (as conceived in Stoic ethics) would characteristically do in the relevant circumstances. We might also say, in the Stoic context, that the right action is one that is done, by the virtuous person, for its own sake,³³ meaning that it is done for reasons specific to the situation or on general principles bearing on the situation. There are, in my view, at least two factors that make Hursthouse's formulations of special interest in this connection. One is that her account, in both respects, corresponds with distinct and well-marked features of Stoic ethical theory, and, in particular, with the presentation of deliberation in *De Officiis*. The other is that

---

³⁰ Hursthouse 1999: 35–42.
³¹ Hursthouse 1999: 126–36. For the Aristotelian notion, see *NE* 2.4, 1105a32.
³² On this topic, see also Annas 2011: 41–51.
³³ For Stoic versions of this idea, see DL 7.89 (LS 61 A) or Cic. *Fin.* 3.21–2 (LS 59 D(4–6)).

her analysis accentuates a conception of right action that is avoided or de-emphasised in the discussions of Barney and Brennan, which are the most detailed treatments of Stoic deliberation to date. Her analysis brings out the ideas that a right action is one which is characteristic of a virtuous person and that it is one which is motivated by reasons (specific and general) characteristic of such a person.

However, a potential problem in correlating the approaches of Hursthouse and Stoicism needs to be considered. Hursthouse assumes that aiming to act rightly (understood as acting as the virtuous person characteristically acts) is a reasonable aim for people in general. However, in Stoic theory the virtuous or wise person is presented as an ideal which virtually no-one achieves in practice; correspondingly, a distinction is drawn between the perfectly correct action (*katorthōma*) performed by a wise person and an 'appropriate action', that is, a prima facie reasonable action, which anyone can aim to perform.[34] Cicero, explicitly, locates *De Officiis* at the non-ideal level, and his advice is directed at anyone aiming to 'make progress' towards virtue.[35] He does not claim to have the expertise to offer a definitive statement of the ideal wise person's reasons for actions but, rather, to provide guidance on prima facie justifications for regarding actions as right. However, the guidance he offers is centred, as brought out shortly, on discussion of the four cardinal Stoic virtues, of actions characteristic of the virtues, and of considerations (both specific and general) that can inform virtuous decision-making. To this extent, Cicero, like Hursthouse, takes the ideas of acting as a virtuous person characteristically acts, and acting for reasons of the type that the wise person has, as providing a valid basis for guidance in practical deliberation. Hence, Hursthouse's criterion for what counts as right action and her account of ethical guidance are useful for analysing the Stoic, and Ciceronian, approaches, despite the difference in conceptual frameworks just noted.

Taking into account these various discussions, I now offer my own analysis of (well-conducted) Stoic practical deliberation. This analysis is couched, for the most part, in general terms. However, I incorporate reference to features of *De Officiis* which I see as expressing standard Stoic thinking on this subject. All practical deliberation (that is, in Stoic terms, all performance of appropriate actions) involves reference to indifferents,

---

[34] See text to n. 6. This distinction underlies the objection of Barney and Brennan to including reference to virtue in Stoic accounts of deliberation (text to nn. 17–19).

[35] *Off.* 1.8, 3.13–16. On ethical progress as crucial for bridging the gap in Stoic theory between the wise and non-wise and resolving the apparent problem of two irreconcilable ethical levels, see Inwood and Donini 1999: 717–35.

both preferred and dispreferred, that is, things such as health and illness, wealth and poverty. Deliberation takes as its starting point the fact that it is natural for oneself and others to be motivated towards preferable and away from dispreferable indifferents. Hence, all practical deliberation properly takes account of the question of what is preferable and not, both for oneself and others involved in the situation. To this extent, I take the force of Barney's model and Brennan's emphasis on this dimension.[36] However, I do not accept that (properly conducted) deliberation is, typically or necessarily, framed solely in those terms. The typical form of such deliberation is addressing the question which appropriate action is right or correct (*kalon* in Greek and *honestum* in Latin) in the relevant circumstances. Put differently, deliberation addresses the question which allocation of indifferents (preferable and dispreferable) to oneself and others is right or correct under these circumstances. Hence, when Stoics refer to 'selection' of indifferents and present this as forming the material or content of practical reasoning, they mean selection between preferables and dispreferables (for oneself and others) and not, invariably, selection of preferables for oneself.[37]

What criteria should be drawn on to determine what selection of indifferents counts as right? In answering this question, Hursthouse provides a helpful framework and one that matches the overall organisation of the topic in *De Officiis*. In determining a right action, as she stresses, the primary question is: what would a virtuous person, characteristically, do in the relevant circumstances? Hursthouse argues that this way of posing the question is as clearly defined and informative as the main modern theoretical alternatives, and that it corresponds to widespread social assumptions and practices.[38] Interestingly, her approach corresponds closely with the framework of *De Officiis*. In offering criteria for what counts as a right (*honestum*) action in Book 1, Cicero refers, primarily, to the virtues. He combines general accounts of the four cardinal virtues with comments, reported cases, and examples designed to illustrate actions characteristic of the virtue in question. The combination of general accounts of the virtue with illustrative discussion matches the presentation of Stoic guidance in terms of *decreta* and *praecepta* ('doctrines' and 'guidance') offered by Seneca and discussed by Inwood.[39] Cicero's extensive use of

---

[36] See text to nn. 11–15.
[37] On this topic, though arguing for a different view, see Barney 2003: 322–5.
[38] Hursthouse 1999: 25–31, 35–9; similarly, Annas 2011: 41–51.
[39] See text to nn. 9–10.

illustrative comment and narrative incorporates the aspect of situational variability stressed by Inwood in his discussion of Stoic guidance, while the accounts of the virtues provide a theoretical and structural framework. Taken as whole, this mode of presentation can be seen as setting out, in Hursthouse's terms, what a virtuous (just, brave and so on) person would, characteristically, do in the circumstances described. This does not mean that the factor of preferability is simply set aside. As brought out later, this feature forms an integral part of the guidance offered in *De Officiis*, though approached somewhat differently in each book. In Book One, for instance, it takes the form of describing the kind of allocation of preferable and dispreferable indifferents to oneself and others that is characteristic of the virtuous person.

There is a second aspect of Hursthouse's analysis which is helpful in making sense of Stoic practical deliberation and Cicero's guidance for this. She highlights the importance of taking account of the virtuous person's reasons for action, including both the person's response to specific features in the situation and recognition of general principles relevant to the action. This also forms part of determining what a virtuous person would, characteristically, do in the relevant situation. This dimension also forms part of Cicero's framework in *De Officiis*, both in its specific and general aspects. One of the general ideas that figure in this role is that of 'nature', meaning, in this context, human nature, understood as a combination of rationality and sociability. 'Nature' is an important normative idea in Stoic ethics; both virtue and (virtue-based) happiness can be characterised in terms of what is 'according to nature', meaning (in some versions of Stoic theory) according to human nature.[40] Hence, for a Stoic, determining what action counts as 'according to nature', in their sense, can form part of determining what action is 'right', and also what is characteristic of the virtuous person. This aspect of practical deliberation corresponds to acting 'in principle' in Hursthouse's analysis, and in this role forms part of what is characteristic of the virtuous person.[41]

So, overall, I suggest, Hursthouse's analysis of what is involved in determining right action can be seen as applying not only to modern virtue ethics but also to at least one ancient form of virtue ethics, namely Stoic ethics as presented in *De Officiis*. It also, I think, helps us to make sense

---

[40] The ethical significance of human nature, conceived as rational and sociable, is emphasised in Stobaeus' summary of Stoic ethics, see sections 5b1, 5b3, 6a, 6e (Inwood and Gerson 2008: 125–6, 132–3); on nature in Stoic ethics as universal or cosmic as well as human, see DL 7.87–9 (LS 63 C).
[41] Hursthouse 1999: 131–6.

of key features of Stoic thinking on deliberation. I develop this view by examining further aspects of *De Officiis*, which provide material for probing further the relationship between the central Stoic concepts of virtue, indifferents and appropriate actions.

3 *De Officiis* as Guidance for Stoic Practical Deliberation

Cicero's *De Officiis* is presented as a version or adaptation of the treatise *On Appropriate Action* (*peri tou kathēkontos*) by Panaetius, the last head of the Hellenistic Stoic school.[42] Although Panaetius has sometimes been seen by scholars as somewhat unorthodox, I share the view of Teun Tieleman (2007) that his views fall firmly within the main lines of Hellenistic Stoic thinking, with relatively small-scale and distinct innovations.[43] Books One and Two of Cicero's work are based on Panaetius' three-book treatise. Book Three is independently composed by Cicero, though he tells us that he has made great efforts to ensure that it draws on the best available Stoic writings on this subject. Overall, then, we have good reason to see Cicero's work, in its main themes and argument, as reflecting Stoic thought, though with illustrations based on his own experience and knowledge.

According to Cicero, Panaetius presented practical deliberation as a response to three kinds of uncertainty: (1) whether an action is right (*honestum*) or wrong (*turpe*); (2) whether or not it confers things that are advantageous or useful (*utilia*), that is, 'preferred indifferents'; (3) when what seems to be advantageous conflicts with what is right. Cicero says that Panaetius dealt effectively with the first two questions and that the first two books of *De Officiis* adopt Panetius' lines of approach. However, he criticises Panaetius for his failure to address the third question, which Cicero tackles in his Book Three.[44] These introductory comments might lead one to assume that these three questions, each taken in isolation from the others, form the subject matter of each of Cicero's three books. However, there are at least two ways in which this impression would be mistaken. The question of the relationship between what is right and what is useful, and how they are to be reconciled, figures in all three books, in different ways, and not just in the third. Also, in all three books, the

---

[42] *Off.* 1.6–10, 3.7–12; also Dyck 1996: 17–24; Veillard 2014. On *Off.* as a whole, focusing on Cicero's authorial and philosophical objectives, see Woolf 2015: 170–200. All subsequent references not otherwise identified are to books and chapters of *Off.*

[43] See also Inwood 1999: 100, n. 14. Panaetius' innovativeness receives greater emphasis in Inwood ch. 3, this volume.

[44] 1.10, 3.7–10.

primary question addressed is what course of action is right; and this, in turn, determines the approach taken to gaining advantages and negotiating between the competing claims of right and advantage. Further, underpinning Cicero's discussion of all three topics is reference to the four cardinal virtues, which form the main normative idea and organising framework in all three books.[45] The preceding discussion of Stoic thinking on practical deliberation and its conceptual and ethical basis clarifies the rationale for these features of Cicero's work; and Cicero's work, in turn, offers detailed illustration of Stoic guidance on deliberation, as interpreted here. I now outline the approach taken by Cicero in each book, referring to certain illustrative passages, and considering how they bear on the interpretative questions about Stoic deliberation raised in the second section of this essay.

The main lines of approach in Book One have already been set out in connection with the earlier analysis of Stoic deliberation. The project undertaken is providing guidance on how to determine what appropriate action counts as 'right' (*honestum*); and the primary reference point is that of general accounts of the four cardinal virtues and comments and narratives showing actions characteristic of each virtue, as so defined.[46] In this sense, in Hursthouse's terms, a right action is conceived as that which a virtuous person would do in the relevant circumstances. This virtue-based framework is supplemented by (broad) treatment of another key Stoic normative idea, namely nature, specifically human nature, conceived as combining rationality and sociability.[47] This idea figures in three main forms: (1) the four cardinal virtues are treated as developed expressions of four primary human motives (1.11–15); (2) the main types of human association are presented as natural, especially the family and humankind as a whole, regarded as a unit or broad family (1.50–9); (3) four roles (*personae*) are described as being common to all human beings, including that of human nature in general and one's own specific, individual nature (1.107–21). These references to the idea of nature have two principal functions, which can be linked with the two kinds of reasons for acting which

---

[45] This is clear from the synopses in Griffin and Atkins 1991: xlvii–li, and Walsh 2000: xlviii–lii. Veillard 2014: 91–3, 102–6, stresses this point.

[46] On the virtues as criterial of correct 'appropriate actions', see 1.15, 152. Book One is structured around these four virtues: wisdom (1.18–19, also 153–8), justice (1.20–60), magnanimity (the Panaetian version of courage) (1.60–92), the fitting (*decorum*, the Panaetian version of moderation) (1.93–151).

[47] On human nature as rational and sociable, see n. 40. Significantly, all four virtues have a two-fold character, involving sociability (actively other-benefiting motivation) as well as rationality. For the sociable strands, see 1.42–59 (generosity), 1.69–91 (the benevolent aspect of magnanimity), 'fitting' treatment of other people (1.99–100, 103–4), sociable expression of wisdom (1.153–8).

Hursthouse ascribes to the virtuous person performing an action 'for its own sake'. They serve, especially in the case of topics (2)–(3), to enable the specification of what counts as a right (virtuous) act in particular situations. Also, given the central role of ideas about nature, in various senses, in Stoic ethics, they highlight the principles (including the 'kinship' of human beings as such) on which a virtuous person may act in any given situation.

How does the discussion of Book One bear on the question of the relationship between the right and the useful, which, I have suggested, arises in different forms in all three books? A helpful example in this connection is provided by Cicero's treatment of generosity, which constitutes the active, other-benefiting, dimension of justice:

> First one must make sure that kindness (*benignitas*) harms neither the very people whom one seems to be treating kindly, nor others; next that one's kindness does not exceed one's capabilities; and then, that kindness is bestowed upon each person according to his standing. Indeed, that is fundamental to justice (*iustitia*), to which all these things ought to be referred. For those who do someone a favour (*gratificantur*) in such a way that they harm the person whom they appear to want to assist, should be judged neither beneficent nor generous, but dangerous flatterers. Those who, in order to be generous towards some, harm others, fall into the same injustice (*iniustitia*) as if they had converted someone else's possessions to their own account.[48]

This passage brings out several important features of Ciceronian (and Stoic) guidance. First, determining what is right (in line with virtue) necessarily involves 'selection between indifferents'. The right (generous) action is one which allocates useful or advantageous things to people appropriately and does so in a way that does not involve injustice to others who are not treated in the same way. The selection is directed at benefiting other people and not oneself; in this respect, Barney's model of deliberation, based on self-directed benefit, does not apply.[49] The passage also indicates ways in which reference to 'nature' supplements the specification of what is right by reference to virtue. The general forms of natural human association outlined in 1.50–9 are presented as helping the donor to determine to whom benefits are given in specific situations.[50] Implicit throughout the discussion of generosity is the idea that

---

[48] 1.42, trans. Griffin and Atkins 1991.
[49] See text to n. 11.
[50] See 1.57–9, on the obligations consequential on different kinds of social relationship, supplementing 1.45–9, on determining 'worth' or 'standing' in those to whom we make donations.

the virtuous person is positively motivated towards acting in line with the virtues (an idea elided in Brennan's 'no-shoving' model of deliberation). The basis for this view is indicated in the opening discussion (1.11–15) of the four virtues as developed forms of four primary motives, which express, in turn, the idea of human nature as rational and sociable.[51] Thus, this example illustrates at least one of the ways in which the determination of what is right involves reference to the factor of preferability and the allocation of preferables (to others in this case). It also gives an example of how reference to the idea of nature, in conjunction with that of the virtues, provides a way of spelling out justificatory reasons why a specific act is rightly adopted in a certain case.[52]

In Book Two, the topic announced is deliberation about what is advantageous, rather than right. From Cicero's initial outline of topics (1.9–10),[53] we might have expected that Cicero's discussion would have been framed as an examination of the various forms of advantages (health, property, welfare of family, for instance) and actions that promote them.[54] This would have formed a parallel to Book One, based on a review of the virtues and actions characteristic of them. This approach would have also matched Barney's interpretative model for Stoic deliberation, centred on the maximisation of preferable things for the person concerned.[55] However, in fact, the standpoint in Book Two forms a linear continuation of that taken in Book One. The type of deliberation envisaged is not based on the question: which actions are likely to bring about the greatest possible advantages for the person concerned? Rather, it is based on this question: how should one deal with advantages, given that the overall aim is to do what is right, that is, primarily, what is in line with the virtues?[56] In fact, as you might expect from this way of framing the topic, the focus is as much, or more, on allocation of advantages to others, rather than oneself. Even when the question turns to gaining advantages for oneself, these are also

---

[51] For Brennan's model, see text to nn. 21–7. The stress on the positive motivation to benefit underlying generosity is paralleled in Seneca's (Stoicism-influenced) treatment of generosity in *De Beneficiis*; see Griffin 2013: 105–7, and 25–9.
[52] For these two factors (specific and general reasons for virtuous action performed for its own sake), see the discussion of Hursthouse 1999 in text to nn. 31 and 41.
[53] There is a brief reference back to this list of topics in 2.9.
[54] There is a brief comparative assessment of different types of advantage (not in Panaetius' book) in 2.88.
[55] See text to n. 11.
[56] This focus is indicated in 2.9–10, underlining the inseparability of the concepts of advantageous and right. Veillard 2014: 91–3 sees this point as crucial for Panaetius' approach; she also underlines the conceptual dependence of Book Two on Book One. See also Woolf 2015: 184–5.

viewed as instrumental for enabling right actions (that is, actions in line with one or other of the virtues).

By contrast with Book One, which discusses three virtues, at least, in some depth, the focus is almost wholly on one type of advantage, namely glory or social approval.[57] Also, there is a recurrent emphasis on the idea that the only effective and reliable way to gain social support, in private or public relations, is to act in line with the virtues. Hence, for instance:

> I count it as the special property of virtue to win over people's hearts and to enlist them in its own service ... it is the wisdom and virtue of outstanding persons that inspire other people to be prompt, ready and devoted in assisting our advancement ... A vigorous love is aroused in the masses, however, by the very reputation and rumour of liberality, of beneficence, of justice, of keeping faith, and of all the virtues that are associated with gentleness and ease of conduct (*mansuetudinem morum ac facilitatem*).[58]

Although Cicero stresses here the social impact of all the virtues, the main focus is on one virtue that, especially, generates such approval, that is, generosity, presented, as in Book One, as the actively benevolent aspect of the virtue of justice.[59] This emphasis reflects, of course, Cicero's outlook as a Roman politician and public figure, and, more broadly, Greco-Roman aristocratic attitudes that seem already to have informed Panaetius' treatment of this topic.[60] However, the focus is also consistent with Stoic guidance on deliberation, as presented here. Acquiring the advantage of social approval is a by-product of doing what is right, that is, performing actions in line with the virtues, especially generosity, properly expressed and performed for their own sake.[61] As we have already seen in the case of generosity in Book One, the 'selection of indifferents' centres, primarily, on the correct allocation of benefits to others.[62] Although the donor gains an advantage too, namely good reputation and approval, this also serves an instrumental role in enabling further such virtuous actions (it serves as the 'material of virtue' in this sense).[63] In this respect, the overall Stoic

---

[57] But see Schofield ch. 4, this volume.
[58] 2.17, 32, trans. Griffin and Atkins 1991; see also 2.16–18, 33–8 (on the social impact of the virtues as a whole).
[59] After a short discussion of justice (2.38–40), there is a fuller treatment of generosity (2.52–85). On generosity as the actively benevolent aspect of justice, see 1.42–59.
[60] See Long 1995: 228; also Dyck 1996: 353–60, 416–17.
[61] For the stress on acting in line with the virtues for its own sake, see 2.17, 32 (just cited) and 2.37–8, on magnanimity.
[62] See text to nn. 48–9. On this theme, see 2.52–5, 61–5, 68–71.
[63] On this point, see 2.36–50; also Long 1995: 230–3; Gill 2019: 64–6. On preferred indifferents as 'the material of virtue' (Chrysippus' view), see LS 59 A.

framework of guidance for deliberation, as framed in Book One, applies here too.

The consistency of outlook between Books One and Two on this point may explain why Panaetius did not write a further book offering advice on conflicts between acting rightly and gaining benefits. However, Cicero feels that this further addition is needed, and composes it independently, though drawing, for the philosophical basis of the book, on Stoic material, including some writings by Hecato, a student of Panaetius.[64] As in Book Two, the conceptual and ethical framework is the same as in Book One and it closely reflects Stoic thinking on deliberation. The book begins, slightly awkwardly, by maintaining that, although the explicit topic is that of conflicts between right and advantage, there can be no real conflict between them but only the appearance of conflict.[65] Although this is, in terms of Stoic theory, a defensible view, on various grounds, Cicero does not explain very clearly the assumption on which this claim is based in this discussion.[66] I think that the premise which is most in line with the approach of the work is that, for someone approaching decision-making in the way he is recommending, there can be no fundamental conflict between the two factors, because the overriding aim is to do the right thing. However, there are situations in which acting rightly involves loss of advantages (actual loss and not just the appearance of loss), and this gives rise to uncertainty (that is, a sense of conflict) about how to weigh the competing factors and reach a decision. Cicero explores such situations with a view to enabling clearer understanding of the ethical weight or value of the factors involved and to reinforcing the motivation to adopt the right course of action, even when this entails reduction of advantages for oneself.[67]

I consider briefly here three major aspects of Cicero's treatment, which illustrate his approach. In doing so, I highlight features which reflect the framework presented in Book One and the linkage with the analysis of Stoic deliberation offered in the second section of this essay. These features are the opening formulation of a 'rule of procedure' (*formula*), the

---

[64] See 1.10, 3.7–10.
[65] 3.11–13.
[66] Two possible grounds are (1) the fundamental difference of value between virtue and indifferents (LS 58); and (2) the point made in Book 2 that the only reliable basis for gaining advantages (preferred indifferents) is the exercise of virtue; but I do not think Cicero has either ground primarily in view.
[67] This line of thought is indicated, but not fully spelled out, in 3.12–14, 17–18, 34; see also Woolf 2015: 192–3. On conflicts of duties in the work as a whole, see Tsouni ch. 2, this volume.

discussion of business ethics, and the concluding example of Regulus. The rule of procedure is presented in this way:

> Now then: for one person to take something from another and to increase his own advantage at the cost of another's disadvantage is more contrary to nature than death, than poverty, than pain, and anything else that may happen to his body and external possessions. In the first place, it destroys the common life and fellowship of human beings; if we are so minded that any one person will use theft or violence against another for his own profit, then necessarily the thing that is most in accordance with nature will be shattered, that is, the fellowship of the human race.[68]

This 'rule of procedure' reflects two key features of the earlier framework. First, the formulation expresses the two main aspects of the virtue of justice, as presented in Book One: that is, the more 'legalistic' aspect, the (negative) avoidance of harm unless unjustly provoked and the positive desire to engage in social association and to give and receive benefits in that context.[69] Secondly, both in this passage and, repeatedly, in the following discussion, Cicero refers to the idea of nature, meaning human nature (conceived as rational and sociable), and especially the idea of the natural fellowship between human beings as such.[70] Hence, as in Book One, practical deliberation is informed by guidance based on an understanding of the virtues (here, justice), supported by reference to one of the main ethical connotations of the idea of nature. In Book One this framework is deployed to guide deliberation about what is right: in this book, the focus is also on doing what is right, but in cases of ethical complexity, such as the ethics of tyrannicide, where killing, normally a wrong action, is presented as justified.[71] The approach deployed here can be correlated (or contrasted) with interpretative options considered earlier. The kind of 'rule' involved is what Inwood characterises as a 'rule of thumb', rather than a definitive or highly codified moral rule; it is one which needs to be worked out in relation to the specific facts of the situation, if it is to be applied correctly.[72] As regards the deliberative models of Barney and Brennan, Barney's model, based on maximisation of advantages for the agent, seems inapplicable for the approach of Book Three as a whole. Brennan's 'no-shoving model' is

---

[68] 3.21, trans. Griffin and Atkins 1991.
[69] For these two aspects, see 1.20, 22–3 (also Woolf 2015: 197). On the importance of the second aspect, and the positive motivation to act virtuously, see text to nn. 23–5, 51.
[70] See 3.21–3, 25–8, 31. See also 1.11–15, 50–9, 98–100, 107–14 (also text to n. 47). The theme of nature is also considered (but differently interpreted) by Barney 2003: 332–6; Brennan 2005: 218–20.
[71] See 3.19, 32 (Cicero has in view the assassination of Julius Caesar in 44 BCE; see Long 1995: 219–24, and cf. Gildenhard ch. 11, this volume).
[72] Inwood 1999: 121–2; see text to nn. 9–10. On this aspect of *Off.*, see Woolf 2015: 179–80, 189.

closer to the approach found here; and Brennan's examples of this model are largely drawn from this book. However, the problems noted earlier appear here too. In the passage just cited and often elsewhere, Cicero's guidance presupposes a positive motivation to act rightly (according to virtue) and not just a readiness to restrain the motivation to maximise advantages, one seen by Brennan as operating in all people, including virtuous ones.[73] Also, although in this instance, the example refers to justice, both as a general idea and its specific indications, in the book as a whole, as well as the other books, the guidance refers to other cardinal virtues.[74] Hence, here as elsewhere, I think that Hursthouse's analysis both matches and illuminates the Ciceronian (and Stoic) framework, in its presentation of right action as characteristic of the virtues and motivated by two related types of reason for acting, which explain why the action is done 'for its own sake'.[75]

In the two other features of Book Three noted earlier, I single out in each case two points that underline the linkage between Hursthouse's analysis and the Stoic approach. The first passage turns on the contrasting guidance of two Stoic heads (Diogenes and Antipater) on how to act in a business situation where openness would involve loss of profit. Both forms of guidance are presented as matching credible norms of right action; however, Cicero, explicitly, favours the guidance of Antipater which accepts loss of the advantage of profit for oneself.[76] He presents two factors as decisive. One is a reference, again, to the idea of nature, in the form of human brotherhood and community, presented as justifying going beyond the legalistic conception of just action advocated by Diogenes.[77] The other is Cicero's depiction of the policy favoured by Diogenes as the mark of someone who is 'not an open or straightforward person …; on the contrary … crafty, devious, sharp, deceitful, malicious'.[78] These two aspects mark parallels with Hursthouse's analysis of a right action as characteristic of a virtuous person (here, *not* characteristic of the vicious person), and also acting on certain types of reasons, including an appeal to a general principle, couched here in terms of human nature (the kinship of human beings as such).[79] The culminating example of Regulus (3.99–108)

---

[73] See 3.21, cited, also 3.23–4, 26, 28.
[74] See Barney 2003: 321–5; Brennan 2005: 206–14; also text to nn. 11, 20–8. In Book 3, as in Book 1, the cardinal virtues form the main structure for the book: justice and wisdom, taken together (3.40–74), magnanimity (97–115), moderation/*decorum* (116–20).
[75] See text to nn. 29–33, 38–41.
[76] See 3.50–7; on this discussion, see also Inwood 1999: 123–4.
[77] See 3.52; for similar ideas, see 1.50–2, 3.26–7, *Fin.* 3.64.
[78] 3.57, trans. Walsh 2000.
[79] See text to nn. 29–31.

represents an extreme ethical case, in that the decisions he takes, especially that of keeping his oath to the enemy and returning to Carthage, require him to give up all possible advantages, including that of life itself. Two points, again, bring out the parallel with Hursthouse's approach. Despite the seemingly extreme, or at least personal, form of the decision, it is presented as justified by general norms. It is cited as exemplifying two of the cardinal virtues, courage or magnanimity, as presented in Book One, and justice or good faith, especially with regard to keeping the oath.[80] Also, Cicero's use of a dialectical format (setting out arguments for and against Regulus' decisions) underlines that his action was based on reasons, some specific to the situation and some more general, underlying his insistence on maintaining his oath.[81] This climactic episode thus exemplifies clearly the value of Cicero's discussion as illustration of the Stoic conception of well-conducted deliberation and brings out the linkage with Hursthouse's suggestive analysis.[82]

---

[80] On magnanimity, see 3.99–102 (also 1.66–7); on justice and good faith, see n. 81.
[81] See 3.101–8, including 102–3, 104, 107–8, for arguments for and against keeping the oath sworn to an enemy. On good faith as integral to justice, see 1.23; Regulus is cited as an exemplar of keeping one's oath to the enemy (as an expression of justice) in 1.39.
[82] See text to nn. 29–33, 38–41.

PART III
Exemplary Ethics

CHAPTER 6

De Officiis *and Exemplary Ethics*

Rebecca Langlands

1 Introduction

It is in *De Officiis*, one of his final works, that we see Cicero's most sustained engagement with and reflection on Roman exemplary ethics. This is an ethics based on exemplary models, often taken from history, but also including admirable family members or mythical characters, whose behaviour is taken to enact particular abstract moral concepts, and therefore to usefully illustrate virtues and vices, and to provide guidance and inspiration for moral behaviour. Cicero several times acknowledges his own role as an *exemplum* for his son in *De Officiis*. However, in the Roman context, such models or *exempla* are usually in the form of short well-known moral tales about the great heroes and villains of history, which constitute an important feature of Roman cultural memory, and are widely used as a persuasive tool in Roman rhetoric, as "evidence" to support arguments and arouse the emotional responses of the audience. Cicero makes extensive reference in *De Officiis* to these kind of *exempla*, from the city's founder Romulus, through giants of the republic such as Fabricius and Scipio Africanus, to the more recent and poignant *exempla* of Cato and Caesar.

Cicero had already spent a lifetime honing skilful deployment of such historical *exempla* within his forensic and political speeches, and experimenting in his philosophical writings with their potential to facilitate the discussion of ethical ideas.[1] His practice had always reflected an innovative synthesis of rhetorical training, Roman *mos maiorum* ("custom of the ancestors") and the popular framework of exemplary wisdom within which Romans were acculturated, as well as strands of philosophical thought. *De Officiis* is a mature work in which, building on his experience, Cicero uses *exempla* in their full range of functions, which include

---

[1] See e.g. Müller 2022, van der Blom 2010 with further bibliography.

rhetorical, illustrative and persuasive, paradigmatic, epistemic, prototypical and injunctive, prompts to creative imitation, and heuristic – often weaving several functions together in one instance, as I shall discuss.[2]

It is not a straightforward matter to distinguish Cicero's innovations here from the existing Stoic model of exemplarity on which he was drawing (any more than it is possible to be absolutely clear about any other philosophical innovation); in addition, it is hard to be sure what the pre-existing tradition of popular Roman exemplary ethics with which he was engaging looked like, and how far his own practices were new or conventional.[3] In all our surviving ancient sources, the elements of Stoicism, wider Roman culture, and Ciceronian thought are already deeply entwined, no doubt to a large extent due to the notable influence of *De Officiis* itself on subsequent approaches to practical ethics and on ancient literature more broadly. In the philosophical sphere Stoicism is especially associated with *exempla*, but this is to a large extent because of Seneca's discussions, which in turn draw on and develop themes articulated in *De Officiis*.

Bearing these difficulties in mind, my broad suggestions here are the following: that, as far as we can tell, Cicero enriched and developed the Stoic modes of using *exempla* that he found in Panaetius; that these included in particular epistemological and casuistic uses of *exempla*, and the particular function of *exempla* within a virtue ethics framework; that he enriches these in a number of different ways, some more fully developed than others; that he does so partly by integrating into his philosophical discussion some key features of Roman exemplary ethics, including a sense of particularity and historical specificity, emotional charge and injunction, and indeterminacy of meaning. Within *De Officiis*, *exempla* play a wide range of different functions, often enmeshed, and not distinct from one another, and we often see *exempla* playing more than one role even within the same passage – I shall endeavour to show this in relation both to Cicero's important passage on the four *personae* theory and to the representation of Regulus.

I will further show that in *De Officiis* ethical exemplarity is a central concern. Cicero both reflects upon the some of the challenges of exemplary ethics when viewed within the Stoic context, and develops new techniques for utilising *exempla* within the Stoic framework. In these respects he anticipates to some extent ideas later developed more explicitly by Seneca; identifying the presence of these features already in *De Officiis*

---

[2] See Müller 2022 for an outline of some of these different modes of exemplarity that Cicero deploys in his works.
[3] On this see Langlands 2018: 227–231, Langlands forthcoming. See also n. 17 below.

enables us to better appreciate the unfolding dialogue between Stoicism and exemplary ethics.

2 Regulus as Stoic *Exemplum*

As a starting point for explicating some of these claims about Cicero's innovations in the work, I shall briefly consider how he handles the example of Regulus, which of course dominates Book 3 of *De Officiis*. Regulus and his choice to return to certain torture and death at the hands of the Carthaginians certainly may be read as a "luminous example of a Roman subordinating his apparent personal interest to that of the state,"[4] displaying the virtues of loyalty and courage, and embodying the importance of keeping one's oath, in the traditional mode of *mos maiorum* and Roman exemplary ethics. So the paradigmatic-normative function is certainly important here.[5] Yet we are also told that his action is highly situated in its historical context, a reflection of an ancestral seriousness about oathtaking as much as of his own outstanding virtue. Within his treatment, then, Cicero allows different exemplary functions to unfold in parallel, from the abstract clarification of arguments, to the inspirational, to the attention to situational ethics which is another key theme of this work. However, I propose here that in addition Cicero crafts Regulus as a Stoic *exemplum* in some quite fundamental and structural ways that go far beyond merely illustrating key Stoic virtues.

We know from a letter to Atticus written in November 44 BCE that Cicero already had his eye on this historical figure as an especially useful case study for tackling the question of the relation between "the good" (*honestum*) and "the useful" (*utile*) that is at the heart of Book 3.[6] It feels significant that in setting off on his own philosophical exploration, compelled to depart from his model Panaetius, Cicero chose to organise his articulation of this question around the extensive treatment of a particular, well-known story embedded in Roman tradition – and one whose heroism is both celebrated and contested.[7] The case of Regulus is not cited as a concise anecdote within a framing argument in a conventional persuasive mode. Rather it is teased apart into an extended dialectical framework,

---

[4] Dyck 1996: 35; he suggests it is offered as a deliberate counterexample to that of Caesar.
[5] Müller 2022 argues that in Cicero's practical philosophy this is the dominant mode of exemplarity.
[6] *Att.* 16.11.4, with Dyck 1996: 487–488.
[7] On the contestation in the Regulus site of exemplarity and its ethical implications see Langlands 2018: 272–290.

where anonymous interlocutors suggest interpretations of Regulus' behaviour that are rebutted at greater length by Cicero. In this way it is presented as a kind of case study, exploiting its controversial elements, matching the casuistic use of hypothetical examples within a debate by the Stoic teachers Diogenes and Antipater that is described earlier in the book.[8]

Drawing on a complex "site of exemplarity" in Roman cultural memory in which Regulus' behaviour is presented in different lights by different voices, Cicero is especially concerned to highlight alternative readings of Regulus' moral choices as *both* wrong *and* highly plausible, emphasising how very easy it is, even for intelligent observers, to mistake the sheen of apparent benefit for the gleam of true virtue. This perceptual challenge is at the heart of the work, and *exempla* prove to be crucial instruments in both articulating and addressing associated anxieties: that imperfect understandings of what is good can easily lead one astray, that it is difficult to distinguish true virtue from counterfeit virtue and deceptive vice, that the embodiment of virtue is manifold and may require radically different choices depending on the individual situation. Cicero builds, then, on a casuistic model which seems to belong to the existing Stoic tradition, in which philosophers debate points of disagreement on abstract questions by applying them to and testing them on specific tricky cases.[9] The use of this model earlier in the same book primes us to recognise the treatment of Regulus as another version of this established Stoic method of argument based on examples. However, Cicero enriches this with the complexity of exemplary ethics.

He also further develops the model so that it provides something else, even more useful in the context of a treatise on how to make good ethical decisions: an illustration of ethical deliberation in action. As Christopher Gill suggests elsewhere in this volume, Cicero's use of a dialectical structure allows him to focus in on what the motivation is for each choice that Regulus makes throughout the unfolding of his story, and allows us to see how and why he makes each choice within the narrative.[10] The extended treatment breaks the story down into a series of decisions. The latter half of Book 3 is essentially an extended exploration of the motives of Regulus at each stage of his story, which serves to make it clear that every action was

---

[8] 3.50–57. Broadly this dialectical technique is one Cicero had used elsewhere in his philosophical works, such as *De Finibus*, where Epicurean and Stoic viewpoints wrangle over the figure of Torquatus (on which see Langlands 2018: 259–266).

[9] See Inwood 1999: 112–127, esp. 120–127.

[10] See ch. 5: 115–116. On the importance of motivation in moral evaluation and its connection to the indeterminacy of *exempla* see Langlands 2018: 141–165.

guided by clear moral principles associated with the cardinal virtues. The reasoning of the text appears to get inside the head of the Roman hero, and expose his mental processes. Regulus emerges from this dialectical treatment as a model of well-reasoned choices.[11] Further, as Gill argues, it aligns Regulus' actions with the idea that *honestum* is generated by a virtue-ethics framework, where virtues are the original source of motivation for every right action (as established in Book 1, see 1.15 and 1.152).[12] The case study of Regulus enacts this principle that right action is always motivated by virtue, and that true benefit can only be a consequence of action according to the principles of virtue.

Breaking the *exemplum* down into multiple ethical choices also has a further consequence, which is again significant in Stoic terms. It allows Cicero to present Regulus as a man of ethical consistency. In this respect Regulus also goes some way towards addressing what Matthew Roller has identified as a limitation of traditional *exempla* from a Stoic viewpoint, what he calls the "insufficient evidence critique," that a single anecdote about an exemplary figure does not provide enough evidence to allow a moral learner to fully evaluate the moral value of the agent and cannot prove the most important Stoic quality – that of consistency.[13] It is unsurprising that this principle might be on Cicero's mind as he crafted his Regulus *exemplum*; *constantia* ("consistency") is systematically presented in *De Officiis* as a core element of *honestum*, vital to *decorum* ("seemliness"): "nothing, however, is so seemly as preserving constancy in everything that you do and in every plan that you adopt," (1.125, cf. 1.111–112, 1.119: *constare in perpetuitate vitae*, "to be constant for our whole length of life");[14] elsewhere in the work Cicero criticises those who show virtue in some circumstances but not in others "and they are not very constant even in this" (1.71).

In another *exemplum* crafted by Cicero in the Stoic mould – that of Cato the Younger at *Off.* 1.112 – Cicero has already had a go at incorporating consistency into the presentation of the story, when part of its rationale is that it was because of his natural characteristics, specifically including *perpetua constantia* ("perpetual constancy"), that Cato could do no other

---

[11] "Cicero's use of a dialectical format (setting out arguments for and against Regulus' decisions) underlines that his action was based on reasons, some specific to the situation and some more general" (Gill in this volume: 116).
[12] Ibid.
[13] Roller 2018: 275–283; "Regarding Fabricius and Horatius, [Seneca] assuredly suggests that we lack the range and number of observations required to support well-grounded moral evaluations" (283). On *constantia* in Seneca's Stoic writings see 281–282.
[14] For *constantia* as indispensable to virtue: 1.17 (where it is part of the fourth cardinal virtue), 1.67 (a key characteristic of a wise person), 1.80, 1.98, 1.102, 1.120, 3.5, 3.35.

than take his life when faced with defeat by the tyrannical Caesar.[15] Cato's *exemplum* – later extremely influential itself within Stoic exemplarity – succinctly conveys the guideline that for a man to be truly virtuous his every deed must be in accordance with his own virtues, even at the cost of his life. Further elaborating this principle in Book 3, Cicero provides evidence of Regulus' consistency *over time* by recrafting the *exemplum* of Regulus into a more drawn-out narrative, in which he repeatedly makes choices guided by the same set of principles aligned with Stoic virtues; he introduces thereby the diachronic dimension that will be identified by Seneca as important in moral evaluation.[16] Regulus emerges as a man who repeatedly performs what Cicero calls here "middle duties" (*media officia*), that is to say the "appropriate actions" (*kathēkonta*) of an ordinary person, rather than the "perfect actions" (*katorthōmata*) that one would find performed by a true Stoic sage. Regulus matches therefore the description of the illustrious men such as Cato and Laelius who, although they are not really sages, take on the appearance of wise men because of their "repeated practice of middle duties" (3.16). Cicero is able in this way to offer Regulus as a workable model for Stoic virtue, comparable to a living role model; he presents a useful appearance of sustained virtue for imitation, even though he has not achieved Stoic perfection.

Regulus' is a slightly unusual case within the work, in that Cicero provides an extended treatment of the *exemplum*, when we more usually find *exempla* appearing in the form of a concise narrative or brief citation. It nevertheless serves to demonstrate how a single *exemplum*, introduced ostensibly to support a particular line of argument, can in fact play multiple roles simultaneously within the work, some pertaining to the specific argument and others belonging to the wider ethical frame. To enable this, Cicero brings into play specific aspects of Roman exemplary ethics, including indeterminacy and interpretation. In fashioning Regulus' *exemplum* in this way he offers a consistent model for good decision-making within a Stoic and virtue ethical framework.

3 Moving Beyond Panaetius

In using *exempla* in his discussion of ethical deliberation, Cicero is of course following in the footsteps of his model Panaetius, and presumably following received Stoic practice in using *exempla* to support the expression of

---

[15] On Cicero's role in creating this episode as Stoic *exemplum* see Rauh 2018.
[16] Roller 2018: 281 on Seneca, *Ep.* 120.10.

philosophical ideas, certainly to illustrate virtues and principles and probably as the focus of casuistic debate, as above.[17] However, notably, in both places where Cicero explicitly cites Panaetius' use of *exempla* he does so critically, as if to distance himself from his source. At 2.16 he describes Panaetius' list of Themistocles, Pericles, Cyrus, Agesilaus, and Alexander as "unnecessary witnesses" to an uncontested claim that individuals need support of their community to excel. Later in Book 2 he makes the repurposing of Panaetius' *exempla* explicit. Panaetius has cited his own Roman contemporary, Scipio Aemilianus, in illustrative and injunctive mode as a paradigm of *abstinentia* ("abstinence") – part of the fourth cardinal virtue: "Panaetius praises Africanus because he was 'uncorrupted by greed' (*abstinens*)" (2.76). Cicero recasts him as a historical *exemplum*, among a cluster of others (his father Paullus and his colleague Lucius Mummius), and raises his significance above the simple illustration of a moral quality: "praise for such incorruptibility belonged not only to the man, but also to his age." In this brief list of well-known *exempla* is conveyed a rich sense of exemplary tradition in Rome, whereby the moderate actions of Aemilianus are not merely recognisable as *officia*, but are historically situated, and bound into a long tradition of emulation; he is described as "imitating his father Paullus": *imitatus patrem Africanus*. They represent the acts not only of individuals but of a community, are a reminder (in conjunction with 2.75) that the vice of *avaritia* ("avarice") is a relatively recent introduction into Roman political life, and in their clustering convey a hopeful sense of virtue's contagion. Moreover, this list touches optimistically on another Ciceronian concern: the motivational idea that virtue attracts recognition and commemoration, which is evoked here by the repeated idea of the *domus* ("family") made illustrious for the future through the virtuous acts of its members.

Through citation of such *exempla*, then, Cicero is not merely drawing on a shared knowledge of Roman history in order to clarify Stoic precepts; he is embedding Stoic ideas into Roman history. Or perhaps, as Jörn Müller has suggested to me, he is extrapolating the principles of Stoic ethics *from* Roman history, stressing the epistemological primacy of the Roman example.[18] Roman history here is not timeless but is characterised by change and transformation. This (moving) situatedness is aligned

---

[17] On the thorny question of how much of *De Officiis* is directly drawn from the writings of Panaetius, and how much is Cicero's innovation, see the discussions of Lefèvre 2001 and Brunt 2013; cf. also the chapters by Inwood and Schofield, this volume.

[18] For more on this model of Ciceronian thought see the reading of the "archaeology" of Cic. *Rep.* 2 in Müller 2017.

with the practical objective of a work that aims to make philosophical ideas applicable *now* (where "now" is constantly changing); with the acute awareness of the importance of situation that underpins the work and is itself expressed and addressed through the citation of particular *exempla*; and with the sense of urgency and specificity of context that is especially evoked by the constant presence of the recently assassinated Caesar under the skin of the text.[19] It is intimately bound up with the idea of situational ethics, and requirements of different moments and contexts (*tempora*), but this abstract ethical concept is rendered especially poignant by the sense of the extreme conditions from which *De Officiis* emerges.

A similar effect of situating abstract (Stoic) ideas in the real Roman world is created when Cicero outlines in some detail one of his most extensive narratives, about the Roman knight Gaius Canius who had been scammed by Pythius about twenty years earlier.[20] The latter sold him a house in Syracuse having led him to believe by means of an elaborate staging that its property included exceptional fishing waters (3.58–61). This is followed (3.62) by a brief story about the property negotiations of Cicero's former teacher Quintus Scaevola, who – to his own detriment, but in accordance with justice – increased the price on a farm he was buying because he thought it was worth more than the asking price. These references supplement and echo the hypothetical cases at the heart of casuistic discussion between Diogenes and Antipater about the situations where benefit seems to conflict with honourableness (especially 3.50–53). These are not *exempla* in the conventional sense of being celebrated tales of ancestral heroism; they look more like entertaining anecdotes about property purchase. As such, they help us clarify how we might define *exemplum* in this context of practical ethics: if a story or individual is cited as a specific case to illustrate a quality, to inspire, to test a principle or a conceptual boundary, or to think with ethically – that counts as an ethical *exemplum*. The hypothetical cases discussed by Diogenes and Antipater count as *exempla* to an extent, situated in a recognisable Mediterranean setting, but for a Roman and within the context of exemplary ethics they cry out for the last touches of realism that a specific instance can confer. Particular instances from real life have that extra element of concreteness that is lacking in a hypothetical case invented for the purpose.

---

[19] Caesar's triumph in Africa and Caesar's tyranny are described as constituting in themselves specific extreme circumstances in which very shocking acts of killing are – unusually – highly virtuous (1.112, 3.19). See further Gildenhard ch. 11, this volume.

[20] Though prior to Aquilius' definition of fraud (3.60) and so before 66 BCE.

4 *Exempla* within Virtue Ethics

The principal concern of *De Officiis* is the question of how to make good ethical choices, and, within this, the particular issue of how to distinguish what is truly "good" (*honestum*) from what only appears to be so, or what appears to be "useful" (*utile*).[21] In his contribution to this volume, Gill shows how illuminating it is to map Cicero's Stoic account of ethical deliberation onto the framework of virtue ethics elaborated by Rosalind Hursthouse. In this model, right actions are characteristic of the four cardinal virtues – wisdom, justice, courage and moderation – which are outlined in Book 1, and it is these virtues that provide both the motivation for all right action and the framework for recognising "the good." In the Stoic context, Gill proposes, the performance of "appropriate actions" (*officia*) or selection of indifferents that constitutes ethical decision making is done according to the requirements of these virtues. For the moral learner, *exempla* are deployed "to illustrate actions characteristic of the virtue in question" (ch. 5: 106). *Exempla* shed light on virtue – help us to see and recognise it; they also help us to recognise the kind of actions that are characteristic of each virtue.

If within Stoic thought one of the central questions for a moral agent is what a virtuous person would characteristically do in these circumstances,[22] then *exempla* offer evidence (at least *prima facie*) of what people have done in other (perhaps comparable) circumstances, which can be used to generate an answer for one's own case, given a sufficient understanding of the implications of context – and this sensitivity to context is a key feature of exemplary ethics. In the case of the exemplary tales of Roman ancestors, famous actions are often helpfully "coded" in their transmission with particular moral qualities. For example, in *De Officiis* Cicero describes the well-known tale of Fabricius' refusal to take unfair advantage of a defector who had pledged to poison his enemy Pyrrhus as "another very great example of justice towards the enemy" (1.40), and Fabricius himself as someone who "is called just" (3.16). In such a case, the famous deed represents an instantiation of a particular virtue – here justice – that provides both a useful illustration of what that virtue might look like in practice, and at the same time a model of how to put virtue into practice for oneself. This is a practical application of *exempla* to moral development and decision-making which is closely aligned with Roman exemplary ethics more broadly, where admirable or detestable figures from history are used

---

[21] Gill ch. 5: 108 argues that "the relationship between what is right and what is useful, and how they are to be reconciled" is central to all three books.

[22] As argued by Gill in this volume, drawing on the work of Hursthouse 1999.

to teach what moral qualities look like in practice, to arouse admiration or outrage, to inspire action, and to provide models for emulation or rejection.[23] In this combination of illustrative and injunctive function, and in a virtue ethics context where virtues constitute the primary motivations (rather than a force of restraining appetite for preferred indifferents), *exempla* can be thought of as embodying the kind of v-rule that is described by Hursthouse in her account of virtue ethics.[24]

Cicero aligns this with the tradition of *mos maiorum*, in which Romans are urged to follow in the footsteps of their own celebrated familial ancestors. In this light he suggests that it falls to his son, his addressee, "both to inherit my glory and to imitate my deeds" by developing his prowess in the fields of oratory and politics. This Roman idea that particular attributes run in specific families (e.g. 1.116) helpfully illustrates the idea that one person might be naturally better suited to shine in a particular way than another, which in turn underpins one of the central Stoic principles articulated in *De Officiis* – that of situational and personal variability. However, Cicero also makes it clear that no man is bound by his inheritance; Africanus is an example of someone who added his own glory in oratory to the family tradition of military glory, and there are yet others (clearly Cicero himself being the prime example) who "decline to imitate their ancestors and pursue a course of their own" (1.116), choosing thereby their own models and modes of excellence to aspire to. Thus the familiar Roman tradition of *mos maiorum* helps to introduce and frame the important Stoic discussion of situational ethics that crowns Book 1.

5 Situational Ethics

A key aspect of Roman exemplary ethics is the principle of situational variability and the importance of context when it comes to deciding what is right, which is also closely associated with the practice of creative imitation of exemplary models.[25] Cicero's discussion of four *personae* at *De Officiis* 1.107–123 is an important early articulation of these principles in relation to Stoic thought, which both models the utility of *exempla* in this context, using a catalogue of diverse *exempla* to illustrate the concept of situational variability, and reflects on the principle of *varietas* ("diversity") more

---

[23] What Müller 2022 identifies as prototypical function, in addition to a simple epistemological role.
[24] On *exempla* and v-rules see also Langlands 2021.
[25] The term "situational ethics" can be used to describe more radical positions, but here I use it simply to refer to theories that recognise the centrality of context in correct decision-making (see Langlands 2018: 112–227).

generally. The core principle is that virtue "looks" different, and needs to be enacted differently, in different contexts and by different people according to their natural individual attributes. This principle will be fundamental to exemplary ethics as it develops after Cicero's day, probably due to the influence of *De Officiis*.[26] It governs the way *exempla* can mediate between general moral ideas and particular cases, and the way that moral learners can apply models to their own behaviour through creative imitation, but it can also only be grasped as a principle through reference to the *varietas* of specific examples. It is related to the wider practice of "clustering" examples, found throughout Roman culture, where groups of *exempla*, inevitably divergent to an extent even when illustrating the same category, thereby convey the scope and breadth of that category.[27]

In a twist on this practice, however, in his own articulation of the principle of situational variability, Cicero begins at *Off.* 1.108–109 by illustrating the principle of *varietas* itself. The implicit category to which all his cited examples belong is therefore notable and admirable men, and the point is that each excels in his own particular way, and sometimes with a quality that is the direct opposite of the excellent quality of another. Cicero's aim here is not to map out the full panoply of admirable qualities, but to demonstrate the distance between one quality and another, and the fact that they can seem to lie at opposite poles; hence he organises the examples around two pairs of opposites, contrasting the naturally light-hearted with the very serious, and the strategic with the straightforward:

> Lucius Crassus and Lucius Philippus had plenty of wit; Gaius Caesar, the son of Lucius, still more, though it was more studied; but in the same period Marcus Scaurus and the youthful Marcus Drusus were showing exceptional seriousness, Gaius Laelius was extremely jolly, his intimate friend Scipio had greater ambition and a more earnest style of life … We hear that Hannibal the Carthaginian was crafty (*callidum*), as was, of our leaders, Quintus Maximus, who found it easy to conceal or keep silent, to dissemble, to set traps (*dissimulare, insidiari*) and to anticipate the enemy's plans… Others are very different from these, being straightforward and open (*simplices et aperti*); they think that nothing should be done through secrecy or trickery, they cultivate the truth and they are hostile to deceit (*veritatis cultores, fraudis inimici*). There are others again who would endure anything you like, devote themselves to anyone you like, provided they acquire what they want; we saw that in the case of Sulla and Marcus Crassus. (*Off.* 1.108–109)

---

[26] Cf. Langlands 2011 on Valerius Maximus' engagement with Cicero's articulation of situational ethics here.

[27] On such clustering and multiplicity see Langlands 2018: esp. 112–114, 122–124 with 124–127 on the way this aligns with Hursthouse's account of Aristotelian virtue ethics.

This catalogue of *exempla* illustrates the point that, while everybody shares in the "same human nature" (*communis persona*), there are wide differences in the nature of individuals: "just as there are enormous bodily differences ... similarly there are still greater differences (*varietates*) in men's spirits" (1.107). This is the basis for the next step in ethical deliberation, which is making sure that one knows one's own characteristics sufficiently to be able to understand what specific actions are appropriate for one in one's own circumstances. The list does not merely illustrate the abstract *point* that there is diversity among men, it also serves to illustrate, if only partially, the *nature* of the diversity itself. In their own diversity the *exempla* begin to map out some of the particular areas in which one person may differ from another, and the various qualities with which one might be endowed. Through this diversity they also inevitably draw the reader into the process of *comparatio* ("comparison"), a key aspect of exemplary ethics and of ascertaining specifically which duties are appropriate for oneself.[28] Reading the passage it is difficult not to begin to wonder: am I naturally witty or serious? Where would I place the people I know within these categories? Which of them do I admire?

Cicero's particular choice of illustrative *exempla* serves to layer a further effect on top of the themes of *varietas* and *comparatio*. On the face of it this passage illuminates diversity with a view to encouraging the reader to recognise that they are an individual with their own natural qualities which will not be the same as other people's, and to recognise and become familiar with their own strengths, so that they do not make the mistake of trying to imitate an unsuitable model. The *exempla* and the qualities with which they are associated are intended to show the wide variation in the ways that admirable people can be endowed. It is asserted that this variation is morally neutral, like the physical properties to which they are initially compared (1.107), and Cicero concludes by saying no particular quality is to be censured (1.109), and that "each person should hold on to what is his as far as it is not vicious, but is peculiar to him, so that the seemliness we are seeking may be more easily maintained" (1.110). The point is to ascertain which good qualities are natural to *you*, not which are the best *in themselves*. Others may lead lives that are more meaningful, but we need not strive to be like them: "even if other pursuits may be weightier or better, we should measure our own by the rule of our own nature" (1.110).

And yet, the natures on display in this particular selection of *exempla* suggest that, while the principle sounds a simple one, the practicalities

---

[28] See Langlands 2018: 92–93.

of following "one's own natural traits but keeping away from vice" (*non vitiosa, sed tamen propria*, 1.110) are not straightforward. What does one do if one is naturally the kind of person who will stop at nothing to get what one wants, like the cited *exempla* of Sulla or Marcus Crassus? How, in this case, might one avoid vice? Is the aptitude for deception and trickery really no less admirable than that for honesty and truthfulness? In other places in the work it is very clear that this is not the case.[29] And why is it that Cicero offers us multiple *exempla* in the more troubling categories of cunning and ruthlessness, but none to illustrate the evidently good nature of "people who cultivate the truth" (*veritatis cultores*), when cultivation of the truth is elsewhere the very essence of the first cardinal virtue?[30] Even though Cicero states explicitly in conclusion that none are to be criticised (1.109), it is difficult not to feel anxious about how one might reconcile some of the natures on display here with virtue and steer them away from vice. Indeed, the way the *exempla* are presented invites the reader's moral evaluation – some ways of being seem evidently more desirable or virtuous than others. In this list, morally neutral talent overlaps uncomfortably with ethical qualities, raising discomfort about how we evaluate the qualities of others, and which we admire and strive for in ourselves, which strikes at the heart of exemplary ethics.[31]

Is this discomfort and lack of fit deliberate? The passage is far from unique in Latin literature in presenting a set of examples that seems less than perfectly suited to the argument that it is apparently supporting.[32] Of course, Cicero drafted this work at speed, striving to articulate complex philosophical ideas as persuasively as possible; this is perhaps not a work that intends itself to be studied for hidden layers of meaning, and perhaps his *exempla* were carelessly chosen. It is also a common feature of *exempla* that their meaning exceeds the frame of argument within which they are cited. Indeed, this is part of what lends them such utility and flexibility, since no author or citation can ever pin down their meaning – a feature that clearly causes Cicero some anxiety in relation to his own attempt to control the legacy of Caesar and the Gracchi as negative

---

[29] E.g. 3.57 where the man who is "open, straightforward, well bred, just or good" *aperti, simplicis, ingenui, iusti, viri boni* is compared to the one who is "a twister, mysterious, cunning, tricky, ill-intentioned, crafty, roguish and sly," with the latter qualities named as vice (*vitiorum*); 3.68, nothing should be done *insidiose*.

[30] E.g. 1.16, 1.63, where being *simplices, veritatis amicos* is required of just men.

[31] See Gill 1988: 180–185 on the discomforting aspects of this passage; Gill's suggestion is that Cicero (and Panaetius) are adopting conventional aristocratic standards rather than Stoic ones.

[32] Often this creative technique is used to significant effect: see e.g. Gazich 1995 on Propertius; Watson 1983 on *Ars Amatoria*; Langlands 2018: 321–326 on Seneca *De Ira*.

exempla. However, the inclusion of the names Hannibal and Sulla, which are inevitably coloured by moral controversy, suggest that the dissonance here is not inadvertent. In addition to supporting his exposition of the idea of variation, this catalogue of *exempla* delivers another layer of moral communication, about apparent moral ambiguity, which ties into running themes of the work as a whole.

For Cicero's decision to display the contrast between *calliditas* and truth here is not arbitrary. In arousing the reader's anxiety about how far cleverness and trickery is to be admired, this sequence of *exempla* picks up a moral theme that runs through the work about the moral ambiguity of cleverness, which is both a fundamental part of the first virtue (wisdom),[33] and at times the worst kind of vice: at 3.57 the "clever person" is associated with trickery and malice, and explicitly contrasted with the "good man."[34] In Book 2 Cicero asserts that "the more cunning and clever a man is, the more he is hated and suspected if deprived of the reputation of integrity" (2.34). As portrayed by Cicero over the course of this treatise, *calliditas* and *sollertia* ("cleverness") provide an opportunity for expressing a fundamental anxiety about the proximity of virtue and vice to one another, and the difficulty of distinguishing one from the other in many circumstances. At the end of Book 3, Cicero again draws attention to the difficulty of distinguishing between good and bad types of cleverness, and knowing precisely where the boundaries lie between true "wisdom" (*prudentia*) and mere "brute cunning" (*stulta calliditas*). By describing the latter as imitating or "taking on the appearance" (*imitata*) of the former, he highlights how difficult it is to distinguish one from the other, as they look so very similar (3.113). The idea that vice can masquerade dangerously as virtue is a pervasive anxiety of the book, and Cicero neatly communicates it here through his deployment of the ambiguous Latin term *imitata*.[35] Imitation is a key part of exemplary ethics; *exempla* are to be aspired to and to be emulated. Yet imitation of virtue or apparent virtue does not always result in reproduction of virtue, and can indeed, as here, result in vice.

Earlier, in his discussion of justice, Cicero used a mini-series of two *exempla* to explore the moral boundaries of *sollertia* and *calliditas* and to set up this idea that both qualities can have positive or negative moral valence (1.33). The first *exemplum* is the case of the man who "during a truce of thirty days which had been agreed with the enemy, laid waste the fields by night, on the

---

[33] *Sollertia* is part of the initial definition of the first virtue, wisdom (*sapientia* or *prudentia*) at 1.15.
[34] *non viri boni, versuti potius, obscuri, astuti, fallacis, malitiosi, callidi, veteratoris, vafri.*
[35] See Langlands 2020 on the ambiguity of imitation in exemplary ethics more broadly. Cf. also White ch. 7, this volume.

grounds that the truce had been established for *days* but not for *nights.*" The second is Labeo's arbitration of a land dispute between Nola and Naples when he stole the land in between them for himself by getting both sides to draw in their boundaries. This kind of *sollertia* is to be avoided in all circumstances – "it counts as deception rather than judgement" (*decipere hoc quidem est, non iudicare*). In these *exempla* we see in operation qualities that are described at the start and end of this section as *nimis callida sed malitiosa*[36] and *talis sollertia* – "too much cleverness" and "cleverness of the wrong kind" – which lead to injustice, and do not fall within the parameters of goodness. Yet in other cases *sollertia* and *calliditas* count as admirable virtues, when they are aligned with justice. These *exempla* help to decide where a line needs to be drawn – or at least, that a line does need to be drawn – distinguishing good from bad cleverness (it is nice that the second story is precisely about contiguity and the act of drawing boundaries).

To return to the catalogue of *exempla* at 1.108–109, we can now contextualise it within a wider set of concerns about moral evaluation and ambiguity which run through the work. Some excellent qualities can fall within the scope of both virtue and vice, and it is not always easy to see where the distinction lies; this is a pervasive issue when it comes to recognising virtue. Underlying this disconcerting catalogue of *exempla* may also be Cicero's recurrent concern about personal attributes that attract admiration of the kind that exemplary virtue should, yet are not in themselves always morally virtuous (although, like cleverness, they can be). Since admiration of prowess is such an important aspect of exemplary ethics, and is what kickstarts the emulative process,[37] it is particularly worrying that it can be aroused by the wrong kind of quality, likely to lead the admiring moral learner astray. It is especially worrying when the admirable quality such as cleverness might in fact count as virtue or as vice depending on the wider context, but it is not always easy to determine which in a particular context. How is one to evaluate the quality of Hannibal's *calliditas* in this passage, which may be admired or deplored depending on perspective? (This dependence on perspective is further emphasised by pairing Hannibal with his enemy Fabius, and allocating the terms with more negative connotations – such as *insidiari* – to the latter.) Another such ambiguous attribute is *magnitudo animi* ("greatness of spirit"), and this latter occasions particular anxiety in relation to ethical exemplarity, expressed several times through the *exemplum* of Caesar.

---

[36] Editors' understandable anxiety about the phrase "*nimis callida sed malitiosa*" rests precisely on an ambiguity about how we are to understand the moral significance of the term *callida*. *Nimis* suggests a negative valence, but the contrast with *sed malitiosa* suggests otherwise. See Dyck 1996 *ad loc.*
[37] Langlands 2018: 86–95.

In 1.108–109 these anxieties are not referred to explicitly, indeed they are barely implied. But as the list moves from a selection of great men it takes the reader on an uncomfortable trajectory that parallels the framing argument about diversity and intersects at the same time with wider concerns of the work, so that the latent ideas about the limitations of both admiration and diversity are activated as we read, and carry through into discussion later in the work. As in the case of Regulus we can see *exempla* taking on multiple roles simultaneously.[38]

Related to these is another concern about exemplary evaluation and emulation, which is articulated through the *exemplum* of Cato cited a little later in the discussion of situational ethics, at *Off.* 1.112: the very same deed which counts as virtuous when performed by one person may be an instance of vice if performed by another. Here, the primary function of the *exemplum* is to support the point that such is the diversity of our individual natures that what is the right thing for one individual is very much the wrong thing for another: "Such differences of nature (*differentia naturarum*) have so great a force that sometimes one man ought to choose death for himself, while another ought not." This *exemplum* conveys poignantly the necessity of being absolutely clear about our own nature in order to understand what action is required of us, since sometimes it will be the very opposite of what is required of another person:

> For surely the case of Marcus Cato was different from that of the others (*ceteri*) who gave themselves up to Caesar in Africa? Indeed, it would perhaps have been counted as a vice (*vitio datum esset*) if they had killed themselves, for the very reason that they had been more gentle in their lives, and more easy-going in their behaviour. But since nature had assigned to Cato an extraordinary seriousness, which he himself had consolidated by his unfailing constancy, abiding always by his adopted purpose and policy, he had to die rather than look upon the face of a tyrant. (*Off.* 1.112)

It is clear that this difference displayed here, while it points to the different appropriate behaviours, is not morally neutral; there is a suggestion that Cato is not merely "different" but may be considered morally superior to the *ceteri* with whom he is contrasted. The citation serves therefore as an implicit exhortation to particular qualities of *gravitas* ("seriousness") and *constantia* ("consistency") which he possesses,[39] even as it communicates the idea that most of us could never aspire to be a Cato – his *gravitas* is *incredibilem* ("incredible"). Yet, a striking point made here by Cicero

---

[38] For this multidimensional use of *exempla* in later Latin literature see Langlands 2018: 335.
[39] Qualities already associated by Cicero with Cato in 46 BCE (*Att.* 12.4.2).

is that it is not merely that the others fall short of Cato's steadfast virtue. Absent his particular personal qualities or these very specific circumstances, if the others had taken the same action as Cato and killed themselves this would have counted as an "immoral act" (*vitium*). In addition to its primary function, this *exemplum* prompts reflection on the very process of exemplary ethics, since it is not enough to be inspired by the impressive acts of other men and strive to equal them; one must sift through a range of available *exempla* very carefully to understand how each might be applicable to one's own *persona* and situation.

6 The Limitations of Exemplary Ethics

The glittering *exemplum* which erupts regularly into the discussion, imbuing the work with a sense not only of political urgency but also of moral anxiety, is Julius Caesar, assassinated earlier that year.[40] Cicero uses Caesar's *exemplum* as a particular means of expressing disquiet about exemplarity itself, and of the role of *exempla* in illustrating virtue. Above all, the haunting figure of Caesar crystallises a set of anxieties about virtue and exemplarity itself which are developed in *De Officiis*: the deceptive glamour of Roman exemplary heroes and the ambiguity of greatness of spirit. *Magnitudo animi* is a core virtue (the third virtue, 1.15) that can also become a vice, specifically when it is not accompanied by justice (1.62). A related anxiety is that certain kinds of deeds tend to inspire more admiration than others, and thus to be recognized as exemplary by the community, yet these are not necessarily the deeds that are in reality the most virtuous[41] – indeed, they can be quite the opposite. This represents, in some ways, the uncomfortable corollary of the idea that actions can count as virtue or vice depending on who performs them; acts which appear to be splendid and virtuous may in fact enact the worst kinds of vice. Cicero's further implication is that what attracts us about such exemplary figures may not always be true virtue, but something else, deceptively appealing.

Caesar is the poster boy for this anxiety. In a significant extended passage in Book 1, Cicero tells us that the deeds and people that shine most brilliantly and are most alluring to us tend to be of a certain type, that is great spirited: "… but we must realise, it is that which is done with a great and lofty spirit (*animo magno elatoque*), one disdaining human affairs, which

---

[40] "The great event that throws its shadow over *De Officiis* is the assassination of Caesar on the Ides of March" with list of references in Griffin and Atkins 1991: xii.
[41] This corresponds to an extent to what Roller calls the "misjudgement critique" developed by Seneca in *Ep.* 94 (Roller 2018: 266–275).

appears in the most brilliant light (*splendissimum*)" (1.61). The particular horror here is that when a man possesses the exciting quality of *magnitudo animi*, but without the mitigating virtues of justice and moderation (*si iustitia vacat*), it is no longer a virtue, it is a vice (*in vitio est*, 1.62). "It is not merely," Cicero tells us, "that it is not virtuous" (*non modo enim id virtutis non est*), but that it is "a savagery which repels all civilized feeling" (1.62).[42] Cicero has the *exemplum* of Caesar in mind here, going on to stress how susceptible such great men are to be led into desire for sole rule, and to be unable to preserve their sense of justice. Cicero's anxiety is that it might in the end be men like Caesar who are the most exciting and inspiring stars, with their impressive courage and intellectual brilliance, and that the quieter virtues (he describes them as *lenioribus*, "gentler", 1.46) do not shine so brilliantly, may not garner praise and glory, and may attract less emulation. Such qualities rest so lightly upon people – the Latin here is *attingere* ("to touch upon") – that they may be barely perceptible.[43]

This potential for the moral learner to be led astray by the misleading surface glamour of outstanding deeds is a challenge to the smooth functioning of exemplary ethics, which relies on the idea that goodness can be recognised as it shines forth from the deeds of virtuous men. However, it is not just that there is the danger of a moral learner being deceived by *exempla* because of the resemblance of vice to virtue and the overlap between them. Cicero makes it clear that within the Stoic framework *all* celebrated *exempla* are deceptive and flawed, since none of the historical figures actually displays the true form of virtue that one would find in a Stoic wise man. The appearance of virtue in them is merely something that looks superficially like virtue:

> When the two Decii, or the two Scipiones, are mentioned as "brave men", or when Fabricius or Aristides is called "just", we are not seeking an example of courage in the former, nor of justice in the latter, as if in a wise man; for none of them is wise in the way that we want to understand wise. Not even Marcus Cato and Gaius Laelius were in fact wise, although they were called and considered wise; and nor were the famous seven. Rather, because of their repeated practice of middle duties (*media officia*), they exhibited a kind of likeness to (*similitudo*) and appearance (*species*) of wise men. (*Off.* 3.16)

In other words, while it may be through *exempla* that we come to recognise what a virtue such as justice or courage looks like, the virtue we perceive

---

[42] The idea is repeated at 1.157, where *magnitudo animi* without *communitas* is "a kind of brutal savagery" (*feritas ... quaedam et immanitas*).

[43] This issue also relates to concerns about the value of glory as an indifferent and as a motivation and reward for virtue, which are addressed in *De Officiis* and presumably also in Cicero's lost work *On Glory*.

is not the real thing. For all that *exempla* are instances of particular virtues and help us to understand the nature of these virtues, they do not in fact display true virtue, but only a semblance of it (*similitudo*, *species*). Earlier Cicero has warned his reader that the wisest people among us are mere *simulacra virtutis* (1.46).

Yet in this respect exemplary figures are comparable to the ordinary moral learner who has not reached perfect wisdom, and therefore cannot attain true *honestum*, but only likenesses of it (*similitudines honesti*, 3.14). The plural "likenessess" here is significant; there can only be one true goodness, but there are many different ways for men striving to be good to approximate to it, just as there are many different *exempla* of courage or justice, none able to embody it to perfection. So *exempla* have a great utility for the student of Stoicism, but their incompleteness needs to be borne in mind if one is to fully appreciate what one can learn from them. While Fabricius isn't truly "just," the apparent justice of his behaviour towards Pyrrhus can help us appreciate what justice looks like. Meanwhile, of his *exempla* of wisdom, Cicero adds a further suggestion about why *exempla* can be useful; it is because of their "repeated middle duties" that Cato and Laelius exhibit a likeness to wise men. In this respect, they can provide a useful model for how to be a good person, by showing what such repeated choices look like in the lives of particular individuals. As we have seen, Cicero develops the *exemplum* of Regulus precisely to address this need within the context of practical Stoic ethics.

Nevertheless, Cicero's analogy with works of art and literature, where "inexperienced people are delighted, praising them when they ought not to be praised" but if they receive education "readily abandon their view," and his allusion to "ordinary people" and their deficient understanding of *honestum* (3.15), leave open the possibility of the moral learner reaching a state of moral enlightenment where they no longer admire the virtues of traditional *exempla*, which are therefore no longer useful in aiding moral progress. It is not clear at what point of moral progress this might happen, and whether it is likely that most or vanishingly few advanced students of Stoicism will end up leaving *exempla* behind in this way. However, this corresponds very closely with the model later articulated by Seneca, in *Ep.* 120, of moral learning as a two-stage process: initially (as children) we learn about the appearance (*species*) of virtue from admirable *exempla* such as Fabricius and Horatius Cocles, which show us "a likeness of virtue," and ignoring their flaws we allow ourselves to be dazzled by the surface glamour (*fulgor*) (*Ep.* 120.5, 8); later, as adults we are able to discern these flaws and to appreciate that true virtue is to be seen in those who act with total consistency in all they do (120.9–11).[44] Moreover at 120.8–9 Seneca expresses precisely the warnings about the proximity between virtue and vice and their resemblance to one another to which we have seen Cicero demonstrate such great sensitivity in *De Officiis*. Indeed *Ep*. 120 seems to engage directly with *De Officiis*, picking up, as it does, on the *exemplum* of Fabricius and some key terms and ideas: *honestum perfectum* (the perfected good), *species* (appearance), *similitudo* (likeness).[45] In other words the rich engagement with exemplary ethics that scholars have found in Seneca's Stoic thought is already clearly visible as mature reflection in *De Officiis*. Through his own crafting of exemplary material in the work, Cicero both explicates some of the limitations of exemplary ethics and offers some practical solutions; his innovations here were influential on later writers.

7 Conclusion

In *De Officiis*, Cicero uses the familiar materials and modes of traditional Roman exemplary ethics to help him articulate the Stoic ideas found in Panaetius and then further develop their implications in Book 3. *Exempla* facilitate, for instance, understanding of the cardinal virtues, what sort of actions are characteristic of each, and how to distinguish them from similar looking vices. They serve to communicate the important principle that in reality different circumstances can require different kinds of actions, and they provide guidance in how to situate oneself in relation to this diversity. Already in *De Officiis* we also see reflection on some of the friction that arises when *exempla* are caught at the nodes of intersection between different traditions of thought and practical ethics. Cicero crafts troubling *exempla* such as that of Caesar to articulate his anxieties about exemplary ethics, and the potential for moral learners to be led astray by surface glamour or misleadingly similar vices, and he also reflects on the flawed nature of all *exempla*, whose apparent virtue is deceptive. Finally, Cicero draws on aspects of Roman exemplary ethics (such as particularity and historical situatedness, *auctoritas*, indeterminacy and interpretability, emotional and injunctive charge) in creative ways, so as to enhance the mode of exemplarity found in Panaetius, and further tailor exemplary materials and models to the Stoic context.

---

[44] Roller 2018: 275–283 and Langlands 2018: 102–109 see the relation of this passage to exemplary ethics and Stoicism slightly differently, but give a similar account of the two-stage process.

[45] See also the naming of Cato and Laelius as efficacious Stoic *exempla* in *Ep*. 11 and 25 and of Caesar as *exemplum* of the troubling glory of the unvirtuous. We can see the presence already in *De Officiis* of both critiques that Roller identifies as Seneca's Stoic critiques of "conventional exemplarity": the "misjudgement" and "insufficient evidence" critiques.

CHAPTER 7

Emulation and Moral Development in De Officiis

Georgina White

1 *Exempla* in *De Officiis*

Quamquam te, Marce fili, annum iam audientem Cratippum idque Athenis abundare oportet praeceptis institutisque philosophiae propter summam et doctoris auctoritatem et urbis, quorum alter te scientia augere potest, altera exemplis ...

Marcus, my son, since you have now been studying with Cratippus for a year – and that also in Athens – you ought to be full to the brim with the precepts and principals of philosophy on account of the utmost authority of both your teacher and the city: the former of which can make you greater with his knowledge, the latter by its *exempla* ... (*Off.* 1.1)

The status of the *exemplum* – "a short, pithy account of a saying or action of a famous man (or less often, woman)"[1] – as a key element of moral education is introduced in the very first sentence of *De Officiis*. Cicero, addressing his son, asserts that Marcus must by now have made great progress in his philosophical studies, not only because of the instruction provided by his teacher Cratippus, but also because of the *exempla* offered by his stay in the city of Athens.[2] As the treatise develops, it becomes clear that *exempla* have an important role not only in young Marcus' studies in Athens, but also in the educational experience offered by his father's text. While the argument of the first two books of *De Officiis* seems to follow a Panaetian model, Cicero often departs from his source material to include *exempla* from recent Roman history that can have had no place in his

---

[1] Morgan 2007: 5.
[2] That the *exempla* here referred to are historical *exempla* is clear both from the examples invoked throughout *De Officiis*, and from *Fin.* 5.2–6, where a more developed description of the use of Athenian historical *exempla* as a starting point for philosophical inquiry can be found.

Greek model.³ In the final book, meanwhile, where Cicero claims independence from Panaetius,⁴ we find some of the most developed instances of historical *exempla* within the work, including the extended discussion of the actions of Regulus at 3.99–115. In a work in which it is often difficult to untangle Cicero's own innovations from vestiges of his source text, then, the *exempla* stand out as a feature that has clearly received particular attention from their Latin author.

Given the apparent importance of *exempla* to Cicero's project, any account of Cicero's philosophical method in this work is forced to grapple with the question of how exactly these historical insets function within the text. From the account of Marcus' education given in the opening sentence, *exempla* are clearly envisaged as having an important didactic purpose: a parallel role is played in Marcus' philosophical development by his studies with Cratippus and the *exempla* offered by the history of the city. In the *De Officiis*, then – a text which self-consciously presents itself as a Latin literary reflection of this Greek educational model – we might similarly expect the *exempla* to play a didactic role parallel to the teachings of Stoic philosophers that are contained within the text.⁵

Yet understanding how, exactly, these *exempla* contribute to the reader's moral progress is an interpretative challenge. As we shall see in Section 2 of this chapter, Cicero's treatment of his *exempla* in this text warns us against taking them simply as models for imitation. Instead, as Sections 3–5 will show, these *exempla* aid the reader's moral progress in other ways: helping her to develop her skills of ethical analysis, and illustrating that the Stoic ethical theory of the *De Officiis* offers a valuable framework within which to approach real world events. They also have the potential to act as a unique spur to ethical action, in that they activate the reader's "emulative" emotions – her desire to gain similar social rewards to the figures described. As we shall see, however, in order to channel these "emulative" emotions into an impulse for ethical rather than unethical action, Cicero needs to redirect our desire away from the counterfeit glory pursued by such villainous figures as Caesar and Sulla, and towards the *true* glory

---

³ These recent *exempla* focus on the Roman civil wars and their aftermath, with Cicero often emphasizing the proximity of these events, e.g. *Off.* 1.26: the potential for the desire for glory to lead people away from justice was shown *modo* ("just now") by the actions of Caesar. For the presence of Greek *exempla* in Panaetius, see *Off.* 2.16. On Cicero's Panaetian model more generally, see *Att.* 16.11 and Dyck 1996: 17–29.

⁴ *Off.* 3.7–10.

⁵ For the status of this text as a Latin version of Marcus' Greek philosophical education, see *Off.* 1.1; for the *praecepta* of philosophers as the primary content of the text, see *Off.* 1.5.

that is achieved only by those who act virtuously. In doing so, Cicero redefines contemporary Roman ideas about glory and, again, it is by appealing to *exempla* that he is able to do this.

2   *Exempla* and Imitation

One possible way of understanding the didactic role of the historical *exempla* in *De Officiis* is that they provide models of correct action that the reader might seek to imitate (or, conversely, of incorrect action that the reader can strive to avoid). On this reading, while the argumentative sections of the text may help the reader to make moral progress by providing her with the tools needed to analyze moral choices and rationally determine the correct course of action, the *exempla* would provide a kind of ethical shortcut, allowing a reader who may not yet have fully internalized the principles of correct moral reasoning nevertheless to engage in virtuous action by imitating the deeds of a virtuous model. If the reader finds herself with the opportunity to break a promise made to an enemy, then, rather than worrying about what action may best promote the community of men and so produce justice (1.20), she can ensure that she takes the virtuous course simply by copying the actions of Regulus (1.39). The idea that these *exempla* are presented as models for imitation by the reader would fit with the use of historical *exempla* in Roman moral discourse more generally, as exemplified in the preface of Livy (1.10) and explored more fully in the work of Matthew Roller and Rebecca Langlands.[6] Indeed, the practice of picking a virtuous figure for imitation is explicitly applauded at *Off.* 2.46, where young men are advised to pick out renowned and wise men *ad imitandum* (for imitation).[7]

---

[6] Each scholar has a slightly different model to explain the function of exemplary discourse in the Roman world, yet both include imitation as an essential aspect. Roller 2004: 4–5 argues that exemplary discourse requires: (1) action (admitting of ethical categorization); (2) audience (to observe the action and evaluate as good/bad); (3) commemoration (a monument showing the deed and the reception of the deed); (4) imitation ("any spectator to such a deed … is enjoined to strive to replicate or to surpass the deed himself, to win similar renown and related social capital"). Langlands 2018 ch. 4 claims that the key aspects of the process of learning from exempla are: (1) admiration, (2) comparison, (3) *aemulatio* (i.e. a feeling of rivalry with the actor in the *exemplum*), (4) modeling (i.e. taking the *exemplum* as a template for imitation), (5) cognition (i.e. increased understanding of the moral quality displayed by the *exemplum*), (6) discernment (i.e. honing the learner's skills of ethical discrimination and judgement).

[7] La Bua 2019: 301 notes the importance of this particular passage to later readers: "a rightly celebrated passage from the second book of the *De Officiis* (2.46) illustrates how imitation of the *exempla* of past generations was thought of as having a great impact on the learning process."

Yet, as Roller and Langlands have emphasized, the didactic role of *exempla* in Roman culture is rarely as straightforward as it may appear. As Roller notes, in many cases Roman exemplary discourse seems to ask the reader to engage in "*categorical*" imitation (i.e. in imitating the *virtuous nature* of a historical deed), rather than "*structural*" imitation (i.e. imitating the *specific actions* involved).[8] If this is what Cicero is asking his reader to do in *De Officiis*, his *exempla* would not provide a shortcut to appropriate action at all – instead, in order to engage in the relevant kind of imitation of Regulus' actions, the reader would require a full understanding of what, exactly, made them just, and so a deep engagement with the more argumentative sections of the text. On this model, then, far from allowing a novice reader to bypass the more difficult sections of the text, an understanding of ethical theory would be a prerequisite for the successful use of these *exempla* as models for correct action.

Interestingly, however, *De Officiis* does not align neatly with the conventions of the exemplary tradition in presenting its *exempla* primarily as candidates for imitation by the reader. Instead, while acknowledging the central role of imitation in early education, Cicero focuses on the problems inherent in taking others as models for imitation.[9] At 1.117–118, Cicero makes it clear that, as we enter adolescence, when there is the "greatest weakness of judgement" (*maxima imbecillitas consilii*) and "before one is able to judge what is best" (*ante… quam potuit, quod optimum est, iudicare*), we *do* indeed make our moral choices on the basis of imitation. But this is a decidedly sorry state of affairs – far better if we were like the divine Hercules, who, as a young man, was able to "debate with himself sitting down for a long time" about whether it would be better to take the path of Virtue or that of Pleasure. Unfortunately, we mere mortals have no such opportunity for prolonged theoretical reflection at a young age, but are condemned to imitate those around us (usually following in the footsteps of our parents). Imitation, then, is presented as an impoverished alternative to theoretical contemplation, but one that we must rely on in our early lives. However, Cicero warns us, even in our youth, when our powers of judgement are underdeveloped, we should not see such imitation as an excuse to bypass our critical skills: instead, adolescents "must not imitate the moral faults" of those they copy (*ne vitia sint imitanda*, 1.121), an injunction which, at the very least, requires the ability to differentiate

---

[8] Roller 2004: 24–25; see Langlands 2018: 95–100 for further Roman concerns about the mechanics of ethical imitation.
[9] See also Langlands' analysis of "the limitations of exemplary ethics," ch. 6 sec. 6, this volume.

Emulation and Moral Development in De Officiis

virtuous from vicious activities.[10] Cicero is clearly not here thinking in terms of Roller's "categorical," as opposed to "structural," imitation – we copy our parents in specific actions, like selecting a career as a statesman, rather than following them only in so far as we aim to be equally just – but nor does he admit of the possibility that uncritical imitation could act as a shortcut to correct behaviour for the novice ethicist.

The theoretical foundations for this concern that any real-life historical *exemplum* is an imperfect candidate for imitation are examined at the beginning of Book 3. Here, Cicero discusses the status of some of the figures held up as *exempla* in the *De Officiis*: the Decii (cited as examples of greatness of spirit at 1.61); the Scipiones (also mentioned as examples of greatness of spirit at 1.61, with the younger featuring again at 1.108–9 and the elder in the preface to Book 3); and Fabricius (who has been invoked as an *exemplum* of justice at 1.40, and will reappear as a figure who correctly judges that the immoral can never be truly expedient at 3.86–87).[11] We are told:

> But indeed, when the two Decii or the two Scipiones are mentioned as "brave men" or when Fabricius is called "just", a model (*exemplum*) of bravery is not sought from the former, nor a model of justice from the latter. For none of these men was wise in the sense that we wish "wise" to be understood. Nor were M. Cato and C. Laelius, those men who were held to be and named "the Wise", actually wise men. Not even the famous Seven were wise. But because of their repeated practice of the middle duties they bore a certain resemblance (*similitudo*) to and appearance (*species*) of wise men. (*Off.* 3.16)

Cicero is here repeating the familiar Stoic claim that the requirements for true wisdom are so stringent that it is either impossible or, at the very least, highly improbable that anyone could actually meet them.[12] But, whereas elsewhere Seneca tries to reconcile Stoic theory with traditional

---

[10] We see similar concerns that the Roman impulse towards imitation can lead us to adopt other's faults at 1.140, where Cicero complains that people imitate the vices of rich men such as L. Lucullus rather than their good traits; at 1.137, where he warns us not to imitate the arrogance of the protagonist in Plautus' *Miles Gloriosus*; and at 2.57, where Cicero complains that each new aedile imitates the excessive expenditure of his predecessor.

[11] The Fabricius passage at 1.40 is omitted by a number of our manuscripts, but, given that all the other figures mentioned in 3.16 have appeared in Book 1 of *De Officiis* it seems likely that Dyck 1996: 151 is correct in his judgement that this excision "surely cuts into living flesh by deleting the example of C. Fabricius."

[12] On this passage see further Langlands ch. 6 sec. 6, this volume. Cf. *Off.* 1.46: "we do not live with men who are perfect and completely wise, but with those who do exceptionally well if there are within themselves images of virtue (*simulacra virtutis*)." See Brouwer 2014: 97–112 and Sellars 2014: 36–41 for the broader Stoic context.

Roman exemplary discourse by saying that the gods have at least given us Cato as an *exemplar* of the wise man (*Const.* 2.1), here Cicero asks his reader *not* to view the *exempla* offered within his text as examples of truly virtuous behaviour. Instead, these illustrious historical personages have been able to attain only the "middle duty" available to the ordinary person.[13] As we become more philosophically schooled, we will be able to see the flaws (*quid vitii*) in the actions of those who achieve this "middle duty," just as, with training, we can come to see the faults in an imperfect painting or poem (3.15). For the student of *De Officiis*, then, the familiar figures of the Roman exemplary tradition can only ever be imperfect models, whose faults we must try to identify and avoid.

In addition to the imperfect nature of the real-life *exempla* provided in *De Officiis*, Cicero raises a further problem with relying on the imitation of our predecessors as a guide to ethical action. Not only are our chosen models likely to admit of flaws that should not be copied, but imitation of a given *exemplum* may not even be possible for us. As Cicero observes, when in early adolescence we try to follow the model of our forefathers, we may find that "our nature does not allow that certain things can be imitated" (1.121). Our own natural capacities may differ from our models to such an extent that we cannot successfully copy them, just as the poor health of the Elder Scipio's son prevented him from following the example of his father (ibid.). While Scipio the Elder may indeed have acted virtuously in defending his countrymen against Hannibal, he was, nevertheless, an inappropriate model of virtuous action for his son, whose ill health prevented him from engaging in these same activities.[14] Moreover, Cicero argues that these differences in individual nature (whether physical or psychological) affect not just the actions that we are capable of performing, but also the ethical value of any given action.[15] As he tells us, "these differences of nature have such force that sometimes one person ought to choose death for himself while another [in the same circumstances] should not" (1.112).[16] While it may have been right for Cato to commit suicide rather than to live under a tyrant, that is only because nature had provided him with a peculiar inflexibility of character. If others had followed his example, we are told, this

---

[13] To use the technical terminology introduced at *Off.* 1.8, they have attained the *medium/commune officium*, or *kathēkon*, rather than the *perfectum officium*, or *katorthōma*.

[14] And it is not just our physical limitations that may prevent us from following a positive *exemplum*. Cicero tells us that he himself cannot follow Scipio's example in taking strength from solitude, because he cannot imitate that figure's "exceptional character" (*ingenii praestantia*, 3.1).

[15] This problem is explored more fully in Langlands ch. 6 sec. 5, this volume.

[16] The words "in the same circumstances" (*in eadem causa*), while present in the codex Harleianus, are absent from other manuscripts and may be a post-Ciceronian scribal addition.

would not have been the correct choice; in fact, for anyone else, suicide may even have been immoral behaviour (*vitium*, 1.112).

This idea that the moral status of an action can change according to the identity of the agent is, as Brad Inwood has noted, a natural extension of the "situation ethics" championed by the Stoics.[17] As he notes, the available evidence suggests that "the Stoics advocated a situationally fluid, heuristic process of choice," which asks its followers to consider the unique circumstances in which they find themselves, rather than mechanically applying general rules for correct behaviour.[18] This aspect of Stoic thought is one that Cicero (presumably following his Panaetian model) embraces in *De Officiis*. As he tells us in his discussion of whether promises should always be kept: "occasions often occur when those things which seem to be most worthy of a just man (whom we call a 'good man') change and turn into their opposites" (1.31).[19] In most cases, Cicero tells us, it is, of course, right to keep a promise, but this is only because doing so usually promotes justice (here formulated as preventing harm from happening to anyone and fostering the common interest). In cases where keeping a promise would cause harm or detract from the common interest, however, this action would in fact be *against* the principles of justice and so would be unethical. Similarly, when Cicero turns to the question of tyrannicide at the beginning of Book 3, he notes that there is usually no greater crime than to kill a friend. Yet, "often it happens, due to the circumstances, that what is usually considered to be immoral is found not to be immoral" (3.19), and the case in which your friend happens to be a tyrant is one such instance. So, then, rather than relying on general rules like "always keep your promises" or "never kill a friend," we need to become "good calculators of our moral duties" (*boni ratiocinatores officiorum*, 1.59), deliberating on what might best promote justice in the particular circumstances in which we find ourselves.[20]

In *De Officiis*, we see this claim that the appropriate action to take can change according to our circumstances extended to include the idea that it

---

[17] Inwood 2005: 95–131 is an important discussion of situational flexibility in Stoic ethics. He turns to the necessity of considering the individual identity of the agent at 129: "another important category of factors to consider in selecting the right action and in giving a reasonable justification of one's selection will be the individual identity and character of the agent and the particular relationships in which she finds herself." Langlands 2011 and ch. 6 sec. 5, this volume, explores the connection between "situational ethics" and the exemplarity of *De Officiis* more fully.

[18] Inwood 2005: 98.

[19] *Sed incidunt saepe tempora, cum ea, quae maxime videntur digna esse iusto homine eoque, quem virum bonum dicimus, commutantur fiuntque contraria...*

[20] Cf. *Off.* 3.32, where we are told we must seek out our duty "based on our current circumstances" (*ex tempore*).

can also change according to the identity of the agent.[21] The "four-*personae* theory," discussed at 1.93–153, argues that when making moral choices we cannot think of ourselves as acting only in our role (*persona*) as rational human being (1.107) – an attitude which might lead us to think that, by virtue of our shared identity as humans, there should be a single appropriate action that anyone should take in a given circumstance.[22] Instead, we need to take into account the other roles that we hold, for example, our natural character as a fast runner or a witty conversationalist (1.107–110); the role we are born into in terms of our wealth and status (1.115); and any social roles we have selected for ourselves in choosing our lifestyle or careers (1.115).[23] Because we differ from each other in each of these roles, there can be no one-size-fits-all rule that prescribes a single correct behaviour for a given set of circumstances; rather, a key aspect of ethical decision-making is working out what action is most appropriate for each of us as an individual, given these various roles. As Cicero tells us, picking up the metaphor of our individual peculiarities as dramatic roles (*personae*), we should make our choices like good actors, who "select not the best plays, but the plays best suited to themselves" (1.114).

The idea that the correct course of action is dependent upon the identity of the agent, then, is a key part of the ethical theory of *De Officiis*. However, as Langlands has observed, this position poses obvious challenges for the traditional Roman view that positive *exempla* provide us with models of appropriate behaviour to be imitated.[24] According to the ethical theory of *De Officiis*, there can be no guarantee that what may have been the most appropriate action for Scipio in light of his peculiar combination of *personae*, would also be the correct course of action for us, given our own *personae*. And this is a consequence to which

---

[21] The extent to which either Panaetius or Cicero himself innovated upon earlier Stoic thought in formulating this position is the subject of debate. See Gill 1988: 174–175 (with references) for a variety of scholarly views. Inwood 2005: 129 is surely right to point out that it would be hard to imagine that Stoics before Panaetius had not taken the character of the agent into account: "… it would be a strange agent-centred ethical theory which did not in its theory of moral reasoning provide for the relevance of the particularities of each agent. The *persona* theory first reported for Panaetius (*Off.* 1.107ff.) is used in exactly this way, but there is no reason to conclude that he is the inventor of the theory."

[22] For the name "four-*personae* theory," as well as a comprehensive overview of the theory and its possible Greek origins, see Gill 1988.

[23] There is a lively debate as to whether this final *persona* pertains to one's individual personality or just one's particular role within society. See Gill 1988: 193 for the view that this fourth *persona* deals with "social roles [that] are correlated with distinct styles of living" and Sorabji 2006 for the view that it deals with the "unique persona" of an individual personality. This debate is continued in Sorabji 2008 and Gill 2008. Either way, this *persona* is clearly highly personalised and unlikely to be shared by the reader of *De Officiis* and an exemplary figure.

[24] Langlands 2011: 109–110.

Cicero draws our attention repeatedly in the text. As well as telling us that Cato's suicide, while the correct course of action for him as a unique agent, would be incorrect for others (1.112), Cicero points to the fact that the different characters of Ajax and Odysseus dictated that they should choose very different courses of action when faced with adversity (1.113). Similarly, at 1.148 we are told that "no-one should be led into the error of thinking that because Socrates or Aristippus did or said something ... it is right for him to do the same himself." Rather, the particular characters of these two exceptional men (their "great and divine goodness") mean that those behaviours, which were correct for them to adopt, would be incorrect for us.[25] Each of these historical figures, then, is invoked by Cicero not as a model to be copied, but in order to illustrate the very problem of taking historical *exempla* as models for imitation. Langlands takes these passages to be a warning from Cicero that we need to think carefully about exactly which *exempla* we should copy and "imitate others and follow their example only if we are equipped by nature to do so"[26] – and this is surely the case for those adolescents, mentioned earlier, whose undeveloped deliberative faculties mean that they must rely on imitation rather than reason (1.117–118).[27] But Cicero seems also to be raising a fundamental challenge to the idea that the mature ethical agent should read the *exempla* of the text primarily as models for imitation. The ethical theory of *De Officiis* is built around the idea that we need to calculate which course of action is most likely to promote virtue in our own unique circumstances; and, as is clear from Cicero's discussion, the imitation of illustrious figures from the past is no substitute for this kind of careful deliberation. As he tells us, you cannot achieve the consistency (*aequabilitas*) characteristic of a good person "if, by copying the natures of other people, you ignore your own" (1.111).

If the *exempla* of the *De Officiis* are not, then, presented primarily as models for imitation by the reader, the question becomes: what is their role in the text? How do they make the important contribution to the moral education of the reader promised in the opening sentences? As we shall see, Cicero focuses on three different, but related, functions for his *exempla*

---

[25] For the special dispensation of exceptional men to break moral taboos, see Inwood 2005: 101.
[26] Langlands 2011: 109.
[27] Cicero's instructions to his son, Marcus, to imitate his own deeds at 1.78 and 3.6 also fall under this category of instruction to the adolescent; but these particular instructions to follow in the footsteps of one's ancestors also avoid the problems in imitation discussed here, in that they focus on achieving the same outcomes (e.g. providing benefit to the Republic and gaining the repute that derives from this) rather than replicating specific behaviours. In doing this they fit in with the emulative use of *exempla* discussed later in this chapter, in Section 5.

within *De Officiis*. In the first instance, we are told that looking at the behaviour of others can help us to *develop the analytical skills* necessary to correctly deliberate about our own actions. Secondly, *exempla* work to *verify* the theoretical claims of *De Officiis*, showing (a) that the theoretical arguments of the text are applicable to real-life situations, and (b) that they reflect our intuitions about what constitutes correct or incorrect action. Finally, they show the *beneficial outcomes* of following the teachings of the text, in terms of the glory and praise that accrues to those who engage in correct action (though, as we shall see, this strategy is only effective because of Cicero's radical redefinition of the concepts of glory and praise in this text).

3 *Exempla* and (Self-)Analysis

As we have seen, the *De Officiis* asks us to determine the correct course of action not by copying the models of our forefathers, but by applying ethical theory to our own particular nature and circumstances. But, as the text informs us, this is not an easy task. Even if we have fully grasped the relevant moral theory, it can still be difficult to know how exactly to apply this to our own personal situation. As Cicero notes, we not only need the theory itself, but also practice in how to apply it:

> But, just as neither doctors nor generals nor orators are able – however well they might understand the general rules of their art – to achieve anything worthy of great praise without experience (*usus*) and practice (*exercitatio*), similarly, general rules on observing duty are handed down, as I myself am now doing, but a matter of such importance also requires experience and practice. (*Off.* 1.60)

It is all very well for Cicero to inform us that it is right to rehearse a court case on a solitary walk, but not at a dinner party; or to flirt at the games, but not at a business meeting (1.144) – but what if we are on a walk with a single close friend; or what if we run into a colleague while at the games? What we need to do is to practice applying this theory to real-life situations in order to develop the deliberative skills necessary to make these kinds of judgements successfully.

One way to get this necessary practice is, of course, by applying the ethical theory of *De Officiis* to the decisions we make in our own lives. But, as Cicero notes, while it may be easy enough for us to tell if we are making obviously poor choices (for example, engaging in the gross misconduct of singing in the forum), it can be difficult for us to identify smaller errors in judgement (1.145). If we want to be "keen and careful discerners of moral faults" (*acres ac diligentes ... animadversores vitiorum*), Cicero tells us, it is easiest to start by analyzing the behaviour of others:

> For somehow it is the case that we detect errors in others better than in ourselves. Consequently, in teaching, those students are most easily improved whose faults the teachers imitate in order to correct. (*Off.* 1.146)

As Cicero notes, we can use the relative ease with which we identify faults in others to our advantage in two distinct ways: we can engage someone else to act like the teacher in the above passage and point out our own flaws to us from a third person perspective (just as painters, sculptors, and poets present their work for public review, 1.147); or we can observe others in an attempt to identify their faults, then apply whatever we learn from this to an analysis of our own actions ("it is advantageous to judge the nature of each action from [the actions of] others, so that, if there is anything unseemly in these, we may ourselves avoid it," 1.146). Assessing the moral quality of the behaviour of others, then, can provide us with the opportunity to practice our skills of ethical analysis, and so enables us to better discern the complexities of our own situation.

The educational experience that is gained by analyzing the behaviour of those around us in real life has its parallel, in the literary world of *De Officiis*, in the analysis of the actions of historical figures. Cicero often asks us to apply our skills of moral judgement to the situations described in his *exempla*.[28] The most developed of these is the *exemplum* of Regulus at 3.99–112, and Cicero's approach here demonstrates how we might sharpen our powers of ethical discernment by analyzing the actions of others.[29] After describing the actions of Regulus, who refused to break an oath given to the enemy to save his own life, Cicero provides a number of possible reasons that someone might think his action was incorrect. Regulus may have erred because he: (a) foolishly chose to engage in an action that caused harm to himself (3.101); (b) misjudged the negative consequences of breaking his oath, by mistakenly believing that he would be the subject of divine anger (3.102); and (c) did not correctly judge the ethical demands

---

[28] E.g. *Off.* 2.25 when he asks us "*quid censemus?*" ("what do we think?") of the life of the tyrants Dionysius and Alexander of Pherae; 3.85 when he asks of Caesar "*quas conscientiae labes in animo censes habuisse?*" ("what stains do you think he had on his conscience?"); or 3.73 when he asks us whether the actions of M. Crassus and Q. Hortensius should be considered immoral (*satin est hoc, ut non deliquisse videantur?* "Is this enough that they seem not to have committed a crime?"). He is even more explicit at 3.81, where he orders his reader: "untangle and work out your own idea, as it seems to you, of what is the form and concept of a good man" in the context of determining whether Marius was a good man.

[29] For a more extensive analysis of the Regulus *exemplum* as "ethical deliberation in action," see Langlands ch. 6 sec. 2, this volume.

of his immediate circumstances, by treating an oath exacted under force by the enemy in the same way as an oath given voluntarily to a friend (3.103). In raising these objections, Cicero demonstrates the kind of considerations we might bring to bear when, as "keen and careful observers of moral faults," we analyze the actions of another.

But Cicero goes a step further in leading us through the Regulus *exemplum* and shows us that, to assess accurately whether any of these factors really did constitute a moral error, we need to refer them back to the fundamental principles of our ethical theory. As he demonstrates, each of these potential objections disappears under a more considered analysis: (a) Regulus would have caused more substantial harm to himself if he had *not* kept his oath, as anything that harms our political community also harms ourselves (3.101); (b) Regulus appropriately judged the negative consequences of breaking his oath, because he understood that committing an immoral act harms the perpetrator spiritually (3.106); and (c) although Regulus' oath was made to an enemy, it was a legitimate enemy in the context of a just war and, as such, he had certain moral responsibilities towards them (3.107). By leading us through this working example of Regulus' actions, then, Cicero shows us how, by looking at the behaviour of others, we can practice applying the moral theory of *De Officiis* to the analysis of real-world situations. And he concludes not by saying that we should imitate Regulus in our own lives, but by highlighting that we should have learned something from this exercise: "it is clear that those things which are done with a cowardly, base, wanting, and broken spirit, such as the deed of Regulus would have been if he had given advice about the captives as seemed to be in his own interest rather than in that of the state, or else he had wanted to remain at home, are not beneficial, because they are disgraceful, shameful, and dishonourable" (3.115).

So, then, we can see in Cicero's treatment of Regulus a model for how we might go about analyzing the behaviours of others, and, thereby, develop the skills needed to assess our own. In doing this, Cicero is careful to point out that the choice of Regulus is as close as one can get to analyzing the actual behaviour of other moral agents within the constraints of a literary text. At 3.99, he notes that this is neither a *fabula* (a myth) nor *externa* (a tale from a foreign land), but rather is *res facta nostraque* (a real, Roman historical event). This, then, leads us to the second role of the *exempla* in *De Officiis*: illustrating that the teachings of the text are practicable in real-world contexts, and that the moral claims of the text are verified by our own experience.

4 *Exempla* and Practical Ethics

An additional important function of the historical *exempla* in *De Officiis* is to bridge the gap between ethical theory and practice. By presenting us with historical examples that are amenable to analysis in the terms recommended by the text, Cicero shows us that the types of moral reasoning advocated in *De Officiis* can be successfully applied to real-world events.

From the very beginning of the work, Cicero is clear to point out that the unique value of this study of moral duty is that it can be applied to each and every situation in which we find ourselves:

> For, although in philosophy many serious and beneficial matters have been discussed accurately and extensively by philosophers, those things seem to be most widely applicable (*latissime patere*) that are handed down and ordered by them concerning moral duties (*officia*). For no part of life – whether public or private, in the forum or at home, in activities you undertake by yourself or those you engage in with others – is able to be free from moral duty. (*Off.* 1.4)

Throughout *De Officiis*, then, Cicero illustrates his claims concerning the universal applicability of the theory contained within the text by presenting us with a range of historical *exempla*: real-life scenarios in which we can see the concerns of Stoic moral theory at work. We find, for example, the general claim of Book 3 that no immoral action can ever be truly beneficial applied to historical situations as diverse as: the forgery of L. Minucius Basilus' will (3.73), Marius' public criticism of his military commander (3.79), and L. Philippus' drafting of financial legislation (3.87). In showing how the concepts of Stoic philosophy can be applied to actual historical situations (and, indeed, to the kinds of mundane ethical decisions that are likely to be familiar from the reader's own life), Cicero demonstrates that the abstract theory of *De Officiis* is relevant to the kinds of everyday decisions that confront his Roman audience.

Of course, at points in the work, Cicero draws upon examples from poetry and myth to illustrate more exotic moral dilemmas;[30] but, as we have already seen in the way that he urges us to move our attention from myths and foreign events to the realities of Roman history when introducing the *exemplum* of Regulus at 3.99, he seems aware that these are often less effective within a text that claims to help us to deal with the kinds of ethical decisions that we confront in our day-to-day lives. Cicero

---

[30] E.g. *Off.* 3.97 for the story that Odysseus feigned madness to avoid going to Troy, as recounted by tragedians.

explores this concern that fictional or hypothetical examples can interfere with our ability to see the practical value of philosophical learning in his treatment at 3.38–39 of Plato's myth of Gyges. Here Cicero presents us with the objections of those who are not morally bad, but are not intellectually sharp enough (*non satis acuti*) to understand the subtleties of Plato's mythological excursus.[31] They complain that Plato's story is a "fictitious and false tale" (*ficta et commenticia fabula*), and refuse to engage with it as a meaningful example of practical ethics on the grounds that the situation described is impossible.[32] This concern that his audience will find it more difficult to engage with the hypothetical than the historical also motivates Cicero's didactic choices in other texts, perhaps most strikingly in *De Re Publica*, where Scipio opts to lay out the political organization of the historical Roman state rather than inventing an imaginary state in the manner of Plato, on the grounds that this will make his argument easier.[33]

Even on those rare occasions when Cicero does provide us with hypothetical rather than historical scenarios, he is careful to demonstrate their connection to the kinds of real-world behaviour described in his historical *exempla*. At 3.75, Cicero introduces his own rival thought experiment to illustrate Plato's claim that an immoral act can never be beneficial, even if it is committed without the possibility of being detected. The scenario ultimately described by Cicero is no less outlandish than that introduced by Plato's Glaucon in recounting the Gyges myth: Cicero asks us to consider whether a good man would take advantage of his powers if he were to find that he could magically appear as a beneficiary in a rich man's will by snapping his fingers.[34] But this imaginary scenario is introduced by Cicero as a stronger version of a situation that exists in real life, following, as it does, directly upon the *exemplum* of L. Minucius Basilus' will (3.73). Marcus Crassus, we are told, thought that he benefitted from being secretly entered into Basilus' will as an heir; in reality, though, he caused harm to himself by committing the immoral act of depriving the true heirs of what was rightly theirs. The man with the power to snap his fingers and appear in a will, then, is, in terms of the moral choice he has to make ("should I commit a crime, knowing I will not be discovered?"),

---

[31] *Off.* 3.39. Interestingly, he attributes these complaints to "certain philosophers" (*philosophi quidam*), presumably, as Woolf 2013: 804 and *passim* has argued, referring to the Epicureans.
[32] For a more complete analysis of the philosophical stakes behind Cicero's insistence on the impossibility of the Gyges story, see Woolf 2013.
[33] *Rep.* 2.3.
[34] Woolf 2013: 804 notes that, in introducing a second magical device to accompany the renewed discussion of the ring of Gyges here, Cicero is imitating Plato, who has Glaucon introduce the cap of Hades when the conversation returns to the ring of Gyges in *Republic* 10 (612b1–4).

presented as a superpowered version of a real-life Roman legacy seeker. Indeed, Cicero highlights the similarity between his historical and hypothetical examples by eliding the distinction between the characters in the real-world *exemplum* and in the thought experiment. At the conclusion of the thought experiment, Cicero asks us to imagine that it is, in fact, Crassus himself who has access to this magic power, and suggests that, in this situation, Crassus would make exactly the same error of judgement as he did in the case of Basilus' will, being so delighted by this apparent benefit that he would dance in the forum (3.75). So, even when *De Officiis* does turn to hypotheticals, Cicero works to show their relevance to everyday life by appealing to the real-life figures of historical *exempla*.

As we have seen, the *exempla* of the *De Officiis* work to illustrate that the moral theory of the text is applicable to everyday life. Furthermore, in allowing us to consider how the teachings of the text might apply to real-world examples, these *exempla* also provide us with an opportunity to assess the effectiveness of this framework in a real-life context. That the *exempla* have this verificatory function – demonstrating that the theory presented in the text makes good sense of the moral choices we face and is in keeping with our intuitions about what behaviours are right or wrong – is something that Cicero draws our attention to at various points. The *exemplum* just discussed, concerning the forged will of L. Minucius Basilus, is introduced with the instruction "let us put this to the test, if you please, also in the case of certain *exempla*, in which perhaps the common man does not think an error is committed" (*Off.* 3.73). The subjunctive "let us put this to the test" (*periclitemur*) directs the reader as to how she is supposed to use these *exempla*: we are asked to view them as hard test cases against which we might judge the success of the text's philosophical claims. The fact that we can all agree that Crassus was wrong to accept a fraudulent inheritance acts as proof for Cicero's claim that there is no true benefit to be gained from crime, even when committed in secrecy. At various other points, *exempla* are introduced as "witnesses" (*testes*) to the veracity of the claims made in the text. To verify his claim that power cannot be long-lasting if it is produced through fear, Cicero adduces the *exemplum* of the tyrant Phalaris as a "witness."[35] To support Socrates' position that true glory can never be won by deception, Cicero says he could appeal to "very many witnesses" but confines himself to *exempla* from the family of the Gracchi.[36] At 3.105, meanwhile, we are asked to consider Regulus (whose exemplary tale was

---

[35] *Off.* 2.26: *testis est Phalaris*
[36] *Off.* 2.44.

discussed in the previous section) as "a not unimportant witness" (*testis non mediocris*) to the Stoic claim that pain is not an evil.

The function that is here attributed to the *exempla* of the *De Officiis*, then, is parallel to that of witnesses in a legal case: they are intended to be taken as proofs of the accuracy of the author's argumentative claims, just as a witness is proof of the accuracy of the orator's. That this use of *exempla* is fundamental to Cicero's didactic strategy in *De Officiis* is clear from the fact that he attributes this same function to the *exempla* contained in his Greek model. At 2.16, he criticises Panaetius for having cited the *exempla* of Themistocles, Pericles, Cyrus, Agesilaus, and Alexander to prove a point that was so obvious as to need no proof: "he calls witnesses that are not needed in service of an issue that is not in doubt" (*utitur in re non dubia testibus non necessariis*).

5 *Exempla* and Emulation

We have seen, then, how the historical *exempla* of the *De Officiis* work to verify the teachings of the text, by acting as "witnesses" to the particular philosophical claims made, for example the idea that pain is not an evil. More generally, however, they also act as collective evidence for the fundamental claim of Book 3 that our lives will be better if we prioritise ethical behaviour: "whatever is morally right is also beneficial, and nothing which is beneficial is not morally right."[37] They do this by illustrating to the reader the desirable consequences of correct action, showing that the rewards of glory (*gloria*), praise (*laus*), and honours (*honores*) come to those who conduct their lives according to the teachings of the text. At 3.85 Caesar's assassins are said to have earned "gratitude and glory in perpetuity" (*in maxima et gratia ... et gloria*) for their services to the Roman people; Aratus of Sicyon, we are told at 2.81, is "rightly praised" (*iure laudatur*) for having justly overseen the redistribution of property after a change in government; at 2.58 we are told that Orestes has recently won great honour (*magnus honos*) on account of his generosity. These examples are representative of a larger pattern.[38] Similarly we are also shown the social sanctions that have accrued to those who make poor ethical choices. The Athenian Cyrsilus was stoned to death by his fellow citizens for proposing surrender to the Persians (3.48); Caesar was subject to loathing (*invidia*) for his ambitions of tyranny (3.82); ill-repute (*infamia*)

---

[37] *Off.* 3.20.
[38] E.g. Fabricius receiving praise from the senate for refusing an offer to kill Pyrrhus by treachery (3.87); Africanus' earning of praise at 2.76; and 3.110–111 for the praise of Regulus and his times.

and hatred (*odium*) fell upon the Roman state when it reneged on a taxation treaty with its allies (3.88).[39] The historical *exempla*, then, show that those who have engaged in ethical behaviour have earned the reward of social approbation, while those who have ignored their moral duties have been punished with infamy, and so support the claim that the morally right is also beneficial.

The focus on the social rewards of an exemplary action is typical of Roman exemplary discourse. As Roller has noted, this emphasis plays a key role in the didactic function of an *exemplum*, in that it can generate in the reader a desire to gain similar rewards to the exemplary figure, and so motivate her to change her own behaviour.[40] In this same way, the *exempla* of the *De Officiis* serve to dramatize the desirable consequences of adopting the teachings of the text, and provide an emotional stimulus to internalise these lessons (namely, the desire to attain these benefits). Langlands terms this emotional response to an exemplary action *aemulatio*, or "emulation," and describes its effect as being "to rouse the receptive moral agent to desire to mould their own behaviour accordingly."[41] At times, we can see Cicero working to rouse this "emulative" emotion in his reader by stressing the desirability of the rewards of correct action. At 3.82, for example, he argues that the social reward of good reputation is not just desirable, but is, in fact, more valuable than anything else: "Is there, then, anything of such great value or any benefit so worth seeking that you would give up the renown (*splendor*) and reputation (*nomen*) of a good man?" The idea that social approval is a uniquely valuable asset finds its fullest treatment in Book 2, where Cicero discusses the relationship between glory and justice. Here Cicero argues not only that good reputation (here a "reputation for justice," *opinio iustitiae*) is the customary source of political power (2.42), but also that it is necessary for survival (2.39). He does this using two complementary sets of *exempla*: the historical *exempla* of the Medes and early Romans who used to select those with the best reputation as their kings; and the hypothetical *exemplum* of the man who lives in voluntary solitude in the countryside but still requires the goodwill of his fellow man to protect him from harm. With these two groups of *exempla* – the former

---

[39] See also e.g. 3.86 where winning a war through treachery is said to be "a great shame and disgrace" (*magnum dedecus et flagitium*).

[40] Roller 2004: 32 argues that exemplary texts often emphasise the glory that accrues to a particular deed, in order to create in the reader "the impulse to imitate, to gain similar glory."

[41] Langlands 2018: 94. The use of the term "emulation" to describe this constructive emotional response is not entirely consonant with Cicero's own view of *aemulatio* (*Tusc.* 4.16–17); instead it seems to be adopted from Kristján Kristjánsson's translation of Aristotle's *zēlos* as "emulation" (2006: 42).

of which serves to highlight the benefits of good reputation and the latter the potentially fatal consequences of its loss – Cicero is activating not just his reader's desires, but also her anxieties. By engaging these "emulative" emotions, then, the *exempla* of De Officiis allow the reader to engage emotionally with the text, as well as intellectually. In doing this, they have the potential to motivate us to adopt the teachings of the text, and so help us on our path to moral progress in a way in which the argumentative sections of the text cannot.

In emphasising the social rewards that come from ethical behaviour and using the promise of such rewards to drive the reader to correct action, Cicero is acting within the framework of typical Roman exemplary discourse, appropriating its "emulative" emotional sway and accompanying didactic power. However, in order to press these into service of the philosophy of *De Officiis*, Cicero needs to challenge the reader's basic assumptions concerning the identity of those social rewards towards which our "emulative" emotions are directed. As A. A. Long has observed, Cicero radically redefines the concepts that lie at the heart of the traditional Roman value system: according to *De Officiis*, the rewards we should be seeking are not the glory, praise, and honours common to everyday language, but *true* glory and the *merited* praise and honours that accompany it.[42] The relationship between true glory and ethically correct behaviour is examined in 2.32–38. Here we learn that virtue (here the *honestum* or *decorum*) is naturally pleasing to human beings, with the result that, whenever we see this quality in others, we are naturally compelled to approve of it (*a natura ipsa diligere cogimur*, 2.32).[43] This form of social approval, which derives naturally from morally correct behaviour, is "*true* glory" (*vera gloria*, 2.43),[44] and it is acquired only by carrying out the moral duties (*officia iustitiae*) laid out in *De Officiis*. So, Cicero tells us, you cannot win true glory by pretending to be good;[45] you cannot win glory through crime;[46] and you cannot win glory from treachery.[47] As for those concomitant social rewards – praise and honours – we find these similarly redefined at the very beginning of *De Officiis*, when Cicero chooses the term *honestum*

---

[42] Long 1995: 217: "Cicero preserves the traditional connotations of the buzz words *laus, decus* etc., but thanks to his use of Greek philosophy he has shifted their denotations."
[43] See also 2.37 where we are told no-one could fail to admire the splendor and beauty of virtue.
[44] At *Off.* 2.31 it is called the "highest and perfect glory" (*summa … et perfecta gloria*).
[45] *Off.* 2.43: "everything false (*ficta omnia*) quickly falls like flowers, nor is anything feigned (*simulatum*) able to be long-lasting."
[46] *Off.* 3.87: "crime must be absent, in which there can be no glory."
[47] *Off.* 1.62: "no-one has attained praise who has pursued the glory of bravery through treachery or bad behaviour, for nothing can be morally right that lacks justice."

to denote something which is *worthy* of honour (i.e. the morally correct), rather than that which actually receives honour in everyday life:

> What we seek is the morally right (*honestum*), which, even if it is not actually treated as noble (*nobilitatum*), is none the less worthy of being honoured (*honestum*); and which, we say truly, even if it is praised by no-one (*a nullo laudetur*), is by its nature praiseworthy (*laudabile*). (*Off.* 1.14)[48]

The objects of our "emulative" emotions – glory, praise, and honours – which, in the traditional exemplary discourse are merely descriptive (denoting that which gains social approval), become, in *De Officiis*, normative (denoting that which *should* gain social approval).[49] So, while Cicero may indeed activate our "emulative" emotions through his use of *exempla*, he also tries to redirect them, pushing us to perform actions which earn the *true* glory reserved for morally correct behaviour, rather than the so-called glory of political power or acclaim by the mob.

In his attempt to draw the distinction between true glory and the so-called glory of everyday language, Cicero runs the risk of appearing problematically circular. Things which are virtuous are "rightly praised,"[50] and it is this true glory that verifies them as being virtuous; but it seems that we can only tell that something is praised "rightly" because this praise is in response to something virtuous – everything else is praised "according to the error of the ignorant mob."[51] So, it seems true glory is being appealed to in order to verify the virtue of an action; yet, simultaneously, we need to know whether an action is virtuous in order to tell whether the praise it receives is true glory, or only so-called glory.[52] One final way in which the *exempla* of the *De Officiis* help the reader to accept the philosophical teachings of the text is to make this relationship between true glory and virtuous action seem less viciously circular, and the distinction between true glory and so-called glory less *ad hoc*. The *exempla* of the text are able to achieve this because they are, themselves, instances of social reward or punishment. The positive *exempla* of the text commemorate and praise the actions of the historical figures they describe, so rewarding them in literary

---

[48] Long 1995: 218: "This punning definition is an indication of [Cicero's] radical attempt to detach 'the honourable' from the traditional honour code and to conceptualize it in terms of what is intrinsically or naturally good."

[49] Long 1995: 229.

[50] E.g. *iure laudatur* 2.81.

[51] *Off.* 1.65: *ex errore imperitae multitudinis*. Cf. 3.15 for the claim that the ignorant (*ignari*) "praise that which does not deserve praise" (*laudentque ea, quae laudanda non sint*).

[52] For a Roman reader, this problem would doubtless have been mitigated by their familiarity with the arguments of Cicero's *De Gloria*, a text which is, unfortunately, no longer extant (see Plasberg and Simbeck 1917 for fragments).

form with the praise, honour, and glory so important to the Roman value system.[53] The negative *exempla*, meanwhile, pick out particular historical figures for criticism, so tarring them with the ill-repute and infamy that engages the reader's "emulative" emotions through its sheer abhorrence. In this way, then, as Cicero criticises those historical figures who have committed immoral actions, he also provides a corrective to any praise they may have received, showing this glory to be improperly founded and unstable, such that it will disappear whenever subjected to rigorous philosophical analysis.[54] In other words, their treatment in *De Officiis* itself reveals them to be recipients of so-called glory, rather than true glory.

We can see Cicero's strategy in his treatment of the *exempla* of the dictators, Caesar and Sulla. In his discussion of these figures, Cicero emphasises that their socially destructive actions were aimed at attaining what they took to be glory. Caesar, we are told, was motivated to pursue one-person rule by the "desire for glory" (*gloriae cupiditas*, 1.26). Caesar and Sulla, meanwhile, undertook the redistribution of property because they were "desirous of renown and glory" (*cupidi splendoris et gloriae*) (1.43). But, the *De Officiis* tells us, Caesar, in his desire for glory, perverted all laws of gods and men under the influence of an "error of opinion" (*opinionis errore*, 1.26); and, along with Sulla, he acted unjustly in depriving his fellow citizens of their rightful property (1.43). Whatever praise the ignorant mob may have bestowed on them at the time, then, is corrected by Cicero's criticism of these figures in *De Officiis*. On this analysis, the glory they aimed at is shown to be hollow and short-lived social approval which they, mistakenly, took to be glory, rather than the true glory championed by the text. Instead, it is Caesar's assassins who will win "gratitude and glory in perpetuity" (*in maxima et gratia ... et gloria*) for their virtuous behaviour in freeing the Roman state from tyranny (3.85). That our approval for the actions of these men is stable, enduring, and survives the thorough analysis of the *De Officiis*, is what marks it out as *true* glory. As Cicero tells us:

> True glory (*vera gloria*) takes root and even spreads out; everything false (*ficta omnia*) quickly falls like flowers, nor is anything feigned able to be long-lasting (*diuturnum*). (*Off.* 2.43)

Cicero's distinction between so-called glory and true glory is, then, revealed to be not just a verbal trick, but a fact of life. There are some real-life figures, such as Caesar and Sulla, who aim at something they take to be glory, only

---

[53] For the status of *exempla* as instances of commemoration, see Roller 2004: 4.
[54] See Section 3 of this paper for an account of the kind of rigorous philosophical analysis Cicero asks us to apply to these *exempla*.

to find themselves marked out by posterity as recipients of blame, rather than the lasting praise associated with true glory – a fact that is proved by their critical treatment in *De Officiis* itself. What Caesar and Sulla took to be glory (and what we call "glory" in everyday language), then, cannot be *true* glory at all, as it results in the punishment of social disapproval rather than the reward of social approbation. Furthermore, this treatment shows that the counterfeit, so-called glory is identifiable not only because it derives from misplaced praise, but also because such praise is short-lived and subject to correction in the later exemplary tradition. The possible circularity of Cicero's treatment of the relationship between true glory and virtue, then, is broken through his appeal to historical *exempla* that show true glory to be differentiated from so-called glory by its enduring nature as well as by having its basis in moral action. Indeed, Cicero appeals to an *exemplum* as a witness (*testis*) in support of his claim that so-called glory is transient while true glory persists: the virtuous Tiberius Gracchus, the son of Publius, will be praised (*laudabitur*) as long as the memory of Rome shall endure; his immoral sons, on the other hand, are held in disrepute by the annals of history.[55]

Cicero's redefinition of glory as something that accrues only to those who engage in morally correct behaviour is, then, shown to be externally supported through the historical record – of which *De Officiis* is itself, in its wide-ranging use of *exempla*, a part. In using historical *exempla* to support this distinction between the lasting approval of true glory and the fleeting reward of so-called glory, Cicero is also able to figure the moral teachings of *De Officiis* as being, in fact, congruent with the traditional Roman value system that he appears to be challenging. Because the true glory that derives from moral behaviour is characterized by its long-lasting nature, we can see it in *exempla* from the more distant Roman past. The mistaken striving for so-called glory, in contrast, is revealed to be an error of recent figures, such as Sulla and Caesar, and it is one that the exemplary tradition will, in time, show to be misguided (as we can see in the treatment of these figures within *De Officiis* itself). Cicero represents the exemplary figures of the ancient past as having their "emulative" emotions aimed in the right direction, being driven by desire for the *true* glory that

---

[55] *Off.* 2.43: "There are many witnesses on both sides, but, for the sake of brevity, I will limit myself to one family. For Tiberius Gracchus, the son of Publius, will be praised for so long as the memory of the Roman state persists; but his sons were not approved of by good men while they were alive, and now that they are dead they are numbered among those who were justly killed." *testes sunt permulti in utramque partem, sed brevitatis causa familia contenti erimus una. Tiberius enim Gracchus, P. f., tam diu laudabitur, dum memoria rerum Romanarum manebit, at eius filii nec vivi probabantur bonis et mortui numerum optinent iure caesorum.*

is earned through virtuous behaviour, rather than the counterfeit glory of short-lived honours or approval. In the good old days before Sulla, we are told, "our magistrates and commanders desired to attain the greatest praise (*maximam laudem capere studebant*) by means of this one thing: if they defended their provinces and allies with justice and fidelity" (2.26). It would be difficult, Cicero tells us, to find an *exemplum* more praiseworthy or outstanding (*aut laudabilius aut praestantius*, 3.110) than his climactic example of Regulus. But, we are told, in conducting his life in the morally correct manner that has earned him the enduring praise of true glory, Regulus was doing nothing that was not characteristic of his time: "this praise," we are told, "belongs to the age, not to the man."[56]

Through his use of Roman historical *exempla*, then, Cicero is able to figure the Panaetian philosophy of *De Officiis* as a return to traditional Roman ethics. In doing so, he reassures his readers that, in redirecting their "emulative" emotions towards the true glory earned by morally correct behaviour, they will not be engaging in a radical overthrow of the traditional Roman value system, but, instead, in a return to the ethos of the noble Roman past. In this way, the *exempla* of the *De Officiis* ask us to look to the figures of the distant Roman past, but, rather than asking us to imitate their actions, it asks us to adopt their definition of glory. In focusing our "emulative" emotions towards true glory, Cicero provides us with a lasting reward for correct moral behaviour, and so provides his reader with a reason to turn her efforts towards making moral progress and to engage fully with the lessons of the *De Officiis*.

---

[56] *Off.* 3.111: *itaque ista laus non est hominis, sed temporum.*

PART IV
Self and Society

CHAPTER 8

Care of the (Written) Self
Literary and Ethical Decorum in De Officiis

Caroline Bishop

1 Introduction

The discussion of decorum in Book One of *De Officiis* (1.93–151) has long been one of the more influential sections of the work. The culmination of its account of the four virtues, it represents a striking innovation in the history of ethical thought – both within Cicero's Roman milieu and in the Greek tradition of his source, Panaetius – for its importation of an aesthetic term, τὸ πρέπον or *decorum* (as Cicero translates it), into the sphere of ethics. In ancient scholarship, this term, used to describe something fitting, appropriate, or coherent, frequently served as a criterion for determining the quality of a piece of poetry; it also held a prominent position in oratory as one of the virtues of rhetorical style. By adopting this aesthetic term as a standard by which one's ethical self should be defined, Cicero advances a conception of the self defined in distinctly literary terms: as, in essence, a text that should be worked up in private until perfected, and only then revealed to the world. This concept proved influential not just upon future generations of Romans, but indeed the Western idea of the self writ large.

In this chapter, I will explore both Cicero's and Panaetius' motivations for adopting τὸ πρέπον as an ethical category. Panaetius, as I will show, was an innovator who foreshadowed several important trends in later philosophy, while Cicero recognized how well-suited Panaetius' innovations were to the dramatic changes in elite Roman life that took place during his lifetime. I will close with a brief consideration of the legacy of this new formulation, by demonstrating how Horace's equally influential *Ars Poetica* evinces a thorough acceptance of Cicero's aestheticized self.

2 The *De Officiis* in Context

I will begin by examining the changing political and social conditions that produced Cicero's *De Officiis,* and that made the importation of this literary/rhetorical term into the field of ethics an especially suitable choice. In the five years that preceded the composition of the work in late 44 BCE, the civil war and Caesar's accession to the dictatorship had profoundly unsettled the typical rhythms of elite life. Its parade of elected offices, priesthoods, and important court cases – all time-honored routes for achieving glory and the moral goodness presumed to go hand-in-hand with it – had been disrupted. New ways of acquiring distinction had to be devised, and the hope that the production of written works might serve as a suitable substitute for the honors that had once been achieved through political life animates many of the works Cicero composed after the civil war.[1]

Writing was a medium that suited the times and the mood: the growing group of Greek intellectuals in Rome and a concomitant increase in scholarly and literary materials had already made literary production an increasingly popular route for acclaim.[2] Moreover, the foreclosure of traditional paths to aristocratic distinction encouraged a shift in the period following the civil war to private self-care and a self-display predicated on activities performed in one's leisure time. The conception in *De Officiis* of an inner self meticulously groomed according to aesthetic dictates before being revealed to the world thus accords nicely with Cicero's larger shift in thinking at this time, when he also began to conceive of literary and rhetorical works being produced in private before appearing in public as a proxy for his former forensic and political activities.

Cicero discusses this shift explicitly in a number of works written after the civil war. In his earliest post-war dialogue, the *Brutus*, he visualizes an "orphaned eloquence ... penned up at home under an honorable guard," a statement that underlines the profound changes that had already occurred in oratorical activity and foreshadows the transition to declamation as the principal source of elite rhetorical display.[3] And at many points in the prefaces to contemporary philosophical works, Cicero describes their publication as a substitute for his political activities, as, for example, in the *De Natura Deorum*:

> Nam cum otio langueremus et is esset rei publicae status ut eam unius consilio atque cura gubernari necesse esset, primum ipsius rei publicae causa philosophiam nostris hominibus explicandam putavi, magni existimans

---

[1] This topic is discussed in detail by Narducci 1997, Dugan 2005, Steel 2005, and Baraz 2012.
[2] Bishop 2019b discusses the increased use of writing as a medium for obtaining glory in this period.
[3] *Brut.* 330: *nos autem, Brute, quoniam ... orbae eloquentiae quasi tutores relicti sumus, domi teneamus eam saeptam liberali custodia.* All translations are my own. Stroup 2003 discusses the implications of this passage.

> interesse ad decus et ad laudem civitatis res tam gravis tamque praeclaras Latinis etiam litteris contineri. (*ND* 1.7)
>
> When I was listless from leisure and the state of the republic was such that it was necessary for it to be ruled by the advice and care of a single man, I thought that for the sake of the republic itself it was worth setting out philosophy for my fellow citizens, judging it to be of great value for the glory and the renown of the state that such weighty matters and such excellent ones be expressed in Latin.

While it is the glory and renown of the republic that Cicero explicitly mentions enlarging here, it is clear that (just as was the case in his political career) by increasing the republic's glory, he adds to his own.[4]

Of course, these philosophical works were not solely devised to regain the prestige Cicero had lost from a stalled career. There is a certain urgency in the choice of philosophy as his subject matter, and especially in the writings composed in the period between Caesar's assassination in March 44 BCE and Cicero's decision to renew his political career by opposing Antony in the winter of 44–43. Of the five treatises written in this span, three – *De Amicitia,* the now-lost *De Gloria,* and *De Officiis* – are concerned with concepts central to elite self-identity.[5] In these works, Cicero not only grapples with the role that these concepts played in the breakdown of civic order at Rome, he also seeks to redefine them in a way suitable to Rome's changed political and social circumstances; the uncertainty that followed the civil war called for a way to practice glory, duties, and friendship (and hence both be, and be recognized as, a morally upright individual) in an environment detached from the traditional paths to obtaining these concepts.[6] Cicero's goal in these works was to place these ideals upon a more philosophically secure foundation, which would also have the benefit of making them practicable in a more private-facing environment.

It is within this context that *De Officiis* must be understood. In the preface to the second book, Cicero provides one of his most explicit statements on how philosophical writing has come to substitute for the activities of his former career:

> Atque utinam res publica stetisset quo coeperat statu nec in homines non tam commutandarum quam evertendarum rerum cupidos incidisset!

---

[4] Similar statements appear in several other works written during Caesar's dictatorship (e.g., *Tusc.* 1.7, *Fin.* 1.10, *Div.* 2.1–7).
[5] Of the other two works written at this time, *De Fato* completes a long-planned trilogy of theological works (as the follow-up to *De Natura Deorum* and *De Divinatione*), while the *Topica*, like the *Brutus* and *Orator*, reconceptualizes rhetoric as more an academic than a practical course of study.
[6] Habinek 1990: 166–67 and Long 1995: 224 note this aspect of the three works.

> Primum enim, ut stante re publica facere solebamus, in agendo plus quam in scribendo operae poneremus, deinde ipsis scriptis non ea, quae nunc, sed actiones nostras mandaremus, ut saepe fecimus. Cum autem res publica, in qua omnis mea cura, cogitatio, opera poni solebat, nulla esset omnino, illae scilicet litterae conticuerunt forenses et senatoriae. (*Off.* 2.3)
>
> If only the republic still stood in its original state and had not fallen among men who wanted not so much to change it as to overturn it! If it did, I would, first of all, be putting my efforts more into pleading cases than into writing, as I was accustomed to do when the republic was standing. Second, I would not be committing to writing the subject matter that I am now, but rather my speeches, as I used to do. But when the republic, into which I used to put all my care, my thought, and my effort, no longer existed, then, as you know, that forensic and senatorial literature of mine fell silent.

Here Cicero puts more frankly than ever what he had largely hinted at in earlier philosophical and rhetorical works.[7] In those works, to be sure, philosophical/rhetorical writing is figured as an alternative source of prestige for the writing and speaking that Cicero can no longer do (as well as something that will ultimately prove beneficial for the changed Roman state).[8] But *De Officiis* represents the culmination of this approach, an attempt by Cicero to reframe Rome's moral code in a way that would make it applicable to a new environment.[9]

The excursus on decorum is central to this project, since it offers an account of proper behavior detailed enough to cover the movements of the body, the nature of one's speech, and even the type and location of one's house. The result is a blueprint for moral conduct in almost any situation, public or private. And indeed, the fact that Cicero discusses behavior in private settings (including a rubric for maintaining decorum in one's private speech) represents an important advance in Roman ethics, which had heretofore been dominated by *exempla*: public acts by exceptional men (and women) acting in some public capacity.[10] By providing a guide that encompasses moral behavior in non-public settings – and one that

---

[7] Similar, more implicit sentiments occur when he laments in the *Brutus* that the forum has been deprived of eloquence (6) and that his own pen had fallen silent (19), and in *Orator* that his forensic skills and civic acts had fallen into ruin (148), and when he calls the subject matter of the *Tusculan Disputations* his *senilis declamatio*, the rhetorical exercise of his old age (7).

[8] In the preface to the *Tusculan Disputations*, Cicero says his hope was that "if in my public career I produced something of value to the Roman state, I might also be of some value, if I am able, in my leisure" (1.5: *si occupati profuimus aliquid civibus nostris, prosimus etiam, si possumus, otiosi*).

[9] Long 1995 argues that the aim of the *De Officiis* was nothing less than the redefinition of central Roman values like *laus* and *gloria*.

[10] On the role of *exempla* in Roman morality, see Roller 2018 and Langlands 2018; and on their treatment in *De Officiis*, the chapters by Langlands and White, this volume. As Morgan 2007: 122–59 notes, *exempla* reflected the values of the ruling class, the very group whose identity was in crisis in this period.

uses the literary/rhetorical concept of decorum as its benchmark – Cicero re-envisions what it means to be a good Roman under a new political system that does not offer the same scope for political or military behavior that could be publicly recognized as a communal good.

Cicero made this intervention in Roman ethics by way of Greek philosophy. According to his own account (*Off.* 3.7), the first two books of *De Officiis* follow closely on the Περὶ τοῦ καθήκοντος of Panaetius of Rhodes (c. 185–110 BCE). In the first, Cicero takes up Panaetius' discussion of the *honestum* (the honorable), while the second is devoted to his account of the *utile* (the useful or expedient). The third book addresses a topic Panaetius had promised (but failed) to discuss, namely how to reconcile these two concepts. Throughout, as is common in all of his adaptations from Greek, Cicero weaves in native ideas and examples to make the work more palatable to a Roman audience. Indeed, even as he offers an alternative guide to moral behavior that moves beyond traditional *exempla*, he incorporates many traditional Roman heroes as ethical examples, including Horatius Cocles (1.61), Scipio Africanus (3.1–4), Cato – both the elder (1.37, 1.104, 3.16) and the younger (1.112) – Regulus (3.96–115), and even himself as an exemplum of courage and glory in his opposition of Catiline (1.77–78).[11] The treatise thus presents itself as a synthesis of the Roman tradition of concrete examples of moral worth with a more abstract approach grounded in Greek philosophical ethics. In this way, it is of a piece with Cicero's other philosophical works from this period, in which Greek philosophy is cast as the means of saving the Roman state from itself.

3 Panaetius and the *De Officiis*

Cicero's innovative response to Rome's political crisis in *De Officiis* builds on the work of a Greek philosopher who was himself an innovator, not least because of his connections to Rome: Panaetius, though trained at Athens by Diogenes of Babylon (the fifth head of the Stoa) and Antipater of Tarsus, actually lived in Rome for some time, where he was attached to Scipio Aemilianus.[12] Along with his teacher Antipater, he is also one

---

[11] Long 1995 discusses how Cicero contrasts his own proper ethical behavior throughout *De Officiis* with the behavior of (would-be) tyrants like Sulla, Caesar, and Antony.

[12] In this respect, Panaetius prefigured the large number of Greek intellectuals who would move to Rome in the following two centuries. Panaetius' relationship with Scipio was much romanticized by Cicero; see, e.g., *Mur.* 66; *Luc.* 5; *Fin.* 4.23; *Rep.* 1.15, 34; *Tusc.* 1.81. Indeed, Cicero's interest in Scipio Aemilianus and Laelius surely owed much to their relationship with Greek (and Roman) intellectuals like Panaetius, Polybius, and Terence, which made them useful *exempla* for his own intellectually inclined career; see van der Blom 2010: 184–85, 232–33.

of the earliest known philosophers whose work signals a shift away from Hellenistic empiricism towards the eclecticism of later antiquity in its incorporation of doctrines from other major philosophical schools, particularly Plato's and Aristotle's.[13] Cicero says that he spoke of Plato as divine (*Tusc.* 1.79), and that a mixture of Academic and Peripatetic figures, including Plato, Aristotle, Xenocrates, Theophrastus, and Dicaearchus, "were constantly on his lips" (*Fin.* 4.79: *semperque habuit in ore Platonem, Aristotelem, Xenocratem, Theophrastum, Dicaearchum*).[14] He also had an interest in rhetoric: Plutarch tells us that he argued that Demosthenes' speeches evinced a philosophical belief that the good was to be chosen for its own sake (*Dem.* 13.4), and it is possible that he was among the earliest philosophers to teach a sort of philosophical rhetoric.[15]

In his eclecticism, his embrace of rhetoric, and his willingness to engage with Rome, Panaetius was at the forefront of several trends in philosophy that only grew more popular in the centuries after his death. His innovation was also on display in the treatise on which *De Officiis* was based, Περὶ τοῦ καθήκοντος. The topic itself, *kathēkonta* (a term adopted by Stoics for the appropriate acts each person should perform) was utterly traditional for Stoic philosophers: prior to Panaetius' treatment, it had already been discussed in treatises by Zeno, Cleanthes, Sphaerus, and Chrysippus.[16] But Cicero's adaptation suggests that Panaetius considered this traditional topic in several novel ways, one of which was his use of τὸ πρέπον as a criterion for guiding one's ethical behavior.[17] An examination of Cicero's

---

[13] For Panaetius' role in this transition, see Frede 1999. For Antipater's role, for which the best evidence is his view that Plato shared ethical doctrines with the Stoa, see *SVF* 3.3.56, Dörrie 1990: 315–17, and Tarrant 2000: 56–58. Panaetius' incorporation of Platonic and Aristotelian figures into his philosophy prefigures the eclectic approach of Antiochus' Old Academy, another important influence on Cicero, since it authorized his ability to embrace Stoic doctrines. On this, see Bishop 2019a: 96–97 and Frede 1999: 776–77.

[14] Philodemus similarly refers to him as "a lover of Plato and a lover of Aristotle" (*Stoic. Hist.* col. I.XI.2–7: φιλοπλάτων καὶ φιλοαριστοτέλης). For more on Panaetius and Plato, see Tieleman 2007: 108–16; Dörrie 1990: 317–23; for Panaetius and Aristotle, see Frede 1999: 775.

[15] As Brittain 2001: 308–9 suggests. In this he may have followed Diogenes of Babylon, who wrote a treatise on voice, and perhaps also one on oratory, in which he argued that only the wise man can speak persuasively (*SVF* 3.237.11–14).

[16] See Dyck 1996: 2–8.

[17] Another common claim for Panaetius' novelty in the work is that he was the first to consider the subject of ethical behavior not from the perspective of the ideal moral agent, the sage, but from the point of view of a typical one; on this see Philippson 1930, De Lacy 1977, and Gill 1988. Further potential innovations are discussed by Dyck 1996: 17–18. See also Inwood ch. 3, this volume. However, Lévy 2003 and Striker 2022 argue that Panaetius was closer to traditional Stoic doctrine than is typically believed. Of course, with the *De Officiis* as our principal witness to Panaetius' work, and so little known about prior treatises on the subject, all claims of innovation remain provisional.

treatment of the subject in light of traditional Greek philosophical ethics offers evidence for how Panaetius incorporated this new principle into his guidelines for moral behavior.

Panaetius' discussion of the moral dimensions of τὸ πρέπον was presumably situated, as Cicero's is, within a larger account of the traditional four virtues (knowledge, justice, courage, and moderation) necessary for leading a morally upright life.[18] If Cicero's account follows his, then he too argued that all four of these virtues flow from reason, which Nature has uniquely bestowed upon humans. First, humans have a rational desire to avoid injury, which, when coupled with the natural impulse to live in communities, produces justice (*Off.* 1.11–12). Next, reason inspires an eagerness for learning about the world in which we live, which produces knowledge, and an independence that leads us to disavow anything unjust or unlawful, which produces greatness of mind or courage (1.13). Finally, humans are the only animals that have the rationality to determine what order is, what is fitting, and how to be moderate in both deeds and words, and this inborn sense produces moderation, or *sōphrosunē* (1.14). Moral goodness is fashioned from the combination of these four elements, and the human being who shapes his or her behavior in accordance with moral goodness will perform the *officia* (or *kathēkonta*) expected of ethical individuals.

It is in the fourth and final virtue that Panaetius diverges most widely from traditional accounts.[19] In earlier philosophy *sōphrosunē* referred to the self-control or temperance that an ethically upright individual practiced in curbing their desires (e.g. Plato, *Phdr.* 237e–238a; Aristotle, *NE* 1117b). It held no special position among the virtues and was simply one of the four, in equal position with the other three. But in Cicero's late philosophical works, *sōphrosunē* is represented as both the incitement to and culmination of knowledge, justice, and courage, a fact that is clear from his description of it in *De Finibus* as the crown of the four virtues (2.47). There, Cicero argues that the knowledge humans gain of the inherent beauty and dignity of the natural world spurs them to beautiful and dignified speech and action; that justice teaches them not to injure anyone with their speech and actions, which inspires them to keep both speech and actions appropriate at all times; and that courage makes them afraid to do or say anything unmanly, and so also has a moderating influence on speech and actions. It is thus appropriate that *sōphrosunē* caps

---

[18] I follow Schofield 2012b for this reading of the role of *decorum*, "the fourth virtue," in *De Officiis*.
[19] For other Stoic accounts of the four virtues, see LS 61, especially 61C and 61H.

the discussion of the four virtues in *De Officiis*, since for Cicero it has a certain universal quality: it is nothing less than behaving in one's speech and actions in a way that is consistent with and appropriate to the three other cardinal virtues.

In both Panaetius and Cicero, this *sōphrosunē* acquires a new name in keeping with its newly expanded nature. Cicero provides this term when he defines the virtue at the outset of his discussion of it:

> Sequitur ut de una reliqua parte honestatis dicendum sit, in qua verecundia et quasi quidam ornatus vitae, temperantia et modestia omnisque sedatio perturbationum animi et rerum modus cernitur. hoc loco continetur id, quod dici latine decorum potest, graece enim πρέπον dicitur. (*Off.* 1.93)

> We must speak about the one remaining part of moral goodness. In it respect and a certain polish to one's life are discerned, as well as self-control and moderation and the calming of every disturbance of the mind and due measure for everything. Under this heading is encompassed what in Latin can be called decorum, since its name in Greek is πρέπον.

Cicero's definition incorporates *temperantia* and *modestia*, the two words he uses elsewhere to translate *sōphrosunē* (e.g., *Tusc.* 3.16), but it is notable that these terms (and the related concepts of equanimity and due measure) are not the only ones that appear. Cicero's understanding of *decorum*, his overarching title for this group of ideas, clearly denotes something more comprehensive, since the concepts of *ornatus* (distinction or polish) and *verecundia* (respect) are also included. *Ornatus* is an especially interesting word for Cicero to use in this setting, since it was also a key term in his discussions of rhetorical style, where it connotes the embellishment or polish applied in the final stage of producing a well-turned speech.[20] In other words, literary-critical and rhetorical elements are present even from the outset of Cicero's discussion of this newly expanded *sōphrosunē*.

This must also have been the case in Panaetius' account, since the word he used for this virtue, τὸ πρέπον, had similar associations. While this term was not without a philosophical pedigree (it is used as a virtual synonym for τὸ καλόν at both Plato, *Hip. Maj.* 293e and Aristotle, *Top.* 135a13), Panaetius was the first, as far as we know, to import it into the realm of ethics by accepting the Platonic/Aristotelian association of it with τὸ καλόν and then applying it to morally fine behavior.[21] Furthermore, by the time he was writing his treatise, τὸ πρέπον was probably better known

---

[20] On the centrality of *ornatus* to Cicero's style, see Dugan 2005.
[21] See Pohlenz 1933: 55–58 and Philippson 1930: 392–94, 401.

Care of the (Written) Self 171

for its poetic and rhetorical senses than its philosophical one. An examination of its use first in Greek rhetorical theory, then in poetics, will offer insight into how these aesthetic senses may have influenced Panaetius' (and Cicero's) understanding of its meaning.[22]

4 τὸ πρέπον in Aesthetic Context

As with so much of ancient scholarship, the application of τὸ πρέπον to the aesthetic qualities of both poetry and rhetoric can be traced back to Aristotle. In the *Poetics*, he uses the term to describe the importance of consistency and appropriateness in poetry: it is applied to characters at 1454a22–28 and to plots at 1455a22–26. In the *Rhetoric* (3.7.1408a10–11), he explains that an oration possesses πρέπον whenever it properly expresses three things: the speaker's emotion (παθητική), his character (ἠθική) – by which Aristotle means that the style of the speech takes into account the speaker's age, personality, and circumstances – and a proper proportion to the subject matter (τοῖς ὑποκειμένοις πράγμασιν ἀνάλογον). Aristotle's three components of rhetorical πρέπον thus connote speech that represents the speaker and the circumstances of his case in a way that is appropriate and easily comprehensible to his audience.

Aristotle's discussion of πρέπον in the *Rhetoric* laid the groundwork for the term's use in later rhetorical theory: his student Theophrastus formalized it as one of the four virtues of style (*Or.* 79), and from there it passed into the mainstream of rhetorical thought, including among Stoics. In Diogenes Laërtius' discussion of Stoic theories of language, for example, which is principally based on the treatise Περὶ φωνῆς by Panaetius' teacher Diogenes of Babylon, πρέπον is included among the Stoic virtues of style, and is defined in essentially Aristotelian terms: it consists of "speech that is fitted to reality" (7.59: πρέπον δέ ἐστι λέξις οἰκεία τῷ πράγματι). In other words, even if Panaetius had not had a particular interest in Aristotle, he would surely have been familiar with the rhetorical sense of πρέπον from one of his own teachers.

Cicero also speaks extensively about πρέπον in his works on rhetorical theory, *De Oratore* and *Orator*. In *De Oratore,* it is treated as one of the traditional Aristotelian/Theophrastan virtues of style (as at 1.144, where one should speak "fittingly and with dignity, as it were," *apte et quasi decore*, and at 3.53, "fittingly and consistently," *aptum et congruens*). The lengthiest

---

[22] Cicero's translation, *decorum*, nicely captures both the philosophical and aesthetic realms of meaning, though it misses the original sense in the Greek of something that shines forth or attracts the eye. See Dyck 1996: 242 and Lévy 2003: 128.

discussion of it in this treatise comes at the end of Book Three (3.210–12), where Cicero explains that determining what is appropriate (*quod decet*) for any given speech requires awareness of a number of different categories that follow upon Aristotle's definition: the subject of the speech, its audience, its circumstances, and the orator's character. But Crassus, the interlocutor here, claims that as a virtue of style, propriety is almost impossible to teach, since these aspects of a case are all highly variable. The only precept he is willing to give for achieving this virtue is that the orator should choose which of the three styles of speaking (plain, middle, or grand) is best suited to the subject matter.[23]

But in *Orator*, written nine years later, Cicero's understanding of rhetorical decorum has changed, and has acquired a philosophical cast that suggests he had become familiar with the work of Panaetius (and others) on the subject in the interim; indeed, his remark in this treatise that a full discussion of the idea would require a *magnum volumen* (73) seems to look forward to the *De Officiis*.[24] This treatise marks the first time that Cicero uses the term *decorum* to describe the concept, and it is now no longer one among several virtues of style. Instead, much as in contemporary philosophical works, it serves as the culmination of the four virtues, here as the foundational principle that the perfect orator uses to determine how best to achieve eloquence in any given situation (69–74); as Cicero puts it, it is applicable to "every type and part of the case" (72: *in omni et genere et parte causarum*). This is because this newly expanded decorum is evident not just in words but even "in one's expression and gesture and gait" (74: *in voltu denique et gestu et incessu*).

The discussion of propriety in *Orator* (written in 46 BCE) thus represents a significant shift from *De Oratore* (written in 55), where it is simply one of the standard rhetorical virtues. It is appropriate to consider this shift in light of the very different political circumstances that lay behind the two works: when *De Oratore* was written, there was still hope that the young men trained in its precepts would use them for the same full range of political and forensic circumstances that Cicero himself had enjoyed. But *Orator* was written after Caesar's accession when, as Cicero puts it, "my forensic skills and public proceedings had fallen into ruin" (148: *meae forenses artes et actiones publicae concidissent*). The oratorical precepts in this work consequently focus less on providing tools for practical

---

[23] Crassus' lack of interest in providing concrete rules and guidelines is typical for *De Oratore*, where rhetorical theory is only one among many tools that the budding orator needs in order to succeed. Fox 2007: 111–41 and Gunderson 2000: 187–222 discuss this ambivalent aspect of the dialogue.

[24] This is clear from Cicero's statement that "the philosophers are accustomed to treat this subject under the category of 'duties'" (72: *philosophi solent in officiis tractare*).

application than on the delineation of an ideal figure, the perfect orator. The expanded function of rhetorical decorum, which Cicero links directly to the decorum treated by "the grammarians in their discussions of poets" (72: *grammatici in poetis* [sc: *solent tractare*]), underscores the fact that oratory has here shifted from a public political and forensic activity to a private literary one.[25]

Cicero's mention in this treatise of the *grammatici* who investigate the role of decorum calls to mind the other aesthetic field to which the term was applied by Aristotle, poetics. Aristotle's insistence on the importance of πρέπον for poetic characters and plots had received fresh and sustained attention from the great literary critic Aristarchus a generation before Panaetius wrote his treatise, and Panaetius' understanding of the topic broadly agrees with Aristarchus' formulation.[26] Aristarchus' views on poetic πρέπον thus offer useful insight into the semantic resonance of the term around the time that Panaetius composed his treatise.

Aristarchus' work on Homer makes it clear that he accepted Aristotle's premise, articulated in the *Poetics*, that a good poem was one that was internally consistent in both plot and character. Both Aristotle and Aristarchus use the term πρέπον at various points to refer to this consistency. For Aristarchus, this concept was particularly applicable to the poem's characters: they needed to be consistent and believable at all times, behaving in a manner suitable to their age, social status, present situation, and mythical model.[27] Any violation of this principle was cause for athetesis (the marking of a passage as spurious): thus, for example, Aristarchus argued that the speech of Achilles to Aeneas where he asks if the Trojans have bribed Aeneas to fight him (*Il.* 20.180–86) ought to be athetized as "not suited to the character of Achilles" (*Sch. Vet. Il.* 20.180–86a: οὐ πρέποντες τῷ τοῦ Ἀχιλλέως προσώπῳ). Aristarchus' reasoning here seems to be that the greatest Greek hero would never have insulted an enemy with vulgar remarks like these.[28]

The connections between Aristarchus' understanding of τὸ πρέπον as a poetic virtue and its role as one of the rhetorical virtues are apparent. In

---

[25] On this see further Guérin 2009, who notes that the emphasis on technically proficient oratory espoused in the work – whose yardstick is decorum – paves the way for the practice of declamation.

[26] It is, of course, impossible to know for certain whether Panaetius was aware of Aristarchus' work, though he was presumably familiar with the preeminent literary critic of the Pergamene school (and a younger contemporary of Aristarchus), Crates of Mallos, who was also a student of Diogenes of Babylon. Furthermore, early Stoic interest in what later came to be called grammar made Stoic work of natural interest to Alexandrian grammarians, and we can assume the same was true of the Alexandrians for the Stoics; see Blank and Atherton 2003.

[27] Schironi 2018: 429–30 discusses this aspect of Aristarchus' poetics.

[28] See Schironi 2018: 710–17 for Aristarchus' understanding of Achilles' character and behavior, including this episode.

both cases, the term refers to the use of language and behavior that suits the speaker's character, his audience, and the circumstances in which he speaks or behaves. There is also a natural affinity between these aesthetic principles and the philosophical tenets of Stoicism, which emphasized the importance of consistent behavior at both a macro level (in the design of the universe) and a micro one (in the modeling of a person's behavior). In fact, Cicero himself offers excellent evidence of the extent to which Stoics connected these two fields in his use of the same two terms, *constantia* and *aequabilitas*, to describe the consistency expected in each.

For Stoics, the consistency at work in the operation of the universe, which they took as a sign of intelligent design, was often illustrated by the movement of the stars. As Cicero puts it in *De Natura Deorum*, "the sight of the uniform (*aequabilitas*) motion and exceedingly regular (*constantissima*) rotation of the heavens is enough to indicate that they are not the product of chance."[29] Strikingly, these same two terms recur in *De Officiis* to describe the regularity of ideal human behavior. Cicero first suggests that "if decorum is anything at all, it is obviously nothing more than uniformity (*aequabilitas*) in one's entire life."[30] A few chapters later, he remarks that "there is nothing, then, that is more fitting than to observe regularity (*constantia*) in everything one does and everything one plans."[31]

These lexical connections demonstrate that consistency was an organizing principle in multiple aspects of Stoicism, from physics and theology to ethics. If a similar embrace of consistency could be found in the fields of poetics and rhetoric, then why not borrow from these more widely studied fields to illustrate the concept's philosophical relevance?[32] This is precisely what Cicero does in his discussion of decorum in *De Officiis*.

5 τὸ πρέπον in *De Officiis*

Throughout *De Officiis*, Cicero relies on the better-known aesthetic senses of decorum to explain its applicability to ethics. Indeed, one of Cicero's earliest explanations of the idea in the work relies on an understanding of

---

[29] ND 2.15: *maximam aequabilitatem motus <constantissimamque> conversionem caeli ... quarum rerum aspectus ipse satis indicaret non esse ea fortuita.*
[30] *Off.* 1.111: *omnino si quicquam est decorum, nihil est profecto magis quam aequabilitas universae vitae.*
[31] *Off.* 1.125: *nihil est autem quod tam deceat, quam in omni re gerenda consilioque capiendo servare constantiam.*
[32] Gill 1988: 195 suggests that Panaetius simply formalized as a matter of philosophical ethics a commonly held emphasis on propriety in every aspect of ancient society. But it is clear that the literary and rhetorical approaches towards decorum in particular played an important role in Panaetius' understanding of the concept.

the poetic dimension of decorum that is essentially identical to Aristarchus' conception:

> Haec [sc. moderatio et temperantia] ita intellegi, possumus existimare ex eo decoro, quod poetae sequuntur … Sed ut tum servare illud poetas, quod deceat, dicimus, cum id quod quaque persona dignum est, et fit et dicitur, ut si Aeacus aut Minos diceret 'oderint dum metuant' aut 'natis sepulchro ipse est parens' indecorum videretur, quod eos fuisse iustos accepimus; at Atreo dicente plausus excitantur, est enim digna persona oratio. (*Off.* 1.97)

> That these things [moderation and self-control] are understood [to be a component of decorum] we can judge from the decorum that poets follow … We say that poets have observed what is proper whenever both actions and words are appropriate for each character. If Aeacus or Minos were to say "let them hate, as long as they fear", or "the father himself is the children's tomb", it would seem inappropriate (*indecorum*), because we have learned that they were just. But when Atreus says them, it provokes applause, because the speech is appropriate to his character.

While this conception of τὸ πρέπον is reminiscent of Aristarchus' manner of evaluating the Homeric poems, Cicero also attaches an openly moralizing aspect to it. His point is that as human beings trying to lead ethical lives, we should act as poets do: just as they recognize that certain words and behavior are appropriate for certain characters and inappropriate for others, so we should shape our words and behavior to fit our ethical "characters."[33] The theatricality latent in this metaphor, and in the lengthy discussion that follows of the four *personae* (literally, masks) that each individual chooses (or has chosen) for himself to comprise the face he presents to the world, has been much discussed.[34] I will not add to that discussion, but Panaetius' innovation in connecting the fields of ethics and poetics should certainly be admired: in order to offer a practical and easily digestible example of the ethical sense he had attached to τὸ πρέπον, he linked it with the word's aesthetic use among literary critics, who employed the term to describe the consistency of characters' speech and actions in the works of Homer and the classical tragedians.[35]

---

[33] While Cicero's quotations here derive from Accius' *Atreus*, he is probably providing a Roman substitute for Panaetius' Greek original, as Jocelyn 1973 demonstrates was his typical practice when adapting Greek philosophical sources. Both Sophocles and Euripides wrote tragedies on Atreus, and we might compare Plutarch *Mor.* 480f–81b, which also uses Atreus as an example of a depraved character.

[34] See, e.g., De Lacy 1977, Gill 1988, Lévy 2003, Dugan 2005, Schofield 2012b. The centrality of this concept to understanding the theory of poetic decorum on display in Horace's *Ars Poetica*, which shows clear links to Cicero's discussion in *De Officiis*, is discussed by Oliensis 1998: 198–223.

[35] As De Lacy 1977: 164–65 and Striker 2022: 240–41 note, there was a philosophical tradition of using dramatic characters to illustrate individual characteristics, but the connection to moral behavior and the specific four-part system of *personae* seems to have originated with Panaetius.

But for Cicero, the connection that could be drawn between the ethical sense of τὸ πρέπον and its use as one of the virtues of rhetorical style was perhaps even more important than the term's poetic resonance. In rhetoric, obeying the dictates of τὸ πρέπον meant adapting one's speech to the character of the orator, the audience, and the circumstances of the case, since, as Cicero puts it in *De Oratore*, "one type of speech is not suited to every case or audience member or character (*persona*) or time" (3.210: *non omni causae nec auditori neque personae neque tempori congruere orationis unum genus*). In this earlier work, Cicero uses the word *persona* as a rhetorical term of art; it does not have the ethical meaning it acquires in *De Officiis*. And yet the rhetorical sense of *persona* – where it denotes the self that the successful orator presents to an audience through his use of appropriate language and body language – is surely latent in Cicero's discussion of ethical *personae* in *De Officiis*. Furthermore, the rigid schematization Cicero applies in *De Officiis* to determining an individual's exact combination of *personae* puts one in mind of nothing so much as rhetorical status theory, the system of extensive categories and subcategories of criminal defense strategies devised by Hermagoras of Temnos. Just as an orator could use the divisions of status theory as a shortcut to determine the best way to argue his case, someone who wished to act appropriately could use the *personae* of the *De Officiis* to determine which behavior best suited his nature and personality.[36] The similarities between the two fields are especially clear in Cicero's account in *De Officiis* of the different duties appropriate for men of different ages and at different times in their lives (1.122–25), which he sums up in language that echoes the discussion of rhetorical decorum in the *De Oratore* passage above: "duties will be clearly discovered when we ask what is fitting and what is appropriate for characters, times, and ages" (1.125: *fere officia reperientur, cum quaeretur quid deceat et quid aptum sit personis, temporibus, aetatibus*).[37]

These echoes show that the rhetorical sense of τὸ πρέπον was at the forefront of Cicero's mind when he wrote *De Officiis*, a fact that is made even clearer by his excursus within this section on the use of decorum in speech (1.132–37). In this discussion, Cicero divides up speech into two main types, oratory (*contentio*) and everyday conversation (*sermo*) (1.132).[38]

---

[36] De Lacy 1977: 170–71 describes *persona* theory as "a formula for discovering for any person in any given situation the appropriate act, *quid deceat*" – a definition that could apply, with a few changes in terminology, to status theory.

[37] See Philippson 1930: 395.

[38] Unlike the neutral or positive word *oratio*, which Cicero contrasts with *sermo* in *De Oratore* (e.g. 2.270), *contentio* can have the negative sense of a struggle or dispute, as Kennerly 2010: 136 notes.

As he notes, oratory – which he links here explicitly to the public apparatus of the state (trials, public assemblies, and speeches in the senate) – is already bounded by a number of rules governing its usage. But everyday conversation (under which heading Cicero includes social gatherings, learned discussions, meetings with friends, and dinner parties) has no such rules, even if, as he has already suggested, adhering to one's duties in these situations requires attention to the same principles of rhetorical propriety that public oratory does.

In the brief account of the observation of propriety in private conversation that follows, Cicero essentially adapts the principles he had delineated in *De Oratore* for public-facing speech to speech performed in a private setting.[39] Indeed, he even mentions three of that dialogue's interlocutors as masters of private conversation, in language that directly echoes his descriptions of their public style in the earlier work. Quintus Lutatius Catulus (along with his son) is lauded for his pure and perfectly spoken Latin (1.133, cf. *De Or.* 3.29 and 3.42), while Gaius Julius Caesar Strabo is singled out for his humor and wit (1.133; cf. *De Or.* 3.30). But the crown in both works goes to Lucius Crassus, who could speak even more copiously and wittily than these two friends of his.[40] It is as if the use of these three men in particular, described in terms that perfectly recall their rhetorical traits in *De Oratore*, is meant to serve as a sort of shorthand for the reader, directing him to the earlier work for a more detailed account of the rules and regulations that govern speech – which are here envisioned as being perfectly commensurate between the public and private spheres.[41] Nor are these the only Roman orators who have excelled at private speech: Cicero too, as he has already explained at the outset of *De Officiis*, is able to move smoothly between an oratorical style and a philosophical one, combining the (public) force of Demosthenes and the (private) elegance of Plato (1.3–4). Here, then, as elsewhere, Cicero's own career, with its shift from public oratory to private-facing philosophy, provides an implicit model for the theoretical account he sketches out.

---

[39] Note, for example, the precept that serious matters should be discussed with the appropriate gravity, while more light-hearted topics can be discussed with charm (*Off.* 1.134). This was a key tenet of literary/rhetorical propriety. In *De Oratore* it is applied to the orator's ability to move an audience to whatever emotions are appropriate for his case (2.72–73); its applicability to the more relaxed conversation used in letters is discussed in *Fam.* 2.4. It is noteworthy too that Cicero discusses propriety in humor (*Off.* 1.144), in a passage that recalls the lengthy excursus on the topic in *De Oratore* (2.217–89).

[40] Crassus (along with Caesar Strabo) is also mentioned for his wit at *Off.* 1.108 in the discussion of the four *personae*. His copiousness is mentioned by Antonius at *De Or.* 3.51.

[41] This accords nicely with one of the central arguments of Book One of *De Oratore*, which is that a good orator can speak well in every type of *sermo* (e.g. 1.71).

In other words, in the *De Officiis,* Cicero has not only adapted the rules governing rhetorical propriety for ethical use in private situations, he has also rhetoricized those situations by treating private conversation as subject to the same detailed theoretical apparatus that had developed around oratory. This is, of course, in keeping with Cicero's general interest in the post-civil war period of reorienting formerly public behavior to a private environment; indeed, as we have already seen, his first work written after the war, the *Brutus,* already makes great strides in this area in its transferral of eloquence from the forum to a private home. *Orator* continues the trend by introducing a purely aesthetic set of standards by which to judge the perfect orator, the chief of which is a newly expanded concept of decorum that now covers every aspect of the orator's performance. *De Officiis* completes this trajectory when its treatment of philosophical decorum expands to include private speech, now conceptualized as being governed by the same set of guidelines that Cicero had formerly applied to a speech before a jury or the Senate. In an environment where opportunities for forensic and deliberative oratory have all but vanished, Cicero has found a way to refocus and thus retain his training in what constituted proper speech. By promoting what is essentially an ethically-oriented, inward-looking oratory – and by expanding its scope to include all aspects of speech, gesture, and expression – he lays the groundwork not just for the practice of declamation, but for the highly aestheticized habits of subsequent members of the Roman elite.

6 The Long Reach of Cicero's Decorum

It is impossible to say which aspects of *De Officiis* originated with Cicero, and which he found in Panaetius. Panaetius certainly transferred the use of τὸ πρέπον employed in the analysis of oratory and poetry to the field of ethics, arguing that the consistency expected of rhetorical style and of poetic plots and characters was of a piece with the consistency of a morally upright person's behavior. But presumably it was Cicero who recognized how well this new conception of self-care might suit a ruling class whose ability to rule – an ability that rested in large part on their mastery of persuasive speech – had been removed from them. Now the tools that they had acquired in pursuit of that goal could be turned inwards for perfecting a self understood in distinctly literary and rhetorical terms.

The conception of the self that Cicero sketches out in *De Officiis* was highly influential upon later Romans. Indeed, although most studies that name ancient Rome as the society in which Western ideas of the self were first shaped have focused on the imperial period, it is clear that Cicero laid the groundwork for that later approach.⁴² His influence on this topic can be felt as early as the Augustan period, an era in which he has not typically been thought to have had much sway. Among Augustan writers, the decorous ethical self he promotes in *De Officiis* can be seen most clearly in another work with a storied history of reception, Horace's *Ars Poetica*.⁴³ In fact, the two texts are in some respects mirror images of one another: where Cicero uses poetry to illuminate philosophical ethics, Horace makes philosophical training the first principle for poetic abilities, a fact that he underlines towards the end of the poem:

> Scribendi recte sapere est et principium et fons.
> rem tibi Socraticae poterunt ostendere chartae,
> verbaque provisam rem non invita sequentur.
> Qui didicit patriae quid debeat et quid amicis,
> quo sit amore parens, quo frater amandus et hospes,
> quod sit conscripti, quod iudicis officium, quae
> partes in bellum missi ducis, ille profecto
> reddere personae scit convenientia cuique.   (Horace, *AP* 309–16)

> Wisdom is the foundation and source of writing well.
> The Socratic pages can indicate subject matter for you,
> and words will not unwillingly follow well-thought-out subject matter.
> He who has learned what he owes to his fatherland and what to his friends,
> with what affection a father, brother, and guest should be loved,
> what is the duty of the senator and of the judge, what
> the tasks are of the general sent into war, that man surely
> knows how to express what is suited to each character.

This passage echoes so many of the tenets of Cicero's two extended discussions of decorum (in *Orator* and *De Officiis*) that it reads as a virtual Ciceronian pastiche.⁴⁴ Allusions in the first and last lines are particularly marked. The first, *scribendi recte sapere est et principium et fons*, recasts a sentence from Cicero's introduction to the topic in Orator: *sed est eloquentiae sicut reliquarum rerum fundamentum sapientia* (70: "but wisdom

---

⁴² Lévy 2003: 127 notes, with puzzlement, the tendency to overlook the *De Officiis* in such studies, citing as examples Foucault 2001 and Hadot 1992 and 2001.

⁴³ Rather than positing a common Greek source for these two works (Labowsky 1934 compares them in an attempt to reconstruct Panaetius' original treatise), it has become increasingly uncontroversial to say that Horace was a reader of Cicero's philosophical works. See, e.g., Grant and Fiske 1924, Oliensis 1998, Feeney 2002, Lowrie 2002, and Dressler 2015. Horace's and Cicero's similar attitudes towards propriety are discussed by Philippson 1930: 408–12.

⁴⁴ The Ciceronian resonances of this passage are discussed by Grant and Fiske 1924 and Philippson 1930: 410–11.

is the foundation of eloquence just as it is of everything else"). The closing clause, *ille profecto/reddere personae scit convenientia cuique*, echoes *Off.* 1.98: *quocirca poetae in magna varietate personarum etiam vitiosis quid conveniat et quid deceat videbunt* ("therefore poets will see what is suited and what is appropriate in a great variety of characters, even wicked ones").

The intervening lines essentially offer a summary of the contents of Book One of *De Officiis*, drawing especially on Cicero's discussion of the different duties propriety demands based on one's age and circumstances at 1.122–25. In this section, Cicero considers proper behavior first of the young (*iuniores*) and the old (*seniores*), then of magistrates, private citizens, and foreigners.[45] Elsewhere he considers the duties one owes to fatherland and to friends (1.21); to country, parents, and friends (1.154); and to one's various connections, including parents, siblings, friends, and country (1.53–60). The overlap between Cicero's and Horace's categories, in addition to the obvious echoes of Cicero's language at the beginning and end of this passage, make Horace's point clear: a good poet is one who has read Cicero's *De Officiis* and absorbed its philosophical principles – most notably its account of propriety, which links ethics and poetics. These are not the only reminiscences of *De Officiis* to be found in the *Ars Poetica*, but they are enough to show that the idea of decorum in Cicero's treatise, which uses poetry to illustrate moral behavior, is employed by Horace to provide precepts for poetic composition itself.[46]

Among the many aspects of Cicero's legacy that were adopted by later generations of Romans, perhaps the most central for the development of Latin literature – and the one that had the most immediate influence among Augustan authors – was his reconfiguration of literary production, after the civil war, as not just an acceptable elite activity, but one that ought to earn its producer the same respect and standing that he might otherwise have acquired through a successful political career.[47] The *De Officiis* is in many ways the cornerstone of this new approach. While its

---

[45] Horace also echoes this passage in his injunction earlier in the work that "different types of propriety must be given to different natures and ages" (*AP* 157: *mobilibusque decor naturis dandus et annis*); he goes on to differentiate especially between youth and old age (161–78).

[46] A few other examples: Oliensis 1998: 199–202 explores the connection between the grotesque hybrid imagined in Horace's opening lines (*AP* 1–5) and the link between embodiment and decorum that recurs throughout the *De Officiis*, especially at *Off.* 1.98; Horace, like Cicero at *Off.* 1.97, uses the tragedy of Thyestes and Atreus to illustrate the importance of propriety in language and character (*AP* 89–90); both authors, moreover, indicate the importance of following the decorum inherent to one's individual nature with the same proverb, that nothing should be done "with Minerva unwilling" (*invita Minerva, AP* 385 and *Off.* 1.110).

[47] As Habinek 1994, Dugan 2005: 13–21, Fox 2007: 22–54, and Bishop 2019a have argued.

main purpose was to impart moral philosophy to the next generation of the Roman elite, the fact that some of its most practical advice for governing one's day-to-day behavior is couched in explicitly literary and rhetorical terms underscores just how much Cicero's definition of the self had changed in this period. He himself might yet be remembered and defined at least in part by his public political career (and indeed, his recollection of his own services to the state in *De Officiis* is clearly designed to facilitate this), but he recognized that that avenue would largely be closed to his son and to others of his generation. And so he himself modeled the path that they could take, turning not just literature and rhetoric, but even one's self-definition, inward, and suggesting that all of the highest values of the public Roman state should be afforded to all three. It would be difficult to overstate how crucial this reconfiguration was, not just for the generation that immediately followed, but also for authors like Seneca and Marcus Aurelius to whom later Western notions of the self have typically been assigned. When we talk, then, about the massive influence that Cicero and the *De Officiis* have had in shaping the way that Western society is structured, we should include among such discussions Cicero's formulation of a self both inward-facing and openly aestheticized.

CHAPTER 9

Cicero and the Cynics

Sean McConnell

1 Introduction

In his opening remarks on the fourth virtue, *decorum* ('seemliness'), Cicero asserts that it is inseparable from what is honourable (*honestum*), being the necessary accompaniment of the first three virtues (wisdom, justice, and greatness of soul) as well as a distinct virtue in its own right (*Off.* 1.93–4).[1] Cicero indicates that *decorum* has two main aspects: (1) a concern for restraint, moderation, due measure, and what is appropriate or fitting, captured in words such as *temperantia et modestia* ('restraint and modesty'), *omnisque sedatio perturbationum animi* ('a calming of all agitations of the spirit'), and *rerum modus* ('due measure in all things'); (2) a concern for appearance and not offending others, captured in words such as *ornatus vitae* ('the ordered beauty of a life') and *verecundia* ('a sense of shame').[2] The two aspects are interconnected: it is through moderation, fittingness, due measure, and the like that one maintains seemliness and so avoids offending others.[3]

In the lengthy discussion of *decorum* that follows, Cicero stresses the general principle that we avoid giving offence to others by following nature as our guide (*Off.* 1.99–100):

> Thus we must exercise a respectfulness towards men, both towards the best of them and also towards the rest (*adhibenda est igitur quaedam*

---

[1] Compare *Off.* 1.11–17, where Cicero demonstrates the virtues' roots in nature and their unity with each other. On the distinctive model of the four virtues in *De Officiis*, which follows the innovations of Panaetius, see further Dyck 1996: 82–102.
[2] Schofield 2012b: 43 puts it well: '*decorum* is what both *is* and *looks* exactly right'.
[3] See also *Off.* 1.15–17. There is detailed commentary on Cicero's treatment of *decorum* in Dyck 1996: 238–352, who is good on Cicero's debt to Panaetius and the Stoic philosophical tradition while finding his account to be largely muddled (here see also Striker 2022). Schofield 2012b is much more sympathetic and teases out the careful logic of Cicero's reasoning; he also helpfully links the discussion of *decorum* in *De Officiis* to related material in *Orator* (70–4), *De Finibus* (2.45–7), and *Tusculan Disputations* (3.16–18). See also Bishop ch. 8, this volume.

reverentia adversus homines, et optimi cuiusque et reliquorum). To neglect what others think about oneself is the mark not only of arrogance, but also of utter laxity (*nam neglegere quid de se quisque sentiat non solum adrogantis est sed etiam omnino dissoluti*). There is a difference between justice and shame when reasoning about humans (*est autem quod differat in hominum ratione habenda inter iustitiam et verecundiam*). The part of justice is not to harm a man, that of a sense of shame not to outrage him (*iustitiae partes sunt non violare homines, verecundiae non offendere*). Here is seen most clearly the essence of seemliness (*in quo maxime vis perspicitur decori*). I think it will be understood from this explanation what kind of thing it is that we call 'being seemly' (*his igitur expositis quale sit id quod decere dicimus intellectum puto*).

The duty which is derived from this follows above all the road that leads to agreeing with and preserving nature (*officium autem quod ab eo ducitur hanc primum habet viam, quae deducit ad convenientiam conservationemque naturae*). If we follow her as our guide we will never go astray; we will follow that which is by nature discriminating and clear-sighted, that which is suited to bonding men together, that too which is vigorous and courageous (*quam si sequemur ducem, numquam aberrabimus, sequemurque et id quod acutum et perspicax natura est et id quod ad hominum consociationem accommodatum et id quod vehemens atque forte*).[4]

This concern about not causing offence to others, bound up with a sense of shame or *verecundia*,[5] is a particularly striking feature of Cicero's moral thinking in *De Officiis*. For Cicero, one's virtue is not merely a private matter concerning solely the health of one's soul; as *decorum* in particular illustrates, it is also a communal or social matter, something seen or on display in public view, and other people's thoughts about what we say, what we do, and how we look have a genuine moral impact on us. But it is not obvious that the offended attitudes of others should be relevant when it

---

[4] All English translations of *De Officiis* are from Griffin and Atkins 1991. When citing the Latin, I use the OCT of Winterbottom 1994. All other translations are my own unless otherwise indicated.
[5] The Latin term is hard to translate since it has various connotations for a Roman (Damon 2010: 388 aptly calls the term 'chameleon-like'). There is detailed discussion of the various social dimensions of *verecundia* at Kaster 2005: 13–27, 61–5. He defines it as follows: '*verecundia* animates the art of knowing your proper place in every social transaction and basing your behavior on that knowledge' (15). This fits well with Cicero's treatment of *decorum*: *verecundia* involves worrying about 'what is proper' or 'what is appropriate' or 'what is fitting' or 'what is seemly' in publicly observable social transactions of all kinds. Kaster 2005: 17–19 also notes that *verecundia* embodies a concern to avoid offence when navigating social space, capturing things such as restraint, modesty, respect, politeness, and etiquette (here see Hall 2009 on how concern for *verecundia* plays out in the carefully calibrated language to different addressees in Cicero's letter-writing; also Damon 2010). A moral sense of shame and honour – caring about being censured and being praised by others, caring about one's social standing and reputation – is also captured by *verecundia* (hence the translation of Griffin and Atkins: 'sense of shame'). Finally, Kaster 2005: 27 notes that *verecundia* 'binds the free members of a civil community'. As we will see, this is a very significant issue for Cicero in *De Officiis*.

comes to a person's moral status – why should the seemliness or unseemliness of one's bodily deportment, facial expression, manner of speaking, haircut, clothing, architectural taste (the kinds of thing that Cicero spends much time discussing in his treatment of *decorum* at *De Officiis* 1.93–151) matter at all from a moral point of view?

In this chapter I explore Cicero's attempt to develop a systematic argument that grounds his concern about the moral importance of offence firmly in nature rather than in convention and arbitrary cultural norms. In Section 2 I outline the Cynics' argument (shared by some Stoics) that there is in fact nothing by nature offensive and that, therefore, concerns about causing offence, bound up with *verecundia*, are morally irrelevant in so far as one seeks to live in accordance with nature. Cicero's treatment of *decorum* is largely defined against the Cynics' challenge, and in Section 3 I examine his argument that *verecundia*, in which the essence of *decorum* is said to be seen most clearly, is in fact grounded in nature.[6] In Section 4 I address further the problem that cultural relativism raises for Cicero's argument – why do different cultures have different norms and standards concerning offence if nature is our universal guide? I suggest that the *personae* theory of *decorum* allows Cicero to account for such differences in a fashion that should appeal, as I spell out in an epilogue, to contemporary thinkers grappling with the social and political implications of offence in liberal multi-cultural societies.[7]

2 The Cynic Challenge

Towards the end of his discussion of *decorum*, Cicero admits that certain individuals are justified in flouting established social customs (*mores*) and civic conventions (*instituta civilia*) by acting and speaking in ways that offend community standards (1.148): Socrates flouted the social customs and civic conventions of Athens and offended his fellow citizens, but he had the license to do so owing to his great and godlike good qualities

---

[6] Griffin 1996: 192–8 stresses the ways in which Roman cultural norms are at odds with Cynicism, particularly the importance attached to reputation, glory, and praise from others. This is certainly an important factor in Cicero's treatment of *decorum* and *verecundia*, but it is significant that his argument against the Cynics appeals directly to nature.

[7] Note that in this chapter, I present and assess things as Cicero's own, leaving aside the traditional dispute about how much he is just reproducing what he finds in Panaetius. On this, see further Brunt 2013; Dyck 1979b, 1984, 1996: 17–29; Pohlenz 1934; who argue that in the first two books of *De Officiis* he is essentially doing just that, with some cosmetic changes to adapt the material to fit a Roman context. On the other side, see Woolf 2015: 170–200; Schofield 2012b; Lefèvre 2001; who argue that Cicero is not uncritical and that his own philosophical views shine through strongly.

(*magna et divina bona*). His exceptional nature makes seemly actions and speech that for others would be unseemly and offensive; once one has recognised the divine virtue of Socrates (which many of his fellow citizens failed to see), one can judge his transgressive actions and words positively, both as befitting his remarkable nature and as reflecting what is *honestum*.[8] But Socrates had an exceptional nature, and Cicero stresses that social customs and civic conventions as a general rule are what one should follow in speech and action.[9] He then turns to the Cynics, who also flout social customs and civic conventions, and asserts that, unlike Socrates, they are not justified in doing so at all (*Off.* 1.148):

> But the reasoning of the Cynics must be entirely rejected (*Cynicorum vero ratio tota est eicienda*); for it is hostile to a sense of shame, and without that nothing can be upright, and nothing honourable (*est enim inimica verecundiae, sine qua nihil rectum esse potest, nihil honestum*).

The Cynics make a universal claim that does not rely on any exceptional attributes or circumstances pertaining to select individuals. For the Cynics, we are all justified in flouting social customs and civic conventions in our speech and actions because there is nothing by nature offensive, and as a result *verecundia* has no true moral force. For this reason, the Cynics argue that we should make a point of adopting an attitude of *anaideia* or shamelessness.[10] Their reasoning is reported and rejected by Cicero at 1.128:

> We must certainly not listen to the Cynics, or those Stoics that were almost Cynics, who criticise and mock us because we think that, though some things are not themselves dishonourable, the words for them are shameful, while we call by their own names those things that are dishonourable (*nec vero audiendi sunt Cynici, aut si qui fuerunt Stoici paene Cynici, qui reprehendunt et inrident quod ea quae re turpia non sint verbis flagitiosa ducamus,*

---

[8] Plato's *Apology* gives a vivid account of the offence that Socrates caused through acting the gadfly with his critical questioning of Athenian norms and values. As part of his defence, Socrates declares that in pursuing the examined life he obeys the god rather than his fellow Athenian citizens (29d). Cicero also reports that Socrates claimed that he was a citizen of the whole world (*Tusc.* 5.108), which implies that he did not consider himself bound to Athenian social customs and conventions. It would seem that Socrates acknowledged the moral force of *verecundia*, but his concern not to cause offence pertained at a higher level than social norms and conventions.

[9] This, it would appear, is because they advise us in the direction that nature points: they capture what is fitting and seemly for people living together in a particular community, in that following them allows us to avoid offending each other and as a result to forge closer social and communal bonds. See further below.

[10] On the Cynics' promotion of shamelessness and their routine flouting of social customs and conventions on the basis that these deviate from the dictates of nature, see further Desmond 2006: 77–161 and Goulet-Cazé 2017: 387–420, 471–510.

illa autem quae re turpia sint nominibus appellemus suis). It is actually dishonourable to rob, to deceive, or to commit adultery, but to speak of them is not indecent. To attend to the matter of children is actually honourable, but the word for it is indecent.[11] They have many arguments to the same conclusion, contrary to a sense of shame (*latrocinari fraudare adulterare re turpe est, sed dicitur non obscene; liberis dare operam re honestum est, nomine obscenum; pluraque in eam sententiam ab isdem contram verecundiam disputantur*).

We can reconstruct the details of the Cynics' reasoning by using this passage as well as a lengthy letter Cicero wrote to his friend Lucius Papirius Paetus (*Fam.* 9.22),[12] in which he says that this position found favour with the Stoic Zeno of Citium, who had a reputation for being very nearly a Cynic and who is most definitely one of the Stoic figures Cicero alludes to at *Off.* 1.128.[13] Cicero opens the letter by drawing attention to a debate between Academics and Stoics on the issue of free and frank speech (*Fam.* 9.22.1),[14] before assertively presenting the case for Zeno's position. He calls the letter 'a Stoic lecture on the thesis that the wise man will call a spade a spade' (*Fam.* 9.22.4),[15] and ends by declaring that he himself upholds a commitment to *verecundia* by moderating his speech when talking about sensitive and offensive things, in the fashion of Plato and the Academy rather than that of the Stoics (*Fam.* 9.22.4).[16] The detailed account in Cicero's letter employs the same terminology that we see in *De Officiis*, and we can present the reasoning of Zeno and the Cynics as follows:

---

[11] Note how Cicero's use of euphemism here exemplifies his own position on *decorum*; cf. Dyck 1996: 303.

[12] The letter's date is uncertain: Wendt 1929 suggests 46 BCE, on the basis of the letter's stylistic similarity to the *Stoic Paradoxes*, and Demmel 1962: 239–43 argues for 44 BCE, on the basis of the affinity to the subject matter in *De Officiis*.

[13] Zeno's teacher was the Cynic Crates of Thebes (DL 7.2–3), and his *Republic* was said to have been written on the dog's tail (DL 7.4); on which, see further Schofield 1991: 10–13 and Goulet-Cazé 2017: 545–606. Zeno also said that the wise man will act like a Cynic (DL 7.121).

[14] *amo verecundiam vel potius libertatem loquendi. atqui hoc Zenoni placuit, homini mehercule acuto, etsi Academiae nostrae cum eo magna rixa est. sed, ut dico, placet Stoicis suo quamque rem nomine appellare* ('I love modesty or rather freedom of speech. And this found favour with Zeno, a clever man by Hercules, even if our Academy has a great fight with him. But, as I say, it finds favour with the Stoics to call everything by its proper name').

[15] *habes scholam Stoicam*: ὁ σοφὸς εὐθυρρημονήσει. Like the English idiom 'call a spade a spade', the term εὐθυρρημονήσει captures the idea of speaking without concerns for upsetting people or overstepping social boundaries. It has a Cynic pedigree (Clem. *Strom.* 2.20.121.2), where it is related to παρρησία (free and frank speech).

[16] *ego servo et servabo (sic enim adsuevi) Platonis verecundiam. itaque tectis verbis ea ad te scripsi quae apertissimis agunt Stoici* ('I retain and will retain (for thus I am accustomed) the modesty of Plato. And so I have written to you with guarded words on topics which the Stoics deal with most openly').

1) If there is something shameful in obscenity, it must either be in the matter or in the word; there are no other alternatives (*nam, si quod sit in obscenitate flagitium, id aut in re esse aut in verbo; nihil esse tertium*, Fam. 9.22.1).
2) It is not in the matter (*in re non est*, Fam. 9.22.2).
3) It is not in the word (*multo minus in verbis*, ibid.).
4) Therefore, there is nothing shameful in obscenity.

This then implies that there is no such thing as obscene or offensive language. Therefore, one should call a thing by its proper, rightful name (*suum nomen*) – there is no need for euphemism, and the wise man will call a spade a spade.

The reasoning here takes the form of a simple logical proof, but the general argumentative strategy is in fact dialectical: Zeno and the Cynics take the opponents' views and practices (held by proponents of the Academy such as Cicero) and show that they are riddled with inconsistencies that render them philosophically untenable. This is also indicated by Cicero's comment at *Off.* 1.128, that the Cynics and Stoics such as Zeno 'criticise and mock us because we think that, though some things are not themselves dishonourable, the words for them are shameful, while we call by their own names those things that are dishonourable'. Thus, they first posit that the shameful property, the thing that makes something offensive, does not lie in the matter itself, because the matter, such as adulterous sex or incest, can, as Cicero and others maintain, be signified by different words, not all of which are obscene. If that which is shameful in obscenity were to lie in the matter, then whichever word is used to signify it would be obscene; but evidently this is not the case: 'Do you see, therefore, that although the matter is the same, because the words are not, nothing is seen to be shameful. Therefore, it is not in the matter' (*vides igitur, cum eadem res sit, quia verba non sint, nihil videri turpe. ergo, in re non est*, Fam. 9.22.2). They then posit that that which is shameful in obscenity does not lie in the word either, because the word merely denotes or signifies the matter, which is not shocking or obscene: 'For if that which is signified by a word is not indecent, the word, which signifies it, cannot be indecent' (*si enim quod verbo significatur id turpe non est, verbum, quod significat, turpe esse non potest*, ibid.). Thus, the view shared by Cicero and others, that certain words signifying honourable things are in fact offensive, is baseless. The crucial claim underpinning the reasoning of Zeno and the Cynics is that the word in all cases appropriates the moral value of the thing that it signifies. Thus, since the matter is not obscene, the word is not obscene either; and, because a euphemistic word successfully signifying adultery, for example, is not obscene or indecent, this implies that the matter it signifies is not obscene or indecent either. It follows that there is nothing obscene by nature, and hence nothing at all that is genuinely offensive (*Fam.* 9.22.2).[17]

However, it is undeniable that people find certain words and matters indecent or obscene and are shocked and offended by them. Zeno and the Cynics insist that there is no real basis for such judgements: 'Therefore, don't you see that there is nothing except for nonsense, that shamefulness is neither in the word nor the matter, and thus it is nothing at all' (*viden igitur nihil esse nisi ineptias, turpitudinem nec in verbo esse nec in re, itaque nusquam esse? Fam.* 9.22.3). In his letter Cicero provides numerous examples that they use to demonstrate that obscenity is really dependent on arbitrary or circumstantial factors. For instance, in a particular culture a contemporary change of fashion may make a previously proper word obscene, such as is the case with the Latin *penis* (*Fam.* 9.22.2). The articulation of certain words that are proper in Latin may be offensive in Greek and vice versa, such as is the case with βινεῖ (*Fam.* 9.22.3). Certain actions may be obscene in certain contexts but not in others (for example, breaking wind in public versus alone in the bath: *Fam.* 9.22.4). Zeno and the Cynics are not concerned with these arbitrary matters but rather with properties in nature that might make something obscene and offensive. It is accepted that if something is 'naturally obscene' it is necessary that it will be judged obscene by all people in all cases, regardless of circumstances or cultural peculiarities, which clearly is not the case with the examples Cicero provides. For Zeno and the Cynics, if we are to live in accordance with nature, we should reject arbitrary cultural concerns and call things by their rightful name; we should speak and act without consideration of offending people – we should dismiss worries about *verecundia* and we should flout social customs and civic conventions, for they have no real moral claim on us at all. If people take offence, then they are simply misguided and wrong, and their censure is morally irrelevant.

In sum, the Cynics, as well as Stoics such as Zeno, use a kind of semantic argument that stresses the arbitrariness of so-called offensive speech, concluding that it is all nonsense – it is all just *typhos* or smoke – once one grasps that there is nothing at all that is by nature obscene or offensive.[18]

---

[17] For detailed critical analysis of the cogency of the argument that Cicero presents in the letter, see McConnell 2014: 169–76.

[18] On the Cynics' notion of *typhos* as a kind of delusion brought about by social conventions, see further Decleva Caizzi 1991.

This poses a challenge to Cicero, who upholds the moral importance of *verecundia* in the strongest terms. As *De Officiis* 1.148 indicates, he asserts that *verecundia* is a necessary condition for things being *rectum* and *honestum* – without a sense of shame that is grounded in nature, there is no genuine moral sphere at all. Both parties to the dispute agree on one thing: *verecundia* requires there to be something truly shameful, if it is to have any real moral significance – things that are by nature obscene or offensive, rather than things that just happen to be thought so arbitrarily. What might such things be?

3 Cicero against the Cynics

At *Off.* 1.126–9 Cicero makes the case that we should all avoid indecency in speech and bodily deportment. He presents an argument that that which is shameful in obscenity lies both in the matter and in the word, *in re* and *in verbo*, not by convention but by nature. Thus, by avoiding obscene language and matters that cause offence to people one acts in accordance with nature. His argument for this does not explicitly rely on a semantic theory about how words acquire moral value from the thing that they signify, but rather it is framed in social terms and rests predominately on the observation of nature's design of the physical human body and what is naturally in public sight and what is naturally hidden from view.

At 1.126 Cicero sets up the topic:

> This seemliness can be seen in every deed and word, and indeed in every bodily movement or state, and the latter depend upon three things, beauty, order and embellishment that is suited to action (*sed quoniam decorum illud in omnibus factis dictis, in corporis denique motu et statu cernitur, idque positum est in tribus rebus, formositate, ordine, ornatu ad actionem apto*). (Such things are difficult to express, but it will be enough if they are grasped.) Furthermore, also contained in these three things is a concern to win the approval of those with and among whom we live (*in his autem tribus continetur cura etiam illa, ut probemur iis quibuscum apud quosque vivamus*). Let us, therefore, say a few things about them as well.

We can see Cicero's concerns about the social impact of *decorum* in this passage: people are worried about the approval of those with whom and amongst whom they live, and, in addition to deeds, this involves our bodily deportment and our speech, how we appear and interact physically and verbally around others in our community. It is implied that we need to maintain *decorum* in all these spheres, avoiding offence by maintaining order and propriety. This recalls Cicero's earlier comments at 1.98 (which set up some key features of his argument against the Cynics at 1.126–9):

> Poets, therefore, will look to what is suitable and seemly for a huge variety of roles (*in magna varietate personarum*), even wicked ones. But our parts have been given to us by nature (*nobis autem cum a natura ... partes datae sint*): since they are ones of constancy (*constantiae*), of moderation (*moderationis*), of restraint (*temperantiae*), of a sense of shame (*verecundiae*), and since the same nature teaches us to be mindful of the way we behave towards other people (*cumque eadem natura doceat non neglegere quemadmodum nos adversus homines geramus*), it becomes apparent how widespread is not only that seemliness (*decorum*) which extends over all that is honourable, but also that which is seen in one part of virtue. For just as the eye is aroused by the beauty of a body, because of the appropriate arrangement of the limbs, and is delighted just because all its parts are in graceful harmony (*ut enim pulchritudo corporis apta compositione membrorum movet oculos et delectat hoc ipso, quod inter se omnes partes cum quodam lepore consentiunt*), so this seemliness, shining out in one's life, arouses the approval of one's fellows, because of the order and constancy and moderation of every word and action (*sic hoc decorum quod elucet in vita movet approbationem eorum quibuscum vivitur ordine et constantia et moderatione dictorum omnium atque factorum*).[19]

At 1.126 Cicero reminds us of the natural sociability we have with other human beings and the ways in which we naturally bond together to form a community. Earlier in *De Officiis* Cicero had stressed that this is done through speech and reason (1.12, 1.50), but now, in the discussion of *decorum*, increasingly *verecundia* is to the fore:[20] Cicero places the concern to avoid offence and gain others' approbation firmly in nature as a dimension of our natural sociability with other human beings.[21]

---

[19] Cicero reasserts many of these points at *Off.* 1.143–6.
[20] Human sociability is a topic that is discussed in detail in the first book of *De Officiis* (1.11–12, 1.50–9, 1.156–60). Cicero essentially recounts and condones the Stoic model of social *oikeiōsis*, on which see further Inwood ch. 3, this volume.
[21] Note that this is completely in keeping with Cicero's treatment of *verecundia* in *De Re Publica*. At the start of the third book he states: 'In truth they are not deterred so much by fear and punishment, as laid down by the laws, as much as by a sense of shame, which nature has given to men as a certain kind of fear of not unjustified censure' (*nec vero tam metu poenaque terrentur, quae est constituta legibus, quam verecundia, quam natura homini dedit, quasi quondam vituperationis non iniustae timorem*, 3.3 Powell). Just as the shared capacity for speech and reason naturally bonds human beings together (3.2 Powell), so a shared concern about justified reproach naturally restrains behaviour and prompts human beings to avoid the dishonourable and strive for the honourable (3.3 Powell). This, in turn, 'is suited to bonding men together' (*ad hominum consociationem accommodatum*), to use Cicero's phrase from *Off.* 1.100. Moreover, the ideal statesman (*rector rei publicae*) strengthens this natural feeling through training (*disciplina*) and codes of behaviour (*instituta*) so that shame (*pudor*) motivates the citizens more than fear of punishment (3.3 Powell).

Cicero and the Cynics

Cicero then attempts to provide an argument within the parameters that Zeno and the Cynics set for the problem, in particular the stress on finding what is offensive to be natural and necessarily so rather than cultural and contingently so (1.126–7):

> From the beginning nature herself seems to have been thoroughly rational concerning our bodies (*principio corporis nostri magnam natura ipsa videtur habuisse rationem*): she has placed in sight those parts of our form and features that have an honourable appearance, but has covered and hidden the parts of the body that are devoted to the necessities of nature and would have an ugly and dishonourable look (*quae formam nostrum reliquamque figuram, in qua esset species honesta, eam posuit in promptu, quae partes autem corporis ad naturae necessitatem datae aspectum essent deformem habiturae atque turpem, eas contexit atque abdidit*). Nature's very careful craftsmanship is mirrored in men's sense of shame (*hanc naturae tam diligentem fabricam imitata est hominum verecundia*). For everyone of sound mind keeps out of sight the very parts that nature has hidden, and makes an effort to obey necessity itself as secretly as possible (*quae enim natura occultavit, eadem omnes qui sana mente sunt removent ab oculis, ipsique necessitati dant operam ut quam occultissime pareant*). Again, concerning those parts of the body that are used out of necessity, they refer by their own names neither to the parts themselves, nor to their uses (*quarumque partium corporis usus sunt necessarii, eas neque partes neque earum usus suis nominibus appellant*). It is not dishonourable to do such things, provided one does them in secret, but it is indecent to speak of them. Therefore, neither such activity, if it is public, nor indecency of speech, is free from scurrility (*quodque facere non turpe est, modo occulte, id dicere obscenum est. itaque nec actio rerum illarum aperta petulantia vacat nec orationis obscenitas*).

First, Cicero asserts that nature has been rational in designing our bodies so as to show openly those aspects that have an honourable appearance (*species honesta*) and to conceal from sight those aspects that are ugly (*deforme*) and dishonourable (*turpe*). The linking of sensory, aesthetic, and moral terms is very significant: what is seemly is honourable and beautiful to behold (hence it is and should be *in promptu* – in plain sight), what is unseemly is dishonourable and ugly to behold (hence it is and should be hidden, out of sight). The operation of the senses, aesthetic judgement, and moral judgement, all fit harmoniously together.[22] Everything

---

[22] Cicero also describes this at *Off.* 1.14: 'No other animal, therefore, perceives the beauty, the loveliness, and the congruence of the parts, of the things that sight perceives (*itaque eorum ipsorum quae aspectu sentiuntur nullum aliud animal pulchritudinem, venustatem, convenientiam partium sentit*). Nature and reason transfer this by analogy from the eyes to the mind, thinking that beauty, constancy, and order should be preserved, and much more so, in one's decisions and in one's deeds (*quam similitudinem natura ratioque ab oculis ad animum transferens multo etiam magis pulchritudinem constantiam ordinem in consiliis factisque conservandam putat*)'. See also see *Off.* 1.98, 1.145–6.

starts with the senses, as Cicero asserts when rejecting the Cynics' reasoning at 1.128: 'For ourselves, however, let us follow nature and avoid anything that shrinks from the approval of eyes and ears' (*nos autem naturam sequamur et ab omni quod abhorret ab oculorum auriumque approbatione fugiamus*). By following the lead of the senses, unsullied by interfering cultural factors, and judging things as honourable and seemly and to be sought, or as shameful and unseemly and to be avoided, a process seemingly captured by the term *verecundia*, one is following the prompting and guidance of nature.

Here Cicero can also be seen as combining empirical observation with teleological reasoning in a manner that should appeal to a Stoic. The Stoics maintain that although the world is ordered rationally and is as perfect as can be, there are unavoidable necessary constraints, and, as a result, negative by-products of nature's good designs are baked into the system.[23] Cicero illustrates that this can be seen with the parts of the human body devoted to the necessities of nature. Just by looking, it is evident that the human form has certain aspects open for all to see, such as our faces and our limbs, and other aspects hidden away. These hidden things, which perform the necessities of nature (digestion, and so forth), could have been placed on public display, but they have been covered – why? Cicero asserts (1.126) that it was designed rationally to be this way by nature owing to aesthetic and moral considerations: nature shows what has an honourable appearance, things such as our faces and limbs, because they are seemly and pleasant to look at, but it hides ugly and dishonourable things as much as possible, because they are unseemly and unpleasant to look at. What is unseemly is what lies under our skin like the viscera, the vital organs, the blood and guts, which nature has hidden from sight because it is shocking and offensive to gaze upon, but also some external bits that are ugly and unsightly – in particular our genitals and excretory orifices, which nature has tucked away as much as possible. Since nature has taken seemliness into account by rational design, there is a powerful compulsion to follow her lead. Indeed, in many ways the most important claim is what follows: *verecundia* imitates nature's rational design (*hanc naturae tam diligentem fabricam imitata est hominum verecundia*, 1.127). This implies that we, as humans,

---

[23] For detailed critical discussion of Stoic views on intelligent design and the rationality of nature, see Powers 2012, with further references. Other bodily examples that the Stoics cite as necessary negative by-products of nature's good designs include the propensity for disease and the vulnerability of the human head (Gell. *NA* 7.1.1–13 = 2.1170 *SVF*). The model of intelligent design constrained by necessity is also Platonic, appearing in the *Timaeus*.

are primed by nature to respond appropriately to the rational design of the human body: there is a natural urge to keep unsightly aspects hidden, both physically and when talking about them – hence why people of sound mind all do it without any other compulsion. And on the flipside, there is also a natural urge to maintain beauty, order, and constancy with regard to our bodies – hence the directives that Cicero lays down at 1.128: 'Let our standing, our walking, our countenances, our eyes and the movements of our hands all maintain what I have called seemliness' (*status incessus sessio accubitio vultus oculi manuum motus teneat illud decorum*).

Cicero further illustrates this point at 1.129 with appeal to the practice of actors on the stage, who wear a breech-cloth 'for they fear if an accident occurred, parts of the body might be revealed that it is not seemly to see' (*verentur enim ne, si quo casu evenerit ut corporis partes quaedam aperiantur, aspiciantur non decore*), and Roman bathing customs, whereby an adult man does not bathe naked with his father or his father-in-law.[24] He concludes: 'We ought therefore to preserve a sense of shame of this sort, especially as nature herself is our mistress and guide' (*retinenda igitur est huius generis verecundia, praesertim natura ipsa magistra et duce*, 1.129). Cicero thus stresses that by following such customary modes of behaviour and keeping unsightly things hidden, we not only avoid offending others, we also find ourselves in tune with the rational design and order of nature, which, as Cicero makes clear earlier in his discussion of *decorum*, is universally seemly and befitting given the rational nature of human beings (1.96, 1.100–7).

At this point, it is important to stress that Cicero's reasoning at 1.126–9 has a universal application that gets real purchase against the Cynics' challenge to find properties in nature that are found offensive by all people in all circumstances: we all by nature possess the same human body (in its fundamentals), and we all by nature should have the same response to its rational design, captured in the term *verecundia*; nothing here relies on convention or arbitrary social customs or specific circumstances pertaining to some people but not to others. The Cynics and certain Stoics of course would deny all this: they maintain that any considerations of shame or *verecundia* are not natural but rather conditioned by other factors, and hence things should be called openly by their rightful names and, indeed, natural bodily functions should be performed openly

---

[24] Griffin 1996: 192 comments: 'The disowning of the characteristic Cynic *anaideia* (shamelessness) is here reinforced by Roman prudery and respect for social convention'.

too.[25] In response to Cicero's argument from design, they might appeal to the new-born infant's behaviour, a kind of cradle argument that is used by the Stoics elsewhere to underpin their model of *oikeiōsis*:[26] evidently human beings do not start with sensory reactions that recoil from natural bodily functions, and indeed they are done quite openly without any sense of shame; moreover, the human body comes naked, with genitalia on display rather than hidden (perhaps why Zeno maintained that no part of the body should be entirely hidden; DL 7.33). Thus, these concerns are just priggish: it is only after social conditioning that such worries about bodily functions and what is seemly arise.

In response Cicero would no doubt assert that performing bodily functions publicly and exposing one's hidden parts to others in fact goes against nature, at least once reason has developed and we are fully human and social creatures rather than infantile and bestial. At *Off.* 1.50 he comments:

> Perhaps, though, we should examine more thoroughly what are the natural principles of human fellowship and community (*sed quae natura principia sint communitatis et societatis humanae, repetendum videtur altius*). First is something that is seen in the fellowship of the entire human race (*est enim primum quod cernitur in universi generis humani societate*). For its bonding consists of reason and speech, which reconcile men to one another, through teaching, learning, communicating, debating and making judgements, and unite them in a kind of natural fellowship (*eius autem vinculum est ratio et oratio, quae docendo discendo communicando disceptando iudicando conciliat inter se homines coniungitque naturali quadam societate*). It is this that most distances us from the nature of other animals (*neque ulla re longius absumus a natura ferarum*). To them we often impute courage, as with horses or lions, but we do not impute to them justice, fairness, or goodness (*in quibus inesse fortitudinem saepe dicimus, ut in equis, in leonibus, iustitiam aequitatem bonitatem non dicimus*). For they have no share in reason and speech (*sunt enim rationis et orationis expertes*).

Although he does not make it explicit, it seems that Cicero would agree that concerns for *verecundia* do not hold sway without reason and speech.[27]

---

[25] Various shocking anecdotes about the Cynics capture this, such as Diogenes shitting in the theatre (Dio Chrys. *Orat.* 8.36) and urinating on people (DL 6.46), and Hipparchia and Crates having sex in public view (Apul. *Flor.* 14). This Stoic practice is also referred to by Cicero at *Fam.* 9.22.4 with the softer examples of public belching and farting.

[26] On the Stoics' use of cradle-arguments, see in particular Brunschwig 1986.

[27] Note that Cicero does connect *verecundia* with reason at *Off.* 1.105: reason motivates humans, as opposed to pleasure, which motivates the animals; humans who are drawn to pleasure realise that they are falling short of what reason demands of a human being, and so they cover it up out of a sense of shame or *verecundia*. At *Off.* 2.15 Cicero also describes *verecundia* as arising for human beings owing to life in a civilised community with laws, customs, and justice.

Along with them, *verecundia* develops over time and underpins moral life in a human community. Here, he could readily appeal to a growing natural concern for modesty and privacy (embarrassment at being observed performing the necessities of nature and so forth) that is observed as a child grows up. On the other hand, animals and infants, who have no share in reason and speech, have no *verecundia* at all. The careful reference to 'everyone who is of sound mind' (*omnes qui sana mente sunt*) at 1.127 can be seen as capturing this precondition: it attributes to the outliers, including the shameless Cynics who are brought to our attention in 1.128, a kind of pathology of reason.

It is striking, however, to see Cicero stress at the end of 1.127 that there is no indecency in performing a natural function or talking about it, so long as the function remains hidden both in deed and in word, as nature intends: in so far as such a thing is private and hidden it is not obscene and offensive, but once it is public it is. Does this fall foul of the Cynic demand that something be offensive for all people in all situations if it is to qualify as natural? Cicero would argue no: this in fact illustrates that the key property in the naturally obscene thing is what might be called 'the on public display property', which nature has taken into account in the rational design of the human body. Public scrutiny is a necessary condition for what is obscene by nature. This is not arbitrary, in that the same thing is sometimes offensive and sometimes not owing to some contingent property; rather, an intrinsic or essential property of the thing is realised in all cases when it is on public display – so it is always offensive in so far as it is seen or heard by a rational person of sound mind. On this model, it is by nature unseemly (and hence a cause of offence) and hence hidden (where its potential to offend is unrealised), but when it is made public is when its potential to offend is realised – for its 'being public' goes against nature, and it is this that generates the feeling of offence (the judgement of *indecorum*: it does not belong here, should not be here, does not fit here, is wrong here, who would do such a thing in plain sight, and so forth).

In sum, Cicero maintains that the hidden, unsightly features of the body are in fact by nature indecent or obscene – that indeed is the reason why nature has made them hidden and not open to view, and that is why they are shocking and offensive to all people with a sound mind when they appear in public view. The offence that people with sound mind feel when exposed to such things is a natural response to a natural property in nature. For Cicero, nature is our guide in this manner: we imitate her in our responses, and we do well to moderate our speech and actions with this in mind, keeping hidden what nature has hidden and hence shown ought to be hidden. A failure to do so is a moral failure, indicative of some deficiency or misuse of reason, and we are judged accordingly. Cicero thus meets the Cynic challenge: *verecundia* is grounded in nature, indeed is fundamentally an imitation or mirroring of what nature does.

4 The Problem of Cultural Relativism

Cicero posits that, as human beings, we all by nature possess a sense of shame or *verecundia*, which demands that we maintain seemliness and due proportion in all things, following nature as a guide. In the course of his treatment of *decorum* in *De Officiis* he applies this to facial expression (1.102, 1.128, 1.131), hand gestures (1.128), bodily appearance (1.128, 1.130–1), the art of conversation (1.132–7), houses (1.138–40), standing (1.128), walking (1.128, 1.131), and dress (1.130); in all these spheres we must avoid offending others by exhibiting moderation and restraint. The particular details, however, are very culture-specific: for Cicero, established Roman social customs and conventions largely set the parameters of what is seemly and what is offensive, and people like his son Marcus will do well to follow them. Thus, Cicero cites the very Roman examples that one should not sing in the Forum (1.145), that agriculture is the most seemly economic pursuit for a free man (1.151), and so on. This all seems quite a leap from the examples of necessary bodily functions, and it raises a worry that Cicero is overclaiming what he is entitled to given the nature of his argument against the Cynics. Despite insisting that nature is a universal guide, such things evidently may be judged seemly or offensive in one society or cultural context and not in another, which is the sort of thing that draws the scorn of the Cynics. Griffin and Atkins identify this as a major problem for Cicero: 'No explanation is given of how the observance of social conventions, fundamental to the notion of "seemliness" (1.99, 1.148), and the adoption of nature as a guide are to be reconciled, given the different (often conflicting) social customs of different societies'.[28] Does Cicero ultimately fall into chauvinism, stressing the superiority of Roman cultural norms and values above all others (we should all really be following them) with a veneer of philosophical rigour? How might Cicero address this concern?

---

[28] Griffin and Atkins 1991: 50 n. 1.

It seems that an answer may lie in his *personae* theory, which explicates how *decorum* applies to individual people (*Off.* 1.100–25). He writes at 1.107:

> Furthermore, one must understand that we have been dressed, as it were, by nature for two roles (*intellegendum etiam est duabus quasi nos a natura indutos esse personis*): one is common, arising from the fact that we all have a share in reason and in the superiority by which we surpass the brute creatures (*quarum una communis est ex eo quod omnes participes sumus rationis praestantiaeque eius qua antecellimus bestiis*). Everything honourable and seemly is derived from this, and from it we discover a method of finding out our duty (*a qua omne honestum decorumque trahitur et ex qua ratio inveniendi officii exquiritur*). The other, however, is that assigned specifically to individuals (*altera autem quae proprie singulis est tributa*).

Cicero addresses *decorum* through two perspectives. First, he identifies the duties that arise from the virtue universally: given our essentially rational human nature, what is seemly for us all as human beings? This is our first and most important *persona* or role to play, and Cicero's central assertion here is that impulse should always obey reason (1.100–6). Secondly, he identifies the duties that arise for each of us individually: just as there are many bodily differences between individuals, so too are there many different character traits, and it is seemly that we each act in accordance with the nature of our particular character – we should follow our own nature and be true to ourselves (1.107–14). He later adds two further roles or *personae*: that which proceeds from the specific (constraining) circumstances that we find ourselves in by fortune (1.115), and that which proceeds from our own free choices about what mode of life we wish to pursue (1.115–17). He uses an analogy with the theatre (1.97–8): in a play there are character roles, and an actor should do what is fitting for his particular character role (and he is applauded and censured accordingly); likewise, we all have certain roles to play, and we should do what is fitting given our role – as humans first and foremost, then as individuals with certain natural character traits (which may differ from those of others), in the (constraining) circumstances we find ourselves (our social class, our youth or old age, and so forth), given our own free choices (what mode of life we have opted to pursue given the possibilities open to us). Using this schema, he offers a host of examples at 1.107–25 to illustrate the ways in which seemliness plays out for different people in different situations.[29]

---

[29] For a range of detailed critical discussion of the four *personae* theory, see further Gill 1988; Dyck 1996: 269–99; Woolf 2007, esp. 334–44; Schofield 2012b; and Hawley 2020.

Societies have customs and standards surrounding what is seemly and what is not, and these clearly differ. But, as the *personae* theory indicates, Cicero would see no problem here: in so far as one is a Roman in a particular moment of Roman cultural history (when he could have found himself in another culture by the lottery of birth, or at another time in Roman history), there are certain things that are seemly for that person; if one is not a Roman but, say, a Gaul or a twenty-first-century New Zealander, then something else will be seemly for that person.[30] All that is changing is the third role or *persona* of a given person, which, in addition to things such as social class and age, is affected to some extent by the nature of the culture or the society in which one happens to find oneself. But the virtue of *decorum* remains constant at the overarching level: for human beings, impulse should always obey reason, ensuring moderation and constancy in all that we do (as Cicero asserts most firmly at 1.100–6 and 1.152–60);[31] moreover, *verecundia*, the concern to avoid offending those with whom we live, remains constant as well. With this in mind, Cicero is writing as an upper-class Roman for upper-class Romans such as his son, and so it is no surprise to see a whole lot of advice pertinent to upper-class Romans living their lives as upper-class Romans in 44 BCE. Some of this may seem strange or inapplicable or embarrassingly snobbish to us today, but that does not really impact on the enduring philosophical value of Cicero's treatment of *verecundia* and *decorum*. For Cicero has left us with a compelling moral framework that can be adapted readily to particular circumstances. As a result, we can take something away from Cicero in our contemporary historical moment, as citizens in liberal multi-cultural societies, by imagining how our own concerns would play out in the schema that he has identified.

---

[30] The alternative is to posit Roman cultural superiority: everyone alike should be aspiring to follow these customs and conventions, for Roman social norms are simply those most in accordance with nature – just as their laws accord most closely with the natural law (*De Legibus*) and their republican constitution most closely with the order of the cosmos (*De Re Publica*). This is a tempting route to take, given Cicero's propensity for championing Roman exceptionalism; however, the *personae* theory suggests a different mode of thinking in *De Officiis*.

[31] Note that Cicero takes care to stress that reason always takes precedence over what a particular society may demand – there are some things that are never honourable and seemly to do, in so far as we are human beings: 'It should perhaps be asked whether this sociability, which conforms so greatly to nature, should always be given precedence even over moderation and modesty. I do not think so: for some things are so disgraceful, or so outrageous, that a wise man would not do them even to protect his country' (1.159). In this way Cicero can also resolve apparent conflict between social convention and nature: it would never be seemly to defecate in public even within a community of Cynics, and so forth.

5 Epilogue: Cicero, Offence, and Multi-Cultural Society

Following Cicero's model, we can maintain that nature remains the universal guide: offence needs to be taken into account by all people, universally, regardless of one's particular cultural context, and not just rejected as the Cynics would have it, for this concern for offence is an integral part of our rational human nature and its concern for sociability. Social customs then advise us in the direction that nature points, for they capture what is fitting and seemly for people living together in a particular community, in that following them allows us, as members of that community, to avoid offending each other and as a result to forge closer social and communal bonds (in an analogous way to how avoiding injustice allows us to avoid harming each other, which in turn fosters closer bonds). As we respect and acknowledge our individual differences and seek to accommodate them as best we can for the good of all in our political community, our social customs and conventions continue to evolve in order best to achieve this outcome: this progressive process is the liberal multi-cultural project, and it may even expand to a cosmopolitan project, whereby all human beings, with all their differences, will ultimately be gathered into one shared political community, flourishing individually and collectively together.

This is great as a vision, but there are worries. For instance, what happens when it comes to interacting with others in multi-cultural society, when some people find certain things about other people unseemly and hence indicative of a real moral deficiency, which weakens communal bonds? Liberal values and customs are designed to mitigate such things by promoting freedom of speech and expression, polite tolerance and respect of others, avoidance of public condemnation for certain personal choices and attributes, anti-discriminatory practices, and so forth. But there is also the reality that there are going to be plenty of instances of people taking offence at each other. Modern liberal societies have traditionally downplayed the importance of offence and instead promoted the good of other values such as individual freedom: thus, one might argue that offence is a sort of unavoidable by-product of freedom, but outweighed by the goods freedom brings. But there is a growing indication that offence as a result of others' speech and actions and 'look' is more and more a serious moral issue for people in so-called liberal societies, on both sides of the political spectrum, with major social and political repercussions. Should we then place more limits on individuals' freedom of personal expression so as to avoid being offended, for offence is more important – perhaps even through legal means? Or, following Cicero's argument against the Cynics, should the offending parties simply be silenced or removed from public view ('cancelled'), hiding them away just as nature hides the excretory orifices? Is this a problem solved ultimately by fragmentation into sustainable smaller and more uniform political communities, where people do not take offence at each other? Or are there novel means to avoid offence and promote social bonds while maintaining individual identities and liberties – through education, public policy, or changes in social customs and civic conventions?

Cicero's treatment of *verecundia* and *decorum* may provide useful conceptual tools for navigating these questions. To give but one example, Cicero stresses that offence is a genuine moral concern, and it is a barrier to the formation of social bonds and political community: being offended by another's *indecorum* is akin to being harmed by another's injustice, and as such it demands to be taken seriously. But being offended is not the same as being harmed, and questions of offence might then be addressed differently from how we address questions of justice. Hence, we might avoid the use of laws, the courts, and the police when dealing with disputes and conflicts in that sphere; and we might take care to tailor our rhetoric to avoid talking about 'harms', which evokes claims of injustice when we are really talking about 'being offended' and issues of *decorum*. This example illustrates one way in which Cicero's *De Officiis* may offer useful conceptual resources as people grapple with these highly fraught social and political issues that promise to be some of the most pressing for the future of liberal multi-cultural societies in the twenty-first century.

PART V

Politics

CHAPTER 10

Patriotism and Cosmopolitanism in Cicero's De Officiis

Jed W. Atkins

1 Introduction

With the possible exception of Aristotle's *Politics*, no ancient text has been more influential in the history of western political thought than Cicero's *De Officiis*. The *De Officiis* is an especially foundational text for two important but seemingly opposed traditions: republicanism and cosmopolitanism.[1] Republicanism identifies the *res publica* (the commonwealth) as the proper object of citizens' greatest allegiance, and patriotism as a central civic virtue. For Republicans, patriotism invokes the "love of the political institutions and the way of life that sustains the common liberty of a people."[2] On the other hand, cosmopolitanism holds that, at minimum, we have meaningful obligations to human beings beyond the borders of our own political community. For many cosmopolitans, patriotism is a potentially dangerous impediment to the wider human community.[3]

Both cosmopolitan and republican traditions find ample support in *De Officiis*. The work clearly articulates a society of all human beings united by justice and common advantage. *De Officiis* 1.50–51 argues for the existence of a fellowship between all human beings. Likewise, 3.27–28 stipulates that human beings have duties to all other human beings simply by virtue of their common humanity and regardless of citizenship or fatherland.[4] On the other hand, *De Officiis* 1.51–57 suggests that a citizen's greatest

---

I presented versions of this chapter at Cornell, Chicago, Princeton, and the Society for Classical Studies 2014 annual meeting. I am grateful to the audiences for feedback. Part of the argument of this chapter was summarized in J. W. Atkins 2022. Some material was previously published there or in Atkins 2023.

[1] For the importance of *De Officiis* to the republican and cosmopolitan traditions, see Viroli 1995 (republicanism) and Nussbaum 1997, 2000, 2019, 2022 (cosmopolitanism).
[2] Viroli 1995: 1.
[3] The best recent work on cosmopolitanism qualifies the sharp dichotomy with republicanism: see especially Appiah 2006 and Nussbaum 2019. Compare the sharp contrast in Nussbaum 1996.
[4] See Nussbaum 2000: 185.

allegiance should be to his own *res publica* and implies that patriotism is a virtue. Likewise, in Book 3, Cicero suggests that whether one keeps one's promise or not depends on whether one is acting "against the interests of the *res publica*, which ought to be dearest (*carissima*)" (*Off.* 3.95).

How, then, does Cicero understand the relationship between the *res publica* and the society of all human beings? In particular, given the existence of a society of all human beings, on what grounds does Cicero argue for the priority of a patriotic allegiance to one's *res publica*? Perhaps this is simply Cicero's Roman patriotism getting the best of him? This for instance is Margaret Atkins' view: "Cicero does not so much argue for patriotism as assume it in his reader."[5] A little later in the same article, citing Cicero's "overtly republican optimate preferences," she concludes that it should be "no surprise that Cicero interprets the sociability that is the natural basis of justice as primarily a desire to live in the *res publica* rather than any other size or type of community."[6]

Despite the strong patriotic impulse among elite Romans,[7] Cicero's prioritization of the Roman *res publica* as the most important *societas* is not simply a function of an unreflective commitment to traditional Roman patriotism. In *De Officiis* Cicero identifies two features of the *res publica* that account for its priority in politics: its status as the locus for, first, fostering natural human loves, and second, for meeting human needs. Responding to these natural loves and meeting these needs is vital for promoting natural human sociability. Since the *res publica* is, according to Cicero, the *societas* that best reconciles these loves and meets these needs, he holds that the *res publica* is the society that best fosters human sociability.

Crucially, however, the very same account of sociability that Cicero claims justifies the priority of the republic also supports the version of cosmopolitanism he advances in *De Officiis*. The basic account of sociability on which Cicero builds his argument derives from Stoicism, and in particular from the thought of the second-century BCE philosopher Panaetius, to whose work *On Proper Functions* (*Peri tou kathēkontos*) the first two books of Cicero's own *De Officiis* are indebted. Thus, Cicero anchors his preference for the *res publica* as the most important *societas* deep within the philosophical project of *De Officiis*. Since Cicero's account

---

[5] E. M. Atkins 1990: 274.
[6] E. M. Atkins 1990: 281.
[7] See Kapust 2020. Kapust discusses Cicero, Sallust, Livy, Polybius, and Vergil. He sees Cicero as presenting a principled patriotism in which one loves one's country inasmuch as it embodies the principles of right reason.

of cosmopolitanism and his justification for the priority of the republic derive from the same philosophical resources, *De Officiis* provides a coherent account of what we might call "patriotic cosmopolitanism." In what follows, we will explore how Cicero sets forth this argument and consider some of the most important philosophical objections that it invites.

2 Natural Loves and the Republic

The Stoics recognize that nature engenders a special love for one's self and one's children, an idea which Cicero captures at the outset of *De Officiis* (1.12). This passage describes how human sociability develops through a process known as *oikeiōsis*, "appropriation" or "making something one's own." Appropriation is a natural process in human beings and other animals whereby they become acquainted with their own interests and the interests of others in their species. Cicero expresses the idea with the Latin verb *concilio*: "nature, by the power of reason, unites (*conciliat*) one human being to another for the fellowship both of speech and of life" (1.12). As human beings mature and develop rationally, they gradually come to identify their own interests with those of others, starting with their immediate family and continuing until they identify with all rational beings, i.e., all mature human beings.[8]

Cicero utilizes the idea of *oikeiōsis* to argue for "the fellowship of all with all," a community bound by justice. In a passage that precedes Cicero's account of political forms, culminating in his defense of patriotic allegiance to the *res publica*, he argues that "reason and speech (*ratio et oratio*)" "unites human beings with one another (*conciliat inter se homines*) through teaching, learning, communicating, debating, and judging. Reason and speech join human beings in a kind of natural fellowship" (1.51). Through *oikeiōsis* (*conciliat inter se homines*), human beings come to develop community. Reason and speech make possible justice, which links human beings together within a common community. Since human beings have the capacity to deliberate about matters of right, which all other animals lack, we begin to develop an affinity with human beings and to identify them with our own interests. This affinity extends to all human beings; thus, there results a fellowship of all among all (1.50–51).

---

[8] Compare the second-century CE Stoic Hierocles' famous and colorful account of *oikeiōsis* at Stobaeus 4.84.23. For bibliography on *oikeiōsis*, see Ramelli 2009 and in Cicero's thought in particular, see Reydams-Schils 2005: ch. 2 and compare Inwood ch. 3, this volume. On family in *De Officiis*, see Wynne ch. 1, this volume.

Cicero next surveys forms of society and offers a genetic account of the origins of the *res publica*.⁹ Fundamental to this account are human beings' natural (*natura*) loves and impulses (*libido*) that unite them into society. Cicero begins with marriage, then moves to the household, which forms the basis of the *res publica*:

> For since this is by nature (*natura*) common to animals, namely, to have the impulse (*libido*) for procreation, the first fellowship (*societas*) exists in marriage itself; the second in children; then a single household, which holds all things in common (*communia*). This is the foundation of the city and, as it were, the nursery of the republic. There follow unions of brothers, later of first and second cousins, who, since they are already unable to be contained in a single house, go out into other houses as though into colonies. There follow marriages and connections from which come even more relations. This stock and progeny is the origin of *res publicae*. (*Off.* 1.54)

Cicero locates the origins of the republic in the household, a move that distinguishes his thought from his later Early Modern liberal admirer John Locke, whose social contract theory begins with the individual.¹⁰ For Cicero, the household, however necessary, is not sufficient for the creation of the republic. He thus introduces another category: the citizen. Cicero had already introduced citizenship earlier in this section, when he reviewed the different forms of society in order from the broadest – the community of all human beings – to the narrowest, the household: "Nearer still is the fellowship of the same city (*civitas*); for many things are shared by citizens (*cives*) among themselves – the forum, temples, porticos, roads, laws, rights, law-courts, elections; in addition, companionship and friends, and commercial and business transactions drawn up by many people with many others" (1.53). At 1.54 he highlights those features of the citizen, which strengthen (and ultimately broaden) the natural benevolence (*benevolentia*) and love (*caritas*) of the family. The *res publica* is held together by natural desires (*libido*) and affections (*caritas*), which it strengthens with conventions that bind citizens to their ancestors and to one another by shared public monuments, rights, tombs, and buildings (1.55).

These foundational loves are natural, but are they rational? After all, on the Stoic account, for mature adults reason supervenes on the original natural drive to love. Cicero finally brings rationality into the picture at 1.57:

> But when you have surveyed everything with a rational outlook (*ratione animoque*), of all fellowships there is none weightier, none dearer (*carior*),

---

⁹ See Dyck 1979a, 78.
¹⁰ For Locke as a reader of Cicero, see Hawley 2022.

than that which exists between each of us and the republic (*res publica*). Dear (*cari*) are parents; dear are children, relatives, and friends; but a single fatherland (*patria una*) has embraced all the affections (*caritates*) of all her inhabitants. On behalf of one's fatherland what good man would hesitate to face death if by doing so he would benefit her? (*Off.* 1.57)

The *res publica* "embraces" "all the affections (*caritates*) of all her inhabitants" (1.57). By this, Cicero means that it makes possible "the Roman's deepest loves" – all the activities and people that make life meaningful.[11] Moreover, the city places a new identity – "citizen" – on top of and beyond the identities and affections generated by the natural bonds of blood. Through the conventional devices of the city – laws, monuments, tombs, and temples – the *res publica* broadens and expands familiar blood relations (1.53–54). At the same time, the boundaries of the *res publica* limit human love and furnish it with intensity.

A "rational outlook" affirms the value of the *res publica* as the dearest and weightiest form of society because of the *res publica*'s unique role in promoting human sociability. To understand Cicero's vision for this role, we need to notice that he is aware of two potential pitfalls in the process of *oikeiōsis*, inasmuch as the process must reconcile two loves: the love for one's own self and its good and the love for others and their good. As we saw at *Off.* 1.12, nature "particularly engenders a special love for one's own children." But Cicero also recognizes that nature stipulates an other-regarding commitment extending outward to any human being. As he writes in Book 3, "if nature prescribes this, namely, that a human being should wish to have regard for another human being, whoever he is, on account of the very fact that he is a human being, it is necessary, according to the same nature, that the advantage of all is common to all" (*Off.* 3.27).

Cicero points out that there is liable to be a tension between these two natural loves, the love of one's own and the love of others. Each, so long as it remains unreconciled with the other, causes problems for political society. The love of one's own keeps us from looking outward to *see* the interests of our neighbors: "We will easily be able to judge what is our duty [to our neighbors] on each occasion," Cicero writes, "*if we do not love ourselves too much*" (*Off.* 1.30). However, there is also a problem native to other-regarding love. If the love of one's own is prone to a nearsightedness that keeps one from *seeing* the interests of others, the love of others is open to a lack of intensity that keeps one from *feeling* the weightiness of those interests. Cicero notes: "It is difficult to be concerned about another's

---

[11] E. M. Atkins 1990: 275.

affairs. Although [the Roman comic poet] Terence's Chremes 'thinks that nothing human is foreign to him', nevertheless we in fact do tend to notice and feel good things and bad things that happen to us more than those things that happen to others, which we see as if a great distance intervenes; accordingly, we judge others differently than ourselves" (*Off.* 1.30).

Political society requires that we not only *see* the needs of others but also *feel* them with some intensity. It requires the broadening of one's natural tendency to love one's own and the intensification of one's natural love for other human beings. The *res publica* achieves precisely this goal. It broadens the love of one's own and strengthens the love of others by giving citizens ties to unite themselves to one another and a sense of a common purpose. But further, insofar as one comes to identify the *res publica* as that which makes possible the loves shared between oneself and one's fellow citizens, the *res publica* makes possible the reconciliation of self-love and other-regarding love, that is, the love of one's own and the love for other human beings. It reconciles these two loves by broadening the former and lending shape and intensity to the latter.

This reconciliation is most clearly manifested in the patriotic sacrifice with which Cicero concludes his defense of the *res publica* as that society to which human beings owe their greatest allegiance (*Off.* 1.57). Cicero asks rhetorically, "On behalf of one's fatherland, what good man would hesitate to face death if by doing so he would benefit her?" In a similar Ciceronian passage, *De Finibus* 3.64, Cato as the spokesman for the Stoic position explicitly draws attention to the connection between the patriotic sacrifice and love. Cato notes that "someone who is willing to die on behalf of the commonwealth ought to be praised, since our country (*patria*) should be dearer (*carior*) to us than ourselves." How does the willingness of a patriot to sacrifice his life for his country indicate the reconciliation of self-love and other-regarding love?[12] This sacrifice of one's life for one's country is other-regarding because one is giving one's life for others; however, it is also self-interested because the patriot is giving his life for what he considers to be his own and holds extremely dear.

Significantly, the patriotic sacrifice is Cicero's second attempt in the section of text ranging from 1.53–58 to reconcile other-regarding love and self-love. The first is found within Cicero's treatment of friendship, immediately preceding his treatment of patriotism. "Nothing is more loveable (*amabilius*) and more uniting than the similarity of good character. Among men who have the same desires and the same wishes, it

---

[12] Cf. the discussion of the patriotic sacrifice at Manent 2006: 205.

comes about that each one is as equally delighted with the other as with himself. The result of this arrangement is that which Pythagoras wanted in friendship, namely, that one comes from many" (1.56). The virtuous admire others who are virtuous precisely because they themselves are virtuous, and they recognize in others the same virtue that they themselves possess. In this respect, the friendship among the virtuous represents an extension of the principle of the love of one's own. It is the most durable form of love of one's own, based not around shared buildings and monuments but around the mutual love of virtue. Insofar as one detects in one's friend a "second self," one finds a marriage between the love of oneself and another. Indeed, Cicero suggests that friendship among the virtuous is the most stable and enduring bond of society (cf. *Off.* 1.56 and *Am.* 56–57, 65–66, 79, 83). However, whether Cicero has in mind the friendship between Stoic sages or a slightly less demanding form of friendship,[13] virtue friendships are relatively rare.

In comparison to virtue friendship, the patriotic sacrifice is a less stable and less perfect union of self-love and other-regarding-love. For one thing, such a sacrifice is liable to be abused, as when a citizen performs a morally reprehensible act in the name of honoring his country. Cicero himself recognizes the potential for abuse and cautions that "some things are so repulsive, so disgraceful, that a wise man would not undertake them even for the sake of preserving his country" (*Off.* 1.159). Still, Cicero's solution to the potential abuse or distortion of patriotic sentiment is not to abandon the fundamental allegiance to the commonwealth but instead to think carefully about where the true interests of the *res publica* really lie (cf. 1.159 and 3.86–88). After all, while the friendship between the virtuous may most securely and completely reconcile self-love and other-regarding love, patriotism, most fully realized in the patriotic sacrifice of one's life for one's republic, represents the reconciliation of self-love and other-regarding love most attainable for the vast majority of human beings, including those for whom Cicero is writing (cf. 1.46, 3.15–16); indeed, it is attainable for every citizen.

Of the various grades of fellowships (*societates*) surveyed by Cicero in Book 1, the association of citizens within the republic best balances the breadth and intensity of love as well as most effectively reconciles self-love and other-regarding love. The familiar bonds of blood are not open to those with whom you do not share these ties; thus, societies based on

---

[13] Dyck 1996: 177 does not think that the sage is in view, but the case is a complicated one: cf. *Off.* 3.15, *Leg.* 1.33–34, and *Am.* 65.

familial ties not only lack the breadth of the *res publica*, but they also do not encompass other-regarding love in the same way as friendship or patriotic allegiance. The ties of friendship, because they come to embrace someone who is not naturally your own by birth, do effectively reconcile the love of one's own with other-regarding love,[14] but friendship is possible only among a few. On the other end of the spectrum, membership in the universal fellowship of human beings, while available to all, is too distant and abstract a concept to generate in individual human beings any strong sense of attachment. Therefore, inasmuch as human society requires some degree of reconciling self-love and other-regarding love, and inasmuch as the *res publica* best accomplishes this reconciliation, then Cicero's account implies that the *res publica* is the political form best equipped to foster human society.

3 Natural Needs and the Republic

In addition to natural loves, for the Stoics sociability also consists of meeting and virtuously responding to our natural needs. So in Cicero's account of *oikeiōsis* at *Off.* 1.12, we read of the adult man, "He devotes himself to providing whatever may contribute to the comfort and sustenance not only of himself, but also of his wife, his children, and others whom he holds dear and ought to protect." In the prior paragraph (1.11), Cicero specifies that human beings possess impulses to fulfill certain natural needs: "From the beginning every species of animal has been assigned by nature to preserve itself, its life, and body; to turn away from those things that seem harmful; and to seek and to provide everything that is necessary (*necessaria*) for living – such as food, dens, and other things of this sort."

The fulfillment of such needs, Cicero makes clear, is not the primary reason why human beings enter into society. As he notes at *Off.* 1.158, "Nor is it true, as is claimed by certain men, that, because of the necessities for life (*necessitatem vitae*), because we are unable to attain or achieve without others those things which nature demands of us, it is for this reason that there was a beginning to community and fellowship among human beings" (cf. *Rep.* 1.39 and *Off.* 1.157).

It is important to distinguish between one's motivations for entering into society and the purpose or function of the resulting society. Once

---

[14] At *Off.* 1.56 Cicero grounds friendship in the mutual love of virtue by men of good character, in which "each one is as equally delighted with the other as with himself." Cf. *Am.* 56–57, 65–66, 79, 83.

political society is formed, one may find that one's reasons for maintaining and perpetuating it are different from the original motivations for founding the society in the first place. Thus, while it is abundantly clear in his account of the formation of political society that Cicero prioritizes the natural human drive to society over fulfilling natural human needs, scholars disagree about whether for Cicero the fulfillment of human need or the promotion of human flourishing is the primary purpose of political society.[15] For reasons that I will explain later in the chapter, I think that on the whole Cicero sees human sociability as the goal of society and so subordinates the meeting of human need to this end. For now, it is enough to note that regardless of where Cicero ranks "need" in terms of the other purposes of human society, his account makes it clear that the fulfillment of human need is *an* important function of political society; indeed, according to Cicero, once human beings are joined together in a community, the natural social drive that brought them together and fosters the new community also meets human needs.

To see why, let's begin with Cicero's suggestive comparison between the collective projects of human beings and other gregarious animals:

> And as swarms of bees herd together, not for the sake of making honeycombs, but since they are gregarious by nature they make honeycombs, so human beings – but to an even greater extent – apply their skillfulness in action and thought, since they have been herded together by nature. (*Off.* 1.157)

Bees "herd together" naturally because they are social, not because together they can better meet their physical needs through the production of honeycombs. Nevertheless, once nature has brought them together, bees produce honeycombs, which serve to meet their needs. Likewise, human beings, who are even more gregarious than bees by virtue of their shared rationality, come together naturally. But their coming together by nature allows for the application of human skillfulness and ingenuity to meet human need.

Of course, need is not explicitly mentioned at 1.157. This is not surprising, given that the emphasis at the end of Book 1 is on the priority of the virtues that regulate human need (justice and liberality) rather than on human need per se.[16] In Book 2, where the focus is placed squarely on those things advantageous for human life, Cicero extends the bee simile's treatment of the relationship between the drive to society and

---

[15] Compare Wood 1988: 132 and the opposing view of Barlow 2012.
[16] For the social virtues such as justice and liberality as regulators of human need, see *Off.* 1.17.

the subsequent enhancement of human skillfulness in a way that brings human need squarely into the picture:

> Indeed, without the gathering of human beings, cities (*urbes*) would not have been built or inhabited. In virtue of this, laws (*leges*) and customs (*mores*) were established, followed by the fair assignment of rights (*ius*) and a fixed way of life. A gentleness of spirit and sense of shame (*verecundia*) followed these things. The result was that life was more secure, and that by giving and receiving and by exchanging our skills and riches we came to lack (*egeremus*) nothing. (*Off.* 2.15)

Just as the natural gregariousness of bees makes possible the production of honeycombs, which in turn serves to meet the needs of bees (1.157), so in this passage natural human gregariousness makes possible the production of cities, which in turn serve as the context in which human skills can make life more secure and reduce human need. Human society helps to enhance human skillfulness, leading thereby to a more secure life and to the reduction of human need.

Cicero argues that a certain type of human society best meets human needs. He makes the point most clearly at *De Officiis* 2.74. Following his own political preferences and Rome's historical practices,[17] Cicero argues that it is best if rulers find ways other than property taxes to meet the needs of the city (such as walls, docks, harbors, aqueducts; cf. 2.60) and its poorer citizens (cf. 2.70, 72). However, he quickly adds that if necessity should require it, those who govern the *res publica* must take heed and make appropriate accommodations if they want the republic to be preserved. Why does Cicero stress the importance of these accommodations? Citizens understand that *an* important function of the *res publica* is the meeting of human need. Therefore, rulers must ensure that this is done, even if doing so means departing from the strict requirements of virtue (cf. 2.60). Cicero admonishes magistrates that they are to govern in such a way that they provide "an abundance of these things which constitute the necessities for sustaining life" (2.74). And, as he emphasizes in this passage, these guidelines are not specific to Rome and Roman magistrates, but to all *res publicae* and those who would rule them. The *res publica*, then, is the social unit that is the primary locus for meeting human needs.

As with its capacity to shape and reconcile human loves, so the *res publica*'s capacity to meet human needs enhances human sociability. Cicero lays the theoretical groundwork for this position in his account of the basic purpose of human society. As he made clear at 1.50–51, the end of society

---

[17] Nicolet 1980: 149–150.

is human sociability. Human beings are rational, social animals and so the meeting of need is connected to, and helps promote, human sociability. This separates Cicero's account from instrumental accounts of the formation of human society, such as those by Protagoras or the Epicureans. When Cicero speaks of society that promotes "advantage" he is construing "advantage" in terms of the "common advantage of human beings" (*ad communem hominum usum*; 1.51). Similarly, humans must make sure that they use the advantages of this life for their own benefit and contribute something "to the common advantage" (*ad communem utilitem*; 1.52).

Cicero elaborates on the connection between human need and sociability in a text discussed earlier, *Off.* 2.15. To our earlier observation that the *res publica* made life more secure as need was met, we must now add two further details. First, Cicero specifies that the polity increases security and reduces need through a particular means: "by giving and receiving and by exchanging our skills and riches we came to lack nothing" (ibid.). This exchange is regulated by the virtues of justice and liberality. Elsewhere Cicero argues that the virtuous – i.e., rational – exchange of goods is nature's way of binding even more tightly human beings together into society and thus enhancing our natural social instinct. Following nature, we ought "to contribute common benefits for the community, and, by the exchange of duties – by giving and receiving – now by skills, now by labor, now by means, to bind together the fellowship of human beings among human beings" (*Off.* 1.22). Cicero's connecting virtuous meeting of need and enhanced sociability is consistent with his earlier suggestion that the social virtues, justice and liberality, have as their object "the necessities (*necessitates*) for preparing and preserving those things that comprise the activities of life, so that ... the fellowship (*societas*) and union of human beings may be preserved" (*Off.* 1.17). What the passage at 2.15 stresses in particular is that natural sociability is enhanced by obeying the conventional laws and customs established by cities to fulfill human beings' natural needs; the exchange of goods and services, so long as most people sense that this is done rationally and fairly, contributes to trust and so builds up society.[18]

Second, *De Officiis* 2.15 specifies that the creation of human cities not only meets human needs but also transforms human nature. Though laws, customs, and habits constituting a "fixed way of life" are conventional, they have a transformative impact on human beings, creating, as it were, a second nature that is more gentle and possesses a heightened sense of

---

[18] See E. M. Atkins 1990.

shame.[19] The city alters human beings so that their natures become more conducive to sociability. Cicero thus suggests that human beings exceed in their capacity for sociability gregarious animals such as bees in two ways: human beings have, as we noted earlier, the additional bond of reasoning about right and wrong to draw them together (cf. 1.50–51); but once they are joined together in a city, the conventions that result from the application of their skills bind them still more deeply. Thus, Cicero identifies the *res publica* as the place where important needs are effectively met and stresses that, when this is done virtuously, human sociability is enhanced.

As in the case of love, so for the socially productive meeting of needs, the size and type of political society matters. Cicero's decision to pick out the *res publica* as the best society to achieve this was not arbitrary (see *Off.* 2.74). On one hand, the *res publica* – the form of society that requires "a union of a great number" (*Rep.* 1.39) – is large enough to have sufficient resources to meet its citizens' needs. On the other hand, it is small enough to provide the knowledge of specific circumstances that Cicero believes is essential for exercising liberality in distributing material resources to the needy (*Off.* 1.59–60). Once again, if the virtuous meeting of human need fosters human society, and if the *res publica* is the particular political society that allows human needs best to be met, then the *res publica* is the political form best equipped to promote human society.

In the final analysis, according to Cicero, one best benefits the universal human society indirectly by making one's first and thickest allegiance to one's own republic. As Cicero declared in a remark at 1.50 that launched his entire discussion of the degrees of fellowship: "Human society and its union will be best preserved if your acts of kindness are conferred upon each person in proportion to the closeness of their relationship to you." Cicero argues for the promotion of general human sociability through the limited, partial, and attached perspective of the citizen rather than from the detached perspective of cosmic justice. Consequently, Cicero's project anticipates what some have called "rooted" or "patriotic" cosmopolitanism.[20]

4 Patriotism, Cosmopolitanism, and Violence

Cicero's defense of the *res publica* on the basis of the same sociability that undergirds his cosmopolitanism is a substantial achievement that in its

---

[19] *Off.* 2.15: "A gentleness of spirit (*mansuetudo animorum*) and sense of shame (*verecundia*) followed these things."
[20] See Appiah 2006.

theoretical sophistication is comparable to or even surpasses influential later accounts.[21] However, several potential objections to Cicero's argument remain: the association of patriotism with violence, Cicero's limited duties of material aid to foreigners, and the challenge posed by slavery to his commendation of citizenship as an instrument to promote human flourishing. Building on the preceding analysis, I will look in the remainder of the chapter at how Cicero answers, or could have answered, these objections. My goal is not to vindicate Cicero on all accounts but through the process of considering these objections to come to a fuller appreciation of the nature of his patriotic cosmopolitanism.

As is clear from the example of the patriotic sacrifice, patriotic attachments may lead citizens at times to harm other members of the larger human *societas* in the defense of their own *res publica*. Isn't this incompatible with Cicero's cosmopolitan commitments?[22]

To this objection, there are two Ciceronian responses. The first is to recall Cicero's extensive account of just war in *De Officiis*. Alongside his general concern with the relationship of the *res publica* to the cosmopolis, Cicero treated the morality of war from various perspectives in his works of political theory of the 50s, *De Re Publica* and *De Legibus*, before taking it up again in *De Officiis*. In the latter work Cicero discusses the grounds for a just cause for declaring war: war should be a last resort when all possible efforts at diplomacy have failed (1.34–35). Following the ancestral Roman fetial law, war requires the identification of an injury and the formal demand for restitution (1.37). War should be guided by its proper purpose: to live in peace without injustice (1.35). Cicero enumerates many restrictions on actions taken within war: war is to be waged by the proper authorities and should be limited to formally recognized soldiers (1.36–37); poisoning is forbidden (1.40; 3.86); soldiers should show leniency in punishment (1.35); truces, treatises, oaths, and promises should be honored (1.38–40); acts dishonoring one's country should be avoided (1.40; 1.159; 3.86); mercy should be given to the loser and refuge to those who seek it (1.35).[23]

Cicero justifies war by grounding it in the same virtue that he believes is the foundation of human sociability – justice. The "first duty" attached

---

[21] For instance, Adam Smith, in his *The Theory of Moral Sentiments* (1976: 219), follows Cicero when he argues for the modern state as the locus of natural human loves but stops short of Cicero's further connection between reconciling these loves and promoting sociability. For similarities with Grotius' later account, see Nussbaum 2022: 290–291.

[22] For this objection, see E. M. Atkins 1990: 277.

[23] For a full discussion of Cicero's account of just war theory, see J. W. Atkins 2023. A briefer account may be found in J. W. Atkins 2022. For the broader context of just war theorizing within Roman political thought, see J. W. Atkins 2018: 176–184.

to the virtue is that "one should not harm anyone unless one has been provoked by injustice" (1.20). The injustice which may rightfully result in punishment may be either to oneself or to one's neighbor. For Cicero, to refrain from acting when you are in position to prevent an injustice to those around you is itself an injustice (*Off.* 1.23, 1.28), and regrettably (so the just-war argument goes) this commitment to justice sometimes requires force.[24]

The second response focuses on advantage. Cicero acknowledges that war takes a horrific toll on the human race: he cites the Peripatetic philosopher Dicaearchus' calculation that more human beings have perished from warfare and human violence than from all natural causes of death combined (*Off.* 2.16). Yet human beings also provide the greatest advantage for one another if their social instinct is fostered (2.17). Since the *res publica* is the form of society best able to foster human sociability, citizens who are devoted to their own *res publicae* are crucial for benefitting the universal human *societas*. To see the logic, let's adapt one of Cicero's own examples, taken in turn from the Stoic Hecato. Just as the *res publica* is generally benefitted by children who revere their parents, even if at times their loyalty to their parents is not in the short-term interest of the *res publica*, so the human fellowship is ultimately best fostered by patriotic citizens who strive above all to see the flourishing of their own various *res publicae*, even if at times this commitment may lead to results (i.e., the use of violent force to take human life) that do not appear to be in the best short-term interest of the human race.[25] In the long run, so Cicero's argument implies, the destructive forces of human violence and natural disasters alike are most reduced through flourishing political societies.[26]

Given Cicero's argument, it is interesting to note that studies by economist Amartya Sen have found that democracies suffer fewer natural disasters than non-democratic regimes. Kwame Anthony Appiah, citing this research, argues that modern cosmopolitans should recognize the importance of healthy regimes for human flourishing.[27] Cicero has a similar view of the republic. The existence of political communities such as the republic that stand between the family, village, and tribe on one side, and the

---

[24] This justification for war entered the later tradition via St. Ambrose's adaptation of Cicero's *De Officiis* in his own *De Officiis [ministrorum]*. For discussion, see J. W. Atkins 2018: 182.
[25] At *Off.* 3.90 Hecato argues that it is in a country's interest for a son to defend his treasury-robbing father out of a sense of *pietas* because having loyal citizens benefits the country in the long run.
[26] Compare *Off.* 2.15 and 2.17 in light of the above argument.
[27] Appiah 2006: 163, 167–168.

cosmopolis on the other, are so vital to human flourishing that a cosmopolitan ethic based on human flourishing should build upon, rather than undermine, republics.

Finally, note that Dicaearchus' calculations about the costs of war are independent of any consideration of political form. By removing the authority to punish, avenge, and defend from the family, village, and tribe, a larger political community such as the *res publica* may in the long term reduce and replace the incessant low-level violent conflict that would otherwise characterize everyday life. Granted, republics' increased size and organizational capacity, features that otherwise contribute to the greater human flourishing, mean that conflicts between republics, while rarer, will be more destructive than those between (say) families or villages. In the Roman context, conflict on a larger scale was enhanced by the imperialism linked to republicanism. Perhaps, considered normatively, republicanism can be separated from militaristic imperialism.[28] For Cicero, commitment to *Roman* republicanism, as an instance of the political form "republicanism" shaped by the unique and irreplicable conditions of Roman history, limits the universal aspirations of republican empire. His logic holds that Roman republicanism could no more be exported wholesale in his day than can American democracy in ours.[29]

5 Liberality and Duties to Strangers

The centrality of the *res publica* for promoting human flourishing is also important for comprehending another place where Cicero has been criticized: the asymmetry of duties of liberality one owes to strangers and to one's fellow citizens. At *De Officiis* 1.51, Cicero cites some lines from the second century BCE poet Ennius to argue "that whatever may be granted without loss should be distributed even to a stranger." One should give freely to strangers common (*communia*) resources, such as running water, fire, or trustworthy advice. "But since the resources of individuals are small but the multitude of those who need them is infinite, liberality that is extended to all (*vulgaris liberalitas*) must be referred to that limit set by Ennius – 'his own light shine no less bright' – so that we may still have the capacity (*facultas*) to be liberal (*liberales*) toward our associates" (1.52).

---

[28] See Nederman 2000, who attributes this position to Cicero.
[29] For a detailed defense of this argument, see J. W. Atkins 2017, followed by Schofield 2021: 125, 140 n. 44.

For Martha Nussbaum, this passage is responsible for perpetuating an unhelpful and false dichotomy that continues to infect our thinking about justice and material aid. "Duties of justice are fully universal, and impose strict, exceptionless obligations…[v]ery different is Cicero's next group of duties, the duties involved in giving material aid to others."[30] Nussbaum is right in noticing a dichotomy in Cicero's texts between one's obligations to fellow citizens and one's obligations to foreigners. In contrast to the positive and thick duties owed to fellow citizens, to once again quote Margaret Atkins, "our duties to the enemy and the passing stranger are minimal and largely negative."[31] However, the contrast between Cicero's accounts of justice and generosity is not quite as stark as Nussbaum suggests.

First, Cicero sees the duties of material aid enjoined by liberality as inseparable from the virtue of justice. The three major constraints that Cicero applies to the duties of liberality are all imposed by the requirements of justice: one should (a) not harm others; (b) not harm oneself or one's own; and (c) take into account what is due to each based on their standing. Cicero is able to insist that liberal acts not be divorced from considerations of justice because he has similar conceptions of the characteristics of these two social virtues. He does not conceive of justice in Kantian terms as strict, universal, exceptionless principles.[32] Instead, he views justice as that which builds up society. This involves some general precepts: give to each what is due to them; do not harm unless harmed; keep trust; contribute to the common good. But each of these requires the exercise of prudence, which in turn requires knowledge of customs, particular circumstances, human nature, and individual persons. While Cicero may be able to give general advice (*praecepta*), he emphatically points out that duties related to "the justice of human fellowship" require "experience and practice" (1.60). Of course, we have much more knowledge about local than national circumstances, which is why, as groups get larger, customs and prudential considerations give way to abstract principles, though even here principles are not absolute, but subject to revision as one learns more about the relevant circumstances and situations.

Cicero's account of liberality mirrors his account of justice in these details. When working out how to distribute our duties within the context of the grades of society within our country, we have a range of customs,

---

[30] Nussbaum 2000: 185. She repeats this critique in Nussbaum 2019: ch. 2 and at Nussbaum 2022: 289–290.
[31] See E. M. Atkins 1990; Atkins' view is endorsed by Schofield 2021: 112.
[32] See Woolf 2007. Contrast Nussbaum 1997.

practices, and experiences to guide us, though these will not be infallible or perfectly consistent guides. In the passage at 1.51–52 Cicero is concerned precisely with those circumstances that take him beyond the laws, customs, and statutes of individual polities. He has in mind duties that are common to all (*vulgaris liberalitas*), that may be extended or applicable to all or many cases.[33] Like the thin "principles" of justice operating beyond our local and national boundaries, the thin "principles" of liberality are operative in situations where we lack the guidance of laws and customs. The reason that we particularly require additional guidance of custom in this area, and struggle if it is absent, is that customs (*more*) and civic codes of behavior (*institutis civilibus*) "are themselves pieces of moral advice (*praecepta*)" (*Off*. 1.148).

What is this thin principle of liberality that may be applied indiscriminately to all in such circumstances? We might summarize Cicero's principle in 1.51–52 as follows: *if a non-citizen has a need, and if you are in a position to meet this need by contributing something advantageous to him or her at little or no cost for yourself, you should do so*. On behalf of this principle, Cicero argues that strict limits must be applied to benefits bestowed on humans by virtue of their humanity alone since, while individual resources are limited, the needs of human beings are infinite. To use our material resources to help every possible stranger with need would require us to exhaust those resources – either entirely or, as Peter Singer and Peter Unger have argued,[34] at least to the point of what we need to survive, i.e., beyond what we would need to continue being liberal. For Cicero, to exhaust one's resources to this degree eliminates one's capacity (*facultas*) to be liberal towards those within the confines of one's own polity. To deny Ennius' limitation while also recognizing a duty to meet human needs throughout the world, as do Singer and Unger, makes it impossible to meet the needs of one's family, friends, city, and country. This in turn is to fail to support, and therefore to be unjust towards (*iniuriosi*), one's own. The result is the inability to heed one of the basic constraints on liberality (*Off*. 1.44): not to be more generous than one's resources allow. Therefore, in situations where we lack the guiding contexts of custom and law, we must limit those benefits that we apportion strictly according to need to resources that cost us little or nothing.

---

[33] *Vulgaris OLD* def. 5: "common to or shared by all; (b) applicable to all or a variety of cases, general."
[34] See Unger 1996 and Singer 2009. Singer argues that infinite need requires us to "keep cutting back on unnecessary spending, and donating what you save, until you have reduced yourself to the point where if you give any more, you will be sacrificing something nearly as important as a child's life – like giving so much that you can no longer afford to give your children an adequate education" (2009: 18).

Whatever one may think about Cicero's argument on this point, we cannot fully appreciate his general position unless we recognize another important distinction in his account: that between the duties that *individuals* owe to outsiders and those that *republics* owe to outsiders. In *De Re Publica* 3, Laelius argues that strong republics may help their weaker allies when they rule for their benefit (*utilitas*). Through looking out for their allies' benefit, republics may "remove from wicked peoples the opportunity to do injury" (August. *Civ. D.* 19.21.34–35 = 3.36 Zetzel). In *De Officiis*, Cicero uses the language of patronage to represent Rome's obligations to its allies; he calls Rome a *patrocinium orbis terrae verius quam imperium*, "a protectorate of the whole world rather than an empire" (2.27). This relationship is characterized not only by the negative and positive duties of justice (to refrain from wronging allies and to protect them from outside aggressors) but also by "acts of kind service" (*beneficia*), which clearly encompass obligations to promote the material aid, and protect the legal rights, of allies.[35] As Malcolm Schofield points out, for Cicero "such corporate responsibilities are conceived as much more substantial than those that individuals should exercise for passing strangers."[36] The greater responsibility that Cicero places on the corporate republic than on the individual human being follows naturally from his argument that the *res publica* as a political form is of the greatest importance for promoting cosmopolitan flourishing.

6 Slavery and Citizenship

Another possible tension within Cicero's patriotic cosmopolitanism concerns his treatment of slavery. Ancient Greek and Roman republicanism traditionally depended upon slavery. Beginning from its presumption of the elevated status of the citizen, there was nothing in the logic of classical republican thought to challenge the dichotomy between "free citizen" and "slave." We might expect to see in Cicero's thought the potential to destabilize this dichotomy. After all, Cicero's justification of the priority of the *res publica* and importance of citizenship derived ultimately from his account of human nature. Citizenship within a *res publica* promotes human flourishing by allowing human beings to fulfill and enrich their social instincts connected to their rational and social natures as *human beings*. If republics promote human

---

[35] For Cicero's use of *patronus* at *Off.* 2.27, see Dyck 1996: 401 and Meyer 1957: 221–223.
[36] Schofield 2021: 112.

flourishing, then one might suppose that Cicero would put a high premium on full membership in a *res publica* (or other such political community) such that slavery would be undermined. What, then, does Cicero say about slavery and citizenship?

Cicero recognizes that his cosmopolitanism implies that the duties of justice must extend to slaves. "Let us remember that justice must be preserved even towards the lowliest. The lowest condition and fortune belongs to slaves. They do not advise badly who order us to treat them as waged employees (*mercennarii*). Work should be required from them and just treatment given to them" (*Off.* 1.41). Here he echoes the Stoic position on several counts. First, Cicero, like the Stoics, rejects Aristotle's view that some could be slaves by nature: slavery was a legal condition brought about not by nature but by fortune. Second, the Stoics recognized that slaves' humanity obligated masters to extend them just treatment. Third, Cicero evokes a saying attributed to the early Stoic Chrysippus, who held that, as subjects of justice, slaves are to be deemed "permanent employees."[37] On this basis, the Roman Stoic Rutilius Rufus is said to have paid his own slaves for the fish that they had caught.

However, Cicero's discussion of justice towards slaves runs up against sharp limits and harsh realities.[38] Slaves were property under Roman law, and as such, completely subject to the arbitrary will of their masters, who could do with them as they pleased, punishing, selling, or even killing them with impunity. For all their talk of justice, Stoics never challenged the legal institution of slavery. Nor could they. Legal slavery impacted the body, and the body for the Stoics was an "indifferent" whose freedom or servitude did not ultimately impact one's ability to be free or flourish. While Cicero's *De Officiis*, written for aspiring statesmen, places more emphasis on indifferents than some other Stoic works such as Epictetus' *Discourses*, its treatment of slavery shares the limitations on challenging legal slavery inherent within the Stoic framework. Hence, Cicero speaks about the ethics of pre-disclosing faults of slaves when buying and selling them, just as one should do with the transactions of other types of "property" such as houses (3.71, 3.91). Cicero agrees with the Stoic Antipater that a master should go beyond the requirements of the civil law in disclosing the faults of a slave at auction, applying his principle of procedure that one

---

[37] Seneca, *De beneficiis* 3.22.1; cf. *SVF* 3.86.20–21. See Dyck 1996: 154 and Griffin and Atkins 1991: 18 n. 3.

[38] Cf. Wynne ch. 1, this volume: 38–9. On Cicero's elevation of slaves to the level of free hired laborers, compare Dyck 1996: 334; Brunt 1973: 29 n. 3; Griffin and Atkins 1991: 18 n. 3.

may not profit at another's expense (3.91). Cicero's acknowledgment of the claims of humanity, including those of the slave's humanity (cf. 3.89), does not for him establish the duty to abolish the legal status of slavery or to extend citizenship to slaves.

Cicero's comparison of slavery to the free wage-laborer (*mercennarius*) incidentally reminds us of another fact sometimes overlooked by Republican theorists.[39] The important slave-free dichotomy should not obscure the fact that there were important gradations within citizenship-status at Rome. Only the adult male paterfamilias had full legal and political rights; all others faced various status-determined "handicaps" to their civil and/or political rights. For instance, the free laborer at Rome was excluded from membership in the Senate.[40] Citizenship for Cicero, as with other elite Romans, incorporated hierarchies of status.

In short, attention to Cicero's discussions of slavery and citizenship in *De Officiis* reminds us of an inegalitarianism that we may miss at first if we read its main republican emphasis on the relative parity of elite citizens through a modern egalitarian lens. For Cicero, as for other elite Romans and (in a different sense) for Stoics, "dignity" (*dignitas*) reflected status. The Roman elite, following the traditional honor code, acquired *dignitas* ("worthy achievement") by progressing through the *cursus honorum*. For the Stoicism on which Cicero drew as he sought to place that code on firmer grounds,[41] "dignity" remained an attribute to be attained, albeit that now one achieved it solely by moral effort. According to Stoicism what is valuable about humanity is our reason. It takes hard work to follow reason, and some of us progress further than others. For Cicero and the Stoics, there remains a sliding scale of value, with the gods and sages on top – even in the *De Officiis* with its more down-to-earth stress on the moral progressor making his way through the world of Late-Republican Roman politics (cf. 1.153). A cosmopolitanism that begins from recognizing the inherent human dignity of all must find its origins in another tradition.[42]

7 Conclusion

In her chapter "Cicero and Twenty-First Century Political Philosophy" in the *Cambridge Companion to Cicero's Philosophy*, Martha Nussbaum

---

[39] Note the (strong) words of caution to republican political theorists posed by Ando 2010.
[40] Cf. 1.150 with Dyck 1996: 335.
[41] See Long 1995, who indicates tensions within Cicero's project. See also J. W. Atkins 2023.
[42] For "dignity" in *De Officiis*, see Griffin 2017. Pöschl 1989 (38–41) mistakenly ascribes the notion of "inherent dignity" to *Off.* 1.106. For "dignity" in the ancient world, see Harper 2016.

writes that Cicero's account at *De Officiis* 1.57 "is still quite possibly the most nuanced account of how a contemporary world citizen should think and feel, in a world where the needs of distant strangers and the institutions of our own nation both demand our concern."[43] As I have argued, the power of Cicero's account lies in showing that citizens' devotion to the flourishing of their own republics is essential for promoting the flourishing of the human society as a whole. Though Cicero's Stoic model has limits (as shown by, e.g., its failure to address slavery), his account in *De Officiis* is still a good starting point for modern cosmopolitans as they reflect on the role of their own nations' institutions and values in promoting human flourishing.

---

[43] Nussbaum 2022: 291.

CHAPTER 11

Cicero's Extremist Ethics

Ingo Gildenhard

1 Introduction

Cicero promotes *De Officiis* as an enterprise in educational activism in the tradition of Cato the Elder: in formal terms a letter addressed to his son Marcus, away in Athens to study philosophy, the work offers instruction to (the next generation of) Roman statesmen more generally.[1] On the syllabus: a civic ethics designed to redress perceived corruptions in Rome's system of values, developed by means of a searching critique of Rome's ruling elite and its political culture that reckons with the defining events of the late republic, in particular the extreme experiences of the 40s – civil bloodshed, expropriations, (the threat of) autocracy, politically motivated assassination.[2] As the most radical aspect of this ethics Cicero endorses protective violence as public duty, up to and including homicide: in Book 3 in particular, but also elsewhere, he maintains that in certain situations each one of us has the right – indeed, the obligation – to kill those (such as Caesar) who pose a lethal danger to communal life.[3] At one level this is

---

The chapter benefitted greatly from feedback provided by audiences at the University of Rome, La Sapienza, University of Durham, University of Konstanz, and University of Toronto (my thanks in particular to Alessandro Schiesaro, Ulrich Gotter, Martin Revermann, Andreas Bendlin, and George Boys-Stones) and the suggestions and editorial attention of Raphael Woolf.

[1] *Off.* 1.1, 3.121. Cf. 2.44–51 (*officia adulescentium*, anticipated by renewed address to his son at 2.42), 1.37, 2.45 (analogy between Cato the Elder's advice on military *ius* to his son and Marcus *filius*' military service under Pompey) and 2.53 (parental epistolary dialogue, in this case Philipp II and Alexander, as a source of general instruction: *hoc ille filio sed praeceptum putemus omnibus*). One particular *iuuenis* (or, indeed, *paene potius puer*: *Phil.* 3.3) very much on Cicero's mind at the time was the young Gaius Caesar, to whom he ascribes many of the virtues lauded in *Off.*: Stone 2008: 223–7. For *Off.* as letter see Gibson and Morrison 2007: 9–10, Ceccarelli et al. 2018: 13.
[2] For *Off.* and contemporary politics (and the *Philippics*), see esp. the excellent studies by Heilmann 1982 and Long 1995, to which the present chapter is much indebted.
[3] *Off.* 1.76–7 explore the analogy Scipio Africanus: Numantia ~ Scipio Nasica: Tiberius Gracchus ~ Cicero himself: Catiline's conspiracy, elevating domestic murder and (if need be violent) suppression of revolution above military achievement abroad. At 2.43 Cicero notes that, while alive, Tiberius and Gaius Gracchus failed to meet with approval from the *boni* and, when dead, were thought to belong among those rightly slain (... *mortui numerum optinent iure caesorum*).

a tall, even counterintuitive, order as Cicero himself acknowledges, asking rhetorically whether there can be any greater crime than to kill not just another human being but a close acquaintance; and yet the Roman people – Cicero goes on to aver, contrary to historical fact – judged Caesar's murder the most illustrious of deeds, achieving a perfect coincidence of the beneficial (*utilitas*) and the honourable (*honestas*).[4]

Cicero's endorsements of the civic commandment 'thou shalt kill (the tyrant)' are not momentary aberrations, unmoored from the rest of the treatise. Rather, the recurrent approval and promotion of ultimate force as a legitimate, or even ethically required, form of communal politics is an integral feature of his overall agenda. Many of the text's most striking conceptual moves are intrinsically related to his effort to come to theoretical and practical terms with the fallout of civil war and the emergence of autocracy (to understand their causes and prevent their recurrence) and to justify tyrannicide, both retro- and prospectively, as a remedial response. His creative play with the (Stoic) concept of *oikeiōsis* ('of how we become familiar with our world'), his investment in justice, his commitment to property rights and his tendentious – if programmatic – identification of the propertied and the just, his theory of double (active and passive) *in*justice, and his authorial positioning vis-à-vis Plato and Caesar as complementary villains, his rhetoric of dehumanization, his drastic use of the metaphor of the body politic, and his ethically motivated exceptions to the binding nature of oaths and other formally sanctioned obligations (to name a few) all help to underwrite the license to kill for the common good. In this sense, *De Officiis* is the philosophical equivalent to his efforts in the *Philippics* to have Antony declared a public enemy (*hostis*).[5] Put differently, politically motivated homicide, as the most extreme yet honourable act endorsed therein, affords a privileged lens through which to read the entire work.

To render this claim plausible, this chapter proceeds in four steps: after a look at the remarkable rift that runs through *De Officiis*, between Cicero's belief in the pro-social nature of humanity and the recognition that no-one inflicts more harm on humans than other humans (2), it surveys the reasons he gives for such perverse and pernicious conduct (3) – as backdrop for an outline of how he imagines a functioning commonwealth grounded in justice (4). This, in turn, sets the stage for a discussion of the

---

[4] *Off.* 3.19. For the aftermath of the assassination see Gotter 1996a.
[5] Heilmann 1982: 172–91.

place of vigilantism up to and including civic-minded murder in his vision of communal life (5).

2 Humanity as Dr. Jekyll and Mr. Hyde, or: The Strange Case of *De Officiis*[6]

Cicero takes it for granted that human nature is inherently pro-social. For philosophical support of this premise, he appeals to Plato and relies heavily on the Stoic doctrine of *oikeiōsis*, suitably reworked. Aspects of it are in play from the outset: after differentiating between human (*homo*) and beast (*belua*) on the basis of our capacity for reason (*ratio*) and speech (*oratio*) (1.11), Cicero asserts our pro-social disposition by variously intertwining references to nature generating harmony between humans more generally (resulting in forms of communal life – *societas, coetus, celebrationes*) and implanting love for our near and dear (offspring, spouse, children, and others in one's care).[7] The ensuing oscillation between kin and community differs from the expositions of *oikeiōsis* we find in other sources, which tend to move methodically outwards in progressively expanding circles from individual to cosmopolis (or *vice versa*).[8] At *Fin.* 3.62–5 (for instance) Cicero starts with the love of parents for their children as a fact of nature and evidence of a *communis hominum inter homines naturalis commendatio* (62–3) and gradually proceeds towards a *communis humani generis societas* (62) or more specifically the cosmopolis of mortals and immortals (64: *communis urbs et ciuitas hominum et deorum*), moving seamlessly across the anthropological-individual, the socio-political and the cosmo-political levels.

Such an orderly procedure, however, would have been at cross-purposes with the priorities of *De Officiis*, focused as it is on socio-political life and *civic* community. Cicero's re-engineering of Stoic *oikeiōsis*, already adumbrated at 1.12, comes fully into its own in 1.50–8:[9] as part of a wider discussion of *liberalitas* and *beneficentia* (1.39–60), i.e. principles that bind

---

[6] For a modern variant on the theme, see Gabbatiss 2017.
[7] *Off.* 1.12. Later in the treatise, the distinction *homo/belua* and related binaries such as *humanitas/immanitas* come to play crucial roles in Cicero's rhetoric of dehumanization, when he (explicitly and implicitly) transforms tyrannical figures into savage beasts, human in appearance only. See May 1996 and below p. 238–40.
[8] *Fin.* 3.16–18, 20–1, 62–5; cf. Hierocles, *Element of Ethics* (Ramelli 2009) with further bibliography at xxxii n. 33).
[9] Discussions include Dyck 1979a, 1996: 165–81, Heilmann 1982, Lefèvre 2001: 36–9. See also Inwood ch. 3, this volume.

humans to each other, these paragraphs offer an account of the different 'societies' in which communal life unfolds, in two movements: in the first, Cicero begins with the broadest form of community, humanity as such, and moves inwards in ever narrowing circles (*gens, natio, lingua; ciuitas; propinqui*) down to our reproductive instinct (1.50–4a), before again circling outwards – but only as far as the citizen community or *patria* (1.54b–8).[10] In the second movement Cicero again oscillates instead of progressing – from household unit (*domus*) to commonwealth (*res publica*) to kinship networks to commonwealth (*res publica*) – and for emphasis reiterates the axiom that kinship relations form the foundation of civic community (1.54: *id autem est principium urbis et quasi seminarium rei publicae; … quae propagatio et suboles origo est rerum publicarum*). The two spheres are here as tightly imbricated as in Roman society, very much in contrast to the sharp separation of *oikos* and *polis* in fifth- and fourth-century Athens.[11]

The account of *oikeiōsis* in *De Finibus* 3 again offers instructive comparison. There, the 'civic' sphere is not entirely absent: Cicero notes that dying *pro re publica* is praiseworthy since the *patria* ought to be dearer to us than we to ourselves (64); but ultimately, the phenomenon of patriotic self-sacrifice remains subordinate to (or, rather, does not seamlessly fit with) the cosmopolitical telos: it is adduced as supporting evidence for the premise (or desirability) of communality at the species level. Otherwise, the social circles on the way from individual to cosmopolis are presented in terms that are semantically bland if deftly alliterated (63: we are by nature suited for *coetus, concilia, ciuitates*; 65: human beings are born to *coniunctio, congregatio, communitas*). *De Officiis* inverts the emphasis: our common humanity only results in relatively weak forms of obligations, such as provision of fire, water or advice – anything that is useful for the recipient without being an excessive burden on the giver. Even if Stoic universalism – and species solidarity – continue to resonate throughout the work, not least in those sections in which Cicero strips tyrant figures of their humanity, our disposition towards sociability is fully realized not in the cosmopolis but in civic community, specifically the shape it takes in Rome.[12]

---

[10] *Off.* 1.22 prepares the ground with the Platonic emphasis on *patria* balancing the species-focus of the Stoics: Cicero argues that we realize our nature and our capacity for reason when putting communal advantages (*communes utilitates*) at the centre of our existence, invoking Plato's doctrine that we are not born for ourselves alone but in equal parts also for our country and our friends and referencing the principles, attributed to the Stoics, that humans are born for the sake of other humans and ought to help each other.

[11] Martin 2002.

[12] On the relationship between cosmopolis and *res publica* see further Atkins ch. 10, this volume.

In the second half of 1.50–8 in particular, Cicero systematically foregrounds the three types of *societas* that define Roman (aristocratic) life: the *patria/res publica*; (extended) family and kinship networks as an integral component of the commonwealth;[13] and friendship.[14] However important kinship relations are, and however privileged a bond (genuine) friendship is, the most important *societas* is the country. Just to make sure, he spells out its absolute priority twice: any evaluation of the matter grounded in reason (*ratio*), he notes (1.57), will rank the *patria* ahead of *parentes, liberi, propinqui*, and *familiares*, before reiterating almost instantly (1.58) that in any contention about precedence, the *patria* comes before *parentes, liberi, domus, bene conuenientes propinqui, amici*.[15] In between the two rankings, Cicero warmly approves of and condemns in the strongest possible terms two complementary extremes (1.57): a good man will not hesitate to sacrifice his life for the common good (*patria ... pro qua quis bonus dubitet mortem oppetere, si ei sit profuturus?*); conversely, those 'who have mutilated their country with all sorts of crime and who have been, and are still, engaged in obliterating her completely' enact subhuman monstrosity (*immanitas*).[16]

These two extreme scenarios – personal self-sacrifice for the common good and monstrous individuals causing societal apocalypse – interlock with central axioms of his civic ethics. *De Officiis* promotes the unconditional priority of the country (*patria*): protecting her well-being outweighs any other obligation including even to one's father – a point spelled out explicitly at 3.82 with reference to the dilemma of father-turned-tyrant.[17] Conversely, preventing her destruction – albeit at the cost of one's own life or, indeed, the lives of those who threaten to destroy her – becomes

---

[13] Cf. Hölkeskamp 2004 on how patriarchy underwrites and unifies the overlapping spheres of *domus* and *res publica*: 'The ideal household also served as the paradigm of authority and of social order in society and in the state as a whole' (114).

[14] On the limits of (Roman) friendship see e.g. Heldmann 1976 and Gotter 1996b. The extensive literature on Roman friendship includes Verboven 2002, Williams 2012 and Rollinger 2014, 2017.

[15] Cf. already *Rep.* 1.1, where Cicero ranks *patria* above parents.

[16] *quo est detestabilior istorum immanitas, qui lacerarunt omni scelere patriam et in ea funditus delenda occupati et sunt et fuerunt.* As *Phil.* 2.52–3 makes clear, Cicero's targets certainly include but are not limited to (Sulla, Catiline and Clodius also fit the bill) the alliance between Caesar and Antony from 49 BCE onwards and Antony's continuation of Caesarian politics in the present: Heilmann 1982: 122, Long 1995: 225, Lefèvre 2001: 37.

[17] If one assumes with Cicero that humans owe their existence to their *patria* and that this constitutes a service that can never be repaid, the willingness to sacrifice oneself for her makes perfect sense within the logic of reciprocity. For the importance of paternal idiom and imagery in Roman culture (*paterfamilias, patronus, patres conscripti, patria*, with the last being 'a sort of collective meta-parent') and the corresponding horror of literal or metaphorical parricide see most recently Lentano 2018: 183–4.

an ethical duty, adumbrated as early as 1.23.[18] Cicero's account of *oikeiōsis*, then, features a distinctive, and distinctively Roman, centre of gravity: the will to self-sacrifice in the service of a mortally threatened *patria*.[19] As the end of *Philippic* 2 and other dramatic passages in the corpus make clear, this is precisely the figure of thought that informs Cicero's political decision-making at the time.[20]

The productive clash of philosophical optimism and historical realism in these paragraphs is typical of the treatise. Despite the axioms of Stoic anthropology, our alleged pro-social instincts, and the dogmatically asserted priority of communal well-being, the world Cicero inhabits and evokes in *De Officiis* is rife with decidedly anti-social phenomena. Violence (*uis*), deception and treachery (*dolus* and *fraus*), barbaric savagery (*immanitas*), and outright delight in cruelty (*crudelitas*) abound. The sense of chaos prevailing is hardly surprising: the Roman commonwealth is no more. Throughout the work, the fact that the most important *societas* for him and his fellow citizens, the *res publica*, is currently in utter ruin – torn to pieces by humans who behave like beasts – functions as leitmotif.[21] In a gradual qualification of the optimistic anthropology endorsed at the outset, *De Officiis* progressively darkens as humanity's paradoxical potential for *in*humanity comes ever more insistently to the fore. Thus when, at the outset of Book 2, Cicero revisits the pro-social nature asserted for humans at the beginning of Book 1 (where he happily highlighted the benefits we derive from each other: 1.22), he adds the sobering observation that the atrocities inflicted by humans on humans through wars and seditions (*bellis aut seditionibus*) exceed those caused by natural catastrophes, such as floods, epidemics, droughts or beasts.[22] The thought is not unprecedented: Plato, for instance, also recognizes that evil outweighs good in human society;[23]

---

[18] *Off.* 1.23: *qui autem non defendit nec obsistit, si potest, iniuriae, tam est in uitio, quam si parentes aut amicos aut patriam deserat.* Dyck 1979a: 79 links these categories to *Off.* 1.58.
[19] If Klein 2016 is right in arguing that the Stoics designed *oikeiōsis* to provide support for the thesis that virtue, conceived of as a correct cognition of the self and the world, is sufficient for happiness, the re-engineering Cicero here performs is stark: the ethical outlook that emerges has closer affinities with Roman military practices such as *deuotio* or *decimatio* than eudaimonistic ethics. On *deuotio*, see Flaig 1991; on *decimatio* as enactment of *utilitas publica* Tac. *Ann.* 14.14, further Hahn 2017.
[20] *Phil.* 2.119, where Cicero announces: 'Give me Liberty or give me Death!' For threatened *libertas* asserting itself against tyrannical power see *Off.* 2.24.
[21] See already 1.35: ... *rem publicam, quae nunc nulla est* ..., further *Off.* 2.3, 2.29, 3.2, 3.4. Cicero makes it clear that the assassination of Caesar, while beneficial, has yet to result in a meaningful revival of the republican commonwealth, very much in line with the views expressed in his contemporary speeches and correspondence.
[22] *Off.* 2.16.
[23] See Plato, *R.* 2.379b–c. Cf. Yong 2016, revisiting Hobbes from an evolutionary perspective.

and Cicero again cites philosophers, in particular Dicaearchus, in support. But subsequent paragraphs (2.23–9) make it clear that this quasi-Manichean vision comes as a direct response to historical experience.

Devoted to the question of how best to generate goodwill, these paragraphs, which form a lexically framed unit, double as a Roman tyrannology, in two parts.[24] In the first (23–6a), Cicero illustrates the importance for those in power of fostering benevolence – ideally by means of their excellence (*uirtus*), if need be also through material resources (*pecunia*) – by bringing into play the chilling example of the tyrant, who generates the opposite of goodwill, i.e. fear and hatred, and gets himself killed as a result. The domestic example of Caesar is again very much to the fore (23, followed by foreign figures in 25–6), with the curious but historically appropriate rider that this tyrant has somehow managed to command obedience from the community that killed him even after his violent death – a topical reference to the contested but continuing validity of the *acta Caesaris* (both real and faked), which dominated Roman politics in the wake of the Ides of March.[25] The inclusion of a protreptic against basing power on fear in a section on how best to win friends and influence people might baffle if it were not for *Philippic* 1, which features an equivalent discussion in its climactic conclusion, addressed to Antony and operating with the same ideas and principles ('tyrants get themselves killed').[26]

Topical negativity is even more pronounced in the second part. In the middle of 2.26 the focus shifts from tyrannical individuals to tyrannical communities, first with reference to the Spartans, then with reference to Rome: Cicero harks back to a period in Roman history when the *populus Romanus* sustained its *imperium* through *beneficia* rather than *iniuria* and justly exercised a 'protectorate of the world', *patrocinium orbis* (27); but it lost sight of this lofty ideal in the wake of Sulla's victory with atrocities perpetrated against both fellow citizens and allies, a process that found its sad conclusion in the triumphant tyranny of Caesar (27–9). Importantly, Cicero implicates himself and any likeminded politician in this story of disaster for not taking action against Caesar's abominable treatment of the Massilians and other allies: sufferance of tyrannical conduct made matters worse. The observation resonates with those passages in the *Philippics* where Cicero expresses regret over his inaction under Caesar and commits himself to the principle 'Never Again!'. *De Officiis*, then, features a

---

[24] See *Off*. 2.23: *diligi* v. *timeri*; 2.24: *ut metus absit, caritas retineatur* and 2.29: *atque in has clades incidimus – redeundum est enim ad propositum –, dum metui quam cari esse et diligi malumus*.
[25] Ramsey 1994.
[26] *Phil*. 1.35, which features the notorious line from Accius' *Atreus* '*oderint dum metuant*'.

conflicted account of human potential tailored to Rome's contemporary political malaise.

3 (Roman) Sociopaths

How does Cicero explain this deplorable discrepancy between norms grounded in nature of how humans ought to interact with each other and organize their communal life and the anomic state of Rome, torn to pieces by tyrannical figures? He nowhere addresses this issue systematically. But his occasional comments add up to a 'psychology of deviance' at the level of the individual, which he explores with specific reference to the socio-political dynamics of late-republican Rome, in particular the interface of wealth and power/status, thus intertwining anthropological and sociological perspectives.

To begin with, Cicero differentiates between the ideal and the real: the perfect human is a notional figure; in actual life, all one can hope for in fellow humans are different degrees of approximation.[27] His universalism is thus one of potential: (most) human beings are by nature capable of living a life in accordance with reason (*ratio*) and nature (*natura*) but may well realize this capacity unequally.[28] Other impulses stand in the way: despite our pro-social nature, altruism is not as obvious a disposition as self-love (in the commonsensical rather than Stoic understanding of the term).[29] And a welter of powerful emotions, such as fear or desire, may drive us to violate the dictates of justice.[30] In addition, Cicero operates with a differential anthropology that recognizes significant differences in the moral disposition of individual human 'natures'. In some humans *uirtus* is all but absent.[31]

Occasionally he brings into view an undistinguished individual unable to resist temptation.[32] But his primary concern are the sins of those who in terms of innate talent count among the very best. His favourite target is Caesar. In *Off.* 1.26, Cicero programmatically exposes his rise to power as making a mockery of three of the four basic aspects of the *honestum*: instead of basing his actions on insight into the truth, Caesar operated in the thrall of a mistaken belief (*opinionis errore*) in his pursuit of supremacy (*principatus*); indifferent to the preservation of *societas*, *fides*, and justice,

---

[27] *Off.* 1.46.
[28] Cf. Forschner 2015: 74.
[29] *Off.* 1.30.
[30] E.g. *Off.* 1.24. Cf. Plato, *Laws* 9.870, where motives for murder include desire for wealth, *philotimia*, and fear of being held to account for earlier crimes.
[31] As implied by the formulation *aliqua significatio uirtutis* at *Off.* 1.46. Cf. 2.84: *ab omni genere hominum et ordine*.
[32] *Off.* 3.79.

he subverted all laws (*iura*); and far from caring for the maintenance of *ordo* and *modus* by way of exercising *modestia* and *temperantia*, he acted out of libidinous rashness (*temeritas*). Yet whereas Cicero has an easy time impugning Caesar for being in violation of truth, justice, and moderation, he found it far more difficult to dispute his claim to the fourth aspect of the *honestum*, namely greatness of spirit (*magnitudo animi*). Indeed, in this respect Cicero counts Caesar among the most gifted individuals Rome had ever seen, a *maximum ingenium*; and he voices, more generally, his irritation (*molestum est*) that the most talented individuals are most prone to fall under the spell of desiring power in its various legitimate (*honor, imperium, gloria*) and illegitimate (*potentia*) manifestations.[33]

Already Plato struggled with this conundrum. In the *Republic*, he too lays the blame for the most catastrophic breakdowns of communal life at the feet of those endowed with the greatest potential, which may manifest itself in deeds of either outstanding goodness or extraordinary evil.[34] If Caesar is a great soul led astray in Book 1, later in the treatise Cicero reassesses his character and motivational profile in a darker key.[35] At 2.28, Caesar's successful *licentia*, which stripped the rest of Rome's ruling elite of its *dignitas*, set an example for other wicked men. He thus left behind a toxic legacy of tyrannical aspiration (*cupiditatum ad multos improbos uenit hereditas*), and even though Cicero uses the plural, the heir apparent of the murdered despot is surely none other than Antony, who, according to Cicero, should long since have suffered the same fate as his lord and master.[36] Towards the end of Book 2, Cicero even implies that Caesar himself became perverted to the point of starting to sin for the sake of sinning, that for him the pleasure of transgression was its own reward.[37] In the course of *De Officiis*, the *magnus animus* and the *maximum ingenium* of Book 1 thus gradually morphs into a psychopath who manifests the same pathologies as individuals wicked by nature (the *improbi*); driven by *libido* he enacts *licentia* and *crudelitas*. Overall, then, a spectrum emerges: Cicero variously attributes anti-social conduct to great natures misled, weak natures tempted or afraid, and perverse natures acting out their wicked instincts – with the categories morphing into one another, especially in the case of Caesar.

---

[33] For the semantics of Roman power terms see Gotter 2008. Cf. *Phil.* 14.18 for *principatus*.
[34] Plato, *R.* 6.489e–91e.
[35] This darkening contrasts with his conception of Caesar in the *Philippics*, where – as foil for Antony and the adoptive father of Octavian – he remains a great soul led astray. See Gildenhard 2011: 96–8 (with reference to *Off.* 1.26 only).
[36] See *Att.* 14.21.3 = 375 SB (11 May 44): *quis enim hoc non uidit, <regem sublatum>* [*add.* SB], *regni heredem relictum?* ('Anyone could see that the king was removed and an heir to the throne was left behind').
[37] *Off.* 2.84. Cf. August. *Conf.* 4.9.

Cicero locates his deviants within wider societal contexts: he is acutely aware that base human instincts and desires find culturally specific articulation and cause culturally specific catastrophes. *De Officiis* is desperately interested in the paradox that members of Rome's ruling elite destroyed their commonwealth (and those of allies) by pursuing the tokens of success their political culture valued most:[38] the text is much concerned with aspects of Rome's political economy, i.e. the interface of wealth and power, and the attendant economics of status.[39] Over the course of the republican centuries pursuit of public office required ever increasing investment of material resources. Cicero brings the relationship of capital and autocracy into explicit focus via the anecdote that the triumvir M. Crassus reckoned anyone under-resourced who was unable to feed an army with the yield of his assets (1.25) just before lambasting the pernicious pursuit of public offices, military commands, glory and Caesar's demented desire for – and attainment of – supremacy (1.26).

What one might label the 'economics of tyranny' remains a preoccupation throughout – from the potentially ruinous finances of maintaining social networks through *liberalitas* or *beneuolentia* to other costly measures of generating public support such as the sponsorship of public games (with excessive investments producing impoverished desperados: see esp. 2.84), from the ruthless conduct of external warfare as a prime enrichment opportunity to the confiscation of private properties to settle veterans. Throughout, ways and means of redistributing wealth (1.43: *pecuniarum translatio*) figure as hallmarks of tyranny, especially those of Sulla and Caesar – from the remission of debt (2.84) to the liquidation of the possessions and estates of adversaries in the preceding civil wars (2.27). The spear (*hasta*) of the auctioneer that advertised the public sale of confiscated goods – not least those of Pompey, sold by Caesar and bought by Antony – stands as one of the most poignant and painful symbols of the lost commonwealth in both the *Philippics* and *De Officiis*.[40]

For Cicero, then, the values of Rome's political culture as misunderstood by wrongheaded or morally weak or otherwise deficient individuals triggered a toxic dynamic, in which the legitimate desire for socio-political rank and standing transmogrified into the unconditional pursuit of supreme pre-eminence and thus ended up destroying a civic community previously grounded in *ratio* and *natura*. How does Cicero propose to fix this problem?

---

[38] Political culture: Hölkeskamp 2017 with further bibliography.
[39] Political economy: Tan 2017; economics of status: Jehne 2016, both with further bibliography.
[40] *Phil.* 2.64, 103–4, 4.9, 8.9; *Off.* 2.27, 29, 83. For Antony's involvement in the transformation of Pompey's assets into Caesarian cash see Ramsey 2004.

In line with his spectrum of human pathologies he opts for a two-pronged remedy: pedagogy, i.e. the re-education of those able to see the error of their ways or the proper induction of the young into the principles of communal life; and, as an emergency measure, the violent elimination of those beyond redemption.

4 The Foundations of Society: Cicero's Justice

Building on the anthropological premise of the pro-social nature of (most of) humanity Cicero grounds his vision of communal life in (a) the foundational importance of justice as the quality that enables human fellowship and (b) the absolute priority of the good of the commonwealth. These two principles enable him to resolve virtually all conflicts of values and ethical dilemmas and impose requisite limits on the immoderate pursuit of wealth, power and prestige. As Margaret Atkins has shown, conceiving of justice as instrumental in realizing our pro-social nature in and through communal life is a distinctive *philosophical* position.[41] Yet her claim that 'the detailed content of the theory itself is strikingly appropriate to the political life and traditions of Rome' (279) needs qualification. It is, to be sure, the impression Cicero would like to convey, and he does his very best to write his theory of justice into the public life and traditions of Rome. Yet under the veneer of tradition he radically innovates, precisely in how he centers the Roman commonwealth in justice. There was no *iustitia*-discourse in Rome before the first-century BCE (as opposed to a legal discourse revolving around *ius* and the principle of *aequitas*) – a fact to be explored in more detail elsewhere.[42] For present purposes what matters is what investment in a Greek-inspired notion of *iustitia* as a foundational principle of community-building affords Cicero in *De Officiis*.[43]

To begin with, it helps him settle tensions between different aspects of the *honestum*.[44] The duties and demands of justice, Cicero argues against those endorsing the philosophical life, take precedence over *cognitio ueri* – just as they need to temper, so Cicero argues against high-minded glory-seekers, the enactment of *magnitudo animi*.[45] The primacy of justice enables Cicero not just to polemicize against the lifestyle of the Greek philosopher,

---

[41] Atkins 1990.
[42] For a brief history of *iustitia* see Thome 1999.
[43] The following paragraphs owe much to Gotter 2003, not least from a methodological point of view.
[44] Outlined initially at *Off.* 1.15.
[45] Tensions between *iustitia* and *decorum* are dismissed as purely notional, though interestingly Cicero concedes that philosophers such as Posidonius imagined certain abstruse scenarios in which a sense of *decorum* might result in someone who is just not doing the just thing – such as saving the *res*

but to reform the common sense, the political economy, and the political culture – grounded as they are in utilitarian reciprocities in interpersonal relationships – of late-republican Rome. In addition, Cicero reconfigures Roman values, placing them 'within an ethical framework which will show that they are proper objectives if and only if they are combined with justice'.[46] With the toxic dynamics of Rome's political economy firmly in mind he invokes considerations of justice to insist on restraint in the exercise of *beneficentia* and *liberalitas*.[47] Other concepts that come in for recoding include *amicitia, fides, gloria,* and *uirtus*. To differentiate the traditional semantics of Roman value terms from the new significance they acquire through their alignment with *iustitia* he uses a Platonizing idiom of seeming and being: understandings grounded in unreformed common sense attract attributes such as *inanis, fictus,* or *simulatus*; philosophically informed redefinitions sport the quality label *uerus*.[48] And just as the universe of Roman values undergoes a 'justification', the 'good man' (*uir bonus*) in the tradition of Cato the Elder morphs into 'the just man' (*uir iustus*): good citizens are not only propertied, they also adhere to a political ethics of justice.[49]

Pervasive appeals to Roman *ius*, in particular the inviolability of property rights, complement the innovative centrality Cicero accords to *iustitia* in how he imagines socio-political community.[50] This may surprise: after all, Cicero concedes that private property does not originate in nature but is the outcome of historical developments and hence societal convention.[51] But he subtly embeds this particular aspect of *ius* within his discourse of *iustitia*, simultaneously conceding that private property is not a 'natural' state of affairs while maintaining that the infringement of property rights violates the *ius humanae societatis* (1.21). The formulation is not *just* 'a *variatio* for *iustitia*':[52] Cicero deliberately opts for a gloss that blurs the boundaries between an aspect of positive *ius* and philosophical *iustitia*. A similar operation occurs at 2.73, where he identifies the protection of property rights as the motivation behind the founding of *res publicae* and *ciuitates*. Conversely, those figures who either agitated for or performed

publica (but, he continues, the actions under consideration are so abhorrent that not even the *res publica* would want the *sapiens* to undertake them): *Off*. 1.159. On *decorum* in the work see further the chapters by Bishop and McConnell, this volume.

[46] Long 1995: 215.
[47] See esp. *Off*. 1.43: *Quare L. Sullae, C. Caesaris pecuniarum translatio a iustis dominis ad alienos non debet liberalis uideri; nihil est enim liberale, quod non idem iustum.*
[48] See esp. *Off*. 2.42–3 with reference to *gloria*; and see White ch. 7, this volume.
[49] *Off*. 2.38, 2.42.
[50] For this emphasis, see Wood 1988: 105–19, further Straumann 2016.
[51] *Off*. 1.21.
[52] Dyck 1996: 112.

redistribution of land or outright expropriations – from the Gracchi to Sulla to Catiline to Caesar and Mark Antony – are all tyrannical figures who threaten to destroy *ius*/*iustitia* and hence also *patria*/*res publica*.[53]

5 Active and Passive Injustice, the Monster and the Body Politic

Ideally, then, communal life relies on positive law (*ius*), legal principles (*aequitas*) and, above all, the ethical concept of justice (*iustitia*) as a normative guide, articulated and reinforced by such educational interventions as Cicero's *philosophica*. Yet in contemporary Rome tyrant figures on the loose have caused (or threaten to cause) communal meltdown. In such situations extreme measures prove necessary to salvage or safeguard the commonwealth. For this purpose, Cicero turns each citizen into a vigilante – a self-appointed activist ready to undertake acts of protective violence also without explicit legal authority. He introduces this civic responsibility early on by identifying two types of injustice: an active one, which consists in harming a fellow human being; and a passive one, which occurs whenever one does not protect a fellow human being from suffering harm even though one could.[54] The example Cicero supplies for each type integrates his theory of double injustice with his overall argument and authorial persona. To illustrate active injustice he invokes Caesar (1.26, discussed above); to illustrate passive injustice he gestures to the philosopher-kings of Plato's *Republic* (1.28), after rehearsing various factors that cause violations of the duty to protect others from harm (fear of incurring enmities, aversion to toil, reluctance to waste resources, or simply sloth or selfishness).

Attacks on philosophers because of their supposed withdrawal from society are a familiar feature of Cicero's writings; but elsewhere he tends to aim his criticisms at Epicurus and his followers – obvious and easy targets given their doctrinal commitment to a life outside the public limelight.[55] Plato and his philosopher-kings make for rather more dubious adversaries. Cicero concedes that *under compulsion* the philosopher-kings *will* get involved in government; but justice, he submits, requires a *voluntary* commitment to do what is right.[56] The disposition of Plato's imaginary rulers – otherwise

---

[53] Gracchi: apart from *Off.* 1.76–7 and 2.43 (above n. 3) see also 2.72–3.
[54] *Off.* 1.23.
[55] See, for instance, the preface to *Rep.* or *Tusc.* 1.6. Already in *Off.* 1.13, Cicero restricted the time to be spent on theoretical studies – despite their foundational importance to what it means to be human and to communal welfare – to those hours that remain available after the satisfactory completion of obligatory affairs in public life (*cum sumus necessariis negotiis curisque uacui* …). In 1.28, he takes the priority of political practice over philosophical theory an important step further.
[56] Cicero here (polemically) ignores the Plato of the Letters, for which see McConnell 2014.

perfect embodiments of justice given their contempt for politics and preference for a philosophical life devoted to theoretical contemplation of the truth – thereby renders them liable to the charge of passive injustice. The attack is rather contrived even though it reinforces the point that no-one who wishes to fulfill the twofold obligation of justice – abstention from harming others, protection of those who may suffer harm – is allowed to disengage from socio-political life: *even* philosophers, who do no-one any harm and single-mindedly pursue, no less, the first requirement of the honourable, i.e. the search for truth, are, through the very existence they lead, potentially guilty of the evil (injustice) that destroys society.

Arguably, the answer to the puzzle is Cicero's desire to intertwine the doctrinal content of his work with his authorial self-fashioning. Setting up Plato's philosophers as a negative foil within his theory of twofold injustice turns Plato into a figure obliquely complementary to Caesar – a ploy that yields a configuration of programmatic significance. The greatest philosopher of Greece and the greatest tyrant of Rome mark the coordinates that allow Cicero to stake out his own position on duties, situated midway between the excesses of both: the Caesarian pursuit of power and the Platonic search for truth. The following table illustrates the point:

	Caesar	Plato	Cicero
Justice	Actively unjust	Passively unjust	Enacting justice
Social type	Rex/*tyrannus*	*Philosophus*	a *princeps ciuitatis*
Terms of existence	Powerbroker in a world of *opinio* and *error*	Passive life in the world of truth (theoretical *ueritas*)	Active life in the world of truth (applied *ueritas*)
Main Activity	Passion-led practice in a world of falsehood	Contemplation of the truth (*theoria*)	Theoretically enlightened practice
Motivation	Self-interest	Self-interest	Communal welfare
Centre of self	Body	Mind	Mind and body
Centre of life	Warfare	Private existence	Peaceful politics
Key ideals	Political office, military commands, power, and glory according to *contemporary* Roman 'common sense'	Pursuit of theoretical truth according to the principles and priorities of Greek philosophy	Statecraft through theoretical insight into (equivalent to ancestral wisdom about) the true nature of things
Affiliated aspect of the honourable	*Magnitudo animi* (untempered by justice)	*Cognitio ueri* (untempered by justice)	*Iustitia* + *magnitudo animi* & *cognitio ueri*

As the table shows, Cicero's theory of active and passive injustice, with its respective figureheads of Caesar and Plato, goes right to the heart of his pedagogy, philosophy and politics – as well as his double mission of asserting Roman superiority over Greece while using Greek conceptual resources to develop an educational programme that can serve as a bulwark against tyranny at Rome. Both Caesar and Plato's philosopher-kings are at cross-purposes with a republican commonwealth grounded in justice: the former through his desire for omnipotence; the latter through their contempt for politics owing to an exclusive interest in *inuestigatio ueri*. But each figure or type represents one key aspect of the *honestum*, viz. greatness of spirit that manifests above all in the willing embrace of political responsibility; and insight into truth. If these temper each other, they yield a truthful politics devoted to justice. Cicero's own position thus integrates the respective virtues of Caesar and Plato while simultaneously avoiding their respective vices.

One form of passive injustice consists in inaction in the face of the most extreme form of active injustice perpetrated by tyrant figures, who destroy the most important *societas* (the *patria*) and the very foundations of communal life (*iustitia*). Cicero renders this fully explicit in Book 3 by inserting elements of tyrannology into the discussion. The avowed purpose of the final book is to explore potential conflicts between the *utile* and the *honestum* or, rather, to show that any such conflicts are only apparent. They disappear if assessed against the foundational significance of *iustitia* and the axiomatic priority of the common good (*communis utilitas*), protection of which is by definition honourable. As part of this agenda, Cicero sets himself a challenge that would seem even tougher than resolving a conflict between the beneficial and the honourable: to show that something seemingly shameful (*turpe*) is in fact both *utile* and *honestum*.[57] And his prime example of an act that looks disgraceful on the face of it (homicide) but may in certain circumstances well be regarded as both beneficial and honourable is the assassination of Caesar. Cicero's attacks on Caesar in *De Officiis* have often been taken as unfortunate personal outbursts motivated by visceral hatred; but such a reading arguably misses the point. His attacks are not so much directed *ad hominem* as *ad genus* – as 3.32 makes clear:

> nulla est enim societas nobis cum tyrannis et potius summa distractio est, neque est contra naturam spoliare eum, si possis, quem est honestum necare, atque hoc omne genus pestiferum atque impium ex hominum communitate exterminandum est. etenim, ut membra quaedam amputantur si et ipsa sanguine et tamquam spiritu carere coeperunt et nocent reliquis partibus corporis, sic ista in

[57] *Off*. 3.19.

figura hominis feritas et immanitas beluae a communi tamquam humanitatis corpore segreganda est.[58]

> For there can be no fellowship between us and tyrants – on the contrary there is a complete estrangement – and it is not contrary to nature to rob a man, if you are able, whom it is honourable to kill. Indeed, the whole pestilential and irreverent kind ought to be eliminated from the community of humans. For just as some limbs are amputated, if they begin to lose their blood and their life, as it were, and are harming the other parts of the body, similarly if the wildness and monstrousness of a beast appears in human form, it must be removed from the common body of humanity.[59]

Cicero here relies on his opening anthropology where he differentiates between human (*homo*) and beast (*belua*).[60] Resorting to the universalizing 'we' (*nobis*), he strips Caesar and his ilk of their humanity, turning tyrannical individuals into a separate 'race' (*genus*) of monsters who, while embedded within human society, are human in appearance only. Cicero follows Plato in dehumanizing the tyrant: in the *Republic*, this figure transforms literally into a wolf;[61] in Cicero, the tyrant retains his human form – but behind the veneer of humanity lurks a savage beast. If the community wishes to survive, such cancerous elements within the body politic – as in the *Philippics* and elsewhere Cicero employs the biological metaphor of the civic community as a corporeal entity – must be exterminated:[62] the gerundive *exterminandum est* has axiomatic force and doubles as a call to arms. It articulates a civic duty and a code of conduct for anyone interested in avoiding the charge of passive injustice by safeguarding communal life.[63]

In the run-up to 3.32, Cicero uses the legendary Sicilian tyrant Phalaris as example. But in *De Officiis* the specimens of the 'breed of tyrants' (*genus tyrannorum*) that matter most are Caesar and his self-appointed successor Antony. Thus, in 3.82 he dismisses, in the form of a rhetorical question,

---

[58] For the text see Dyck 1996: 535: 'I adopt (with Muretus) the correction *humanitatis corpore* offered by some *recentiores* for *humanitate corporis*; if taken literally, this latter reading results in absurdity'. Cf. Winterbottom's OCT apparatus: 'humanitatis corpore *1469, Muretus, fort. recte*'.

[59] Translation by Griffin and Atkins, adjusted.

[60] May 1996 traces the ramification of this initial distinction throughout *Off.* and shows how it culminates in this passage and 3.84, with the monstering of the tyrant and in particular Caesar. For Antony as monster in human form (*belua*) see *Phil*. 3.28 with Manuwald 2007: 426–7, listing further bibliography. See esp. Lévy 1998.

[61] Plato, *R*. 8.565d–6a.

[62] For the body politic see Koschorke et al. 2007, Gildenhard 2011: 125–32, Walters 2020.

[63] See *Phil*. 8.15, linking his own action against Catiline to the current fight against Mark Antony: 'If something in the body is causing harm to the rest, we allow it to be cauterized and cut so that this or that member may perish rather than the whole body. Likewise in the body politic (*in rei publicae corpore*): let whatever is noxious be amputated (*quicquid est pestiferum, amputetur*) so that the whole may be saved'. I cite the translation of Manuwald 2007.

the difference between Plato and himself in conceptualizing the monstrosity of the tyrant (actual transformation into a beast or enactment of the qualities of the *belua*, in particular savagery) as backdrop for putting Caesar in the dock:[64] he claims that verses from Euripides' *Phoenissae*, in which Eteocles claims that the pursuit of absolute power (if nothing else) justifies the violation of *ius*, inspired the dictator to the point of perpetrating the foul and abominable murder of his country (*foedissimum et taeterrimum parricidium patriae*):[65] Caesar, who had once been hailed as father of his country (*parens patriae*), is charged with the murder of the parent of all, the *patria* – for which he rightly suffered the death penalty in turn.[66]

To gain scope for such salvific acts of protective violence Cicero further argues that the ethical duty to uphold the demands of justice overrides formal obligations of friendship, law or religion. The discussion of oath-taking in Book 3 is a case in point. *Generally speaking*, Cicero endorses the binding nature of the oath as an important commitment not to be violated. But his treatment also comprises unconventional emphases that downplay the formally binding nature of oath-taking and, in special circumstances, even advocates oath-breaking. To allow for this possibility Cicero internalizes and secularizes the oath. God becomes a cipher for something else: our mind or conscience.[67] The ties at issue are not so much religious as ethical (and hence socio-political). These considerations form the basis for identifying situations in which a formally correct oath is not binding: if one is in the power of a pirate, who like the tyrant is an enemy of everyone (*communis hostis omnium*), standard protocols of trustworthiness that underwrite and inform social life cease to apply: in Cicero's terms, there is no *societas* between 'us' and specific figures who, on account of their anti-social and monstrous actions, do not belong to any human community.[68] Personal conscience thus becomes the ultimate arbiter of action, which entails the dismissal of the gods as guarantors of oaths and the redefinition of perjury: *non enim falsum iurare periurare est, sed quod* EX ANIMI TUI SENTENTIA *iuraris, sicut uerbis concipitur more nostro, id non facere periurium est* ('to swear something false is not perjury; but not to do what

---

[64] *Off.* 3.82: *quid enim interest, utrum ex homine se conuertat quis in beluam an hominis figura immanitatem gerat beluae?*

[65] *Off.* 3.82–3. For Cicero's use of tragic citations in *Off.* see Gildenhard 2007.

[66] *Parricidium* (of the *patria*) is a leitmotif in the *Philippics*: 2.17, 3.18, 6.4, 11.14, 11.27, 11.29, 12.15, 13.20, 13.22, 13.48, 14.32, 14.35. Cf. already *Cat.* 1.17 and 1.33; *Rab. Perd.* 27; *Sul.* 6 and 76, *Dom.* 133, as well as *Tusc.* 5.6 and *Att.* 10.10.5. For patriarchy (and homicide) in Rome see e.g. Martin 2009, Bauman 2002: 55, Sigismund 2008: 16, Gaughan 2010.

[67] *Off.* 3.44.

[68] *Off.* 3.107–8.

one swears "in accordance with your mind's opinion" – to use our customary expression – *that* is perjury').[69] This line of argument frees prospective tyrannicides to take action – even when they happen to have sworn an oath of loyalty to the tyrant or are bound to him through ties of friendship and as recipients of benefactions.[70]

In his late *philosophica* more generally and *De Officiis* in particular, Cicero launches a considered assault on formal obligations of any kind, including the logic of reciprocity that sustains friendship, formally binding religious speech acts such as oaths, or legislative measures and legal procedures *if* – and this proviso is of course all-important – these are at variance with basic principles of his civic ethics. He does not dismiss the principle of reciprocity, or formal religion, or positive law; but ethical judgment overrules formal obligation.

6 Conclusion

From 133 BCE onwards, when the tribune Tiberius Gracchus and scores of his followers were slaughtered by a faction around Scipio Nasica, the killing of fellow citizens – and the attendant need to justify it – became a defining feature of Roman public life: a range of murderous practices and legal and constitutional measures and counter-measures, such as politically motivated murder, violent insurrection, civil war, proscriptions, the *senatus consultum ultimum*, or *hostis*-declaration, entered Rome's political playbook and fundamentally reshaped its cultural imaginary.[71] Reaching political maturity during Sulla's reign of terror Cicero in due course became himself a major contributor to these developments, with the transformation of Catiline from *ciuis* into *hostis* and the execution of his followers without trial. After his return from exile, suffered for those very acts that gained him the title of father of his country, appearances in court on behalf of defendants accused under legislation against public violence, notably Publius Sestius and Titus Annius Milo, afforded him the opportunity for revisiting his consular actions against Catiline and his followers in an auto-apologetic mode and for developing distinctive theories that justified the use of (murderous) violence in a civic context.[72] *De Officiis*

---

[69] *Off.* 3.108.
[70] The problematics Cicero rehearses with reference to pirates and tyrants – and the idiom he developed for doing so – have resonated down the centuries and remain alive in contemporary definitions and discussions of crimes against humanity in international law and terrorism: see e.g. Heller-Roazen 2009; Luban 2018a, 2018b; de Wilde 2018.
[71] Murder: Sigismund 2008; *hostis*-declaration: Ungern-Sternberg 1970.
[72] For *Sest.* see Kaster 2006; for *Mil.* Forschner 2015.

(and the *Philippics*) are simply his *consultum ultimum* in this respect, his most coherent and ambitious attempt to articulate a personal vision of the principles that sustain civic community and to give his particular perspective on Roman politics an ethical-philosophical underpinning both for ordinary times and in the current crisis.

Although – or perhaps precisely because – he did not partake in the conspiracy against Caesar, he adopted an extremist position on the issue of 'legitimacy beyond the law' in the aftermath of the assassination, which seems to have left most of his contemporaries, even those who sank their daggers into the dictator, cold.[73] Those involved in the conspiracy had no-one else on their kill-list and wanted to return to constitutional politics much to Cicero's regret.[74] *De Officiis* tries not only to elevate what happened on the Ides of March into an exemplary deed and inspiring historical precedent but to validate the event with reference to philosophical principles, in an effort to render tyrannicide a *repeatable* option in Rome's political arsenal. Cicero endeavours to convince Rome's ruling elite that in certain circumstances (such as those that apply at the time of writing ...) extra-legal and extra-constitutional measures might well be required and are fully justified to safeguard the commonwealth. The outcome is a vigilante ethics for the politics to which he had committed himself in the very moment he opted to pen the treatise: fighting Antony as an aspiring autocrat. Ultimately, of course, the one who ended up murdered was Cicero himself.

---

[73] Gotter 1996a, Christian 2008.
[74] Cf. *ad Brut.* 1.4 = 10 SB, where Brutus insists any action taken against Antony required a senatorial decree or popular decision: see Christian 2008: 165–7 for discussion.

References

Algra, K. et al. eds. 1999. *The Cambridge History of Hellenistic Philosophy*. Cambridge: Cambridge University Press.
Ando, C. 2010. '"A Dwelling beyond Violence": On the Uses and Disadvantages of History for Contemporary Republicans', *History of Political Thought* 31, 183–220.
Annas, J. 1989. 'Cicero on Stoic Moral Philosophy and Private Property', in Griffin and Barnes, 151–73.
  2011. *Intelligent Virtue*. Oxford: Oxford University Press.
Appiah, K. A. 2006. *Cosmopolitanism: Ethics in a World of Strangers*. New York: W. W. Norton & Company.
Atkins, E. M. 1990. '"Domina et Regina Virtutum": Justice and Societas in *De Officiis*', *Phronesis* 35, 258–89.
Atkins, J. W. 2017. 'Natural Law and Civil Religion: De legibus Book II', in Höffe, 167–86.
  2018. *Roman Political Thought*. Cambridge: Cambridge University Press.
  2022. 'Empire, Just Wars, and Cosmopolitanism', in Atkins and Bénatouïl, 231–51.
  2023. 'Cicero on the Justice of War', in N. Gilbert, M. Graver, and S. McConnell eds. *Power and Persuasion in Cicero's Philosophy*. Cambridge: Cambridge University Press, 170–204.
Atkins, J. W. and T. Bénatouïl eds. 2022. *The Cambridge Companion to Cicero's Philosophy*. Cambridge: Cambridge University Press.
Baraz, Y. 2012. *A Written Republic: Cicero's Philosophical Politics*. Princeton: Princeton University Press.
Barlow, J. 2012. 'Cicero on Property and the State', in Nicgorski, 212–41.
Barnes, J. 1989. 'Antiochus of Ascalon', in Griffin and Barnes, 51–96.
Barney, R. 2003. 'A Puzzle in Stoic Ethics', *Oxford Studies in Ancient Philosophy* 24, 303–24.
Bauman, R. 2002. *Crime and Punishment in Ancient Rome*. London: Routledge.
Bishop, C. 2019a. *Cicero, Greek Learning, and the Making of a Roman Classic*. Oxford: Oxford University Press.
  2019b. '*Magnum Opus*: Atticus, Cicero, and Eratosthenes' *Geography*', *Rheinisches Museum für Philologie* 162, 265–91.

Blank, D. and C. Atherton. 2003. 'The Stoic Contribution to Traditional Grammar', in B. Inwood ed. *The Cambridge Companion to the Stoics*. Cambridge: Cambridge University Press, 310–27.
Blundell, M. 1990. 'Parental Nature and Stoic Οἰκείωσις', *Ancient Philosophy* 10, 221–42.
Brennan, T. 1996. 'Reasonable Impressions in Stoicism', *Phronesis* 41, 318–34.
  2005. *The Stoic Life: Emotions, Duties, and Fate*. Oxford: Oxford University Press.
  2014. 'The *kathēkon*: A Report on Some Recent Work at Cornell', *Philosophie Antique* 14, 41–70.
Brittain, C. 2001. *Philo of Larissa: The Last of the Academic Sceptics*. Oxford: Oxford University Press.
Brouwer, R. 2014. *The Stoic Sage*. Cambridge: Cambridge University Press.
Brunschwig, J. 1986. 'The Cradle Argument in Epicureanism and Stoicism', in M. Schofield and G. Striker eds. *The Norms of Nature*. Cambridge: Cambridge University Press, 113–44.
Brunt, P. 1973. 'Aspects of the Social Thought of Dio Chrysostom and of the Stoics', *Proceedings of the Cambridge Philological Society* 19 (199), 9–34.
  2013. 'Panaetius in *De Officiis*', in M. Griffin and A. Samuels eds. *Studies in Stoicism*. Oxford: Oxford University Press, 180–242.
Ceccarelli, P. et al. 2018. 'Introduction', in *Letters & Communities: Studies in the Socio-political Dimensions of Ancient Epistolography*. Oxford: Oxford University Press, 1–39.
Christian, E. 2008. 'A Philosophy of Legitimacy in Cicero's *Philippics*', in Stevenson and Wilson, 153–67.
Coates, T.-N. 2015. *Between the World and Me*. London: The Text Publishing Company.
Cole, T. 1967. *Democritus and the Sources of Greek Anthropology*. Cleveland: Western Reserve University Press.
Cooper, J. 1999. *Reason and Emotion*. Princeton: Princeton University Press.
Damon, C. 2010. '*Quid tibi ego videor in epistulis*? Cicero's *verecundia*', in R. Rosen and I. Sluiter eds. *Valuing Others in Classical Antiquity*. Leiden: Brill, 375–90.
Decleva Caizzi, F. 1991. 'τῦφος contributo alla storia di un concetto', in M. Billerbeck ed. *Die Kyniker in der modernen Forschung: Aufsätze mit Einführung und Bibliographie*. Amsterdam: Grüner, 273–85.
De Lacy, P. 1977. 'The Four Stoic *Personae*', *Illinois Classical Studies* 2, 163–72.
Demmel, M. 1962. *Cicero und Paetus* (ad fam. IX 15–26). Diss. Cologne.
Desmond, W. 2006. *The Cynics*. Stocksfield: Acumen.
de Wilde, M. 2018. 'Enemy of All Humanity', *Netherlands Journal of Legal Philosophy* 2, 158–75.
Dörrie, H. 1990. *Der Platonismus in der Antike. Band II: Der hellenistische Rahmen des kaiserzeitlichen Platonismus*. Stuttgart: Frommann-Holzboog.
Dressler, A. 2015. 'Cicero's Quarrels: Reception and Modernity from Horace to Tacitus', in W. Altman ed. *Brill's Companion to the Reception of Cicero*. Leiden: Brill, 144–71.

Dugan, J. 2005. *Making a New Man: Ciceronian Self-Fashioning in the Rhetorical Works*. Oxford: Oxford University Press.
Dyck, A. 1979a. 'On the Composition and Sources of Cicero, *De Officiis* 1.50–58', *California Studies in Classical Antiquity* 12, 77–84.
  1979b. 'The plan of Panaetius' περὶ τοῦ καθήκοντος', *American Journal of Philology* 100, 408–16.
  1984. 'Notes on Composition, Text and Sources of Cicero's "De Officiis"', *Hermes* 112, 215–28.
  1996. *A Commentary on Cicero, De Officiis*. Ann Arbor: University of Michigan Press.
Feeney, D. 2002. 'The Odiousness of Comparisons: Horace on Literary History and the Limitations of Synkrisis', in M. Paschalis ed. *Horace and Greek Lyric Poetry*. Rethymnon: University of Crete, 7–18.
Flaig, E. 1991. 'Amnestie und Amnesie in der griechischen Kultur: das vergessene Selbstopfer für den Sieg im athenischen Bürgerkrieg 403 v. Chr.', *Saeculum* 42, 129–49.
Forschner, B. 2015. *Die Einheit der Ordnung. Recht, Philosophie und Gesellschaft in Ciceros Rede Pro Milone*. Munich: Beck.
Foucault, M. 2001. *L'herméneutique du sujet*. Paris: Le Seuil-Gallimard.
Fox, M. 2007. *Cicero's Philosophy of History*. Oxford: Oxford University Press.
Frede, M. 1999. '*Epilogue*,' in Algra et al., 771–97.
Gabbatiss, J. 2017. 'Is Violence Embedded in Our DNA?', *Sapiens*, www.sapiens.org/biology/human-violence-evolution.
Garnsey, P. 2009. 'Cicero on Property', in J. Carlsen and E. Lo Cascio eds. *Agricoltura e Scambi nell' Italia Tardo-Repubblicana*. Bari: Epiduglia, 157–66.
Gaughan, J. 2010. *Murder Was Not a Crime: Homicide and Power in the Roman Republic*. Austin: University of Texas Press.
Gazich, R. 1995. *'Exemplum' ed esemplarità in Properzio*. Milan: Università Cattolica del Sacro Cuore.
Gibson, R. and A. Morrison. 2007. 'What Is a Letter?', in R. Morello and A. Morrison eds. *Ancient Letters: Classical and Late Antique Epistolography*. Oxford: Oxford University Press, 1–16.
Gildenhard, I. 2007. 'Greek Auxiliaries: Tragedy and Philosophy in Ciceronian Invective', in J. Booth ed. *Cicero on the Attack: Invective and Subversion in the Orations and Beyond*. Swansea: The Classical Press of Wales, 148–82.
  2011. *Creative Eloquence: The Construction of Reality in Cicero's Speeches*. Oxford: Oxford University Press.
Gill, C. 1988. 'Personhood and Personality: The Four-*Personae* Theory in Cicero, *De Officiis* I', *Oxford Studies in Ancient Philosophy* 6, 169–99.
  2008. 'The Ancient Self: Issues and Approaches', in Remes and Sihvola, 35–56.
  2019. 'Stoic Magnanimity', in S. Vasalou ed. *The Measure of Greatness: Philosophers on Magnanimity*. Oxford: Oxford University Press, 49–71.
  2022. *Learning to Live Naturally: Stoic Ethics and Its Modern Significance*. Oxford: Oxford University Press.

Görler. W. 1995. 'Silencing the Trouble-maker: *De Legibus* and the Continuity of Cicero's Scepticism', in J. Powell ed. *Cicero the Philosopher*. Oxford: Oxford University Press, 240–67.

2004. 'Ein sprachlicher Zufall und seine Folgen: "Wahrscheinliches" bei Karneades und bei Cicero', in C. Catrein ed. *Kleine Schriften zur hellenistisch-römischen Philosophie von Woldemar Görler*. Leiden: Brill, 60–75.

Gotter, U. 1996a. *Der Diktator is tot! Politik in Rom zwischen den Iden des März und der Begründung des Zweiten Triumvirats*. Stuttgart: Steiner.

1996b. 'Cicero und die Freundschaft. Die Konstruktion sozialer Normen zwischen römischer Politik und griechischer Philosophie', in H.-J. Gehrke and A. Möller eds. *Vergangenheit und Lebenswelt. Soziale Kommunikation, Traditionsbildung und historisches Bewußtsein*. Tübingen: Narr, 339–60.

2003. 'Ontologie versus *exemplum*: Griechische Philosophie als politisches Argument in der späten römischen Republik', in K. Piepenbrink ed. *Philosophie und Lebenswelt in der Antike*. Darmstadt: WBG, 165–85.

2008. 'Cultural Differences and Cross-Cultural Contact: Greek and Roman Concepts of Power', *Harvard Studies in Classical Philology* 104, 179–230.

Goulet-Cazé, M.-O. 2017. *Le cynisme, une philosophie antique*. Paris: Vrin.

Gourinat, J.-B. 2014. 'Comment se détermine le *kathekon*? Remarques sur la conformité à la nature et le raisonnable', *Philosophie Antique* 14, 13–39.

Grant, M. and G. Fiske. 1924. 'Cicero's "Orator" and Horace's "Ars Poetica"', *Harvard Studies in Classical Philology* 35, 1–74.

Griffin, M. 1996. 'Cynicism and the Romans', in R. Bracht Branham and M-O. Goulet-Cazé eds. *The Cynics: The Cynic Movement in Antiquity and Its Legacy*. Berkeley: University of California Press, 190–204.

2003. '*De Beneficiis* and Roman Society', *Journal of Roman Studies* 93, 92–113.

2008. '*Iure plectimur*. The Roman Critique of Roman Imperialism', in T. C. Brennan and H. I. Flower eds. *East & West: Papers in Ancient History presented to Glen W. Bowersock*. Cambridge MA and London: Harvard University Press, 85–111.

2013. *Seneca on Society: A Guide to De Beneficiis*. Oxford: Oxford University Press.

2017. 'Dignity in Roman and Stoic Thought', in R. Debes ed. *Dignity: A History*. Oxford: Oxford University Press, 47–65.

Griffin, M. and J. Barnes eds. 1989. *Philosophia Togata. Essays on Philosophy and Roman Society*. Oxford: Oxford University Press.

Griffin, M. T. and E. M. Atkins eds. and trans. 1991. *Cicero on Duties*. Cambridge: Cambridge University Press.

Guérin, C. 2009. 'Philosophical Decorum and the Literarization of Rhetoric in Cicero's *Orator*', in F. Woerther ed. *Literary and Philosophical Rhetoric in the Greek, Roman, Syriac and Arabic World*. Hildesheim and New York: Georg Olms, 119–39.

Gunderson, E. 2000. *Staging Masculinity: The Rhetoric of Performance in the Roman World*. Ann Arbor: University of Michigan Press.

Habinek, T. 1990. 'Towards a History of Friendly Advice: The Politics of Candor in Cicero's *de Amicitia*', *Apeiron* 23, 165–85.
  1994. 'Ideology for an Empire in the Prefaces to Cicero's Dialogues', *Ramus* 23, 55–67.
Hadot, P. 1992. *La citadelle intérieure*. Paris: Fayard.
  2001. *Qu'est-ce que la philosophie antique?* Paris: Gallimard.
Hahm, D. 2007. 'Critolaus and Late Hellenistic Peripatetic Philosophy', in Ioppolo and Sedley, 47–101.
Hahn, J. 2017. 'Rituals of Killing: Public Punishment, *munera*, and the Dissemination of Roman Values and Ideology in the *Imperium Romanum*', in W. Vanacker and A. Zuiderhoek eds. *Imperial Identities in the Roman World*. London and New York: Routledge, 36–60.
Hall, J. 2009. *Politeness and Politics in Cicero's Letters*. Oxford: Oxford University Press.
  2014. *Cicero's Use of Judicial Theatre*. Ann Arbor: University of Michigan Press.
Harper, K. 2016. 'Christianity and the Roots of Human Dignity in Late Antiquity', in T. Shah and A. Hertzke eds. *Christianity and Freedom, Volume 1: Historical Perspectives*. Cambridge: Cambridge University Press, 123–48.
Hawley, M. 2020. 'Individuality and Hierarchy in Cicero's *De Officiis*', *European Journal of Political Theory* 19, 87–105.
  2022. *Natural Law Republicanism: Cicero's Liberal Legacy*. New York: Oxford University Press.
Heilmann, W. 1982. *Ethische Reflexion und Römische Lebenswirklichkeit in Ciceros Schrift de Officiis*. Wiesbaden: Steiner.
Heldmann, K. 1976. 'Ciceros Laelius und die Grenzen der Freundschaft. Zur Interdependenz von Literatur und Politik 44/43 v. Chr.', *Hermes* 104, 72–103.
Heller-Roazen, D. 2009. *The Enemy of All: Piracy and the Law of Nations*. New York: Zone Books.
Höffe ed. 2017. *Ciceros Staatsphilosophie: Ein Kooperativer Kommentar zu De republica und De legibus*, Klassiker Auslegen 64. Berlin: De Gruyter.
Hölkeskamp, K.-J. 2004. 'Under Roman Roofs: Family, House, and Household', in H. I. Flower ed. *The Cambridge Companion to the Roman Republic*. Cambridge: Cambridge University Press, 113–38.
  2017. *Libera Res Publica: Die politische Kultur des antiken Rom – Positionen und Perspektiven*. Stuttgart: Steiner.
Hursthouse, R. 1999. *On Virtue Ethics*. Oxford: Oxford University Press.
Ierodiakonou, K. ed. 1999. *Topics in Stoic Philosophy*. Oxford: Oxford University Press.
Inwood, B. 1983. 'The Two Forms of *Oikeiōsis* in Arius and the Stoa', in W. Fortenbaugh ed. *On Stoic and Peripatetic Ethics: The Work of Arius Didymus*. New Brunswick: Transaction Books, 190–201.
  1985. *Ethics and Human Action in Early Stoicism*. Oxford: Oxford University Press.
  1995. 'Politics and paradox in Seneca's *De beneficiis*', in Laks and Schofield, 241–65.

1999. 'Rules and Reasoning in Stoic Ethics', in Ierodiakonou, 95–127.
2005. *Reading Seneca: Stoic Philosophy at Rome*. Oxford: Oxford University Press.
2009. 'Why Physics?', in R. Salles ed. *God and Cosmos in Stoicism*. Oxford: Oxford University Press, 201–23.
2014. *Ethics after Aristotle*. Cambridge MA and London: Harvard University Press.
2016. 'The Voice of Nature', in J. Annas and G. Betegh eds. *Cicero's De Finibus: Philosophical Approaches*. Cambridge: Cambridge University Press, 147–66.
Inwood, B. and P. Donini. 1999. 'Stoic Ethics', in Algra et al., 675–738.
Inwood, B. and L. Gerson. 2008. *The Stoics Reader: Selected Writings and Testimonia*. Indianapolis: Hackett.
Ioppolo, A.-M. and D. N. Sedley eds. 2007. *Pyrrhonists, Patricians and Platonizers*. Naples: Bibliopolis.
Jehne, M. 2016. 'The Senatorial Economics of Status in the Late Republic', in H. Beck, M. Jehne and J. Serrati eds. *Money and Power in the Roman Republic*. Brussels: Latomus, 188–207.
Jocelyn, H. 1973. 'Greek Poetry in Cicero's Prose Writing', *Yale Classical Studies* 23, 61–112.
Kapust, D. 2020. 'Roman Patriotism', in M. Sardoc ed. *Handbook of Patriotism*. Cham: Springer, 47–67.
Kaster, R. 2005. *Emotion, Restraint, and Community in Ancient Rome*. Oxford: Oxford University Press.
2006. *Cicero, Speech on Behalf of Publius Sestius*. Oxford: Oxford University Press.
Kennerly, M. 2010. '*Sermo* and Stoic Sociality in Cicero's *De Officiis*', *Rhetorica* 28, 119–37.
Klein, J. 2015. 'Making Sense of Stoic Indifferents', *Oxford Studies in Ancient Philosophy* 49, 227–81.
2016. 'The Stoic Argument from *Oikeiōsis*', *Oxford Studies in Ancient Philosophy* 50, 143–200.
Konstan, D. 2015. 'Cicero on Grief and Friendship', in A. Tutter and L. Wurmser eds. *Grief and Its Transcendence: Memory, Identity, Creativity*. New York: Routledge, 3–14.
2017. 'Cicero's Two Loves', *Ciceroniana On Line* I.2, 291–305.
Koschorke, A. et al. 2007. *Der fiktive Staat: Konstruktionen des politischen Körpers in der Geschichte Europas*. Frankfurt: Fischer.
Kristjánsson, K. 2006. 'Emulation and the Use of Role Models in Moral Education', *Journal of Moral Education* 35, 37–49.
Labowsky, L. 1934. *Die Ethik des Painaitios: Untersuchungen zur Geschichte des Decorum bei Cicero und Horaz*. Leipzig: Meiner.
La Bua, G. 2019. *Cicero and Roman Education*. Cambridge: Cambridge University Press.
Laks, A. and M. Schofield eds. 1995. *Justice and Generosity*. Cambridge: Cambridge University Press.

Langlands, R. 2011. 'Roman *Exempla* and Situation Ethics: Valerius Maximus and Cicero *de Officiis*', *Journal of Roman Studies* 101, 100–22.
  2018. *Exemplary Ethics in Ancient Rome*. Cambridge: Cambridge University Press.
  2020. '*Aemulatio & Imitatio* in Roman Exemplary Ethics', in A. Bettenworth, D. Boschung and M. Formisano eds. *Students, Followers and Disciples. Aemulatio and Imitatio of Role Models in the Ancient Mediterranean*. Paderborn: Fink.
  2021. 'Roman Exemplary Ethics: Rules and the Unruly', in M. Clarke and E. Corran eds. *Rules and Ethics: Perspectives from Anthropology and History*. Manchester: Manchester University Press, 103–23.
  forthcoming. 'Sites of Exemplarity and the Challenge of Accessing the Cultural Memory of the Republic', in M. Dinter and C. Guérin eds. *Cultural Memory in Republican and Augustan Rome*. Cambridge: Cambridge University Press.
Lefèvre, E. 2001. *Panaitios' und Ciceros Pflichtenlehre: vom philosophischen Traktat zum politischen Lehrbuch*. Stuttgart: Steiner.
Lentano, M. 2018. 'Kinship', in M. Bettini & W. Short eds. *The World through Roman Eyes: Anthropological Approaches to Ancient Culture*. Cambridge: Cambridge University Press, 171–90.
Lévy, C. 1998. 'Rhétorique et philosophie: la monstruosité politique chez Cicéron', *Revue des Études Latines* 76, 139–57.
  2003. 'Y a-t-il quelqu'un derrière le masque? A propos de la théorie des *personae* chez Cicéron', *Ítaca: Quaderns Catalans de Cultura Clàssica* 19, 127–40.
Long, A. A. 1967. 'Carneades and the Stoic telos', *Phronesis* 12, 59–90.
  1995. 'Cicero's Politics in *De officiis*,' in Laks and Schofield, 213–40.
Long, A. A. and D. N. Sedley. 1987. *The Hellenistic Philosophers*, 2 vols. Cambridge: Cambridge University Press.
Lowrie, M. 2002. 'Horace, Cicero and Augustus, or the Poet Statesman at *Epistles* 2.1.256', in A. Woodman and D. C. Feeney eds. *Traditions and Contexts in the Poetry of Horace*. Cambridge: Cambridge University Press, 158–71.
Luban, D. 2018a. 'The Enemy of All Humanity', *Netherlands Journal of Legal Philosophy* 2, 112–37.
  2018b. 'On the Humanity of the Enemy of Humanity', *Netherlands Journal of Legal Philosophy* 2, 187–99.
Lutz, C. trans. and G. Reydams-Schils ed. 2020. *Musonius Rufus: That One Should Disdain Hardships: The Teachings of a Roman Stoic*. New Haven: Yale University Press.
Manent, P. 2006. *A World beyond Politics? A Defense of the Nation-State*. Princeton: Princeton University Press.
Manuwald, G. 2007. *Cicero, Philippics 3–9*, 2 vols. Berlin: de Gruyter.
Martin, J. 2002. 'Familie, Verwandtschaft und Staat in der römischen Republik', in J. Spielvogel ed. *Res publica reperta: Zur Verfassung und Gesellschaft der römischen Republik und des frühen Prinzipats*. Stuttgart: Steiner, 13–24.
  2009. 'Das Vaterland der Väter: Familie, Politik und cognatische Verwandtschaft in Rom', in *Bedingungen menschlichen Handelns in der Antike: Gesammelte Beiträge zur Historischen Anthropologie*. Stuttgart: Steiner, 311–27.

May, J. 1996. 'Cicero and the Beasts', *Syllecta Classica* 7, 143–53.
McCabe, M. M. 2005. 'Extend or Identify: Two Stoic Accounts of Altruism', in R. Salles ed. *Metaphysics, Soul, and Ethics in Ancient Thought: Themes from the Work of Richard Sorabji*. Oxford: Oxford University Press, 413–43.
McConnell, S. 2014. *Philosophical Life in Cicero's Letters*. Cambridge: Cambridge University Press.
  2017. 'Demetrius of Laconia and the Debate between the Stoics and Epicureans on the Nature of Parental Love', *Classical Quarterly* 67, 149–62.
  2018. 'Lucretius on the Nature of Parental Love', *Antichthon* 52, 72–89.
Meyer, H. D. 1957. *Cicero und das Reich*. Diss. Cologne.
Miller, W. trans. 1913. *Cicero: De Officiis*. Loeb Classical Library. Cambridge MA and London: Harvard University Press.
Mitsis, P. 1986. 'Moral Rules and the Aims of Stoic Ethics', *Journal of Philosophy* 83, 556–8.
  1999. 'The Stoic Origin of Natural Rights', in Ierodiakonou, 153–77.
Morgan, T. 2007. *Popular Morality in the Early Roman Empire*. Cambridge: Cambridge University Press.
Müller, J. 2017. 'Ciceros Archäologie des römischen Staates in De re publica II: Ein Exempel römischen Philosophierens', in Höffe, 47–72.
  2022. 'Vorbilder – und wie man ihnen folgen soll: Exemplarität in Ciceros praktischer Philosophie', in M. Summa and K. Mertens eds. *Das Exemplarische: Orientierung für menschliches Wissen und Handeln*. Paderborn: Brill Mentis, 217–39.
Narducci, E. 1997. *Cicerone e l'eloquenza romana: Retorica e progetto culturale*. Rome: Laterza.
Nederman, C. 2000. 'War, Peace, and Republican Virtue: Patriotism and the Neglected Legacy of Cicero', in N. Thompson ed. *Instilling Ethics*. Lanham MD: Rowman and Littlefield, 17–29.
Nicgorski, W. ed. 2012. *Cicero's Practical Philosophy*. Notre Dame: University of Notre Dame Press.
Nicolet, C. 1980. *The World of the Citizen in Republican Rome*, trans. P. S. Falla. Berkeley: University of California Press.
Nussbaum, M. 1996. 'Patriotism and Cosmopolitanism', in J. Cohen ed. *For Love of Country: Debating the Limits of Patriotism*. Boston: Beacon Press, 2–17.
  1997. 'Kant and Stoic Cosmopolitanism', *Journal of Political Philosophy* 5, 1–25.
  2000. 'Duties of Justice, Duties of Material Aid: Cicero's Problematic Legacy', *Journal of Political Philosophy* 8, 176–206.
  2019. *The Cosmopolitan Tradition: A Noble but Flawed Ideal*. Cambridge MA: Harvard University Press.
  2022. 'Cicero and Twenty-First Century Political Philosophy', in Atkins and Bénatouïl, 284–300.
Oliensis, E. 1998. *Horace and the Rhetoric of Authority*. Cambridge: Cambridge University Press.
Philippson, R. 1930. 'Das Sittlichschöne bei Panaitios', *Philologus* 85, 357–413.

Plasberg, O. and K. Simbeck. 1917. *M. Tulli Ciceronis scripta quae manserunt omnia, Fasciculus 47, Cato maior. Laelius. De gloria*. Berlin and Boston: Teubner.
Pohlenz, M. 1933. 'τὸ πρέπον: Ein Beitrag zur Geschichte des griechischen Geistes', *Nachrichten von der Gesellschaft der Wissenschaften zu Göttingen aus dem Jahre 1933*, 53–92.
  1934. *Antikes Führertum: Cicero De officiis und das Lebensideal des Panaetios*. Leipzig: Teubner.
Pöschl, V. 1989. *Der Begriff der Würde im antiken Rom und Später*. Heidelberg: Winter.
Powers, N. 2012. 'The Stoic Argument for the Rationality of the Cosmos', *Oxford Studies in Ancient Philosophy* 43, 145–269.
Ramelli, I. 2009. *Hierocles the Stoic: Elements of Ethics, Fragments, and Excerpts*, trans. D. Konstan. Leiden and Boston: Brill.
Ramsey, J. 1994. 'The Senate, Mark Antony, and Caesar's Legislative Legacy', *Classical Quarterly* 44, 130–45.
  2004. 'Did Julius Caesar Temporarily Banish Mark Antony from his Inner Circle?', *Classical Quarterly* 54, 161–73.
Rauh, S. 2018. 'Cato at Utica: The Emergence of a Roman Suicide Tradition', *American Journal of Philology* 139, 59–91.
Rawson, B. 1991. *Children and Childhood in Roman Italy*. Oxford: Oxford University Press.
Remes, P. and J. Sihvola eds. 2008. *Ancient Philosophy of the Self*. New York: Springer.
Reydams-Schils, G. 2005. *The Roman Stoics: Self, Responsibility, and Affection*. Chicago: Chicago University Press.
Roller, M. 2004. 'Exemplarity in Roman Culture: The Cases of Horatius Cocles and Cloelia', *Classical Philology* 99, 1–56.
  2018. *Models from the Past in Roman Culture: A World of Exempla*. Cambridge: Cambridge University Press.
Rollinger, C. 2014. *Amicitia sanctissime colenda. Freundschaft und soziale Netzwerke in der Späten Republik*. Heidelberg: Verlag Antike.
  2017. 'Beyond Laelius. The Orthopraxy of Friendship in the Late Republic', *Ciceroniana On Line* I.2, 343–67.
Schauer, F. 1991. *Playing by the Rules: A Philosophical Examination of Rule-Based Decision-Making in Law and in Life*. Oxford: Oxford University Press.
Schironi, F. 2018. *The Best of the Grammarians: Aristarchus of Samothrace on the Iliad*. Ann Arbor: University of Michigan Press.
Schofield, M. 1991. *The Stoic Idea of the City*. Cambridge: Cambridge University Press.
  1995. 'Two Stoic Approaches to Justice', in Laks and Schofield, 191–212.
  1999. *Saving the City: Philosopher-Kings and Other Classical Paradigms*. London and New York: Routledge.
  2012a. 'Antiochus on Social Virtue', in D. Sedley ed. *The Philosophy of Antiochus*. Cambridge: Cambridge University Press, 173–87.
  2012b. 'The Fourth Virtue', in Nicgorski, 43–57.
  2021. *Cicero: Political Philosophy*. Oxford: Oxford University Press.

Sellars, J. 2014. *Stoicism*. Abingdon and New York: Routledge.
Shackleton Bailey, D. R. 1971. *Cicero*. New York: Scribner.
Sigismund, S. 2008. *Der politische Mord in der späten Römischen Republik*. Hamburg: Kovac.
Singer, P. 2009. *The Life You Can Save: Acting Now to End World Poverty*. New York: Random House.
Smith, A. 1976. The Theory of Moral Sentiments, Vol. 1 of D. D. Raphael and A. L. Macfie eds. *The Glasgow Edition of the Works and Correspondence of Adam Smith*. Oxford: Oxford University Press.
Sorabji, R. 2006. *Self: Ancient and Modern Insights about Individuality, Life, and Death*. Chicago: University of Chicago Press.
   2008. 'Graeco-Roman Varieties of Self', in Remes and Sihvola, 13–34.
Steel, C. 2005. *Reading Cicero: Genre and Performance in Late Republican Rome*. London: Duckworth.
Stevenson, T. and M. Wilson eds. 2008. *Cicero's Philippics: History, Rhetoric and Ideology*. Auckland: Prudentia, 37–38.
Stone, A. M. 2008. 'Greek Ethics and Roman Statesmen: *De Officiis* and the *Philippics*', in Stevenson and Wilson, 214–39.
Straumann, B. 2016. *Crisis and Constitutionalism: Roman Political Thought from the Fall of the Republic to the Age of Revolution*. Oxford: Oxford University Press.
Striker, G. 1996. *Essays on Hellenistic Epistemology and Ethics*. Cambridge: Cambridge University Press.
   2022. 'Panaetius *Peri tou kathēkontos* in Cicero's *De Officiis*', in *From Aristotle to Cicero: Essays on Ancient Philosophy*. Oxford: Oxford University Press, 222–44.
Stroup, S. C. 2003. '*Adulta Virgo*: The Personification of Textual Eloquence in Cicero's *Brutus*', *Materiali e Discussioni per l'analisi dei testi classici* 50, 115–40.
Tan, J. 2017. *Power and Public Finance at Rome, 264–49 BCE*. Oxford: Oxford University Press.
Tarrant, H. 2000. *Plato's First Interpreters*. Ithaca: Cornell University Press.
Thome, G. 1999. '*Iustitia* – Geschichte eines Wortes und einer Idee', *Anregung* 45, 150–68.
Tieleman, T. 2007. 'Panaetius' Place in the History of Stoicism', in Ioppolo and Sedley, 103–42.
Treggiari, S. 1991. *Roman Marriage: Iusti Coniuges from the Time of Cicero to the Time of Ulpian*. Oxford: Oxford University Press.
   2005. 'Putting the Family Across: Cicero on Natural Affection', in M. George ed. *The Roman Family in the Empire: Rome, Italy, and Beyond*. Oxford: Oxford University Press, 9–35.
   2007. *Terentia, Tullia and Publilia: The Women of Cicero's Family*. Abingdon: Routledge.
Tsouni, G. 2019. *Antiochus and Peripatetic Ethics*. Cambridge: Cambridge University Press.

Unger, P. 1996. *Living High and Letting Die: Our Illusion of Innocence*. Oxford: Oxford University Press.
Ungern-Sternberg, J. von. 1970. *Untersuchungen zum spätrepublikanischen Notstandsrecht: Senatus consultum ultimum und hostis-Erklärung*. Munich: Beck.
van der Blom, H. 2010. *Cicero's Role Models: The Political Strategy of a Newcomer*. Oxford: Oxford University Press.
Veillard, C. 2014. 'Comment définir le devoir? Le *peri kathēkontos de Panétius*', *Philosophie Antique* 14, 71–109.
Verboven, K. 2002. *The Economy of Friends: Economic Aspects of Amicitia and Patronage in the Late Republic*. Brussels: Latomus.
Viroli, M. 1995. *For Love of Country: An Essay on Patriotism and Nationalism*. Oxford: Oxford University Press.
Visnjic, J. 2021. *The Invention of Duty: Stoicism as Deontology*. Leiden: Brill.
Walsh, P. G. 2000. *Cicero: On Obligations*, translated with introduction and notes. Oxford: Oxford University Press.
Walters, B. 2020. *The Deaths of the Republic: Imagery of the Body Politic in Ciceronian Rome*. Oxford: Oxford University Press.
Watson, P. 1983. 'Mythological Exempla in Ovid's *Ars Amatoria*', *Classical Philology* 78, 117–26.
Wendt, W. 1929. *Ciceros Brief an Paetus IX 22*. Diss. Giessen.
Williams, C. 2012. *Reading Roman Friendship*. Cambridge: Cambridge University Press.
Winterbottom, M. ed. 1994. *M. Tulli Ciceronis De Officiis*. Oxford: Oxford University Press.
Wood, N. 1988. *Cicero's Social and Political Thought*. Berkeley: University of California Press.
Woolf, R. 2007. 'Particularism, Promises, and Persons in Cicero's *De officiis*', *Oxford Studies in Ancient Philosophy* 33, 317–46.
  2013. 'Cicero and Gyges', *Classical Quarterly* 63, 801–12.
  2015. *Cicero: The Philosophy of a Roman Sceptic*. London: Routledge.
Yong, E. 2016. 'Humans: Unusually Murderous Mammals, Typically Murderous Primates', The Atlantic, www.theatlantic.com/science/archive/2016/09/humans-are-unusually-violent-mammals-but-averagely-violent-primates/501935/.

Index

animals, 23, 25–26, 32, 65–68, 75, 80, 169, 194, 205–6, 210–11, 213, 214, 226, 229, 239, 240
Antipater of Tarsus, 9, 57–59, 82, 115, 122, 126, 167, 221
Antipater of Tyre, 84
Antony, Mark, 54, 165, 167, 225, 228, 230, 232, 233, 236, 239, 242
appropriate actions. See kathēkonta
appropriation. See oikeiōsis
Aristarchus of Samothrace, 173, 175
Aristotle, 16, 22, 71, 75, 95, 97, 104, 168–73, 203, 221
Atkins, E. M., 36, 91, 196, 204, 218, 234
Atticus, 18–21, 23, 25, 37, 44, 121

Barney, R., 99–103, 105, 106, 110, 111, 114
beneficence, 7, 8, 15, 29, 31, 36–39, 45, 74, 85–89, 93–96, 226, 235. See also liberality
Brennan, T., 99–103, 105, 106, 111, 114–15
Brunt, P., 63, 89

Caesar, Julius, 3, 11, 47, 51, 53, 56, 83, 114, 119, 121, 124, 126, 131, 134–36, 138, 140, 149, 154, 158–59, 164, 165, 167, 224, 225, 228–33, 236–40, 242
Carneades, 21, 43, 56, 57, 82
Catiline, 90, 167, 224, 228, 236, 239, 241
Cato the Elder, 124, 137, 138, 144, 167, 224, 235
Cato the Younger, 51, 119, 123, 124, 134–35, 144, 147, 167
children, 6, 16–21, 23–34, 36–41, 52, 53, 65, 66, 68, 69, 205, 207, 210, 216, 226
Chremes, 23–24, 30, 40, 208
Chrysippus, 23, 42, 57, 76, 77, 101, 102, 112, 168, 221
citizenship, 11, 35, 36, 39, 52, 83, 86–90, 95–96, 206–209, 214, 217–18, 220–23, 227, 229, 235, 236, 241
commonwealth. See res publica
convention, 10, 11, 184–85, 188–89, 193, 196, 198–200, 206, 213, 214, 218–19, 235

Cooper, J., 101
cosmopolitanism, 11, 199, 203–205, 214–17, 220–23, 226–27
courage, 45, 64, 69, 74, 109, 116, 127, 136, 137, 167, 169. See also greatness of soul
Crassus, M., 131, 149, 152, 153, 233
Cratippus, 2, 4, 19, 139, 140
custom. See convention
Cynics, 10, 184–88, 190–96, 198

decorum, 10, 47, 65, 82, 96, 109, 115, 123, 130, 156, 163, 166–67, 169–76, 178–80, 182–86, 189–200, 234
Dicaearchus, 81, 168, 216, 217, 230
Diogenes of Babylon, 9, 57–59, 82, 115, 122, 126, 167, 168, 171
duties. See officia
Dyck, A., 89, 91, 92

emotion, 26, 68, 119, 140, 155–60, 171, 231
emulation, 125, 128, 133, 134, 136, 140, 155–60
Ennius, 217, 219
Epictetus, 20, 21, 24, 26, 65, 97, 221
Epicureanism, 16, 20–21, 26, 55–56, 213, 236
Epicurus. See Epicureanism
expedient. See utile

Fabricius, 119, 127, 137, 138
family, 6–7, 15–18, 26, 28–41, 52, 53, 68, 109, 125, 205, 206, 216, 217, 219, 228
friendship, 36–37, 40–41, 50, 52–54, 83, 95, 145, 150, 165, 180, 208–10, 219, 228, 240–41

generosity. See liberality
glory, 8, 10, 51, 56, 84–86, 90–92, 94–95, 96, 112, 136, 138, 140, 141, 148, 153–60, 164–67, 233
gods, 16, 24, 27, 40, 50, 53, 80, 81, 158, 222, 240
Gracchi, 89, 131, 153, 159, 224, 236, 241
gratitude, 8, 83, 93–96, 154
greatness of soul, 64, 69, 70, 74, 115, 116, 133, 135, 136, 143, 169, 182, 232, 234, 237, 238

254

Index

greatness of spirit. *See* greatness of soul
Griffin, M., 81, 85, 91, 196

happiness, 8, 56, 60, 72, 80, 98, 100, 107, 229
Hecato of Rhodes, 42, 47, 49, 57, 58, 113, 216
Hierocles, 16, 52, 53, 68, 205
honestum, 2, 7, 42, 45–46, 55–60, 64, 72, 79, 96, 106, 108, 109, 121, 123, 126, 127, 137, 156, 167, 182, 185, 187, 190–92, 225, 231, 232, 234, 237–39
honourable. *See honestum*
Horace, 163, 179–80
human nature. *See* nature
Hursthouse, R., 8, 103–107, 109, 110, 115, 116, 127, 128

indifferents, 8, 22–23, 80, 97–102, 105–108, 110, 112, 113, 127–28, 136, 221
injustice, 12, 29–30, 56, 94, 102, 103, 110, 133, 199–200, 215–16, 225, 236–39. *See also* justice
Inwood, B., 7–8, 98–99, 106–107, 114, 145
ius. *See* law, justice
iustitia. *See* justice

just war. *See* war
justice, 7, 12, 24, 29–30, 38, 39, 45, 49, 56, 64, 69, 74, 84–86, 94, 96, 103, 110, 112, 114–16, 126–27, 132–33, 135–37, 140, 141, 143, 145, 155, 169, 182, 203–205, 211–16, 218–21, 225, 231–32, 234–38, 240

kathēkonta, 2, 42–44, 47–50, 52, 95, 97–100, 105, 106, 108, 109, 124, 127, 144–46, 168, 169
katorthōmata, 44, 98, 105, 112, 124, 144

Langlands, R., 141, 142, 146, 147, 155
law, 24, 27, 32, 36, 59, 74, 98, 158, 190, 194, 198, 200, 207, 213, 219, 221, 232, 234–36, 240–42. *See also* convention
Lefèvre, E., 91, 92
liberality, 8, 37, 38, 52, 64, 84–89, 91–95, 109–12, 154, 211, 213–14, 217–19, 226, 233, 235. *See also* beneficence
Livy, 141
Long, A. A., 92, 156

magnitudo animi. *See* greatness of soul
Marcus Aurelius, 65, 97, 181
Marcus Cicero, 2–6, 18, 19, 27, 38, 41, 43, 54, 139, 140, 147, 224
middle duties, 2, 44, 124, 137, 144. *See also officia*
moderation, 45, 64, 109, 115, 127, 136, 169, 182, 198, 232
mos maiorum, 119, 121, 128

nature, 6, 10–11, 17–29, 31–34, 36, 38–40, 45, 46, 48, 50–52, 57, 58, 64, 66–71, 73, 75–77, 80–82, 96–98, 100, 101, 106, 107, 109–11, 114–15, 130–31, 134, 144, 147–48, 169, 180, 182–85, 188–200, 204–208, 210–15, 218, 220–21, 225–27, 229, 231–35, 239
Nussbaum, M., 218, 222

obligations. *See officia*
offence, 10–11, 182–93, 195–96, 198–200
officia, 2, 5–7, 31, 36, 38–40, 42–54, 58–60, 64, 74, 95, 124, 125, 127, 144, 145, 151, 156, 169, 176, 180, 197, 215, 217–22, 237
oikeiōsis, 7, 8, 23, 52, 65–66, 68–71, 74–77, 102, 194, 205, 207, 210, 225–27, 229

Panaetius, 2, 7–10, 17, 42–47, 49–51, 54, 57, 60, 63–66, 69, 71, 74–82, 84–85, 87, 89, 108, 111–13, 120, 121, 124–25, 131, 138–40, 146, 154, 163, 167–75, 178, 179, 182, 184, 204
parents, 6–7, 17–18, 20–31, 33–41, 52–54, 66, 96, 142–43, 180, 216, 226, 228
personae theory, 4, 9, 11, 50, 65, 74, 109, 120, 128, 135, 146, 175–77, 184, 197–98
Plato, 5, 16, 47, 76, 81, 90, 152, 168–70, 177, 185, 186, 192, 225–27, 229, 231, 232, 236–40
plausible. *See probabilis*
Posidonius, 42, 46, 47, 76, 77, 234
practical reason. *See* reason
prepon, 10, 65, 169–71, 173–76, 178
probabilis, 2, 5–7, 43–44, 55
property, 31, 33, 37–40, 57, 88–90, 94, 98, 100, 111, 126, 154, 158, 212, 221, 225, 235

rationality. *See* reason
reason, 2, 4–6, 8, 11, 24–28, 32, 33, 36, 41, 48, 66–68, 75, 98–99, 104–109, 111, 114–15, 123, 141, 147, 151, 169, 190–91, 193–98, 205–207, 211, 213, 214, 220, 222, 226, 228, 231
Regulus, 9, 50, 59, 100, 114–16, 120–24, 134, 137, 140–42, 149–51, 153, 154, 160, 167
republicanism, 11, 203–204, 217, 220, 222
res publica, 11, 35, 36, 52–54, 59, 83, 87–90, 94–96, 203–10, 212–17, 220–21, 225, 227–29, 233–36, 238, 239, 242
right actions. *See katorthōmata*
Roller, M., 123, 141–43, 155
rule of procedure (*formula*), 49, 113, 114, 221

sage, Stoic, 2, 9, 24, 26, 27, 40, 44, 49, 50, 54, 57–58, 100–101, 105, 124, 136, 144, 168, 186, 187, 198, 209, 222
sapientia. *See* wisdom
scepticism, Academic, 5–6, 17, 43–44, 64, 75
Schofield, M., 220

seemliness. *See decorum*
self-love, 7, 208–10, 231
Seneca, 9, 65, 68, 71, 73, 95, 97, 99, 106, 111, 120, 124, 135, 137, 138, 143, 181
shame, sense of. *See verecundia*
Singer, P., 219
slavery, 7, 16, 38–39, 215, 220–23
Socrates, 5, 79, 85, 147, 153, 184–85
sōphrosunē, 169, 170. *See also* moderation
Sulla, 83, 131, 132, 140, 158–60, 167, 228, 230, 233, 236, 241

temperance. *See* moderation
Terentia, 18, 28
theoretical reason. *See* reason
Tullia, 3, 18–19, 29, 41

Unger, P., 219
useful. *See* utile
utile, 2, 7, 42, 45–46, 54–60, 79, 80, 82, 87, 89, 91, 93, 96, 108, 110–13, 121, 127, 143, 167, 225, 238

verecundia, 10, 11, 74, 170, 182–86, 188–96, 198, 200, 214
violence, 215–17, 224, 229, 230, 234, 236, 240, 241
virtue, 2, 5, 7–10, 15–16, 22, 24, 26–27, 29, 31, 39–41, 45–46, 55–56, 64–65, 69–75, 77, 81–83, 85–86, 88–90, 92, 96, 98–116, 119, 121–25, 127–29, 131–38, 141–44, 147, 156–60, 163, 169–73, 176, 182, 183, 185, 190, 197–98, 203–204, 209–16, 218, 229, 238
virtue ethics, 8, 98, 103, 104, 107, 120, 123–24, 127–29

Walsh, P., 91
war, 50, 59, 83, 140, 150, 155, 164–65, 178–80, 215–17, 225, 229, 233, 241
wisdom, 8, 24, 27, 28, 45, 56, 64, 65, 69–73, 75, 109, 115, 127, 132, 137, 143, 179, 182
wise person. *See* sage, Stoic

Zeno of Citium, 42, 64, 168, 186–88, 191, 194

CAMBRIDGE CRITICAL GUIDES

Titles published in this series (continued):

Aquinas's *Disputed Questions on Evil*
EDITED BY M. V. DOUGHERTY
Aristotle's *Politics*
EDITED BY THORNTON LOCKWOOD AND THANASSIS SAMARAS
Aristotle's *Physics*
EDITED BY MARISKA LEUNISSEN
Kant's *Lectures on Ethics*
EDITED BY LARA DENIS AND OLIVER SENSEN
Kierkegaard's *Fear and Trembling*
EDITED BY DANIEL CONWAY
Kant's *Lectures on Anthropology*
EDITED BY ALIX COHEN
Kant's *Religion within the Boundaries of Mere Reason*
EDITED BY GORDON MICHALSON
Descartes' *Meditations*
EDITED BY KAREN DETLEFSEN
Augustine's *City of God*
EDITED BY JAMES WETZEL
Kant's *Observations and Remarks*
EDITED BY RICHARD VELKLEY AND SUSAN SHELL
Nietzsche's *On the Genealogy of Morality*
EDITED BY SIMON MAY
Aristotle's *Nicomachean Ethics*
EDITED BY JON MILLER
Kant's *Metaphysics of Morals*
EDITED BY LARA DENIS
Spinoza's *Theological-Political Treatise*
EDITED BY YITZHAK Y. MELAMED AND MICHAEL A. ROSENTHAL
Plato's *Laws*
EDITED BY CHRISTOPHER BOBONICH
Plato's *Republic*
EDITED BY MARK L. MCPHERRAN
Kierkegaard's *Concluding Unscientific Postscript*
EDITED BY RICK ANTHONY FURTAK
Wittgenstein's *Philosophical Investigations*
EDITED BY ARIF AHMED
Kant's *Critique of Practical Reason*
EDITED BY ANDREWS REATH AND JENS TIMMERMANN
Kant's *Groundwork of the Metaphysics of Morals*
EDITED BY JENS TIMMERMANN
Kant's *Idea for a Universal History with a Cosmopolitan Aim*
EDITED BY AMÉLIE OKSENBERG RORTY AND JAMES SCHMIDT
Mill's *On Liberty*
EDITED BY C. L. TEN
Hegel's *Phenomenology of Spirit*
EDITED BY DEAN MOYAR AND MICHAEL QUANTE

For EU product safety concerns, contact us at Calle de José Abascal, 56–1°,
28003 Madrid, Spain or eugpsr@cambridge.org.

www.ingramcontent.com/pod-product-compliance
Ingram Content Group UK Ltd.
Pitfield, Milton Keynes, MK11 3LW, UK
UKHW022040110326
468905UK00020B/2367